CompuServe®
for Europe

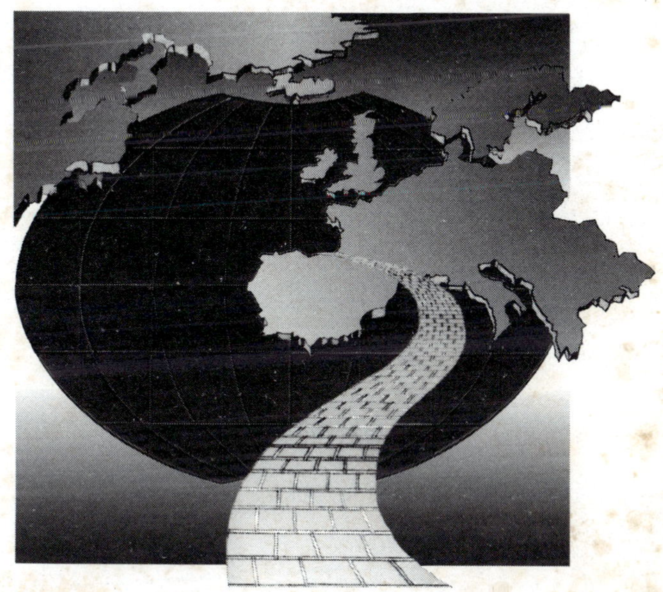

A GUIDE TO THE INFORMATION SUPERHIGHWAY

CompuServe®
for Europe
A GUIDE TO THE INFORMATION SUPERHIGHWAY

Roelf Sluman

INTERNATIONAL THOMSON PUBLISHING

I(T)P An International Thomson Publishing Company

London • Bonn • Boston • Madrid • Melbourne • Mexico City • New York • Paris • Singapore
Tokyo • Toronto • Albany, NY • Belmont, CA • Cincinnati, OH • Detroit, MI

CompuServe® for Europe
A Guide to the Information Superhighway

Commissioning Editor: Samantha Whittaker
Editorial Assistant: Jonathan Simpson

Made in Logotechnics C.P.C. Ltd., Sheffield
Project Management: Sandra M. Potestà
Production: H.-D. Rauschner + Team
Artistic Direction: Stefano E. Potestà
Cover Illustration: William Smith

First printed 1995

Printed in the U.K by Logotechnics C.P.C. Ltd., Sheffield.

International Thomson Publishing
Berkshire House
168–173 High Holborn
London WC1V 7AA

ISBN 1-850-32121-3

British Library Cataloguing-in-Publication Data
A catalogue record for this book is available from the British Library

Contents

Preface

To all of you: thank you for purchasing this book! I had a really fun time writing it, and I hope it will help you get to know CompuServe or, if you have been a member for quite some time already, give you plenty of new things to do online. There's a whole world out there to discover, with new experiences waiting for you all the time!

As European members, we have to deal with CompuServe quite differently from people in the United States. They often benefit from freebees that we have to do without, like free local calls, no surcharges because of independent network usage, and so on. Therefore, I have tried to provide you with lots of information about ways to keep your wallet happy. Automated access programs like CompuServe Navigator for Windows and TapCIS get a lot of well-deserved attention in this book. And if you are a new CompuServe member who is about to get acquainted with the 'online community', you'll find plenty of tips about the program you will most probably use during your first explorations: the CompuServe Information Manager for Windows (WinCIM).

The first four chapters are aimed at new members of CompuServe. You will learn how to get online, how to sign up for membership, and how to find your way around the enormous amount of information and products available to you. We'll use the WinCIM program (which is provided with this book) to do that, although you can use other versions of CIM as well.

Chapters 5 and 6 deal with software that is high on the 'top ten' list of CompuServe members: WinCIM, CompuServe Navigator for Windows and TapCIS. Consult these chapters if you are looking for general information about these programs, whenever you are looking for an explanation of a particular program feature, or if you need instructions on how to use these programs to access certain parts of CompuServe.

Chapter 7 discusses electronic mail or e-mail, as it is often called. Besides covering the most important aspects of CompuServe Mail, we'll also dig into external mailing systems like the Internet, CCMAIL and X400.

If you are interested in forums, the 'meeting places' on CompuServe, read Chapter 8. It contains in-depth discussions about all the forum features that are available, as well as guidelines to help you use the forums as a tool, as a means of recreation, or simply as a way to get to know other people.

Chapter 9 focuses on a number of popular CompuServe products. Don't expect a complete list of everything that's available; it is simply impossible to cover every aspect of CompuServe. Besides, new features are added every day, so this book would be out of date before it even hit the shelves! However, this chapter also shows you how to find out about new developments yourself, and it contains a comprehensive summary of available CompuServe GO words and public forums.

In the final chapter, we'll expand on a new aspect of CompuServe: Internet access, namely the facility to read messages posted on USENET newsgroups. Although people often compare USENET newsgroups to CompuServe forums, they are actually an entirely different form of communication. Before you start exploring, you might like to read this chapter to learn more about them.

Naturally, I am a CompuServe member, just like you. If you'd like to drop me a note, my CompuServe User ID is 71333,1443. Or you might like to visit me and a nice bunch of other people on the Netherlands Forum. Don't worry if you don't speak Dutch: we have sections for English-speaking members, too. I'm looking forward to meeting you online!

And here they are: the paragraphs that most readers skip. Too bad, because your name might be in them!

When I was writing this book, and a long time before then, I enjoyed the help and advice of a lot of nice people. I would like to express my sincere thanks to everyone listed below:

Bob Bolick, Samantha Whittaker and Jonathan Simpson at ITP: thanks for your confidence in me.

LogoTechnics, especially Hans-Dieter Rauschner: thanks for putting up with what must have been some of the weirdest English sentences that you guys have ever seen!

Martin Turner and Neil Laver of CompuServe: thanks very much for providing me with all the information that I needed, often before I even requested it. I hope we can do this again, sometime!

Jaap Bloem, Hans Peters, John Duzs, Clarissa Pinkola Estes (your book or mine?), Dick Lodge, Mary Mitchell, Sonya Stroud, Jeff Gulliford (yep, I do other things besides gardening), Rick Wilkes, Sue Thornburg (keep practising!), the members of the 'NLTeam', and all other CompuServe members that I have had the pleasure of meeting online (and often offline as well): thanks for everything!

My parents, family, and all my friends: thanks for being there. My goal for the year 2000: visiting the birthday parties of all of you!

And finally, the one and only person in the world who can make me forget about CompuServe altogether: the love of my life, Andrea Mayer. Lehetetlen lett volna nélküled! Szeretlek, Szivem.

1 Welcome to the electronic highway

Welcome to the electronic highway

First of all, welcome to CompuServe! If you haven't been 'online' before, you are about to go on a great and endless journey. Comfortably seated behind your computer keyboard, you will travel through a digital world that could change your live dramatically. As a member of the 'online community', your own User ID enables other CompuServe members to get in touch with you easily. You will have permanent access to information that was previously very hard, or even impossible, to get. You will meet new people, maybe even talk to celebrities, exchange messages with CompuServe members that you will probably never meet in person, read up-to-date articles about new developments in your professional field, and so on. Before long, you can't imagine how you ever managed without your CompuServe membership!

1.1 How it all started

When you connect to CompuServe these days, using an elegant access program like WinCIM or CompuServe Navigator, you use pull-down menus and dialogs to perform your online activities. But it all started quite differently. Back in July 1970, an online service called MicroNET was announced. Actually, MicroNET wasn't an online service by today's standards.

Becoming a member of MicroNET meant that you were assigned a project, programmer number (PPN), the predecessor of today's User ID. That project, programmer number enabled you to use computer time on a series of DEC mainframes.

MicroNET consisted of a series of programs that could be run much like DOS programs, complete with a 'DOS-like' prompt (OK, followed by a flashing cursor). There were MicroNET members that wrote their own programs (in a language called XBASIC), which is actually how forums came into existence. In the early 1980s, a series of ASCII menus was added to this interface, which made CompuServe easier to access for non-literate computer users. New services were added as well, making CompuServe the vast source of information it is today.

The next step involved the development of the CompuServe Information Manager: a series of software programs (originally written for Apple Macintosh computers) that use an interface called HMI (Host-Micro Interface) and translate those ASCII menus into nice dialog boxes and pull-down menus. Today, there are three interfaces for accessing CompuServe: the old OK prompt (which is hardly used any more), the ASCII menus (often referred to as the ASCII Interface or Terminal Emulation) and the HMI interface.

1.2 Information and more at your fingertips

The amount of information available on CompuServe is so vast that you wouldn't be able to read it all, even if you wanted to. Each day, thousands of messages are posted on the several hundred forums, databases are updated, and hundreds of programs, articles and other text files are uploaded.

In practiced terms, this means that you have to be selective. After you have determined what you are looking for, you will go online and see how CompuServe can help you get to that information. During that process, you will benefit from the structured way in which all information is organized. Typically, each CompuServe member builds his or her own list of 'popular places' that he or she visits on a regular basis.

If you are like most members, you will want to 'go hiking' from time to time, to discover new features and places to visit. Useful programs like WinCIM, included with this book, assist you by offering a user-friendly interface, with dialog boxes, menus, and so on. During those trips, you will often encounter new services that you want to add to your list of popular places.

1.3 What's all this going to cost me?

One of the questions most frequently asked by new CompuServe users is 'How much am I going to pay for this?'. Unfortunately, this one can't be answered in just one sentence, and not even in one paragraph. For novice users, CompuServe's billing method is something that takes some time to get used to. There are quite a number of different charges to know about, enough reason to spend a large section of this chapter discussing them!

Let's start with the caveat that CompuServe doesn't even mention: your telephone bill. Compared to American CompuServe members, who very often have the luxury of a (free!) local access number, we often have to deal with interlocal, and sometimes even international, telephone connections. Even before going online for the first time, you should try to calculate the average telephone costs per hour. Better still, check whether your telephone company provides cheaper rates when you call in the evening hours – in some countries savings can be up to 50 per cent!

1.3.1 Charges and surcharges

After you have calculated the telephone costs per hour, it's time to look at the charges that will show up on your CompuServe bills. These can be divided into the following categories:

- **Communication surcharges**, sometimes referred to as Network charges: you pay for the use of so-called 'leased lines' that CompuServe, sometimes in cooperation with a telecommunication company, has established for you. Thanks to these leased lines, you don't have to make the call to Columbus, Ohio (where the CompuServe computers are located) directly. Instead, you share a communications link with a lot of other users. Although you might be led to think otherwise, you actually communicate with the CompuServe computers in the USA, instead of using some kind of 'shadow system' in Europe!
- **Connect charges**, which you pay while using the extended services that CompuServe provides. Most forums and other CompuServe facilities are part of the extended services. CompuServe uses a special symbol to indicate an extended service in menus: the plus sign (+).
- **Premium surcharges**, on a number of special services, like Executive News, the Database Plus facilities, and so on. You are always warned when you are about to incur such surcharges. In addition, the Dollar sign (**$**) is used to indicate them in menus.
- **Mail charges**, for sending (and sometimes receiving) electronic mail. You thought that sending and receiving mail was free, right? Well, it is, to a certain entent. As a member of the Standard Pricing Plan, you'll receive a monthly mail credit of $9, and the charges for every mail message that you send are deducted from this sum. When you receive mail that's postage due (which means that you have to pay for it, either because the sender didn't, or because it comes from another network and travelled a long way to reach you), you'll have to pay for that as well. Some members never reach the magical limit of $9.00 per month, others use it up after only two or three days. You'll see why in a few moments.

- **And, finally, the monthly charges**: your 'membership fee'. There are two so-called pricing plans: the Standard Pricing Plan and the Alternative Pricing Plan. The Standard Pricing Plan carries a monthly fee of $8.95. In return, you get a monthly mail credit of $9, plus a vast amount of so-called Basic Services for free. (You don't pay connection charges for using those services, although communication surcharges still apply.) Some of these Basic Services justify a CompuServe membership by themselves! Members of the Alternative Pricing Plan pay only $2.50 per month, but don't benefit from free Basic Services. These 'Pay-as-you-go' members simply pay for almost everything they do online. Also, the hourly connection charges are much more expensive for Alternative Pricing Plan members.

That leaves us with an additional membership facility: Executive Membership. If your CompuServe bill exceeds $10 per month (which is the case for most CompuServe members), you can become an Executive Member for no extra charge. There's only one condition: CompuServe will charge you at least $10 per month, even if you didn't go online in that month. In return, you get access to some services that are off-limits for other members. Note that Executive Membership in itself doesn't cost anything at all. It's simply a matter of calculation: if your CompuServe bill is higher than $10, you can switch over to Executive Membership without incurring extra charges. If you pay less, you probably spend so little time online that it's not worth bothering with the extra services.

1.3.2 Communication surcharges

As you might have guessed, there's a lot going on when you send your e-mail messages to the other side of the world, or even to your neighbour next door. The information you send to CompuServe leaves your computer *via* your modem and arrives at a dial-in node, where it waits to be sent (together with information from a lot of other members) to one of CompuServe's central computers, somewhere in Europe. From there, these data packets are transferred to CompuServe's main computers on the other side of the ocean, in Columbus, Ohio, where they are stored. As soon as the addressee of your e-mail message empties his or her electronic mailbox, your message is sent in a similar way, using the same data communication methods.

The technology used to accomplish this is, to say the least, astounding. And it is expensive, very expensive. But because of the increasing number of CompuServe members worldwide, these services can be provided for less and less cost. Only a few years ago, the communication surcharges were so high that only large companies and privileged computer users could afford to be part of the so-called 'community online'. Quite a contrast with today, where CompuServe members in more and more countries pay very low surcharges, and sometimes don't even pay them at all!

Nowadays, communication surcharges have dropped to a level that makes them affordable for almost every computer user. If you connect to CompuServe through one of its European access numbers, the communication surcharges are $7.70 per hour during office hours (on weekdays between 8:00 a.m. and 7:00 p.m.). During all other hours, the communication surcharges are waived.

Communication surcharges and your network

If you live in a country that doesn't have a direct CompuServe dial-in number, the chances are that you use a so-called external network to get through to CompuServe. Examples of such networks are INFONET and Sprintnet. CompuServe has to pay charges to those networks, and passes those charges on to you. Once online, you can learn more about those charges: just `GO RATES`.

1.3.3 Connect charges

Every member of the Standard Pricing Plan has access to a large number of free CompuServe facilities: the Basic Services. Apart from communication surcharges, you don't pay anything beside your monthly fee while you access those services.

As soon as you leave Basic Services and enter the Extended Services, the 'meter starts running'. CompuServe will charge you a certain amount per minute you spend in Extended Services. At the time this book was written, those charges were $4.80 per hour ($0.08 per minute) for modem speeds up to 2400 bps, and $9.60 per hour ($0.16 per minute) for modem speeds higher than 2400 bps.

Let's say you visit a few forums that are part of Extended Services (almost all forums are, with the exception of forums that support CompuServe products). You have spent 15 minutes in those forums, downloading a few files, reading some messages, and conferencing with other forum members all around the world. The modem speed was 2400 bps. In that case, you would be charged 25% of $4.80: $1.20. Note that communication surcharges (refer to Section 1.3.2) would be added to that amount.

Watch the + sign!

If you are a member of the Standard Pricing Plan, CompuServe will use a plus sign (+) to indicate Extended Services. Also, if you use a program like WinCIM to access CompuServe, you will see status messages like `'You have left Basic Services'` and `'You have entered Basic Services'` when appropriate.

1.3.4 Additional surcharges

For a few CompuServe facilities, you have to pay extra surcharges: so-called premium surcharges. Examples of these facilities are the Executive News Service (ENS) and online databases like Magazine Database Plus and IQuest. Before you enter a premium service, CompuServe will advise you that you are about to incur surcharges. In most cases, you will see a summary of all premium surcharges before you leave the service. In CompuServe menus, premium services have a **$** sign added to their name.

1.3.5 Mail charges

As a member of the Standard Pricing Plan, you receive a mail allowance of $9 per month. For every e-mail message that you send, and for some e-mail messages that you receive, a certain amount is deducted from that mail allowance. Once you have used up your mail allowance for a particular month, CompuServe will charge you for all additional e-mail messages you send (as well as some you receive) during that month.

Your mail allowance expires at the beginning of each new month, and will be replaced by a new $9 mail allowance.

So how is your mail allowance affected by the mail you send and receive?

- For each e-mail message that you send, you pay a minimum amount of $0.15, for which you can send 6,000 bytes (about three pages). Each additional 2000 bytes cost $0.05. Thus, sending a message of 10,000 characters in length costs $0.25. A message that is 50,000 characters long will cost $1.25.
- Apart from regular messages, you can send files as well. The same calculation is applied: $0.05 per 2000 bytes, with a minimum of $0.15.
- Receiving e-mail is essentially free, except for messages sent to you from the Internet. When receiving Internet e-mail messages, you pay $0.05 per 2000 bytes, with a minimum of $0.15.
- When you send messages *via* CompuServe Mail, you can reverse the charges (the receiver pays), or split the charges (you and the receiver each pays half the costs).
- If you send a message *via* CompuServe Mail, you can ask for a confirmation of receipt: as soon as the addressee gets the message (that is, when he or she either reads or deletes it), you will receive a small informative message from CompuServe. You pay an extra $0.15 for this service, which will be deducted from your monthly mail allowance as soon as you send the message.
- Note that communication surcharges still apply!

You could save some money!

Sending large e-mail messages can be expensive if you are a member of the Standard Pricing Plan. Suppose that you need to send three files, each with a length of 1MB. In that case, you would end up paying about $75, minus what is left from your monthly mail allowance. In practice, you would be charged anything between $66 and $75, depending on the amount of other mail you have sent during that month. (For simplicity, we will ignore communication surcharges in this example.)

Members of the Alternative Pricing Plan don't have mail allowances. Instead, they pay $12.80 per hour for access up to 2400 bps, or $22.80 per hour for access with modem speeds higher than 2400 bps. Sending those three files at 9600 bps would take a little bit less than an hour. The total cost therefore would be $22.80.

1.3.6 Monthly charges: the pricing plans

Until a few years ago, pricing plans didn't exist on CompuServe. Members basically paid for each minute they spent online, and didn't have any Basic Services at their disposal. After receiving a lot of requests from members, CompuServe introduced a new pricing plan structure. Members can now choose from the following pricing plans:

- **The Standard Pricing Plan**: This is the default pricing plan. When you sign up, you will automatically become a member of this pricing plan. You pay a $8.95 monthly fee, for which you get the following:
  - A monthly $9 mail allowance which expires at the end of each month.
  - Free access to a large number of Basic Services, like AP News, weather information, online columns, and magazines.
  - Low hourly rates for using Extended Services: $4.80 for modem speeds up to 2400 bps and $9.60 for modem speeds higher than 2400 bps. You will be charged for each minute that you spend in Extended Services.
- **The Alternative Pricing Plan**: The monthly fee is only $2.50, but the 'meter starts running' as soon as you get online. Except from a few free services, you pay high hourly rates for everything you do online: $12.80 for modem speeds up to 2400 bps and $22.80 for modem speeds higher than 2400 bps. You will be charged for each minute that you spend in Extended Services.

Some things online are free

CompuServe offers four kinds of services: free services (free for all members, regardless of their pricing plan), basic services (free for members of the Standard Pricing Plan), extended services (billed at the rates discussed above) and premium services (billed at the rates discussed above, plus a surcharge).

The free services include several forums (the Practice Forum and the CompuServe Help Forum, as well as the support forums for access programs provided by CompuServe, such as the WinCIM Support Forum), as well as membership assistance options.

It is possible to switch plans: **GO CHOICES** to do this. Note the following:

- If you change from the Alternative Pricing Plan to the Standard Pricing Plan, you will be charged the $8.95 membership fee at the end of the billing month, regardless of when you made the change. Generally, the best time to change to the Standard Pricing Plan is as early in the billing month as possible.
- If you change from the Standard Pricing Plan to the Alternative Pricing Plan, you will still be charged the $8.95 at the end of the billing month. Generally, the best time to change to the Alternative Pricing Plan is as late in the billing month as possible.

Once you are signed up to one of the two pricing plans mentioned above, you can decide whether you want to benefit from one of the additional pricing plans. A few examples:

- If, generally, you spend more than $10 per month (including the $8.95 or $2.50 'flat fee', depending on your pricing plan), you can select the Executive Service Option. CompuServe will charge you at least $10 per month (even if you didn't spend any time online), but in return you get access to an additional series of services, of which the Executive News Service is the most famous.
- If you like to spend time on CB (a service that lets you 'chat' with people all around the world) or at the Entertainment Center (where you can play chess, backgammon and a number of other games with people around the world), you could join the CB/Entertainment Center Club. Non-members are charged $4.80 or $9.60 per hour (depending on modem speed) for accessing those services, but as a member of the CB/Entertainment Center Club you pay only $3 per hour (with a flat fee of $25 per month) or $1 dollar per hour (with a flat fee of $50 per month).

How to get information about the current rates

CompuServe changes constantly. Therefore, it is possible that the actual rates have changed since this book was written. For free information (note that communication surcharges still apply) about the current rates, **GO RATES**.

1.3.7 How and when am I billed?

There are three ways to pay your CompuServe bills:

- **By credit card**: This is by far the most popular method. CompuServe will charge your card each week. Don't forget to update your billing information when your credit card expires: `GO BILLING` and select `Changing Your Billing Information` to do this.
- **Via direct debit**: In some countries, you can have CompuServe debit your bank account automatically. `GO BILLING` and select `Changing Your Billing Information` to check whether direct debit is available for your country.

  Normally, you will get an account limit of $300 per month. If you want to spend more, you will need to request a higher account limit. This request will be granted only if your payment history is good.

  Payments will be made every week, provided that there is something to charge, of course. Your monthly membership fee will be billed at the end of the billing month.
- **Via a Business Account**: Qualified businesses can choose to be invoiced by CompuServe. The minimum monthly charges per User ID are $10. To establish a Business Account with CompuServe, you need to `GO FEEDBACK` and request an application.

Typically, you will be billed at the end of each week: your credit card or bank account will be charged with the costs that you have incurred during that week, plus (at the end of the billing month) the fee for your pricing plan. The billing month ends on the last Saturday of the calendar month, at midnight American East Coast time (0500 GMT).

CompuServe maintains records of all costs that you have incurred. To review them, or to change or update your billing information (credit card specification, address information, and so on.), `GO BILLING`. The CompuServe Billing Menu contains the following options:

- **Current Rates**: Displays a menu with rates information. The same menu can be reached by the `GO RATES` command.
- **Review Your Charges**: Displays a list of charges to your credit card, or to your bank account (if you use direct debit to pay your CompuServe charges).
- **Direct Debit Status**: If you use direct debit (not available in all countries) to pay your CompuServe charges, you can get information about the current status of your account *via* this option.
- **Billing Options Explained**: Select this option to get more information about the available billing options.
- **Pricing Plans Explained**: Selecting this option will give you additional information about the pricing plans available on CompuServe.

- **Changing Your Billing Address**: Select this option when you need to change your address information. Note that CompuServe Magazine, the free magazine for CompuServe users, will be sent to the address that you have specified here.
- **Changing your Billing Information**: Select this option when you want to choose another billing method, or when you need to update your credit card information.
- **Executive Service Option**: Select this option if you want the Executive Service Option to be applied to your membership. You will pay a minimum fee of $10 per month; in return, you get access to an additional number of services.
- **General Billing Information**: Select this option for information about your direct debit status, to request detailed billing information, and for other information regarding your account.

The things that you need

The things that you need

CompuServe has been set up to make access as easy as possible, irrespective of the computer configuration that you work with. Regardless of whether you use an MS-DOS compatible computer, a sophisticated PowerPC, an Amiga, or maybe a small PDA like the Psion Series 3a or the Casio Zoomer, there is always a way to get connected.

In this chapter, we will focus on the hardware and software that you need to access CompuServe, and provide information that pertains to the various platforms. Note that some of the information here can be more or less out-dated: you might be able to find newer versions of existing programs on CompuServe, as well as new software for operating systems that weren't supported at the time this book was written.

2.1 Computers and modems

If you can connect a modem to your computer, you can use it to access CompuServe. It's that simple! Basically, you need the following hardware and software to get you online:

- As stated, a computer. Although the majority of CompuServe members use an MS-DOS compatible system, there are also a lot of people online who use Macintoshes, or one of the models that were introduced (and were more popular then than they are now) in the 1980s, like the Atari ST, Commodore Amiga, and a number of 8-bit systems. With hardware and software developments going on all the time, it won't surprise you that a growing number of PowerPC and OS/2 users are finding their way to CompuServe as well.

The only requirement is that your computer can be connected to a modem. This is the case for all computers equipped with an *RS-232 serial port*. In some cases, like the older Atari 8-bit and Commodore 64 models, you need a special expansion module for this. The same applies to palmtop computers like the Psion Series 3a. Consult your dealer for more information.

- A special device that *modulates* bytes into audible tones and *demodulates* those tones back into bytes: a *modem*. After connecting your computer to a modem, and the modem to the telephone line, you are basically ready to communicate with any other computer that is connected in the same way (like CompuServe's computers, for instance).

2.1.1. More on modems

Modems have come a long way since they were first introduced to the general public, about 15 years ago. The first modems were large, clumsy cases that took a great deal of effort to connect to a computer. Direct connections to the telephone line weren't common yet: most modems were actually *acoustic couplers*. You placed the telephone receiver onto an acoustic coupler and pressed firmly, thereby establishing a more or less 'direct' connection. Needless to say, you had to be quiet while data transmission was in progress – any external sound would disturb the communication.

The revival of acoustic couplers

In some countries, it is still considered illegal to connect a modem to a telephone line directly. Other countries allow it on certain conditions only. For example, in the British version of a modem that is manufactured in the United States, some options have been disabled to comply with UK regulations. Although you might be able to obtain a 'non-censored' version of the same modem somewhere else in Europe, you are technically not allowed to connect that modem to the British telephone network. A work-around for this problem is the use of *acoustic couplers*: devices that allow you to establish a connection without actually 'wiring' your modem to the telephone line. Acoustic couplers were once the only affordable way to make a connection with another computer; the advanced versions of these devices could very well become popular tools for the travelling computer user.

When you are considering the purchase of a (new) modem, the chances are that you are overwhelmed by what's available on the market these days. Modems can be divided into three categories:

- *Internal modems*: These come on a card that needs to be plugged into an empty slot in your desktop computer, or into a slot in your notebook computer. The most important benefit of internal modems is that they come with their own serial interface: you don't need an extra communications port. In most cases, you simply install the modem, connect it (*via* a special cable) to the telephone line, and that's it. After the installation, internal modems form an integral part of the computer. This can pose a drawback, especially when you use more than one computer (a desktop and a notebook, for example). In that case, it might be more economic to buy an external modem, for instance a 'pocket' model, that you can take with you when necessary.

- *External modems*: These are connected to your computer *via* one of the communication ports. Two kinds of external modems exist: table models and 'pocket' models. Pocket modems often run on batteries as well, which makes them an ideal travel tool.
* *PCMCIA Modems*: These modems are credit card size, and can be placed into slots known as 'PCMCIA slots'.

Once you have decided into which category your new modem should fall, it's time to consider the following:

- *Compatibility*: To work flawlessly with most communication programs on the market today, your modem should support the Hayes command set.
- *Speed*: The faster the modem, the less time you spend online. When this book was written, CompuServe supported modem speeds up to 14,400 bps (*bits per second*).
- *Error checking*: If you use the ASCII interface to access CompuServe (that is, if you don't use programs like WinCIM and CompuServe Navigator), note that CompuServe's modems support the MNP-5 error checking protocol. (When you use an HMI access program like WinCIM or CompuServe Navigator, you don't have to worry about this: HMI uses its own error checking protocol.)

2.1.2 Connecting in foreign countries

Have you ever tried to connect to CompuServe from a hotel in a foreign country? If so, you will probably never forget the trouble you had to go through – if you succeeded at all! Most hotels are still amazingly ignorant when it comes to the data communication needs of their guests. Experienced travellers who need to stay in touch often carry tools like screwdrivers (to dismantle telephone receivers and/or wall outlets) and a special cable with them. This cable has a standard RJ-11 connector on one end, and two alligator clips on the other. In most cases, you can simply unscrew the telephone mouthpiece and connect the alligator clips directly to the contacts of the mouthpiece.

When you need to be absolutely sure that you will be able to connect to CompuServe from your hotel or foreign office, there is a company called *TeleAdapt* that may have the solution to your problem. TeleAdapt supplies special 'TeleDaptors' for almost every country in the world. They can be reached as follows:

Tel +1 (408) 370-5105
+44 (081) 421 4444
Fax +1 (408) 370-5110
+44 (081) 421 5308

And, of course, *via* CompuServe: the User ID of Gordon Brown at TeleAdapt is 100111,2713.

2.1.3 Helpful files on CompuServe

Before you plan to travel to a foreign country, be sure to take a look at some files on CompuServe that contain very useful information. A few examples are listed below.

Forum: The TapCIS Forum (GO TAPCIS)
Filename: PHONE.PLG
Bytes: 7409
Title: Describes telephone plugs used around the world
Description: A text file that details the telephone plug used in most of the countries of the world with some additional hints for successful international communications. Upload/Author Gordon Brown [100111,2713].

Forum: The TapCIS Forum (GO TAPCIS)
Filename: LAPTOP.ARC
Bytes: 10904
Title: Info about telecomputing while on the road
Description: Information on using hotel phones with laptop computers and modems, airport security, X-ray and magnetic hazards, foreign electrical power, tools and devices to carry, using computers in-flight. Incorporates most or all of the information in a number of previous files on CIS, and attempts to answer some of the most common questions asked by people travelling with computers. Upload by author, John Deakin.

Forum: The TapCIS Forum (GO TAPCIS)
Filename: TRAVEL.KIT
Bytes: 6454
Title: Sysop Joan Phriedman's phamed phone-busting kit
Description: A description of the various phone cords and connectors I carry in my 'travel kit', to be assured of being able to connect my modem regardless of the hotel phone set-up. The file contains an explanation of how all this stuff is used. The necessary equipment can be acquired at Radio Shack at low cost. An ASCII text file, uploaded by Joan Friedman.

Forum: The Europe Forum (GO EURFORUM)
Filename: GERHOT.TXT
Bytes: 26,187
Title: Text telephone help file 'GERHOT.TXT'
Description: A complete description of how to connect PC modems to German telephone lines found in hotels and offices for data and fax comms. Details on VDO4, TAE6, ADO and other connectors, with diagrams. Hints for pay telephones, digital and ISDN phones, and so on.

Forum: The Europe Forum (GO EURFORUM)
Filename: TRAVEL.ZIP
Bytes: 12,152
Title: Connecting Your Computer to Hotel Telephones
Description: Travel Kit for connecting your computer to a hotel/motel phone while you are away from home. Discusses many of the problems one can encounter and methods for getting around them. Includes several common-sense precautions and approaches. Information is included for US and foreign phone and power environments.

Don't forget the Travel Forum!

One of the places you can't afford to miss when you are planning to travel is the Travel Forum on CompuServe (GO TRAVSIG). The forum libraries are filled with invaluable information. To name but a few: airport procedures, hotel recommendations, tips to make travelling more comfortable, details about 'must-see' attractions, and so on.

2.2 Software

There are hundreds of programs available that let your computer communicate with other computers: so-called *communication programs* or *terminal programs*. Some computers (like the Commodore Amiga) come with a terminal program that can be used for basic communication. The same applies to some operating systems: Microsoft Windows' Terminal application is a good example.
Another operating system that provides communication software to access CompuServe is the new version of OS/2. This version comes with a copy of the CompuServe Information Manager for OS/2, a special access program that makes it very easy to use CompuServe.

2.2.1 A frequent route: standard communication software

Unlike some other popular online services, CompuServe can be accessed with every communication program available. When you use a general communication program, you will use CompuServe's ASCII interface. In practice, this means that you will see standard ASCII menus, and that you are required to type commands yourself. Special benefits like dialog windows and pull-down menus (which make CompuServe a lot easier!) are available only when you use special CompuServe access programs like the CompuServe Information Manager (CIM) or CompuServe Navigator. These programs use a special protocol, *HMI*, that is not supported by general communication software.

When you use standard communication software to access CompuServe, set it to use the following parameters:

- 7 data bits
- 1 stop bit
- Even parity
- ANSI
- Local echo off

How to get online

For more information about making the actual connection, refer to chapter 3, 'Getting online'.

2.2.2 The easiest route: the CIM software packages

As you will have noticed, this book contains a Windows version of the CompuServe Information Manager, or WinCIM for short. WinCIM makes access to CompuServe very easy, providing conveniently arranged pull-down menus and dialog windows. If you don't use Windows, you can download copies of CIM for other operating systems from CompuServe. Refer to Section 5.2, 'How to obtain the program', for more information.

2.2.3 The cheapest route: offline readers

Most members need some time to get used to CompuServe. During that period, they often work with one of the CIM programs to make access easy and straightforward. But sooner or later, they feel the need to *automate* their online activities. The time has then come to make the switch to one of the so-called *auto-access* programs.

Auto-access programs, also called *offline readers*, reduce the time you spend online, and thereby reduce your CompuServe and telephone bills. Basically, the programs spend as little time online as possible, retrieving information (like message topics and file descriptions) for you to review offline. Two of the most famous auto-access programs, *CompuServe Navigator* and *TapCIS*, are discussed throughout this book. CompuServe Navigator, provided by CompuServe, is written for the Windows operating system; TapCIS is aimed at DOS users.

Apart from these two programs, there is a lot of auto-access software available on CompuServe, for a number of platforms. An overview of the most popular auto-access programs is given below, as well as information about how to obtain them. A few important remarks are in order. First, it is impossible to cover all the software that is currently available. If you are looking for a particular auto-access program for the computer or operating system that you use, consider visiting the appropriate support forum. Next, some of the 'shortcomings' that are discussed below may well have been eliminated in newer versions of the software that weren't available at the time this book was written. Visit the appropriate forum for details about the latest version of a particular auto-access program. And finally, you will have to pay a charge to use or register most of these programs. Because those charges are subject to change, they aren't listed in this book. To learn more about the costs for a particular program, visit the appropriate forum.

CompuServe jargon

Don't worry if you don't understand all the terms that are used below. *Message threads, file libraries* and other examples of the 'CompuServe language' are discussed in the following chapters.

MS-DOS

Because most CompuServe members use an MS-DOS computer, it will come as no surprise that a lot of auto-access programs have been written for this operating system. The most famous are:

- *TapCIS*: One of the oldest and most famous auto-access programs. Because it uses little memory, it can be used on computers with limited capacity (like older portable computers, and even some palmtop computers) as well. TapCIS is undoubtedly one of the fastest

auto-access programs available. It is, for instance, much faster than CompuServe Navigator. There is one drawback, however: its rather archaic user interface makes this program rather hard to master. But most, if not all, experienced TapCIS users take this interface for granted because of its unrivalled speed.
More information about TapCIS can be found throughout this book, as it is one of the access programs covered in detail. See Section 6.2, 'TapCIS', for additional information.

- *OzCIS*: This program started as freeware, programmed by one of CompuServe's 'celebrities': Steve Sneed. Meanwhile, OzCIS has become a very sophisticated piece of shareware, which can be used to automate almost all facilities that CompuServe offers. In that respect, OzCIS is much more powerful then competing programs like TapCIS. But there is one important drawback: OzCIS doesn't run on XT computers. Apart from that, its memory requirements are huge.
  Currently, there are two versions of OzCIS available. Version 1 works on computers with a 286 processor or better, and requires at least 485 kB system memory. This is an absolute minimum: the program really begins to shine when your system has at least 520 kB system memory and 1 MB EMS or XMS memory at its disposal.
  Version 2 has even more features than version 1. Its message and library archiving system is one of the best on the market, and the program has a very powerful script language that enables you to automate virtually all CompuServe facilities.
  However, these features don't come without a price: you need at least a 286 computer, while a 386 or higher processor is recommended. Memory requirements are high as well: your computer needs at least 2 MB extended memory to be able to run OzCIS.
  Although both OzCIS versions have a friendly and modern user interface, things can get quite confusing for new users. But help is nearby: the OzCIS Forum on CompuServe provides support by experienced OzCIS users as well as by the programmers. If you need more power than programs like CIM and TapCIS can provide, give OzCIS a try. You won't regret it.
  More information about the available OzCIS programs can be found in the OzCIS Forum: `GO OZCIS`. Both versions can be downloaded from this forum as well.

HINTS & TIPS

OzCIS in German

There is a German version of OzCIS available. For more information, `GO OZCIS`.

- *TeePee*: This is an original British shareware program, with very modest system requirements: TP (for short) runs on computers that contain a hard disk and minimal 460 kB system memory. It automates reading and writing e-mail and forum messages, as well as file downloads. TeePee is one of the few programs that can also be used if you 'emulate' MS-DOS on another computer. A trial version of TeePee is available on the UK Communications Forum: `GO UKCOMMS` for more information.

- *NavCIS*: One of the newer auto-access programs, supported by American computer publicist and consultant John Dvorak. NavCIS, available in DOS and Windows versions, contains a few options that no other auto-access program has. One of the most eye-catching features is the possibility of using several fonts in e-mail and forum messages. When you send a message to another NavCIS user, you can apply bold and italic attributes to your text, and you can even choose from a range of character sizes and fonts. If the recipient of your message doesn't use a NavCIS program, he or she sees a string with seemingly random characters, applied to the end of your message. This characters contain the actual formatting commands.
  The NavCIS user interface is very intuitive, although some things work quite differently than in other programs. Unlike programs like TapCIS and TeePee, NavCIS automates one of the most cost-intensive features of CompuServe: the File Finders. After you have entered a search specification, NavCIS will go online and retrieve information about the files that match this specification. Offline, you will be able to mark the files you are interested in for automatic retrieval.
  NavCIS is available for DOS as well as for Windows. Basically, there are two versions. The *Timed Edition* (TE) is a fully fledged version of the program, which expires after 30 days. If you want to continue to use the program, you will have to register it. Its counterpart is the *Special Edition* (SE): this is a limited edition of the program, which you may use as long as you wish. Some of the more important features of the regular program, however, are not available in this special edition. Visit the Dvorak Forum for more information, and to download the program(s): **GO DVORAK**.

Windows

The number of auto-access programs for the Windows operating system is growing rapidly. The most famous titles are listed below:

- *CompuServe Navigator*: This is by far the most famous program, developed by CompuServe and data-compatible with all CIM programs. CompuServe Navigator is discussed extensively throughout this book: Section 6.1, 'CompuServe Navigator', contains detailed information.

- *WigWam*: A British product, of which English- and German-language versions are available. One of the most eye-catching features of this program is its speed: it reads forum message threads as quickly as DOS programs like TapCIS and OzCIS. It is therefore much faster than CompuServe Navigator for Windows, but the user interface needs a little more time to master.
  Compared to DOS programs like OzCIS, WigWam lacks thread management facilities (when this book was written, version 2 of WigWam had just been released.) Although you can mark message threads that you are not interested in, there is no way to avoid the program downloading new messages in the same thread. (Although those messages won't

be displayed on your screen, they are retrieved anyway, which takes additional time.) But the chances are that this feature will be improved in future versions of the program, which might very well be available by the time this book is published.
Trial versions of WigWam (in English and German) are available on the UK Communications Forum: **GO UKCOMMS** for more information.

- *NavCIS*: This program, which is available in DOS and Windows versions, is discussed in more detail above. German-speaking Windows users have an advantage: there is a special German version of this program available. For more information, and to download the program: **GO DVORAK**.

- *OzCIS*: When this book was written, a Windows version of OzCIS was in development. This version, released in July 1994, supports all features of the DOS version and more. For instance, OzCIS uses the HMI protocol to establish a reliable connection, and to allow support for typical CompuServe facilities like the Member Directory, library downloads, and so on. The most revolutionary feature is that the program does this without the time penalty that other programs (like WinCIM and CompuServe Navigator) pay. OzCIS for Windows is a very impressive program; if you want to become a CompuServe power user, you should take a look at it. More information can be found in the OzCIS Forum: **GO OZCIS**. Both versions can be downloaded from this forum as well.

OS/2

- *Golden CommPass*: This is considered to be the 'number one' auto-access program for OS/2 users. Because of its data-compatibility with TapCIS, one of the most famous DOS auto access programs, you can use both programs simultaneously (TapCIS on your laptop computer and Gold CommPass on your desktop computer, for instance). Golden CommPass supports automatic processing of forum messages, file libraries and e-mail. 'Intelligent' thread management is incorporated: Golden CommPass remembers which message threads you have read during a previous session, and will retrieve the new messages in those threads automatically. Because Golden CommPass takes full advantage of OS/2's multithreading and multitasking capabilities, you can start reading messages downloaded from one forum while Golden CommPass processes messages for another forum.
  To download a trial version of Golden CommPass, **GO GCPSUPPORT**. This will bring you to the Golden CommPass Support Forum. Information about obtaining the full version of Golden CommPass can be found in this forum as well.

Apple Macintosh

- *CompuServe Navigator*: This is the Macintosh counterpart of the CompuServe Navigator for Windows program, discussed throughout this book. To order this program, **GO ORDER**. It is not possible to download a complete version of Navigator: it will be sent to you *via* mail. However, updates can be downloaded: **GO NAVIGATOR** for more details.

Commodore Amiga

- *AutoPilot*: A very famous auto-access program amongst Amiga users. Like all auto-access programs, AutoPilot automates the processing of forum messages, file libraries and e-mail. But one of the most powerful features of this program is *ARexx*, the built-in script language that can be used to automate almost all CompuServe features. AutoPilot can be downloaded from the AutoPilot library in the Amiga Vendor Forum (**GO AMIGAVEND**). Full program functionality is available only after you have registered the program, something that you can do online. After you have registered it, you will receive a binary e-mail message that will automatically update AutoPilot to the registered version.

Atari ST

- *QuickCIS*: Atari ST users can download this auto-access program to automate message and file processing as well as e-mail. Registration of QuickCIS is free. A number of (freeware) applications have been developed to make QuickCIS even easier and more versatile. To download QuickCIS, **GO ATARIPRO** to visit the Atari Computing Forum.

3 Getting online

Getting online

If you are already a CompuServe member, most of the material discussed in this chapter may not apply to you. It contains information about signing up and getting online for the first time. But if you travel a lot, and if you would like to access CompuServe from other countries as well, you might be interested in information about external networks, provided in this chapter.

3.1 Want to sign up?

If you aren't a CompuServe member yet, it is time to take the bull by the horns and sign up! As you will see, signing up is not difficult at all. It basically consists of the following steps:

- Finding a CompuServe access number.
- Establishing a connection with CompuServe.
- Specifying necessary name, address and billing information.
- Writing down your User ID (your personal 'address' on CompuServe) and password.

In the next sections, we'll go through all of these steps in detail.

3.1.1 Finding a CompuServe access number

If you have installed WinCIM, provided with this book, the first step is easy. WinCIM contains a built-in list with access numbers for most countries. If you use another program, it is probably best to use a direct CompuServe dial-in node, even if that node is located in a foreign country, for your first few sessions. Once you have managed to get online without any problems, you can `GO PHONES` to get more information about network access numbers and login procedures for your country. A summary of some CompuServe dial-in nodes in Europe is given below:

Country	*Access Number*	*Speed*
Austria	*+43 1 505-6178*	*300, 1200, 2400, 9600*
Belgium	*+32 2 215-0530*	*300, 1200, 2400, 9600*
France	*+33 1 4789-3940*	*300, 1200, 2400, 9600*
Germany	*+49 89 6653-0170*	*1200, 2400, 9600, 14,400*
Netherlands	*+31 20 688-0085*	*300, 1200, 2400, 9600*
Spain	*+34 3 487-3888*	*300, 1200, 2400, 9600*
Sweden	*+46 8 - 140 500*	*300, 1200, 2400, 9600*
Switzerland	*+41 1 273-1028*	*300, 1200, 2400, 9600*
United Kingdom	*+44 171 490-8881*	*300, 1200, 2400, 9600, 14,400*

3.1.2 Making the connection

The steps involved in connecting to CompuServe depend on the access program you use. Refer to the appropriate section.

Connecting with WinCIM

After you have installed WinCIM (*refer to* CHAPTER FIVE *for details*), double-click on the WinCIM icon to launch it. If this is your first WinCIM session, the `Setup Session Settings` window will appear automatically. If it doesn't, select the `Session Settings` option on the `Special` menu. Section 5.9.1 contains additional information about this window. If you are an existing CompuServe member (that is, if you have a User ID and password), be sure to enter at least the following information:

- Your name.
- Your User ID.
- Your password.

- The phone number that should be dialled to access CompuServe.
- The communication port to which your modem is connected (in the `Connector` field).
- The baud rate.
- The network you will use to access CompuServe. If you have specified one of the telephone numbers listed above, you can select `CompuServe`. If not, select the network from the Network combo box.
- When you have finished this dialog, you are ready to connect to CompuServe.

Connecting with regular communication software

Set up your communication parameters as follows:

- Data bits: 7
- Stop bits: 1
- Parity: Even

Now, instruct your communication software to dial one of the access numbers listed above. As soon as one of CompuServe's modems has picked up the phone, you should see the following:

```
07AMU
Host Name:
```

The first line contains information about your connection: the modem number and the CompuServe node. The second line asks you to enter a `Host name`. Do one of the following:

- Enter CIS and press the Enter key.
- Press Ctrl-C.

You will see the following:

```
User ID:
```

This is CompuServe's request for a User ID. If you are already a member, type your User ID and press Enter. CompuServe will now ask for your password; after you have typed it and pressed the Enter key, you'll end up in the CompuServe Top Menu. If you aren't a member yet, proceed at Section 3.1.3, under the heading '*Signing up with a regular communications program*'.

3.1.3 The actual sign-up procedure

Signing up with WinCIM

WinCIM makes signing up to CompuServe very easy. When you install the program, it asks whether or not you would like to install the Sign-up files. If you have chosen to do so, open the CompuServe program group and double-click on the CompuServe Sign-up icon. If you didn't install the Sign-up files, just install WinCIM again.

The CompuServe Sign-up application guides you through a series of windows. After you have entered your membership details and selected a CompuServe telephone number, WinCIM will connect and sign you up automatically. It will also inform you of your temporary password. That password will be valid for ten days. Your second password, which gives you access to some facilities that are restricted for members with a temporary password, will arrive *via* regular mail (or 'snail mail', as some CompuServe members call it).

Signing up with a regular communications program

After you have connected to CompuServe, you type in the following *sign-up User ID* and the *sign-up password* at the prompts:

```
User ID: 177000,5606
Password: EXPLORE/WORLD
```

After you have entered the User ID and password, CompuServe 'knows' that you want to sign up. It responds as follows:

```
Select a Language for Signup

1 Sign me up in English
2 Anmelden in Deutsch
3 Exit Signup

Enter Choice :
```

Type [1] and press the [Enter] key if you want to use the English sign-up procedure. If you'd prefer this to be done in German, type [2] and press the [Enter] key. (In this example, we'll use the English version.)

```
Enter Choice : 1

Please Enter:

Agreement #:
```

It is time to enter the Agreement and Serial Numbers. Please DO NOT use the Agreement and Serial Numbers found on the diskette that comes with this book when you sign up with a regular communications program. (The numbers on the diskette work only if you sign up using WinCIM!) Use the following numbers instead:

```
Agreement #: UKITP
Serial #:    93006
Welcome to CompuServe!  Please answer the following questions so
that we may begin your membership.  The registration process is
free.
Press <CR> for more !
```

<CR> means the Enter key ('Carriage Return'). After you have pressed it, CompuServe displays the following:

```
Please select the area where your mailing address is located:
1 United States
2 Canada
3 Africa/Middle East
4 Asia
5 Australia/Oceania
6 Latin America
7 Europe
8 Other
9 Exit Member Registration
Enter Choice:
```

Select the area that applies to you and press Enter. If you selected 'Europe', CompuServe continues as follows:

```
Europe

1 France
2 Germany
3 Hungary
4 Italy
5 Netherlands
6 Sweden
7 Switzerland
8 United Kingdom
9 Other
10 Exit Member Registration

Enter Choice:
```

After you have selected the country that you live in, CompuServe displays the following:

```
Your package includes a usage credit of $15.00 (US). You will not
be billed for usage until you have used up this credit. However,
usage credits are not applied towards your Standard Pricing Plan
monthly membership.

Throughout this registration, you will be asked to supply
information.  Each time you see a colon (:), please make an entry.
Always follow your entry by pressing the carriage return key.
You may stop the process at any time by typing in the word EXIT at
any prompt. This will erase ALL of your entries.  If you
subsequently wish to cancel your membership, please notify us
through online Feedback (GO FEEDBACK) or by letter.
```

Please note: When you sign up with a regular communications program, you will have to return the filled-in reply card supplied with the book to gain the $15 of usage credit.

Next, CompuServe will ask you how you should be billed:

```
Please Select the Desired Billing Method
CHARGE CARD
1 Visa
2 Mastercard/EuroCard/Access
3 American Express/Optima
4 Diners Club
5 Discover
6 Explanation of Charge Card

BUSINESS ACCOUNT INVOICING
7 Choose Business Account Invoicing
8 Explanation of Business Account
9 Exit Member Registration
Enter Choice:
```

Note that this list can contain more or fewer options than listed in this menu, depending on the country where you are located.

When you have indicated that you want to pay *via* credit card, CompuServe will prompt you to read the official Service Agreement:

```
Be sure to read and understand our Service Agreement Terms,
billing options, and rates because they may be different than the
ones printed in your membership materials. You can review our
current rates by typing GO RATES at any ! prompt once you have
logged on with your permanent User ID number. The current billing
options and Service Agreement Terms can be reviewed by selecting
options from the next menu. Prior to completing the member
registration, you will be asked to review the Service Agreement
Terms and the Operating Rules.
Do You Wish to
1 Review Service Agreement Terms
2 Review Operating Rules
3 Proceed With Member Registration
4 Select a Different Billing Option
5 Exit Member Registration
Enter Choice:
```

Select options 1 and 2 to review the Service Agreement Terms and Operating Rules, respectively. Once you select 3 to proceed, CompuServe displays the following message:

```
By moving beyond this page you are indicating your acceptance of
our Service Agreement Terms covering your use of the Service.
Indicate your acceptance by typing the word AGREE at this prompt
and pressing the carriage return key.
:
```

After you have typed `AGREE` and pressed the [Enter] key, CompuServe will ask you whether or not you want to select the Executive Option. Next, you need to enter your address and credit card information. When you have finished, CompuServe displays the following:

```
By completing the member registration, you are also requesting a
free subscription to CompuServe Magazine, the definitive monthly
guide to using our many products and services. The subscription to
CompuServe Magazine is of no additional cost to you, and can be
cancelled at any time. We reserve the right to limit or modify
this offer at any time.
Do you wish to receive CompuServe Magazine at no additional cost?
(Yes or No) :
```

Type [Y] and press [Enter] to indicate that you would like to receive CompuServe Magazine.

You are now entering the final part of the sign-up procedure. CompuServe displays information about the Standard Pricing Plan and Extended Services:

```
Standard Pricing Plan:

Your CompuServe Standard Pricing Plan membership of $8.95 per month
includes unlimited connect time to access a variety of basic
services. You will not be charged your membership of $8.95 until your
second month of membership.  Refer to the CompuServe basic services
menu (GO BASIC) for a complete listing of services in the plan.

Telecommunications surcharges apply to all online usage and vary
based on the network you use to connect to CompuServe.
CompuServe's own European network currently provides the least
expensive access and is FREE during the evenings and weekends in
the UK and Europe.
For a complete list of all telecommunications surcharges, Type GO
RATES at any ! prompt.  For a list of access methods for your city,
type GO LOGON.
```

```
CompuServe Extended Services:

Extended services are priced at hourly connect charges based on
baud rates and you are only charged for what you use.  Connect
charges are billed in one minute increments with a minimum of one
minute per session. Connect charges do not include communication
surcharges. Your introductory credit will apply toward any usage
of extended services.  A "+" on a menu indicates you will enter a
CompuServe
extended service if you select that choice.

300/1200/2400 baud  $ 4.80/hour
9600/14400 baud  $ 9.60/hour

Some of these CompuServe extended services have additional premium
surcharges associated with them.  They are indicated by a "$" on
the online menus.  For a listing of these services and these
surcharges, type GO RATES once online.
```

You are almost there! CompuServe will display the following:

```
Your name, city, and country will normally be included in the
online Member Directory. If you do not wish to be included, you
may indicate your preference now.
1 List in Directory
2 Do NOT List in Directory
3 Information about Directory
4 Exit Member Registration
Enter Choice:
```

The online Member Directory can be accessed by all CompuServe members. Unless you have very urgent reasons not to, I'd recommend that you select the first option, '`List in Directory`'. You can always remove your entry later: just **`GO DIRECTORY`**.

Next, CompuServe informs you that your name will be put on mailing lists:

```
We occasionally make our membership mailing lists available to
other companies to provide information, about products and
services.
Most members enjoy receiving such offers. You may, however, have
your name excluded by typing GO MEMBER once you are online.
```

After having asked you what equipment you generally use to access CompuServe, CompuServe provides you with your User ID and a *temporary password*:

```
Thank you. We will verify your member registration entry.

We will now provide you with your PERMANENT User ID number and a
TEMPORARY password which you can use to access the Service. After
your initial usage credit is used up, you may continue to access
the Service subject to our current billing rates and account
limitations.  You will be billed for this usage.

Your User ID Number is: 000000,000
Please write your User ID Number down
Your confidential password is: XXXXX?XXXXX
Please write your password down
```

Naturally, your screen will show a different User ID and password.

After you have typed in your User ID and password to confirm, CompuServe informs you that your account is restricted in certain ways, until you receive your second password:

```
NEVER give your password to ANYONE, verbally or through the
Service.
*** PLEASE NOTE ***
As part of processing your member registration, we are creating
and mailing you a new password to be effective 10 days from today.
(Your User ID number will remain the same and will not be mailed
to you). The new password and its effective date will be sent
through Postal Mail to the address you have entered.
```

Until you receive this second password and it is effective, certain restrictions will apply to your account.

You have completed your member registration and may now log on the Service and begin using your introductory usage credit. At the next User ID number and password prompts, enter the new permanent User ID number and temporary password which you have just obtained. Note that your password does not print out as you enter it – this is a security precaution for your protection.

That's it! You are now a member of CompuServe. The first time you log on using your new User ID, you will receive a short explanation about often-used commands and terminology.

3.2 It doesn't work – what now?

If you experience problems while you try to connect to CompuServe, or while you try to sign up a new membership, you first have to determine at which level the problems occur. Use the following checklist:

- Do you actually manage to connect to CompuServe? If you use WinCIM, you should see a few informative messages during the connect process, followed by a 'Connected' status message. If not, check if you have specified the right telephone number and modem speed (baud rate), and that your modem is switched on and attached to the communications port you have specified. If you use an external network, try using an official CompuServe node instead. If that works, you know that the problem is caused by the external network connection.
- Do you get error messages during the sign-up procedure? Check that you have specified the correct information. To sign up, you need to specify two or more of the following:
  - The temporary User ID (only if you use regular communication software; WinCIM users don't need to specify it).
  - The temporary password (again, only if you use regular communication software).
  - The Agreement Number and Serial Number. Note that these numbers can only be used once: it is not possible to sign up several times using the same set of numbers.
- Do you get error messages during the actual login procedure (that is, after you have become a member)? In that case, are your User ID and password correct? Did you remember to replace your temporary password (after ten days) with the new one you received by regular mail?

If your problems still persist, pick up the phone and dial one of the following numbers during local office hours. You will be connected to a member of CompuServe's support staff, who will assist you. Don't worry: you'll be online shortly!

France:	*AZUR number: 36-63-81-31*	*Direct: +33 1 47-14-21-60*
Germany:	*Freephone: 0130-86-46-43*	*Direct: +49 (0)89 66 535-222*

Switzerland:	*Freephone: 155 31 79*	
United Kingdom:	*Freephone: 0800 289 458*	*Direct: +44 (0)272 760 680*
United States:	*+1 614 529-1340*	

3.3 OK, so now I'm there, what am I looking at?

Once you are connected to CompuServe, there are a lot of ways to navigate. The following chapter will give you a good impression of what to expect online, but if you can't wait to explore what's ahead of you, just try the following suggestions:

3.3.1 Using WinCIM

From the main WinCIM window, there are several ways to connect to CompuServe. A few examples:

- Click on one of the icons in the `Services` window. If the `Services` window is not displayed, select the `Browse` option on the `Services` menu. After WinCIM has connected to CompuServe, it (or rather, CompuServe) will display a list with menu options that correspond to the icon you selected.
- Select the `Get New Mail` option on the `Mail` menu. After WinCIM has connected to CompuServe, it will display a list of waiting CompuServe Mail messages (if any).
- Select the `Find` option on the `Services` menu and enter a keyword. WinCIM will connect to CompuServe; after a few moments, you will see a list with services that match your keyword.
- If you know the '`GO` word' of a service you would like to visit, select the `Go` option on the `Services` menu and enter that word. After connecting to CompuServe, WinCIM will take you to that service. A nice example is `GO TOUR`, which starts an 'online tour' of CompuServe facilities.

Disconnecting from CompuServe

Don't disconnect by just 'hanging up the phone', or by switching off your modem. Instead, select the `Disconnect` *option on the* `File` *menu, or press* Ctrl-D*. You can also click on the special* `Disconnect` *button, displayed on the WinCIM Ribbon. Note that when you exit WinCIM without disconnecting, the program will do so automatically.*

3.3.2 Using regular communication software

- Select one of the menu options. To get to the top menu, type TOP and press the Enter key. To get to the 'parent menu' (the menu from which you selected the option that led to the current menu), type M and press the Enter key.
- Use the FIND command to look for services that might interest you. After you have typed a keyword, CompuServe will list all services that match that keyword. You can then use the GO command to visit that service directly.
- Type the GO command, followed by a space and the 'GO word' for a particular service. For instance, to check if you have mail: type GO MAIL (you may use capitals as well as lower case letters) and press the Enter key. Another useful GO word for new CompuServe members is GO TOUR: you will be taken on an 'online tour' and get a good impression of available CompuServe services.
- To get a complete index of all public GO words on CompuServe, type GO INDEX and press the Enter key.

HINTS & TIPS

Disconnecting from CompuServe

Don't disconnect by just 'hanging up'! Instead, type off *and press the* Enter *key. In some cases (depending on whether you pressed* Ctrl-C *to get past the* 'Host name' *prompt), you will see the text* 'Host name' *appearing again. In that case, type* off *again to disconnect.*

4 Welcome to our Guided Tour!

Welcome to our Guided Tour!

Now that you have established a CompuServe account, come and join our Guided Tour! In this chapter, we will visit some of CompuServe's Basic Services. As a member of the Standard Pricing Plan, all Basic Services are free (although communication surcharges still apply).

In this Guided Tour we will visit the following Basic Services:

- *Weather Reports*
- *News*
- *The Academic American Encyclopedia*
- *The Practice Forum*

Although all these services can be accessed using Terminal Emulation (The 'ASCII Interface' of CompuServe), we assume that you use a version of the CompuServe Information Manager: WinCIM. However, you can also use CIM for the Macintosh, CIM for OS/2, or DOSCIM to go on tour with us.

4.1 Ready? Set, GO!

To start our Guided Tour, select the `Browse` option on the Services menu. This will display the Services window. Click on the `Basic Services` option; WinCIM will now connect to CompuServe. After a few moments, the 'connect' message will appear, indicating that you are online. The Basic Services menu will appear shortly thereafter. If you wish to go directly to one of the services discussed, use the listed GO word for that service.

4.2 Weather Reports

(Route: `GO WEATHER`, `GO MAPS`, or *via* WinCIM's Browse menu)

We'll start with a brief look at the current weather. As you will see, you are not limited to the weather in your own country: you can check the current weather anywhere in the world. From the Basic Services menu, select the `News/Weather/Sports` option. This causes the News/Weather/Sports menu, listed in Figure 4.1, to appear.

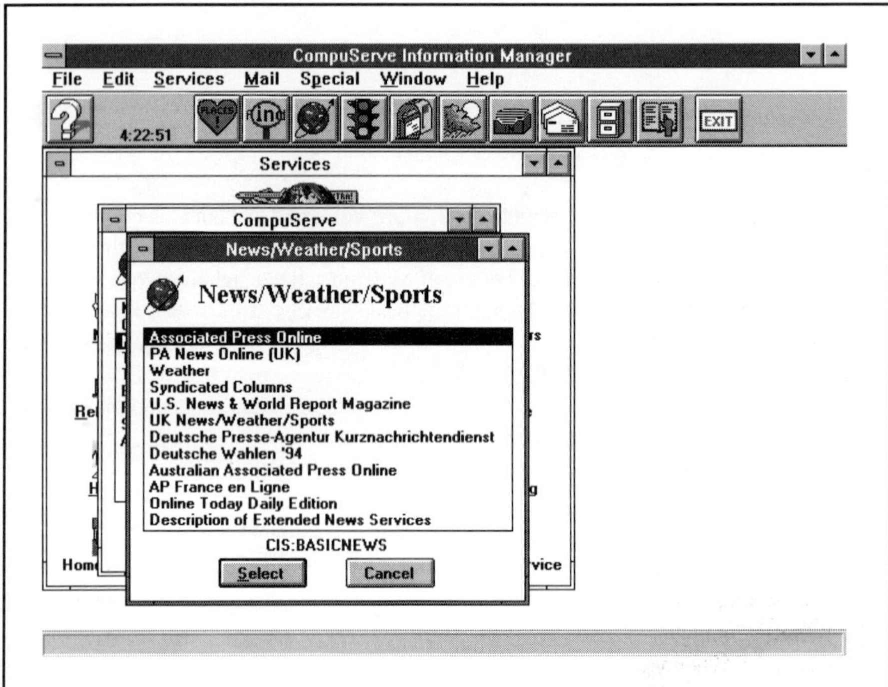

Figure 4.1 This menu sums up the News, Weather and Sports facilities that are part of Basic Services

Select the `Weather` option. After a few seconds, the CompuServe Weather Reports dialog appears, as shown in Figure 4.2.

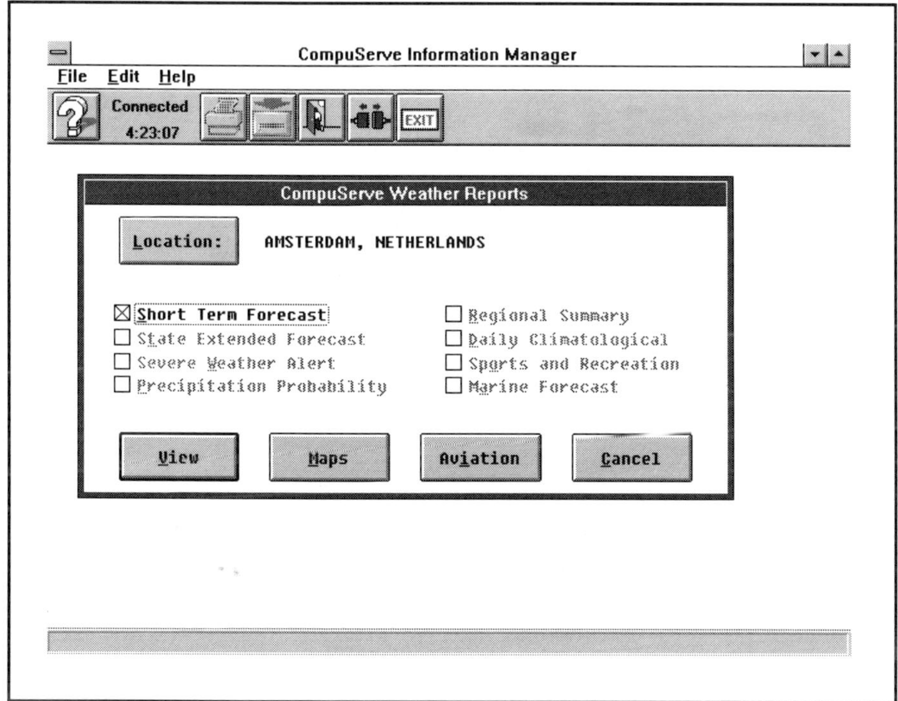

Figure 4.2 The CompuServe Weather Reports dialog

If you have connected to one of the regular CompuServe nodes in your country, the Location field will probably contain the name of the city in which that node is located. To select another city, press the `Location` button. You have to specify country information; if you wish, you can leave the City and State/Province fields blank.

The number of available check boxes in the CompuServe Weather Report dialog depends on the location you have selected. For some locations, like most cities in the United States, all options are available; if you have selected a European city, you have at least the option Short Term Forecast available.

Check, if necessary, the Short Term Forecast box. Next, press the `View` button. After a few moments, CompuServe will display text information pertaining to the current weather and the expected weather for the next few days.

Because CompuServe can send graphical information to your computer, you can also view *weather maps*. When you use one of the CIM programs, this is actually very easy to do. From the CompuServe Weather Report dialog, press the Map button. You will see a list of regional weather maps. After you have selected the map you would like to view, press the `View` button. CompuServe will now transfer the graphical information to your computer; you will see the map appear on your screen. Thanks to the built-in compression that the CompuServe graphic format provides, this takes only a few seconds, even on low communication speeds.

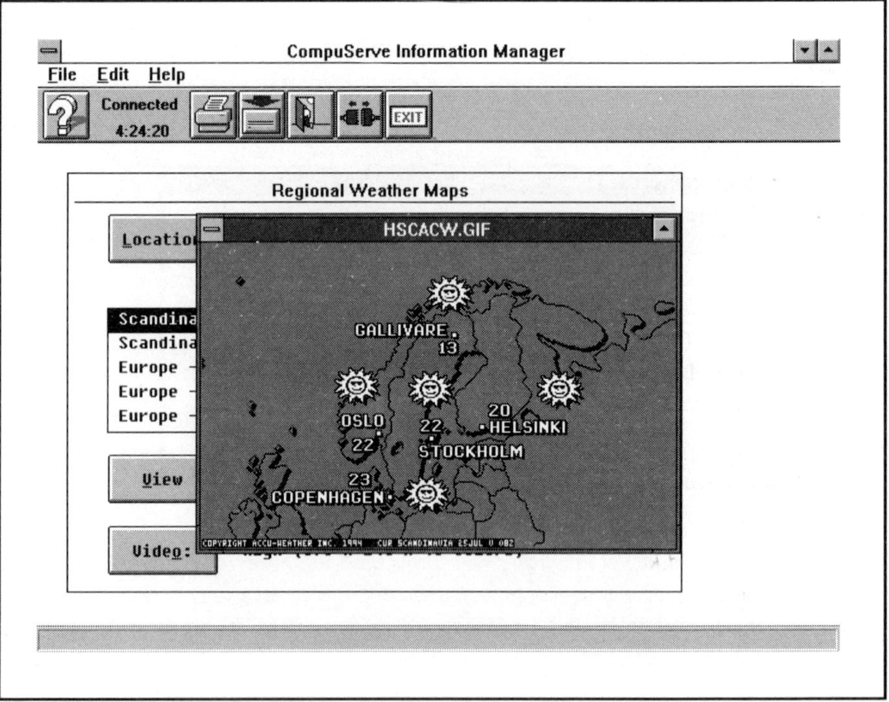

Figure 4.3 Weather information at your fingertips: CompuServe has just sent a map to your computer

Saving the information to disk

Normally, you would select the `Save` or `Save As` option on the `File` menu to save the displayed information. However, WinCIM's menu options are not available while one of CompuServe's Weather Reports dialogs is displayed. To save the information, press the `'Save'` button that is part of the WinCIM Ribbon. You can also print the displayed information (text as well as weather maps) by pressing the `Print` button.

When you have finished using the Weather Reports, press the `Leave` button (on the Ribbon): the button with the 'open door' symbol. Or you can press the `Cancel` button(s) in the current dialog(s).

4.3 News

(Route: `GO BAS-5`, or *via* WinCIM's `Browse` menu)

If you are new to CompuServe, you will probably be surprised to learn how many news facilities are available as part of Basic Services. It doesn't stop with news in the English language: you can read news from the Deutsche Presse-Agentur Kurznachrichtendienst, in German, or news from AP France en Ligne, in French. And because the Basic Services are continually being expanded, the chances are that you either already can, or shortly will be able to, read news in other languages too!

From the Basic Services menu, select the `News/Weather/Sports` option. You will see a list with available options; most of them pertain to news facilities. A few examples:

- *Associated Press Online*: One of the most popular Basic Services. Although it focuses on American news, it also covers 'world news'. The bulletins are updated every hour, or more often if necessary.
- *PA News Online (UK)*: Especially for British members, PA News Online covers news topics specific to the United Kingdom, like politics, financial news, royalty and sports. However, there is also a 'general' section that deals with events all over the world.
- *U.S. News & World Report Magazine*: Select this option to review the current issue of this famous American magazine. Apart from magazine text, you can also view photos, graphics, and sometimes even animated sequences. There is a direct link to the accompanying forum, which, however, is part of Extended Services.
- *Deutsche Presse-Agentur Kurznachrichtendienst*: If German is your mother language, you may not miss this one! Although the main focus is on events in Germany, world news is covered as well.
- *Australian Associated Press Online*: News pertaining to Australia, mainly about business and sports.
- *AP France en Ligne*: French CompuServe members have the option of reading online news in French. Apart from specific French economic, sports and cultural news, you can also read international news.
- *Online Today Daily Edition*: This is one of those services that are often overlooked. Too bad, because OLT, as it is often called, can provide very valuable information! For instance, you will find announcements and reviews of upcoming software, hardware and computer books, as well as important computer news.

Let's try one of the facilities listed above: Associated Press Online. In the News/Weather/Sports window, double-click on `Associated Press Online`, or select this option with the cursor keys and press [Enter].

After you have read the copyright alert, press Enter to proceed. You will see the AP Online menu. When you select an option from this menu, a new menu will appear. This second menu contains the actual news items; select an item by double-clicking on it, or by moving to it with the cursor keys and pressing Enter.

To get updated on the latest news events as quickly as possible, select the first option on the AP Online menu: `Latest News - Updated Hourly`. You will get a list of 'AP Top News' items; the first item in the list contains an overview of the most recent news. Note that the times listed after the news items are in American east-coast format: five hours before GMT, six hours before CET.

Urgent news

If there is late-breaking news, the items in the Latest News – Updated Hourly window will be updated as often as necessary.

You don't have to read the news online. Instead, press the `File It` button to store the news item in one of your Filing Cabinet folders. After you have disconnected, you can read the articles without having to worry about your telephone bill.

The Filing Cabinet will be discussed in more detail in Chapter 5. However, the following should get you going. After WinCIM displays an article, proceed as follows:

1. Press the `File It` button. WinCIM will display the Filing Cabinet: a list of personal folders which are actually subdirectories on your hard disk.
2. Make a new folder: press the `New` button. The `Add New Folder` dialog is displayed. Enter a folder name, for instance 'AP News'. Press `OK` to close the dialog.
3. You will see that the AP News folder is added to the list of folders in the Filing Cabinet. (Because it starts with an A, it will probably be somewhere at the top of your list.) Make sure that the folder name is selected, and press `Save`. The article will now be saved in your AP News folder. After WinCIM has saved the article, a confirmation message is displayed on the status bar.
4. Now, disconnect from CompuServe. Because the article is actually stored on your hard disk, you will be able to read it offline.
5. Open your Filing Cabinet. There are three ways to do this:
   - Select the `Filing Cabinet` option on the Mail menu.
   - Press Ctrl-F.
   - Click on the special `Filing Cabinet` button, displayed on the WinCIM Ribbon.
6. Select the AP News folder and press the `Open` button. It will show one article: the one that you retrieved just a few minutes ago. Press the `Open` button to read it. Take your time: you are not online any more!
7. When you have finished with the article, close its window. If you wish, you can delete the article by pressing the Del button.

The Filing Cabinet storage facility is supported by the majority of online news services. For those services that don't support it, you can press the 'Save' button on the Ribbon to save the article as an ASCII file. (The file will be stored in your `\CSERVE\DOWNLOAD` directory.) After you have disconnected, you can open the file (select the `Open` option on the File menu) to read it.

Try to experiment a little with the Filing Cabinet. It is a handy tool that you will use very often in the future.

4.4 Encyclopedias and dictionaries

(Route: `GO REFERENCE`, or *via* WinCIM's `Browse` menu)

If you are doing research, or if you are looking for the meaning of a particular word, the chances are that CompuServe can help you. Some of the most valuable features of Basic Services are *reference products*. You can actually access one of the world's most famous encyclopaedias, the Academic American Encyclopedia, online! Also, you can improve your knowledge of the English language with the American Heritage Dictionary, while German users have an electronic version of the Bertelsmann Lexikon at their disposal. And, again: all these products are part of Basic Services.

When you select the `Reference` option on the Basic Services menu, a list with options is displayed. The following list shows some of those options:

- *Academic American Encyclopedia*: A perfect tool when you have to prepare essays and suchlike: the online edition of what is often referred to as the 'Grolier's Encyclopedia'. It contains more than 35,000 articles, and it is updated every three months. Because it is updated frequently, you are likely to find articles that are not available in regular encyclopaedias.
- *American Heritage Dictionary*: The online version of one of America's most famous dictionaries: the same one that is included on the Microsoft Bookshelf CD-ROM. It is easy to use, comprehensive and fast.
- *Bertelsmann Lexikon*: Aimed at German-speaking users, this electronic lexicon contains more than 120,000 keywords and is updated regularly. For each keyword entered, a list of items is displayed. When you select an item, CompuServe displays a comprehensive definition.
- *Consumer Reports*: This service contains a series of articles in which new and existing consumer products are discussed. Although some of the products aren't even available in Europe, it can help you to create a list of points to check when you are planning to purchase an expensive product.
- *HealthNet*: If you are looking for medical information, HealthNet is the place to go. It contains a comprehensive reference library, with an additional section containing information about sports injuries and treatments.

- *Handicapped Users Database*: If you are handicapped, you might want to visit the Disabilities Forum (`GO DISABILITIES`), a part of Extended Services. Or maybe you would like to take a free look in this free database, with, amongst other features, an extensive reference library and a list of organizations that make products especially for handicapped people.

Again, we'll try one of the products named above: the Academic American Encyclopedia. Either select the corresponding option on the Reference menu, or `GO ENCYCLOPEDIA`. After a few moments, the Groliers menu is displayed.

If you would like to read a brief introduction, select `Introduction`. (Don't forget to store this text in your Filing Cabinet, instead of reading it online.) Or go straight to the Users Guide, which contains articles that you can place in your Filing Cabinet as well.

After you have read those articles, you are probably ready to start searching. Select the last option on the Groliers menu: `Search Encyclopedia`. CompuServe will now ask for a search term. Be as specific or as brief as you like! For instance, if you would like to see a list of topics that pertain to Hungary, entering 'hung' would be sufficient.

After a few moments, you will see a list of topics that contain information about the keyword you specified. Here is where the fun starts! As you will notice, the descriptions of some of those end with a colon, indicating that these are *referrals* to other topics in the Encyclopedia.

After you have selected a topic, CompuServe displays an *outline*. By browsing through the outline, you can decide what part of the actual article you would like to read. This saves you the trouble of going through the whole article; instead, you can focus on the information you really need. A typical outline contains the following items:

- *Section headers*: Items in capital letters. These items often contain general information.
- *Sub-section headers*: Items that are preceded by a dot. These contain detailed information about a particular subject.
- *General commands*: These are written in mixed case, and can be selected to issue commands. Whether or not a general command is available depends on the topic. Examples of such items are:
  - *Begin New Search*: Select this item to return to the `Search` dialog.
  - *Overview*: Select this item to view short, to-the-point information about the current topic.
  - *Bibliography*: Select this item to review a list of books and magazines that contain additional information about the current topic.
  - *Fact box*: Select this item if you need summarized information about the current topic.
  - *Table*: Select this item to view information about the current topic in tabular form.

What if you wish to store a part of the article? In that case, press the `File It` button to save it in your Filing Cabinet. After you have retrieved all the information that you wish, disconnect to read the contents of your Filing Cabinet offline.

4.5 The Practice Forum

(Route: `GO PRACTICE`, or *via* WinCIM's `Browse` menu)

Newcomers to CompuServe, are you ready to visit your first forum? In that case, let us escort you to the free Practice Forum! In that forum, you will be able to read messages from CompuServe members all over the world, and to learn from the questions and answers posted in the several message sections.

During our visit to the Practice Forum, we will do the following:

- *Join* the Practice Forum.
- *Read messages* posted on the forum.
- *Post a message* in one of the forum's sections.
- *Download a file* from the forum libraries.

If you are reluctant to use the CompuServe forums, you will see how easy it really is. And because the Practice Forum is free, you can worry a little bit less about the charges. Here we go!

4.5.1 Joining the Practice Forum

When the Services window is displayed, select `Basic Services`, followed by `Member Assistance`. Next, select the `Practice Forum` option.

Of course, you can also go to the forum directly: select the `Go` option on WinCIM's Services menu, and enter `PRACTICE` as the destination. And there you go, on your way to what is probably the busiest forum on CompuServe...

As soon as you arrive at the forum, you will see a welcome message. You are informed that you are not a member yet, but that you can *join* any time you wish. As you see in Figure 4.4, you can specify the name you wish to use in the forum. Type your first and last name in the Name field (if they aren't there already). If you like, you can type some information about yourself in the 'Interests' field. If you do so, you will be added to the *Membership List* of the forum. Forum visitors often browse through that list, searching for people with the same hobbies and interests as themselves.

When you have entered the information, press the Join button. Welcome to the Practice Forum! You are now a member, and you can start using all the facilities that this forum has to offer.

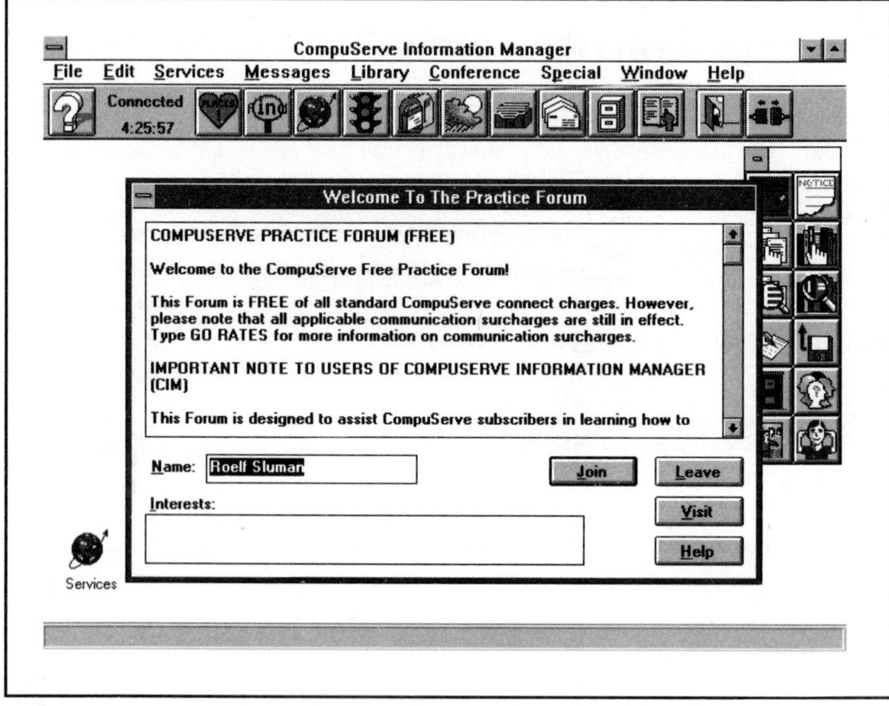

Figure 4.4 You are about to join the Practice Forum

What's this 'Visit' button?

Just ignore it. It is there for people who are not sure if they would like to join the forum, and who choose to look around a little bit before they make their decision. However, the things that a visitor can do in a forum are very limited. For instance, most forums don't allow visitors to read and post messages, or to access the libraries. Because it doesn't cost anything extra to join a forum, don't bother about that 'Visit' button.

4.5.2 You're in!

Because the forum recognizes you as a newcomer, you will see some guidelines for new members of the forum. These guidelines are part of the forum's *notices*; you will learn more about them in a moment.

If you would like to save this notice for future reference, select the `Save` option on the WinCIM's File menu. After you have disconnected, you can read it by selecting the `Open` option on the File menu. (Saved text files have the extension TXT.)

After you have either read or saved the notice, press the OK button.

Because you are in a forum, WinCIM's menu structure has changed. There are now three additional menus: Messages, Library and Conference. In addition, the Special menu contains options that are not available outside forums.

Most forum sysops expect you to read the available notices before you start using the forum. That's right: there are more notices than the one you just saw. To see a list of them, select the `Notices` option on the Special menu. If you wish, read the notices one by one, or store them in a file. When you have finished, you are ready to participate in the forum.

4.5.3 Reading forum messages

First, let's take a look at the available message sections. Those sections are where it all happens: members and forum staff exchange messages, in this case about forums in general. To prevent you from having to go through hundreds of messages, they are ordered logically, in so-called *sections*. Every forum has a number of sections, varying from 1 to 24. (There are even some forums that don't have any message sections at all, but we leave those out of this discussion.)

To see a list of available forum sections, select the `Descriptions` option on the Message menu. As you can see in Figure 4.5, there are a lot of sections!

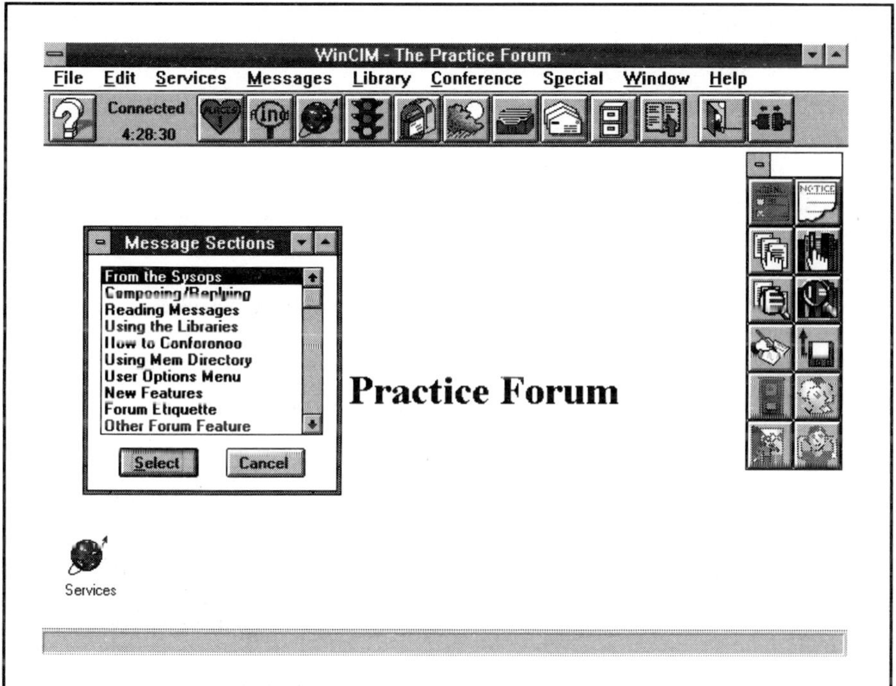

Figure 4.5 The available message sections in the Practice Forum

To learn more about a particular section, select it and press the `Select` button.

In a section, messages are divided into *threads*. When someone composes a forum message, adds a message subject (*topic*) and addresses it (to someone in particular, or to *all*), he or she starts a new thread. When someone replies to that message, he or she adds a message to that thread, and so on. The principle of threads is not as complicated as it seems, as you will learn soon.

We'll start by reading a few forum messages. However, instead of reading them online, we'll *mark* them and *retrieve* them to our computer's hard disk. Proceed as follows:

1. From the Messages menu, select the `Browse` option. You can also click on the `Messages` button on the forum Ribbon: the three documents with the pointing finger.
2. After a few moments, a dialog appears (see Figure 4.6). This dialog contains an overview of all sections in the forum. For each section, you see the number of topics (threads) that contain new messages, as well as the total number of messages. 'New' pertains to the following:

   - If this is the very first time that you select the `Browse` option, you will see all public messages that have been posted (as well as any private messages to you). Note that a forum can only contain a certain number of messages; if the board is filled completely, the first new message that is posted results in the oldest message 'scrolling off' the forum. That message is gone for ever, unless you saved a copy of it, of course.
   - If you selected the `Browse` option in a previous section, and return to the forum later, you will only see the messages that have been posted since. Note that this *doesn't* include the messages you posted yourself: we'll come to that later.
   - If you have reset the message date, you will see a list of all messages available on the forum that have been posted since that date. Although you normally won't need to do this, it is an easy way to catch up with earlier messages, or to look at all the messages in a particular thread. To reset the message date, select the `Set Date` option on the `Messages` menu.

Displaying all forum messages

If you don't see an impressive number of messages (several hundred at least), select the `Set Date` option on the Messages menu and enter a new starting date (1-1-94 will do nicely). The contents of the dialog will be updated immediately.

3. Now, select a section that deals with a topic you are interested in and press the 'Select' button. After a few moments, a new dialog appears. This dialog contains information about all threads in that section: the name of the thread, and the number of messages it currently contains. An example is shown in Figure 4.7.

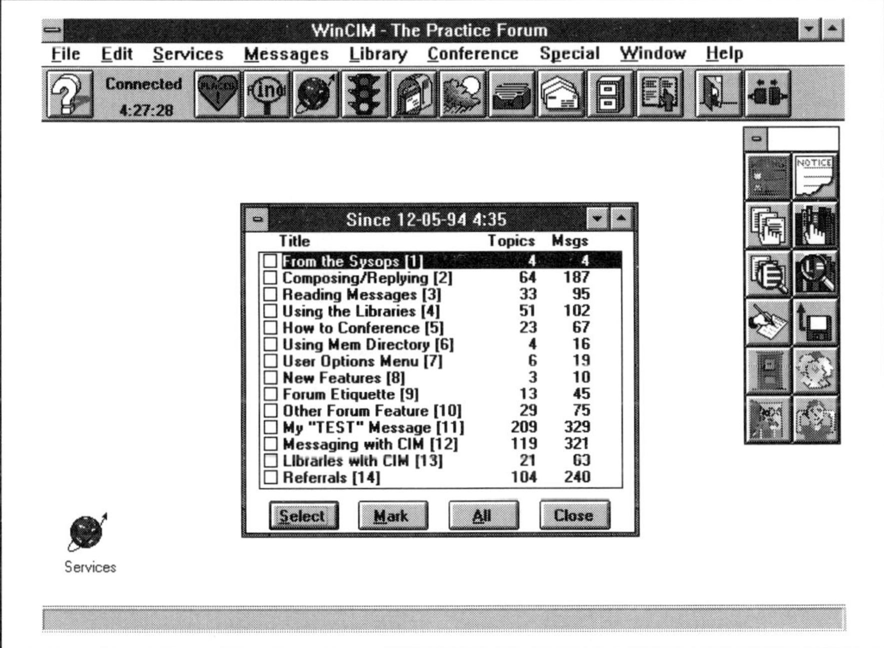

Figure 4.6 Information about the message sections

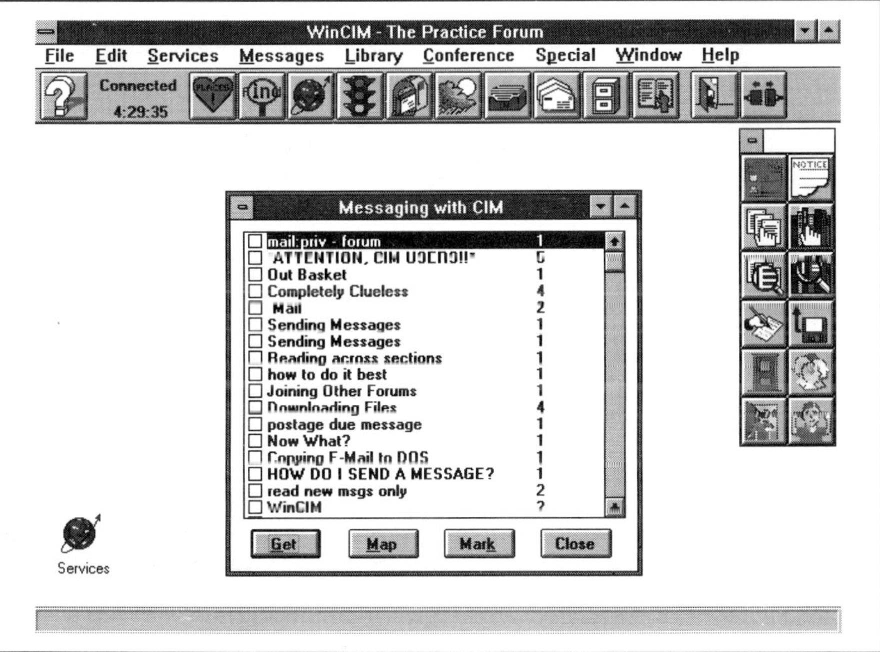

Figure 4.7 Current threads in a message section

4. Now, go and look for one or more threads that interest you. Use the mouse or the cursor keys to scroll through the list; the number of items might be too large to fit on the screen! When you have found a thread that you would like to read, *mark* it: press the 'Mark' button. For the sake of this example, be sure to select one or more threads that contain a large number of messages.

5. After you have marked the threads, you can close this dialog. If you wish, mark some threads in one or more other sections as well.

6. Next, you will *retrieve* the marked messages to your hard disk. To do this, select the `Retrieve Marked` option on the Messages menu. Figure 4.8 shows the accompanying dialog.

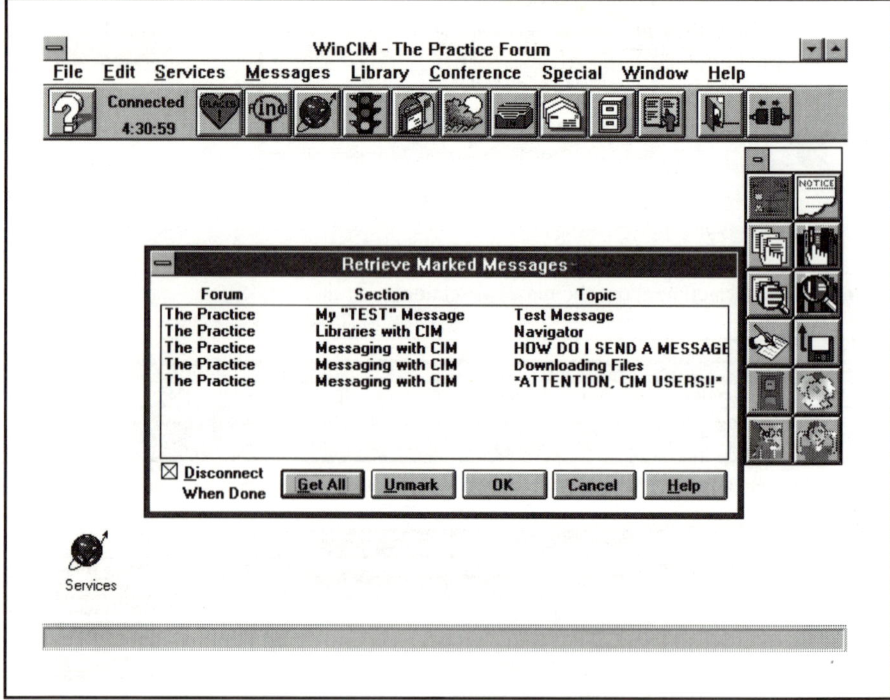

Figure 4.8 You are about to retrieve the marked messages to your hard disk. Once they are stored there, you can disconnect, and read them offline.

7. If you want WinCIM to disconnect automatically when it has retrieved all messages, be sure to check the Disconnected When Done box. Next, press the 'Get All' button. WinCIM will now start retrieving the messages. This can take a while, depending on

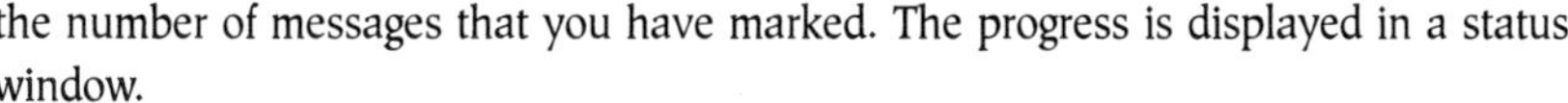

the number of messages that you have marked. The progress is displayed in a status window.

8. When WinCIM has finished, you can start reading the messages at your own pace. (Are you sure that you have disconnected? If not, select the **Disconnect** option on the File menu. If it is greyed out, you are already offline. WinCIM has retrieved the messages into your *Filing Cabinet*. To start reading them, select the **Filing Cabinet** option on the Mail menu, press Ctrl-F, or press the special **Filing Cabinet** button on the WinCIM Ribbon.
9. The Filing Cabinet contains a number of *folders*. If you haven't used it before, there will be only one folder, which WinCIM has created for you. It is probably called 'The Practice'. Select it and press the **Open** button.
10. And there they are: your messages! The first message will be selected. Press the 'Open' button to start reading it. It will be displayed in a dialog, which also contains a number of buttons. You can use these buttons to navigate through the retrieved messages and threads:
    - If a message has replies, press the **Next** button (the button with the arrow to the right) to read them. To return to the *parent message* (that is, the message to which this reply applies), press the arrow-up button.
    - To see a graphical *map* of the current thread, press the **Map** button. You will see the names of everybody who posted messages in this thread, together with their place in the 'thread tree'. To read a message directly, select it and press the **Get** button.
    - To read the *next thread*, press the **Topic** button. If there are no more threads available, this button is greyed out.
    - To reply to the current message, press the **Reply** button. Replying to a message works the same way as posting a new message, except that you don't need to specify certain information. Refer to Section 4.5.4 for more information about posting forum messages.
11. When you have read all the messages, press the **Cancel** button to close the dialog. You can leave the messages in your Filing Cabinet, or you can delete them.

HINTS & TIPS

Messages waiting!

If you have waiting messages (that is, forum messages that were posted to you directly), you will see a notice on the status bar. Also, the **Waiting** button on the Forum Toolbar can be selected. To read all waiting messages, select **Read Waiting** on the **Messages** menu, or press the **Waiting** button.

Note that you have to visit a forum to see if there are any messages waiting for you.

4.5.4 Posting a message

The time has come to introduce yourself to the other members of the Practice Forum – and to try out posting messages yourself!

You don't have to be online to be able to write the message. After you have finished, you can connect to CompuServe, send the message to the forum, and disconnect immediately afterwards. Proceed as follows:

1. Select the `Create Forum Message` option on the `Mail` menu. The Create Forum Message dialog appears (see Figure 4.9).
2. First, make sure that the message will be sent to the right forum, and to the appropriate section in that forum. To do that, use the Forum and Section fields of the dialog. Select 'The Practice' (it might be called something different on your computer) as the forum, and 'My "TEST" Message' as the section.

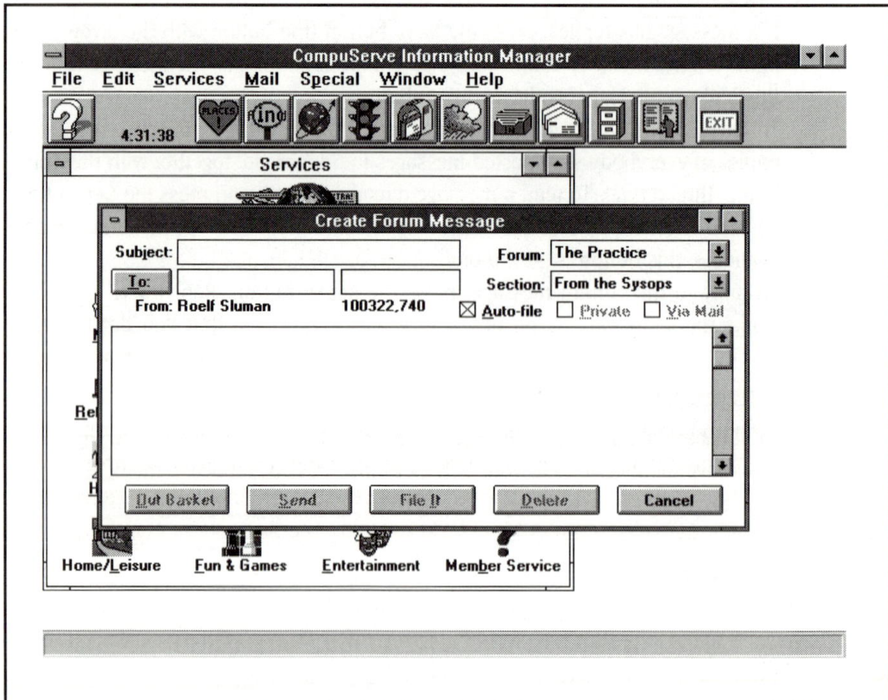

Figure 4.9 Use this dialog to create forum messages

3. When you post a new message (as opposed to *replying* to someone else's message), you actually create a new message thread. In that case, you have to provide WinCIM with information about:

- The *subject*: the actual name of the thread. Use the Subject field to do this.
- The *recipient*: the name and User ID of the person to whom you want to send the message. If you want to send the message to a particular forum member, you have to enter his or her name (in the first field) and User ID (in the second field). However, you can also send a message to *All*, or to *Sysop*. In those two cases, you don't have to specify a User ID.

4. After you have entered information into the 'Subject' and 'To' fields, you are ready to compose your message. Since this will be a short test message, enter something like 'This is my first message to a forum'.

5. When you have finished your message, press the `Send` button. (It will only be available when you have entered valid information in the 'Subject' and 'To' fields, and if you have written an actual message text.) WinCIM will now connect to CompuServe, go to the Practice Forum, and place the message into the right section. Don't forget to disconnect afterwards, as WinCIM will not do so automatically.

6. That's it! Your message has been sent to the Practice Forum. Check for a reply next day. There are a lot of friendly sysops there, and one of them will definitely react to your message.

HINTS & TIPS

Hey, where is my message?

A lot of CompuServe members are confused when they start to look for their own message. Because they don't see it appear in the list of new messages, they tend to think that it was lost somewhere. Some forum sysops even get accused of censorship!

However, there is nothing wrong with your message. It all has to do with the so-called *high message number*.

To every message that is posted on the forum, a number is applied: the *message number*. When you leave the forum, CompuServe automatically attaches the number of the highest message currently in the forum to your name. Next time you enter the forum, CompuServe checks for that high message number and displays only the messages numbered higher than your personal high message number. That way, you only see the new messages, and not all those old messages that you have browsed through before. For example, let's say that the message posted by you gets the number 12345 assigned to it. When you leave the forum immediately afterwards, your high message number will be set to 12345 as well. When you next enter the forum, you will only see the messages numbered 12346 and higher.

If you wish to see older messages as well, there are two things you can do. You can either set the Message Date, *via* an option on the Messages menu, or you can set a new personal high message number (for instance, 12300). Select `Forum Options` on the Special menu to do this. When you leave the forum, CompuServe sets your high message number to the number you specified; next time you enter the forum, CompuServe will use the new high message number to display messages (in this case, all messages from 12301 up).

4.5.5 Downloading files

Finally, we will download a file from the forum libraries. With WinCIM, this is very easy to do. Proceed as follows:

1. First, `GO` to the practice forum. You have to be in the forum to be able to download files from it.
2. Select the `Browse` option on the Library menu, or click on the special `Browse` button, located on the Forum Toolbar (the button with the books and the pointing finger). You will see a list of available libraries (see Figure 4.10).

Figure 4.10 The available libraries for the Practice Forum

3. To review the contents of a library, select it and press the `Select` button. You will see a list of files in the library, as shown in Figure 4.11.
4. When you see a file that you are interested in, press the `Description` button to learn more about it. If you want to download the file, press the `Retrieve` button. WinCIM will now retrieve the file and store it on your hard disk. (Depending on your WinCIM settings, the program will ask you for the name that should be assigned to the file). When the download is finished, you will find the file in your download directory: typically `\CSERVE\DOWNLOAD`.

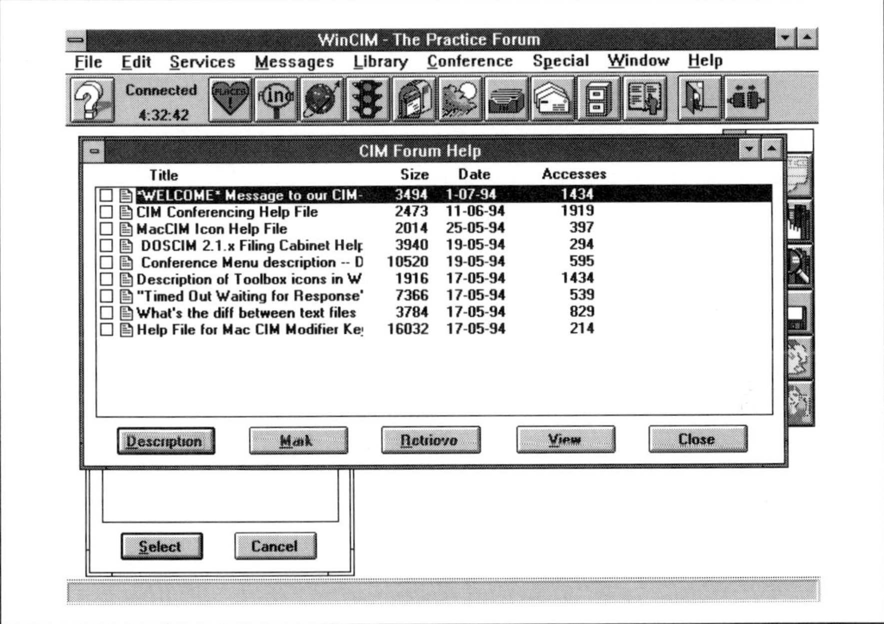

Figure 4.11 A list of library files. Pick and choose!

Marking files for retrieval

If you wish, you can *mark* files instead of downloading them immediately. After you have marked all files that you wish to download, you select the `Retrieve Marked` option on the Library menu. You will see a list of files that you have marked. If necessary, you can 'unmark' one or more files. To start downloading the files, press the `Retrieve All` button. If you wish, you can check the 'Disconnect When Done' box, in which case WinCIM will disconnect automatically after it has downloaded all the files. You will find the downloaded files, as usual, in your `\CSERVE\DOWNLOAD` directory.

4.6 The end

And that completes our Guided Tour through some of the Basic Services! You should now have enough experience to start experimenting on your own. Exploring new services is a great thing to do. Regardless what you are looking for, you are bound to find it on CompuServe.

If you are looking for more information about new CompuServe services, there are a number of places to go to. A few of them are listed below. Good luck on your travels!

- *Browse* through the Services window of the CIM products. Newly added services will appear automatically in the appropriate menus.
- *Read* the 'What's New' announcements which are updated every Monday. They contain valuable information about newly added services, as well as updates of existing products. Reading 'What's New' is free of connect charges.
- *FIND* a service: If you use WinCIM, select the `Find` option on the Services menu and enter a keyword. CompuServe will show you a list of all services that pertain to that keyword. Finding a service is free of connect charges.
- *GO INDEX* to review a list of all public **GO** words. To give you something to start with, a copy of this list is included in Chapter 9. The CompuServe Index is free of connect charges.
- *GO PRACTICE* to visit the Practice Forum. This forum is free of connect charges, and its libraries contain a file with a list of all forums on CompuServe, complete with descriptions of sections, libraries and conference rooms. This file is a definite 'must have'!
- *GO TAPCIS* to visit the TapCIS forum, and search the libraries for the latest editions of TapNews, the electronic magazine of the TapCIS Support Group. Generally, new and interesting CompuServe services are announced in this magazine. Note that the TapCIS Forum is part of Extended Services.
- *GO NLFORUM* and visit us on the Netherlands Forum! Although the main language is Dutch, we also have message sections and libraries for those who speak English. The libraries contain timely information about new CompuServe features. And while you are there, don't forget to post a message to me. We would be honoured to have you as a member! Note that the Netherlands Forum is part of Extended Services.
- If you use CompuServe to access the Internet, you might consider subscribing to the USENET newsgroup 'General' library called *compuserve.announcements*. More information about accessing USENET newsgroups from CompuServe can be found in Chapter 9, 'The Internet'.

5 Getting to know WinCIM

Getting to know WinCIM

CompuServe can be accessed *via* almost all communication programs available on the market. Using the *ASCII Interface*, members can carry out all online actions from virtually any computer available. There are plenty of CompuServe members who log in using first-generation home computers, palmtop computers like the Psion Series 3, and all kinds of other systems, and who use the ASCII Interface to do their work online.

As CompuServe grew, more and more members called for special programs that could help them get the most out of CompuServe, without using the rather archaic ASCII Interface. One of the most famous results of those requests is a collection of access programs called CIM. At the time this book was written, CIM existed for four platforms:

- Apple Macintosh computers
- MS DOS computers
- Computers running under Windows
- Computers running under OS/2

Apart from some differences due to the various operating systems, all four programs basically share the same structure, menus and options.

5.1 The CIM philosophy

The CIM programs, developed by CompuServe, were written to simplify access to CompuServe. Instead of using the often intimidating ASCII Interface, members can take advantage of the conveniently arranged menus, windows and icons of CIM to access almost all CompuServe services. All CIM programs use a special protocol called HMI that reduces the chance of transmission errors and saves time online by working around the normal menu prompts.

Although four CIM programs were in existence at the time this book was written, we focus on the most popular: the Windows version, called WinCIM. If you use one of the other versions, note that most, if not all, of the options discussed are available in your program too.

Program versions

In this book, we discuss version 1.3 of WinCIM, a version that 'went into beta' at the time this book was written. With newer versions coming out on a regular basis, the chances are that your copy of CIM contains options that are not discussed here. Whenever you have questions that are not answered in these pages, consider visiting one of the special support forums: WCIMSUP for WinCIM, DCIMSUP for the DOS version, OCIMSUP for the OS/2 version and MCIMSUP for the Macintosh version.

Go international!

If your native language is German or Spanish, you might consider downloading the special 'localized' version of WinCIM or DOSCIM for your language, from the regular WinCIM and DOSCIM download areas. You can then benefit from translated menus, dialogs and ... Help text! However, there is a downside. It normally takes some time before a new version is localized. Therefore, versions in local languages often lack some of the functionality that is present in the most recent English-language updates.

5.2. How to obtain the program

If you own this book, you own a copy of WinCIM as well. If you borrowed this book, or if you need one of the other CIM packages, you can download it as follows:

- *WinCIM*: `GO WINCIM` to access the WinCIM download area. There is a $10 download charge, but your account will be credited by the same amount. So essentially, downloading WinCIM is free. There are no connect charges for downloading WinCIM, although communication surcharges still apply.

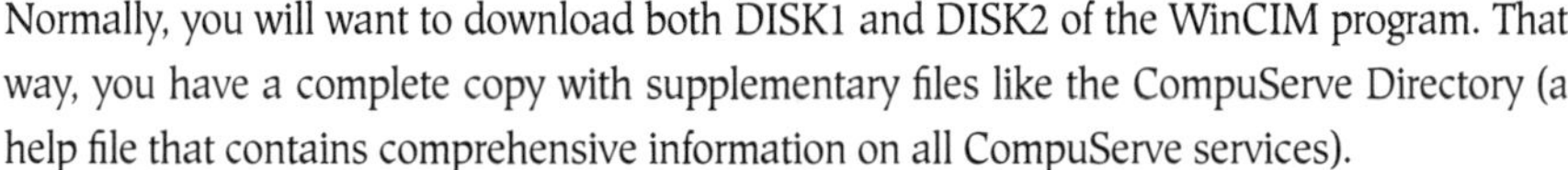

Normally, you will want to download both DISK1 and DISK2 of the WinCIM program. That way, you have a complete copy with supplementary files like the CompuServe Directory (a help file that contains comprehensive information on all CompuServe services).

If you already own a copy of WinCIM (for instance, the copy that you obtained when you bought this book), you can choose to download one or more of the supplementary files. If you don't know whether or not you will need them, don't worry about them now: you can always download them later.

Note that you can also obtain the latest version of WinCIM by ordering it online: **GO ORDER**. The program will be sent to you on disk, in the format you prefer.

- *CIM for DOS*: **GO DOSCIM** to access the DOSCIM download area. Downloading the latest version of DOSCIM costs you $10, but because your account will be credited by the same amount, the program is essentially free.

  There are two versions available: a *standard version* that you can use on IBM compatible computers that don't contain a hard disk, and the *advanced version*, which will only work if you have a hard disk.

  The standard version is free of charge: you don't pay anything (except communication surcharges) for downloading it.

  Note that you can also obtain the latest version of CIM by ordering it online: **GO ORDER**. The program will be sent to you on disk, in the version and format you prefer.

- *CIM for the Macintosh*: **GO MACCIM** to download the Macintosh version of CIM. You will be charged $10 for the download, but your account will be credited by the same amount, making this essentially a free program.

  Note that you can also obtain the latest version of CIM by ordering it online: **GO ORDER**. The program will be sent to you on disk.

Other CIM versions

From time to time, CompuServe releases versions of their CIM software for other computers and operating systems. Examples are the new OS/2 version, released in September 1994, and CIM for the GEOS operating system, which can be used on a range of PDA systems. To learn about new versions, **GO CISSOFT**.

If something went wrong

If there were problems during the download, you can try again for free. When you download the program again in the first 30 days after the first download, your account won't be charged. Of course, communication surcharges still apply.

5.3 How to get online support

Every version of CIM has its dedicated support forum, to which you can turn with all your questions about the program. The forum also contains files of additional information, updated scripts, and so on. Look for support in the following forums:

- *WinCIM*: `GO WCIMSUPPORT`. The WinCIM Support Forum consists of the following message sections:

  1 General Questions
  2 Common Solutions
  3 Install/Upgrade
  4 Modems/Hardware
  5 Forums
  6 Mail
  7 Filing Cabinet
  8 Printing
  9 Online Services
  10 Terminal Emulation
  11 Networks
  12 WinCIM Under OS/2
  14 French WinCIM
  15 German WinCIM
  16 European Support
  17 Suggestions

- *CIM for DOS*: `GO CIMSUPPORT`. The following message sections are available in the DOS CIM Support Forum:

  1 General Questions
  2 Common Solutions
  3 Install/Upgrade
  4 Modems/Hardware
  5 Forums
  6 Mail
  7 Filing Cabinet
  8 Printing
  9 Online Services
  10 Terminal Emulation
  11 Networks
  12 V1.X Specific
  14 French DOSCIM
  15 German DOSCIM
  16 European Support
  17 Suggestions

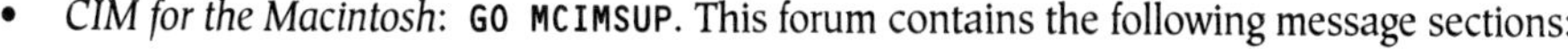

- *CIM for the Macintosh*: `GO MCIMSUP`. This forum contains the following message sections:

  1 General Questions

  2 Common Solutions

  3 Install/Upgrade

  4 Modems/Hardware

  5 Forums

  6 Mail

  7 Filing Cabinet

  8 Printing

  9 Online Services

  10 Terminal Emulation

  16 European Support

  17 Suggestions

5.4 The main elements

WinCIM's main window is shown in Figure 5.1. Although you can configure this window, it will initially contain the following elements:

- A *Services* window, sometimes also referred to as the *Browse* window. This window contains a summary of often used CompuServe services, represented by icons. When you click on an icon, WinCIM will go online and retrieve further information for the service you selected.

Alternative Services windows

Some versions of WinCIM, like the special ZiffNet version, contain alternative Services windows. If you want to work with the normal WinCIM window instead, delete or rename the `CUSTOM.DAT` file, which can be found in the `\CSERVE\WINCIM` directory. Next time you start WinCIM, the program will display the normal Services window.

- A *Ribbon*, which contains buttons for frequently used WinCIM options. You can, within certain limits, change the contents of the Ribbon, as you will see later in this chapter.

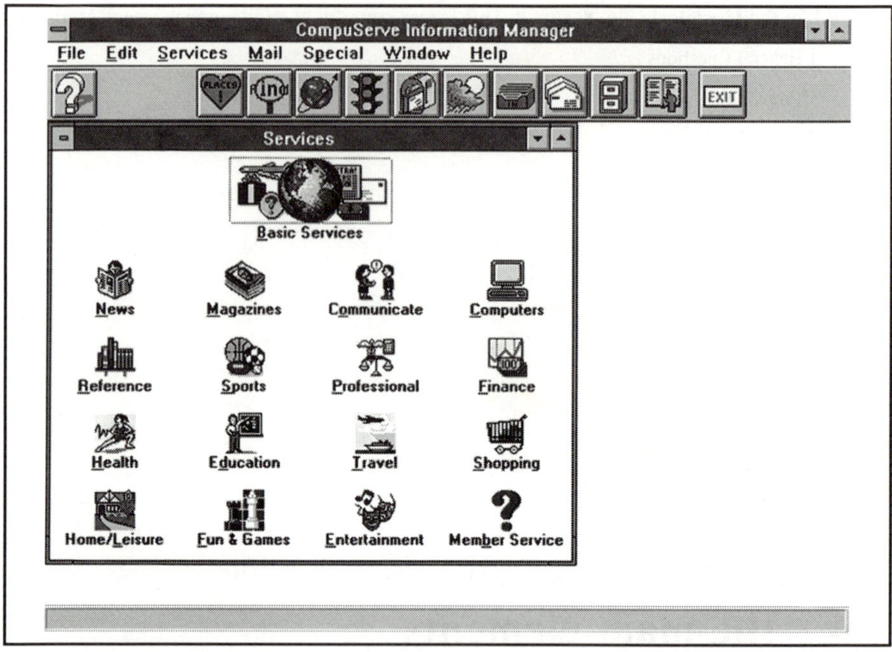

Figure 5.1 The WinCIM main window

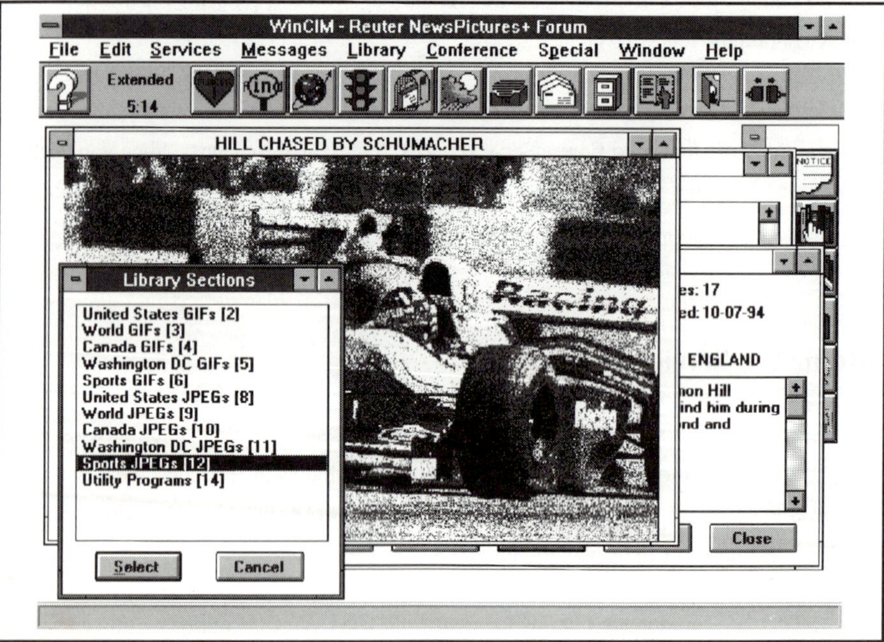

Figure 5.2 WinCIM in action

As you get online, the number of windows in WinCIM will increase rapidly. An example is shown in Figure 5.2: several windows are opened, containing images, menus and retrieved text. Sometimes, WinCIM will close windows for you, but most of the time it is up to you to decide when you no longer need a certain window. You can then either minimize it or close it altogether.

5.5 The first step: installing WinCIM

If you have already installed WinCIM (or tried to), you will have noticed that the actual installation consists of two parts: after installing the actual program onto your hard disk, you enter your personal parameters (like your User ID, password, modem, and so on). You are then ready for your first online session with WinCIM. If you feel that you have installed the program correctly, you can skip the next section.

5.5.1 Installing WinCIM onto your hard disk

To install WinCIM onto your hard disk, proceed as follows:

- If you use the program disk that was included with this book: insert it into your drive. Start the Setup program, either by double-clicking on its filename from within File Manager, or by selecting the `Run` option on the `File` menu in Program Manager. (Users of foreign-language Windows versions are advised to consult their manual for the appropriate commands.)
  The Setup program will ask you for the drive and directory where WinCIM should be installed. Normally, you will want to accept the proposed settings: that way, you are assured that the program will work together with other official CompuServe access programs, like CompuServe Navigator. These programs can share resources like Address Books, In-Basket and Out-Basket, and so on.
  When Setup has finished, it will have created a new CompuServe program group with some icons, or added some icons to your existing CompuServe program group. You can start WinCIM by double-clicking on its icon, as you would do with any Windows program.
- If you have obtained the program by downloading it: copy both `.EXE` files to a temporary directory (for instance, `C:\TEMP`), and decompress them by typing their names. (Both `DISK1.EXE` and `DISK2.EXE` are self extracting archives.) You can do this from Windows (use the `Run` option on the File menu) or from `DOS`. After you have decompressed both `.EXE` files, you can store them on floppy disks for backup purposes.
  Note that `DISK1.EXE` is basically enough to get you up and running. However, you might want to take a look at the supplementary files available, which can be downloaded for free. (`GO WINCIM` for additional information).

To install WinCIM, you will have to start the Setup program which is now located in your temporary directory. You can do this from within File Manager or, again, by selecting the Run option on Program Manager's File menu.

After asking you for the drive and directory where the program should be installed (in most cases, you don't need to change the proposed settings), the program will install itself. The result is a new program group, called 'CompuServe', with some icons in it; if you already had a CompuServe window, it will now contain some additional icons. To start WinCIM, double-click on the appropriate icon.

WinCIM and CompuServe Navigator

WinCIM can share its file structure with another famous access program: CompuServe Navigator, Windows version. CompuServe Navigator is a little bit more complicated to use than WinCIM. However, because it can do a lot of work offline, it lets you save substantial amounts of money. If you have only limited experience with CompuServe, give yourself the time to get acquainted with the use of WinCIM. Once you are feeling confident, however, consider using CompuServe Navigator for your regular business online. More information about CompuServe Navigator can be found in Section 6.1.

Initial configuration

When you run WinCIM for the very first time (and if you haven't used another official CompuServe program like DOSCIM or CompuServe Navigator before), the program will go through an initialization procedure, asking you for your user name, password and modem settings. If you aren't a member yet, you can use the sign-up procedure to get online as quickly as possible. More information about the configuration of WinCIM can be found in Section 5.9, 'Configuring WinCIM'.

5.6 Getting online and offline with WinCIM

WinCIM has been written to make access to CompuServe as easy as possible. You can use WinCIM to visit each and every online service. Most of the time, you will be able to use menus and dialogs to access these services, but there are a few cases where you will use the so-called terminal mode.

5.6.1 Getting online

There are a lot of ways to get online. The most often used methods are:

- Click on one of the icons in the Services window. If this window isn't visible on the screen, select the `Browse` option on the Services menu to display it. Each icon represents a menu of CompuServe services. After you click on an icon, WinCIM will go online and bring you to the corresponding menu.
- Issue the `Go` command and specify the name of the service you want to visit. There are a few ways to issue the `Go` command:
    - Select the `Go` option on the Services menu.
    - Click on the `Go` button (the traffic light) on the Ribbon.
    - Press Ctrl-G.
- Open your personal list of favourite places and select the service you want to visit. There are two ways to open the Favorite Places list:
    - Select the `Favorite Places` option on the Services menu.
    - Click on the Favorite Places button (the pink heart) on the Ribbon.
- Choose one of the appropriate menu options. For instance, the Mail menu has options to check for mail waiting.

Want to get online now? GO Basic!

If you are anxious to get online for the first time, but want to keep the costs within limits, experiment with some of the Basic Services that CompuServe offers. Open the Services window and click on the Basic Services icon. As long as you remain in the Basic Services area, you won't incur any connect charges. But note that communication surcharges still apply, and that your telephone company will be more than happy to charge you as well.

When you have finished, don't forget to disconnect properly. Never disconnect by simply 'hanging up' (by means of one of your modem switches, for instance). Instead, select the `Disconnect` option on the File menu, press Ctrl-D, or click on the special Disconnect button on the ribbon.

WinCIM will show status information while it attempts to get online. The number of messages shown depends on the network you are using to access CompuServe, but the following is a typical example of the messages that are displayed when you connect to a direct CompuServe node:

- *Initializing modem*: WinCIM tries to reset the modem according to the settings in the Modem Control Strings window. Select `Session Settings` on the Special menu and press the Modem button to see this window. After resetting the modem, WinCIM will perform some modem testing procedures.

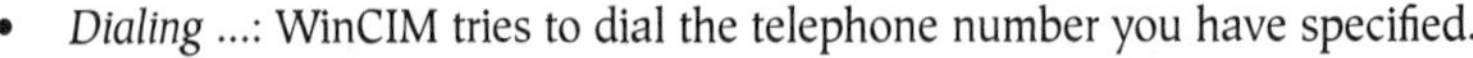

- *Dialing ...*: WinCIM tries to dial the telephone number you have specified.
- *Connecting to CompuServe Network*: When this message appears, WinCIM has succeeded in establishing a connection with another modem. The program will now try to make a connection with the CompuServe network, by sending some special control strings and/or commands.
- *Logging onto CompuServe*: WinCIM is now actually connected to CompuServe, and will send your User ID and password.
- *Waiting to Establish protocol*: Your User ID and password were accepted by CompuServe. Next, WinCIM tries to establish the HMI protocol, which enables an error-free connection and provides easy access *via* the WinCIM menus and windows.

5.6.2 Getting offline: the Disconnect option

When you have finished your business online, you need to tell CompuServe that you are about to hang up. To do this, select the `Disconnect` option on the File menu. As a result of this, WinCIM will exchange some last-minute information with CompuServe (for instance, section and library information about the forum you are in) and tell CompuServe to disconnect.

Yes, that's right: although you might be led to think otherwise, it's actually CompuServe that hangs up on you! After CompuServe receives the 'disconnect' command from WinCIM, it will officially log you out, thereby preventing your account from being charged too much. You should avoid disconnecting by 'pulling the plug' yourself. So don't reset your computer or switch off your modem while you are still online. Although CompuServe will eventually find out that you are not online any more, it can take up to 15 minutes before your sudden departure is noticed. Needless to say, those 15 minutes could be pretty expensive!

Don't do this!

With computers, anything can go wrong. Therefore, it could be that, due to a program error or another cause, you will have to disconnect 'the hard way', thereby taking the risk of incurring extra charges before CompuServe notices that you have gone. Whatever you do, resist the temptation to get online again, only to disconnect immediately thereafter. CompuServe will simply regard this as a new session, and charge your account accordingly.

5.7 WinCIM tools for data management

Once you start collecting information with WinCIM, you will appreciate the powerful storage tools that you have at your disposal. These storage tools serve two purposes. First of all, you

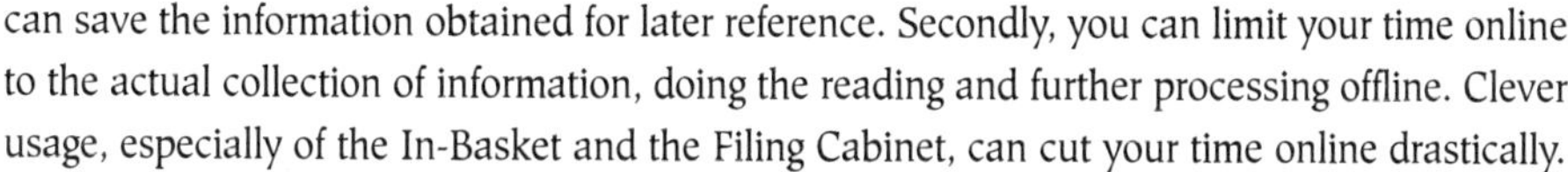

can save the information obtained for later reference. Secondly, you can limit your time online to the actual collection of information, doing the reading and further processing offline. Clever usage, especially of the In-Basket and the Filing Cabinet, can cut your time online drastically.

HINTS & TIPS

Save money with the In-Basket facility

Before you start reading forum messages, take the time to get acquainted with the In-Basket. This powerful WinCIM feature can store the messages you want to read very quickly. Once disconnected, you have all the time you need to read those messages.

The Out-Basket, In-Basket, and Filing Cabinet can be considered as database files, which can be used to store virtually every text you either compose or read. Their individual purposes are listed below:

- The *Out-Basket* can be used to store all e-mail and forum messages you compose offline. When you have finished writing messages, you can send them directly from your Out-Basket. If your Out-Basket contains only regular e-mail (that is, no forum messages), you can have WinCIM send and receive your e-mail automatically. If your Out-Basket contains forum messages, you will still have to visit the forum(s) manually, and direct WinCIM to send all the messages that the Out-Basket contains for that forum. You will still save a lot of time and money, because you actually wrote the forum messages offline!
- The *In-Basket* stores all the e-mail messages that WinCIM retrieves automatically. After disconnecting, you can read the contents of the In-Basket at your own pace.
- The *Filing Cabinet* can be regarded as a digital version of the filing cabinet in your office or study. If you encounter an interesting article or forum message you want to save for future use, you can store it in one of the Filing Cabinet folders. You can make as many folders as you wish. It is also possible to move messages to another folder, and to delete messages and/or complete folders from the Filing Cabinet. Because the Filing Cabinet is supported by a lot of CompuServe services, you can use it to save your time online. Every time you see an article you are interested in, just put it into one of the Filing Cabinet folders. Once offline, you can take your time to read it, and then either dispose of it or store it.

HINTS & TIPS

The Filing Cabinet and your research work

The Filing Cabinet is a real power tool when you do go online for research purposes. Use a Filing Cabinet folder to store all information that looks interesting. Afterwards (and offline), you can process the retrieved information, move it to another folder, or delete it altogether.

5.7.1 The Out-Basket

You use the Out-Basket to store e-mail and forum messages that you are composing offline. Once you get online, you can have WinCIM send the contents of the Out-Basket in one or more *batches*.

Let's assume you want to write an e-mail message. When you have finished writing, WinCIM gives you two options. You can either send the message directly, or you can store it temporarily in your Out-Basket. Next, you can write another e-mail message, or compose a forum message. As soon as you have written all your messages, you can go online and let WinCIM do its work. It will send all regular e-mail messages (files as well as normal messages) automatically. To have it send forum messages as well, you just visit the particular forum and instruct WinCIM to send the messages you want to post on that forum.

As stated before, the Out-Basket is actually a series of files on your hard disk, stored in the directory `\CSERVE\FCABINET\BASKET.OUT`. You can use WinCIM to review the contents of the Out-Basket and/or delete items from it, providing the Out-Basket contains at least one item. It is not recommended that you delete files directly from your hard disk! If you accidentally do this, use the `Rebuild Cabinet Indexes` option on the Special menu to repair the internal data structures.

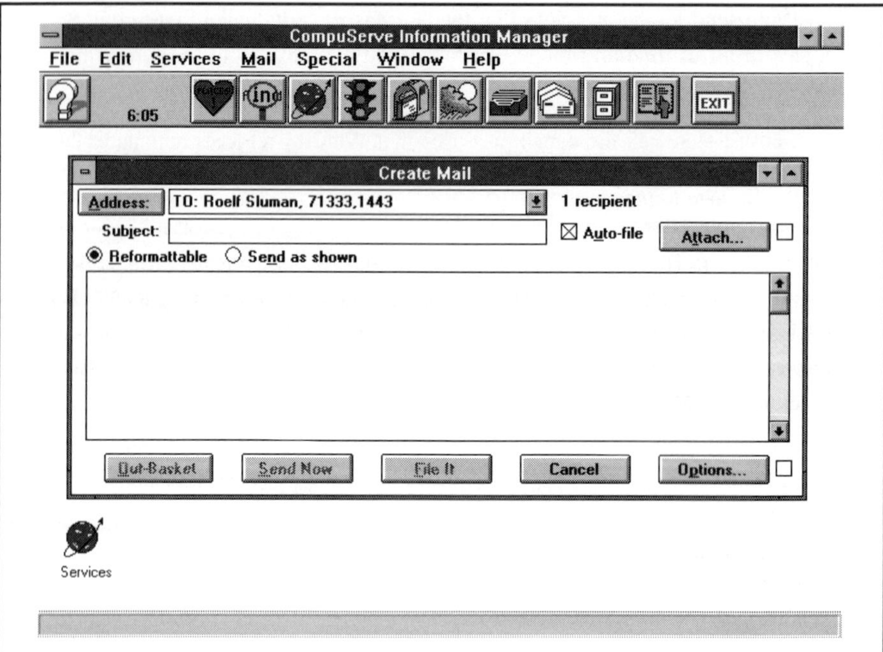

Figure 5.3 The Create Mail window

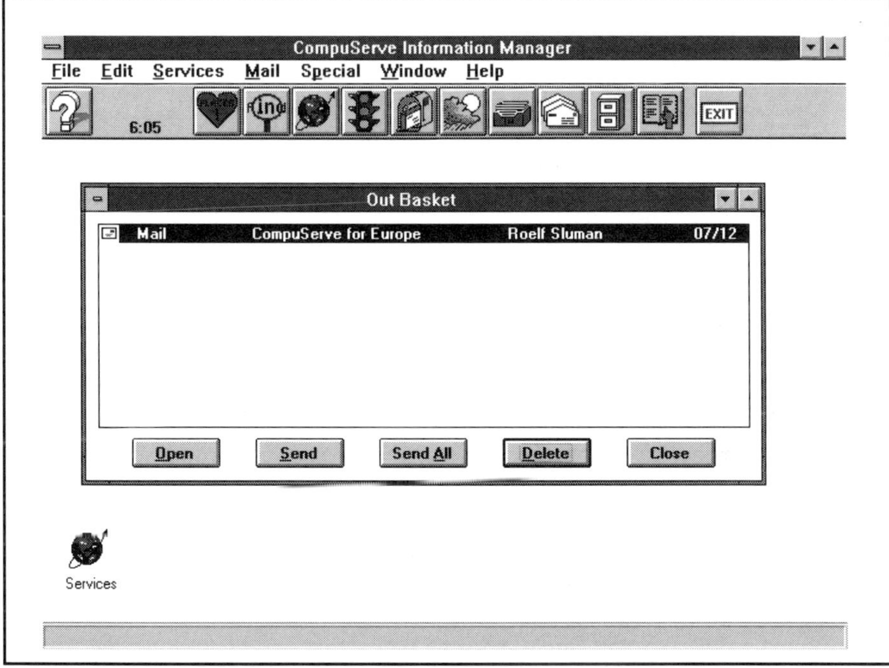

Figure 5.4 The Out Basket window

The following list contains an overview of the most important actions that you can perform on the Out-Basket.

- *Adding an item to the Out-Basket*: To write a message, you use one of the special dialogs that WinCIM provides. For instance, when you compose an e-mail message, you select the `Create Mail` option on the Mail menu. After you have entered the address of the message's recipient, the Create Mail window appears, as shown in Figure 5.3. When you have finished writing, you can press the Out-Basket button to place the message in the Out-Basket. In a similar way, you can press the Out-Basket button after you have written a forum message.
- *Reviewing the contents of the Out-Basket*: If the Out-Basket contains at least one item, the Out-Basket button on the Ribbon can be selected. You can either press this button or select the Out-Basket option on the Mail menu. The Out-Basket window, shown in Figure 5.4, appears. All the items in the Out-Basket are listed. You can send an individual item, send all items (of one category, for instance all e-mail items, or all items that belong to the forum you are currently in), delete an item, or open an item to edit or review it.
- *Deleting an item you have placed in the Out-Basket*: If you have second thoughts about a message you have put in the Out-Basket, you can delete it. Press the `Out-Basket` button

on the Ribbon, or select the `Out-Basket` option on the Mail menu. Next, select the item you want to delete and press the Delete button.

- *Reviewing an item you have placed in the Out-Basket*: If you want to make some changes to an e-mail or forum message that you have stored in the Out-Basket, press the Out-Basket on the Ribbon, or select the `Out-Basket` option on the Mail menu. After you have selected the item you want to edit, press the `Open` button. When you have finished editing the item, press the `Out-Basket` button again to place the new version of the item in the Out-Basket, thereby replacing the old one.
- *Sending all items currently in the Out-Basket*: This is a tricky one! The first time I saw this option, I thought that WinCIM actually would send off all my new messages. That is, it would send all my regular e-mail messages and my newly written forum messages as well. I'll save you the disappointment of finding out the truth yourself: WinCIM will only send the items that are appropriate for the CompuServe service you are visiting.
When you are offline, the Send All option is only available when the Out-Basket contains regular e-mail messages. In other words: when you are offline, the Send All option will only send your e-mail. Once you get online, the Send All option will only send the items that belong to the service you are currently visiting.
Suppose that you have placed three forum messages in the Out-Basket: one that should be posted on the Practice Forum, and two others that are intended for the Foreign Language Forum. To send these messages, you have to visit both forums and, while you are in the forum, press the `Send All` button.

HINTS & TIPS

Time to make a change?

The chances are that you consider this limitation an important drawback. In that case, maybe you should consider using one of the so-called auto-access programs, like TapCIS or CompuServe Navigator. Because the latter can share its data files with WinCIM, you can use both programs simultaneously. You could use CompuServe Navigator for all the things that can be automated, like sending and receiving e-mail, forum visits and weather reports. Every time you want to discover new areas of CompuServe, or do things online that cannot be automated (like attending forum conferences, playing games online, and chatting), you switch back to WinCIM.

5.7.2 The In-Basket

The In-Basket is a very powerful facility to keep your time online within limits. It serves as a storage space for automatically retrieved e-mail messages. Instead of reading those messages online, you can choose to have them automatically stored in your In-Basket. Once offline, you review the contents of the In-Basket and decide what to do with the individual messages after you have read them: delete them, or store them in one of the Filing Cabinet folders.

Just like the Out-Basket and the Filing Cabinet, the In-Basket, shown in Figure 5.5, is really a collection of database files, stored in the `\CSERVE\FCABINET\BASKET.IN` directory. To review the contents of the In-Basket, press the special `In-Basket` button on the Ribbon, or select the `In-Basket` option on the `File` menu.

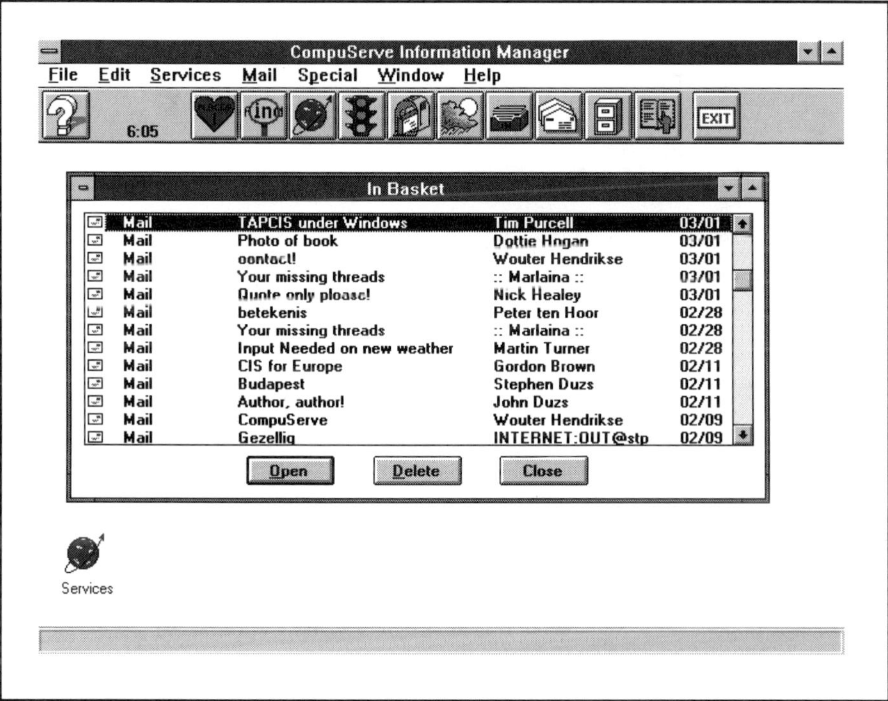

Figure 5.5 A typical example of a heavy-duty In-Basket: my own!

There are two ways to retrieve e-mail messages into your In-Basket:

- *Send and receive your e-mail automatically*: Offline, compose the e-mail messages you want to send and place them in the Out-Basket. Next, select the `Send/Receive All Mail` option on the Mail menu. As a result of this, the Send and Receive All Mail dialog appears, shown in Figure 5.6. If you want WinCIM to disconnect after it has finished, check the 'Disconnect when Done' box.

  After WinCIM has done its job, check the contents of the status bar: this tells you how many e-mail messages were sent and received. Any received messages will be placed in your In-Basket, waiting for you to read them.

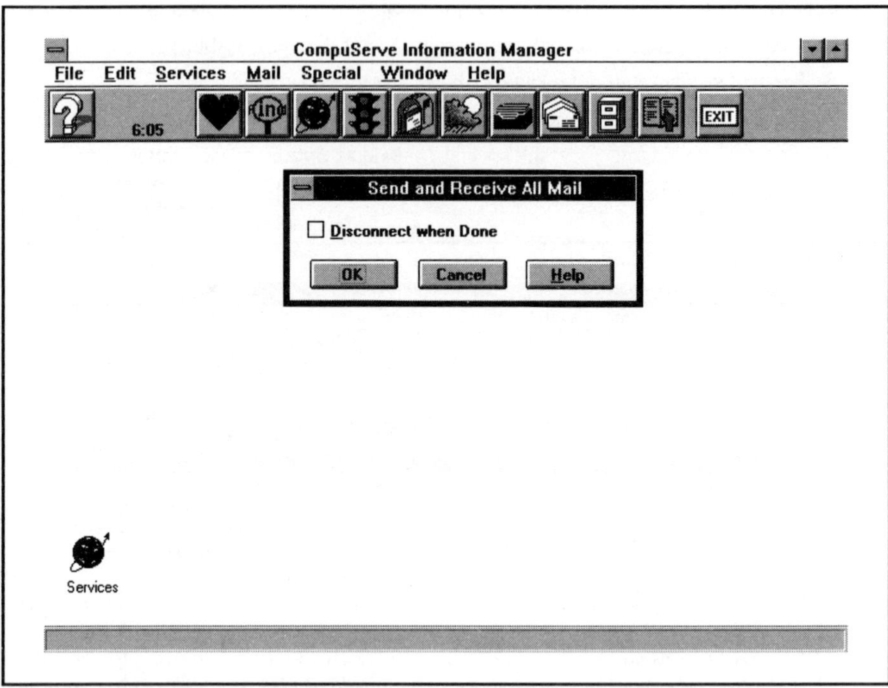

Figure 5.6 One of the few automated actions that WinCIM supports: sending and receiving e-mail messages

- *Retrieve your e-mail messages interactively*: Either offline or online, visit CompuServe's e-mail department by clicking on the Ribbon's special mailbox button, or by selecting the `Get New Mail` option on the Mail menu. If there is e-mail waiting, WinCIM will list the subjects and senders of all individual messages. By selecting the `Get All` option, you instruct WinCIM to retrieve all messages and place them in your In-Basket, for further processing offline.
  Note that you can also select the `Get` option to retrieve only the selected message, and still have it placed in your In-Basket by selecting the `In-Basket` option.

Once offline, you can review the contents of your In-Basket by pressing the appropriate 'Ribbon' button, or by selecting the `Out-Basket` option on the `Mail` menu. To review an individual message, select it with the mouse or the arrow keys, and click on the `Open` button, or press the Enter key.

Mail from WinCIM!

In some circumstances, you will receive 'direct' e-mail from WinCIM itself. WinCIM uses the In-Basket to inform you about system status, errors, and so on. An example of such a message is shown in Figure 5.7.

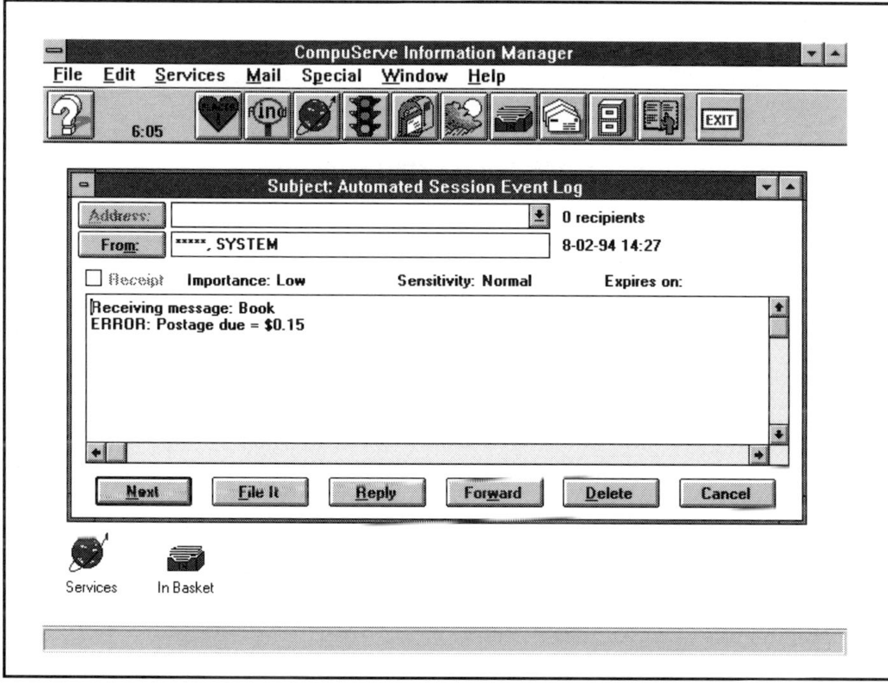

Figure 5.7 WinCIM uses the In-Basket to 'send' you informative messages

Important mail? Let your Filing Cabinet assist you

If your In-Basket contains an important message, you might consider transferring it to a special Filing Cabinet folder, named 'Important' or something similar. You could even expand this system if necessary. For example, because I receive a lot of e-mail messages, I have to divide them according to their urgency. That's why I have four Filing Cabinet folders: Urgent Mail, Mail From Readers, Regular Mail, and Processed Mail. When I have read the actual messages (which are initially stored in my In-Basket), I immediately move them to one of these folders. Once I have either read or processed all retrieved information, I turn to the Mail folders in my Filing Cabinet and start writing answers. Needless to say, the Mail From Readers folder is the first in the queue...

5.7.3 The Filing Cabinet

Once you start taking advantage of your CompuServe membership, a *lot* of information will land on your hard disk. Loads of regular e-mail messages, forum messages, and articles call for a structured solution!

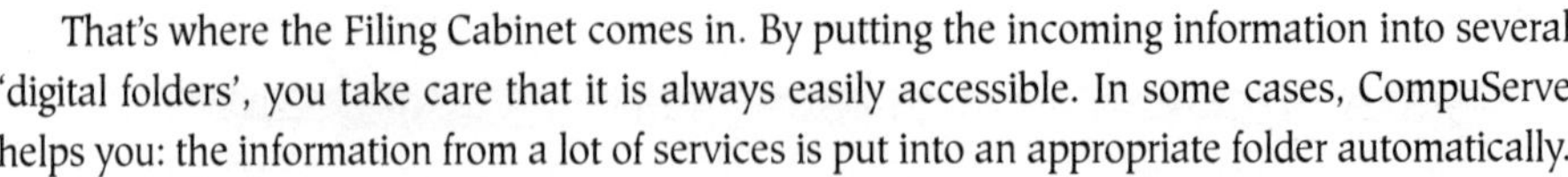

That's where the Filing Cabinet comes in. By putting the incoming information into several 'digital folders', you take care that it is always easily accessible. In some cases, CompuServe helps you: the information from a lot of services is put into an appropriate folder automatically.

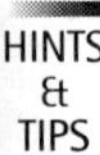

HINTS & TIPS

I retrieved something. Why can't I find it in my Filing Cabinet?

Some WinCIM users have problems tracking down information that they retrieved during an online session. Because they can't find that information in the Filing Cabinet, they assume that it has gone: a frustrating experience!

In two cases, information will be stored in the Filing Cabinet automatically: when you press the File It button, or when you select the `Retrieve All` option on the Messages menu. But note that retrieved *e-mail messages* can be found in WinCIM's In-Basket, and that retrieved *files* will be stored onto your hard disk.

Working with the Filing Cabinet is actually very easy. Basically, it consists of the following three steps:

1. You *create* one or more folders. Or you let WinCIM (or CompuServe) create them for you.
2. You *store* appropriate information, like messages and articles, in those folders. Or you let WinCIM (or CompuServe) do that for you.
3. Offline, you *process* the information stored in the folders. This process could include replying to messages, creating new folders, deleting old ones, and moving or deleting processed information.

As I mentioned before, the Filing Cabinet is supported by a lot of CompuServe services, provided you use WinCIM, of course. Examples of these services are:

- *Forum message sections*. You can *mark* all messages, message threads and/or sections you want to read. This is a very powerful option. Instead of reading forum messages online, you can instruct WinCIM to retrieve them and place them in your In-Basket. You can select individual messages, message threads, and even all messages in one or more sections.
  To have WinCIM retrieve forum messages automatically, go to the appropriate forum and either browse through or search for messages. (More information about typical forum commands can be found in Section 5.8, 'Overview of WinCIM menus and options'.) Next, mark the headers of messages you would like to read. Marking message headers is easy: just check the box in front of every message or topic you would like to read. Figure 5.8 shows a few examples. When you have marked everything you want to read, select the `Retrieve Marked` option on the Messages menu. WinCIM will start retrieving (downloading) the marked messages, placing them in a folder named after the forum.

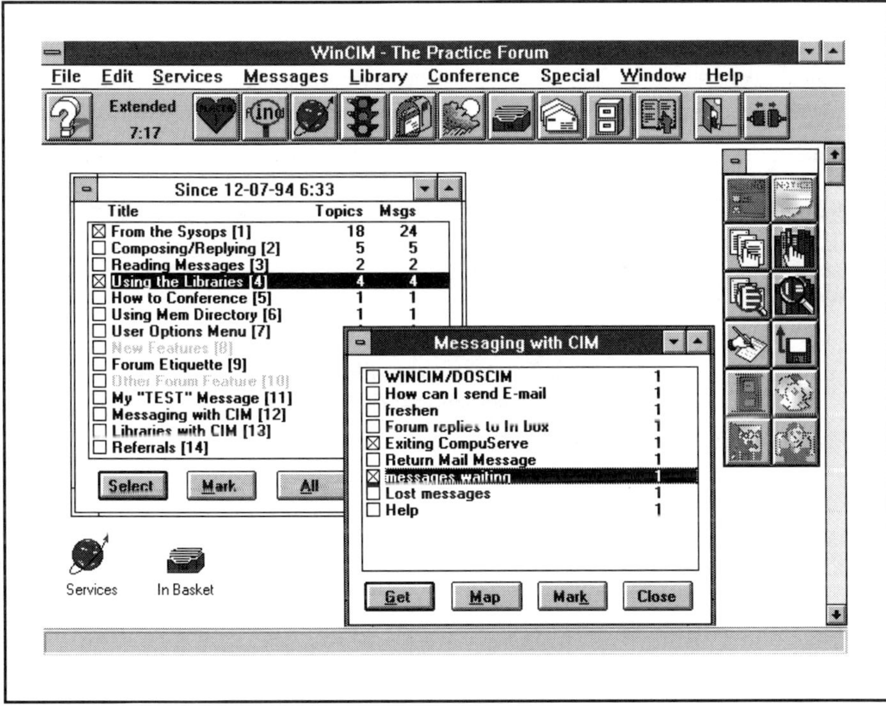

Figure 5.8 You can mark individual messages, threads, and even complete sections for retrieval

- *ENS, the Executive News Service.* After you mark the news articles you are interested in, one command suffices to download them to your Filing Cabinet. WinCIM even creates folders with the same names as your online ENS folders. Refer to Section 9.1.2, for more information.
- *Most of the articles you read online.* If you start reading an article online and then decide you want to have a closer look at it offline, you only have to press the `File It` button. WinCIM will ask you for the folder in which you want to store the article, and retrieve it for you.

What to do when there is no 'File It' button

In some cases, the window in which the article text is displayed does not have a `File It` button. If you do need to store the text on disk, you can always select the `Save` option on the `File` menu. WinCIM will store the text into a `.TXT` file that can be read by all word processors, and by the Windows Notebook application.

To access the Filing Cabinet, press the special `Filing Cabinet` button on the Ribbon, or select the `Filing Cabinet` option on the `Mail` menu. If you use the keyboard, you can also press Ctrl-F. An example of a typical Filing Cabinet is shown in Figure 5.9. The Filing Cabinet window also appears after you press the `File It` button when an article or message is displayed.

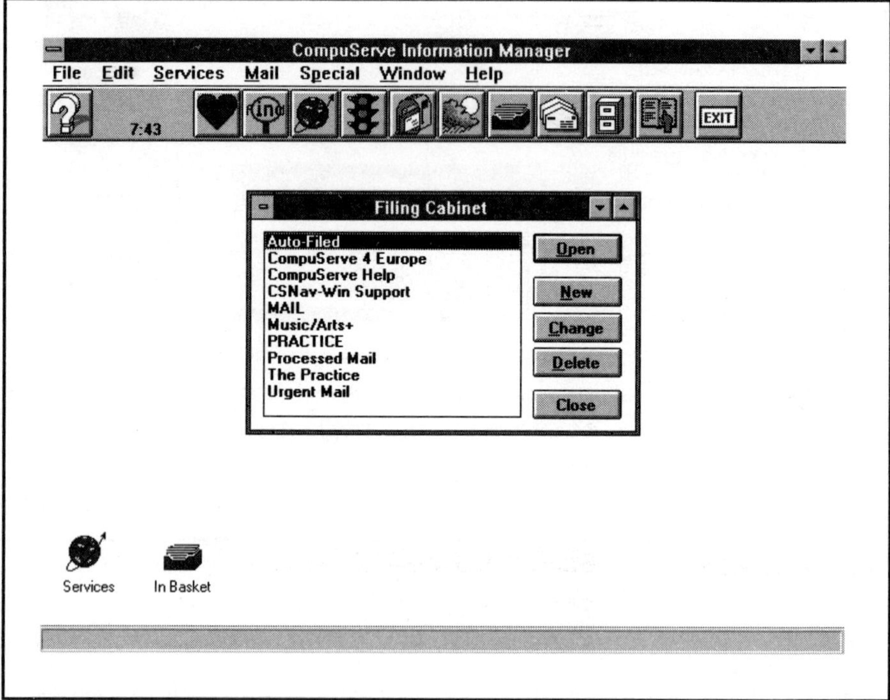

Figure 5.9 The Filing Cabinet dialog

The 'Filing Cabinet' window contains the following options:

- *Open*: This option is not available when you access the Filing Cabinet *via* the `File It` option. It shows the contents of the selected folder: a collection of messages and/or articles. After you have selected an item, select `Open` again to review it, `Delete` to delete it from the Filing Cabinet, or `Close` to return to the main Filing Cabinet window.
- *Store*: This option is only available when you use the `File It` option to access the Filing Cabinet. You can use the option buttons at the top of the window to indicate whether you want to move the message (it will be placed in the selected folder and deleted from its original location) or copy it.
- *New*: Use this option to create a new folder. WinCIM will ask you for a folder name. If you want to rename the folder, you can do so by selecting the `Change` option.

When Filing Cabinet installs a new folder, it will create a directory in the `\CSERVE\FCABINET\CABINET` directory. To see the name of that directory, select the `Change` option.

- *Change*: Use this option to change the name of the selected Filing Cabinet folder. All items in that folder are stored in a directory: the name of that directory is shown as well.
- *Delete*: You can use this option to delete either one or more items currently in a folder, or the complete folder.
  After you select this option, WinCIM lists all items in the current folder. You can mark one or more items, either by checking the box in front of them, or by using the arrow keys to select an item and pressing the `Mark` button. You can also mark all items at once, by selecting the `Mark All` option. When you have finished marking the items you want to remove, select the `Delete` option. If you have deleted all items from the folder, WinCIM will ask if you want to delete the folder as well.
- *Close*: When you select this option, the 'Filing Cabinet' window will be removed from the screen.

Moving items from one folder to another

Although there is no direct option available in the 'Filing Cabinet' window, it is possible to move or copy items between folders. To do this, open the item in the normal way. You will see that the window in which the item contents are displayed contains a `File It` option. Select it and specify the folder to which you want to move or copy the item. After you have indicated whether you want to move or copy the item, select `Store`.
By the way: use as many folders as you like. With its limit of 247 folders, the Filing Cabinet has plenty of room available.

5.8 Overview of WinCIM menus and options

This section contains an overview of the most important WinCIM menus and options.

WinCIM's variable menus

Some of the menus discussed in this section are only available when you visit the corresponding services. For instance, when you visit a forum, the Mail menu disappears, the Message, Library and Conference menus become available, and the contents of the Special

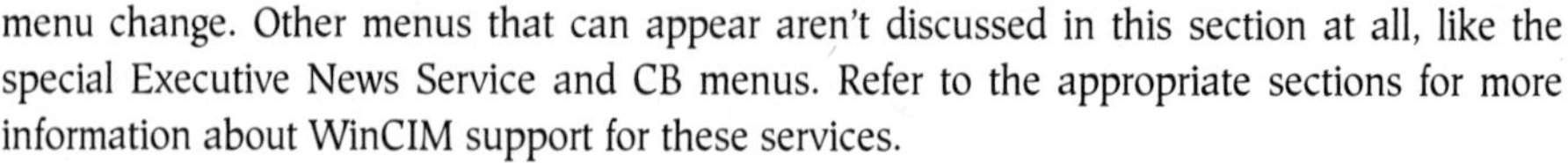

menu change. Other menus that can appear aren't discussed in this section at all, like the special Executive News Service and CB menus. Refer to the appropriate sections for more information about WinCIM support for these services.

5.8.1 The File menu

The File menu contains the following options:

- *New*: Select this option to create a new text file. To edit this file, you use the Windows Notepad application. WinCIM will launch a copy of this application automatically.
  Note that because WinCIM uses the regular Windows Notepad application, you can take advantage of the multitasking facilities of windows and switch back to WinCIM, even without closing the text file.
- *Open*: Use this option to review the contents of a `.TXT` file. Because WinCIM launches a copy of the regular Windows Notepad application, the file size is limited to about 64,000 characters.
  Although, most of the time, you will use the Filing Cabinet to store messages and articles, there are some situations where you will have to use the options `Save` and `Save As` on the File menu. When you use those options, WinCIM will create `.TXT` files.
- *Save* and *Save As*: Use these options to save a message or article as a regular `.TXT` file, which can be read by word processors and Windows applications like Notepad. The options `Save` and `Save As` are especially useful when you want to store information that, for one reason or an other, can't be saved in your Filing Cabinet.
- *Connect*: To get online using WinCIM, you normally select an option that corresponds to the activity you went to perform. For instance, if you would like to access your mailbox, you will choose one of the options on the Mail menu. To browse through the list of forums and other services, you will normally select an option in the Services window. Likewise, you can access services like ENS and CB directly *via* corresponding options on the Services menu.
  If you just want to get online without selecting a service (yet), you can use the `Connect` option. This will bring you to the What's New feature, an online facility that contains information about the latest developments on CompuServe. From there, you can travel to whatever CompuServe service you prefer.
- *Disconnect*: This is one of the most important options on the File menu: it disconnects you from the system. If you use the mouse, you can also press the special Disconnect button on the Ribbon. Keyboard users can press Ctrl-D.
  Note that it is not a good idea to hang up manually, for instance by switching off your modem. Because it will take CompuServe a few minutes to discover that you are not online any more, you could incur a few minutes of additional charges. Always disconnect the proper way, either by selecting this option, or by selecting the `Exit` option.
- *Exit*: Select this option to exit WinCIM.

Disconnecting? Watch your screen!

Make a habit of following the disconnection process on your screen. I once remained online accidentally for no less than 15 minutes (until CompuServe discovered that I wasn't active anymore and eventually logged me off). The reason: I didn't notice that my Out-Basket still contained a message that I forgot to send. In such a situation, WinCIM will ask if you want to disconnect anyway. However, because I wasn't paying attention to my screen, I missed this question completely. WinCIM just waited for me to answer, while the online meter kept running.

Only when the `Disconnect` button on the Ribbon has disappeared, can you rest assured that you are not online any more.

5.8.2 The Edit menu

The options on the `Edit` menu are listed below. Not all of these options are available all the time.

- *Undo*: This option restores the last edit action you performed on the current text. Everything you do between two commands is considered an edit action. For instance, if you type a message without selecting text and/or using the options on the `Edit` menu, you can undo all your typing by selecting this option. (Selecting it again restores the previous undo.) If you use the keyboard, pressing [Ctrl]-[Z] has the same result.
- *Cut*: Use this to cut the selected text out and place it on the Windows Clipboard. If you use the keyboard, you can also press [Ctrl]-[X]. To select text for cutting, drag the mouse over it, or hold down the [Shift] key while you press the arrow keys.
  To paste the Clipboard text back into your message (or into any text you are working on, and even into other applications), select `Paste` on the Edit menu, or press [Ctrl]-[V]. The text will be inserted at the current cursor position.
  Note that the previous contents of the Clipboard will be destroyed when you cut text to it.
- *Copy*: With this option, you copy the selected text to the Windows Clipboard. (The selected text will remain in your document as well.) You can select text by dragging over it with the mouse, or by holding down the [Shift] key while you press the arrow keys.
  You can paste the Clipboard text back (in the same text, another text, or even another application) by selecting `Paste` on the Edit menu, or by pressing [Ctrl]-[V].
  Note that the previous contents of the Clipboard will be replaced by the selected text.
- *Paste*: Use this option to place a copy of the Clipboard text at the current cursor position. The contents of the Clipboard remain unaltered, therefore you can paste as many copies of the Clipboard text as you wish. If you use the keyboard, pressing [Ctrl]-[V] has the same result.

- *Clear*: Select this option to delete the selected text, without placing it on the Clipboard. If you use the keyboard, pressing the [Del] key performs the same action.
- *Select All*: With this option, you select all text in the current edit box at once.
- *Copy To*: This option allows you to copy the complete contents of the current window (including address information, if you are writing an e-mail or forum message) to either an e-mail or forum message. You could use this option to *forward* an article (taking copyrights into account) or another text to someone else.
- *Paste From*: When you select this option, the `Paste From` dialog is displayed, as shown in Figure 5.10. This dialog allows you to copy information from any of the archives created by WinCIM or CompuServe Navigator, the official CompuServe auto-access program.
- *Fixed Font*: If you use the Terminal Emulation feature of WinCIM to work with the CompuServe ASCII Interface, you can change the proportional font that is normally used (the width of the individual characters differs) into a non-proportional font (every character has the same width). If you use the keyboard (and who doesn't, in Terminal Emulation), you can also press the special Fixed Font hotkey: [Ctrl]-[T].

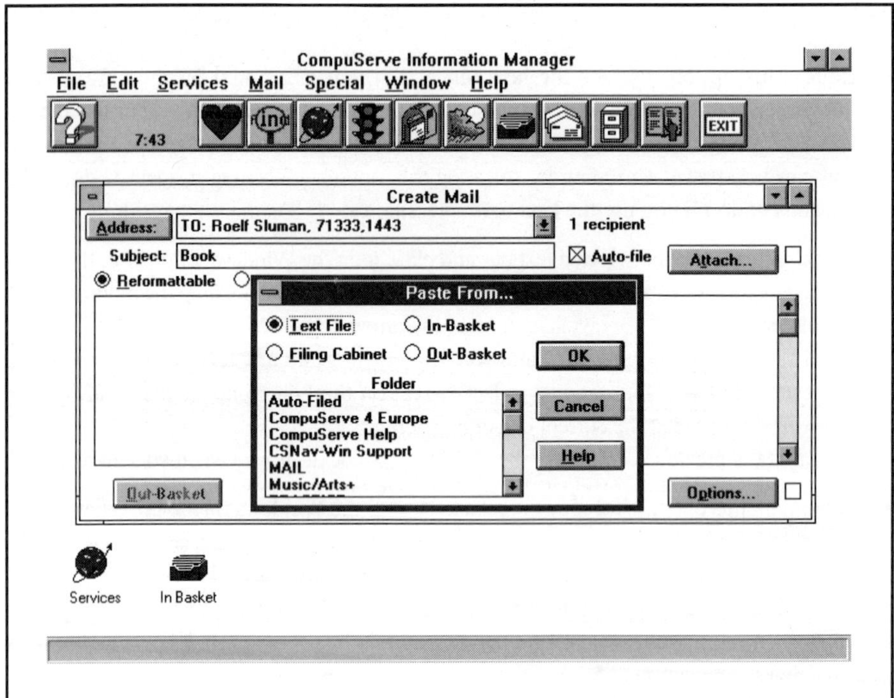

Figure 5.10 The Paste From dialog

5.8.3 The Services menu

Almost all options on the Services menu take you online. In other words: the fun begins! If you would like to try out the examples in this section yourself, don't forget to disconnect when you have finished.

The Services menu contains the following options:

- *Favorite Places*: You can maintain a list of CompuServe services you often visit. This list of Favorite Places is very useful, because you don't have to remember all the GO words for those services.
  When you access the list of Favorite Places for the first time, you will see that it already contains a few initial items. However, feel free to add your own services and delete services you don't like (any more). Refer to section 5.9.2 for more information about the Favorite Places option.
- *Find*: Every service on CompuServe has its own GO word (some services can even be accessed *via* more than one GO word, as you might discover eventually). A list of available GO words is printed in this book, but you can always `GO INDEX` to obtain an updated list. New services are added all the time, 24 hours per day: as soon as they become available, they appear in the CompuServe Index. Refer to Section 9.6 for a hard copy.

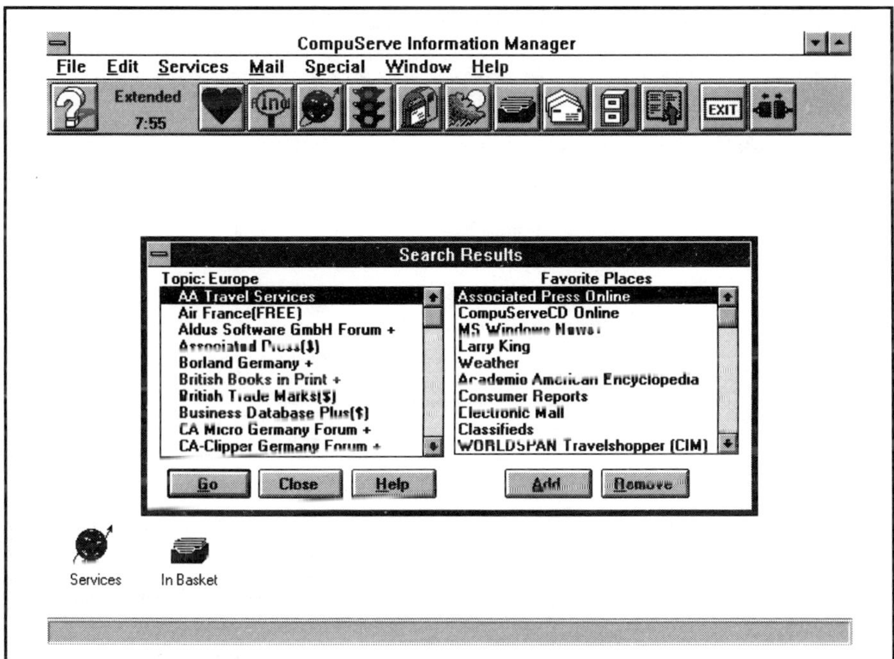

Figure 5.11 A list with services that match the keyword 'Europe'

The GO command is very useful, providing you know the GO word of the service you want to visit. But what if you don't? In that case, you can use the `FIND` command and specify a *keyword*. Most forums and other CompuServe services are registered with a large list of keywords, to ascertain that you can find them if you need them.
After you select the `Find` option, WinCIM asks for a search string. Enter a search string, for instance 'Europe', and press Enter, or click on the OK button. WinCIM will go online and look for all services that match your keyword. Don't be surprised if there is more than one service available. Take a look at Figure 5.11. You wouldn't have thought that this search generated *that* many services, would you?

When CompuServe (or rather, WinCIM) shows a list of available services, you can choose to add them to your list of Favorite Places, or to go to one of those services directly.

Adding Favorite Places while you are online

If, while you are visiting a CompuServe service, you want to add that service to your list of Favorite Places, just select the Favorite Places option on the Services menu. In most cases, WinCIM will have filled in the dialog for you; you only have to click on OK or press Enter.

Figure 5.12 The WinCIM Services Window

- *Browse*: Use this option to open the Services window (see Figure 5.12). This window contains a number of icons that refer to a group of services. You can double-click on one of the icons to get online and review the menu for that particular group of services. If you are a member of the Standard Pricing Plan, you are not billed during this time, although communication surcharges still apply.

- *Go*: If you know the GO word of a particular service, you can use this option to access that service directly. After you select this option, WinCIM will ask for the name of the service. After you have typed the name, press Enter or click on OK. If you are not online already, WinCIM will establish the connection automatically.

HINTS & TIPS

Save your favourite services

As you get more experience online, it won't take long before you start to collect your own favourite services. Instead of learning the `GO` words for these services by heart, you can add them to the WinCIM list of Favorite Places. Select the `Favorite Places` option on the Services menu, or click on the `Favorite Places` button on the Ribbon to access this feature. More information on the `Favorite Places` option can be found in Section 5.9.2.

- *What's New*: Every week, normally on Thursday, CompuServe releases an online bulletin with information about added services, changes, and so on. To get access to this What's New section, select the option of the same name on the Services menu.

HINTS & TIPS

New on CompuServe? Browse through the old What's New bulletins

If you are new to CompuServe, or if you have been away for a while, take the time to browse through some of the old What's New bulletins, *via* an option in the What's New list. These bulletins bring you up to date on the latest developments. Other good information providers about new CompuServe services are the free Help forum (`GO HELPFORUM`), the free Practice Forum (`GO PRACTICE`) and the TapCIS forum (`GO TAPCIS`).

- *Special Events*: From time to time, CompuServe organizes special events like conferences with important politicians, business executives and Hollywood stars. Every CompuServe member can attend these conferences, and even ask a question or two. Use the `Special Events` option to get information about upcoming events, and to reserve a digital seat.

- *Executive News*: One of the special, surcharged news services that CompuServe provides is called Executive News, abbreviated to ENS. For a $15 per hour surcharge, you get access to the latest news bulletins of the major news agencies. The Executive News Service is always up to date: the new stories are available the moment the agencies put them 'on the wires'.

If you are a member of the Executive Pricing Plan, you can make your own ENS folders, with one or more keywords to indicate the news items that interest you. After you have created one or more folders, ENS will scan the news wires continuously and place all articles that match your search criteria in your personal ENS folder.

The Executive News Service is covered in more detail in Section 9.1.2, on page 352.

- *Quotes*: This option shows you the most recent stock market quotes for one or more securities, which you specify.

  After you select the `Quotes` option, WinCIM displays the Stock Quotes window, displayed in Figure 5.13. This window displays a list of available *ticker symbols*: symbols that correspond to a company of whose latest quote information you would like to review. You can review the information for one particular ticker symbol (select the appropriate symbol and press the `Get` button), or you can retrieve information for all listed symbols. You can also add new ticker symbols. To get the ticker symbol for a particular company, `GO LOOKUP`.

  Note that Quotes is part of CompuServe Basic Services. However, you are charged extra for retrieving graphical information *via* the `Maps` option. More information about retrieving quotes *via* CompuServe can be found in Section 9.1.3.

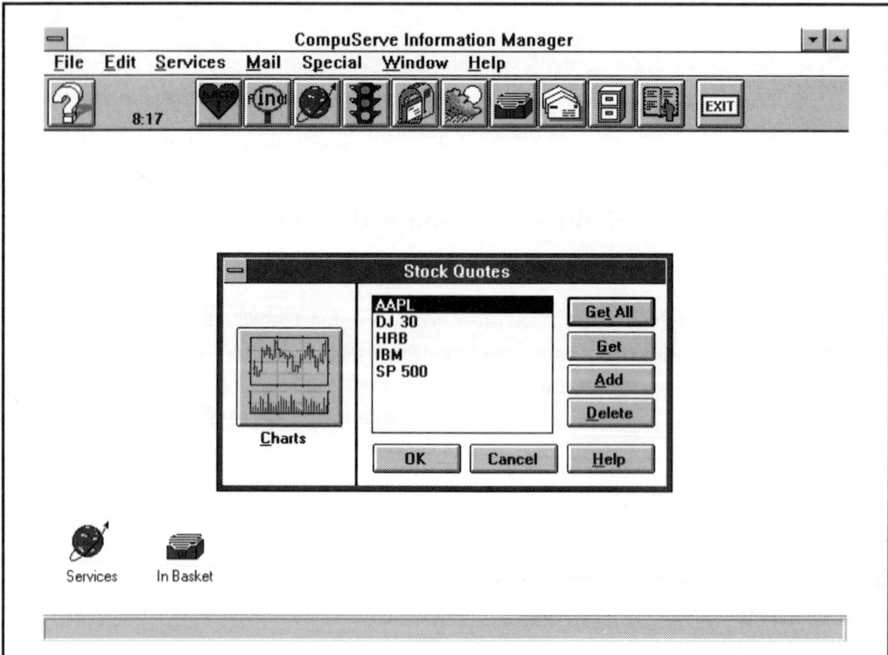

Figure 5.13 The Stock Quotes window

- *Portfolio*: Select this option to get the latest information about your stock purchases from exchanges all over the world, including Europe! You use the Stock Portfolio dialog, shown in Figure 5.14, to request information about particular stocks. In the Add Portfolio Entry field, you enter the necessary information for all stocks you wish to review. Note that you can `GO LOOKUP` to retrieve company ticker symbols.

  The portfolio entries you have specified are listed in the main part of the Stock Portfolio dialog. To generate a report for the listed portfolio entries, press the Report button. WinCIM will go online, retrieve the requested information, and display it in a Portfolio Report window. If you have entered information about the original value of your portfolio entries, your total gain or loss will be displayed as well.

  This BASICQUOTES service is a part of CompuServe Basic Services. Note that the requested information is always at least 15 minutes late, to comply with official exchange regulations.

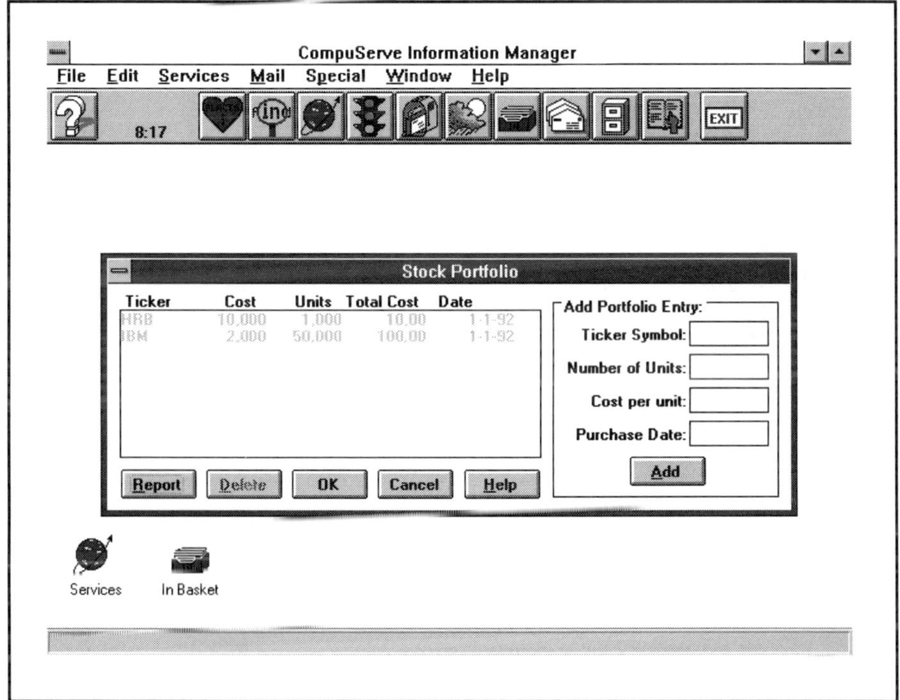

Figure 5.14 The Stock Portfolio dialog

- *Weather*: Use this option to get access to an incredible number of weather reports and maps, from places all over the world. After you select this option (offline as well as online), WinCIM will show the Weather dialog (see Figure 5.15). You can either review information about the weather at your current location, or you can choose from an extensive list of available locations (press the `arrow` button).

Apart from text reports, it is also possible to download *weather maps*: graphical information (in a special CompuServe format, called GIF: *Graphical Interchange Format*). Press the `Maps` button to do this: WinCIM will go online and look for available weather maps.

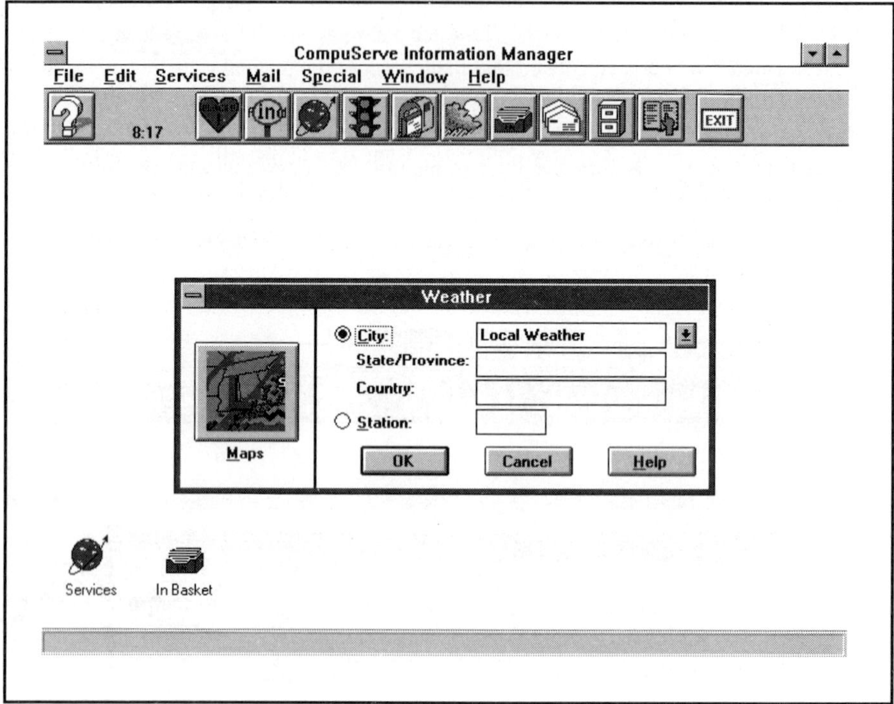

Figure 5.15 Obtain the latest weather information *via* this dialog

- *CB Simulator*: Although the forums are the most popular means of communicating with other CompuServe members, there is also a large group of people who meet each other on CB: CompuServe's digital 'Citizen Band'. Although CB can be quite expensive, especially for European members, a lot of people consider it a very nice way to meet new online friends. It is even possible to play games like chess, checkers and backgammon *via* a CB-related service: the CompuServe Entertainment Center.

  When you select the `CB Simulator` option, WinCIM will go online and display the CB Main Menu. This menu is your entry to the special CB forum, the three CB bands (each band has 36 channels – a CB channel resembles a conference room in a forum) and some special CB features, like the online magazine and some special pricing plan offers. Refer to Section 9.3.1 for more information.

5.8.4 The Mail menu

For most users, this is one of the most important WinCIM menus. The options on this menu allow you to access your In-Basket, Out-Basket and Filing Cabinet, and to send and receive e-mail and forum messages.

Most of the options on the `Mail` menu are discussed in other places in this book. We therefore confine ourselves to a short list of the available menu options.

- *Get New Mail*: After you select this option, WinCIM will go online and check the contents of your mailbox. If you have mail waiting, you can decide to read one or more messages online, to delete messages, or to retrieve them: WinCIM will place them in your In-Basket. See Section 7.5.2 for more information about receiving e-mail with WinCIM.
- *Search New Mail*: If you use CompuServe extensively and receive lots of e-mail messages per day, you can select this option to scan for particular e-mail messages only. It is possible to search for messages written by a particular person, on a specific subject, or with certain *flags*. Refer to Section 7.5.2 for more information.
- *Create Mail*: Use this option to write e-mail messages to other CompuServe members, and to practically anyone that has an e-mail address. Detailed information about sending e-mail with WinCIM can be found in Section 7.3.2.
- *Send/Receive All Mail*: This option is very useful if you want to perform a quick 'e-mail session', in which you send off all newly written e-mail messages and retrieve all messages sent to you. You can even indicate that you want WinCIM to disconnect automatically after performing these duties. I use this option quite often to check for new e-mail messages during the day, while I leave other things like forum visits to the evening hours.
  Note that this option is discussed in Section 7.3.2 as well.
- *Send File*: Apart from regular e-mail messages, you can use CompuServe Electronic Mail to send files as well. WinCIM uses a special protocol to transfer these files; you can therefore be certain that no bits will be lost on the way.
  However, there is an important factor to consider: the price. Because, for Standard Pricing Plan members, e-mail messages are charged according to their length, you could end up paying a small fortune for sending those ten disks with illustrations... Refer to Section 7.4.2 for more information about sending files *via* electronic mail.
- *In-Basket*: Select this option to review your WinCIM In-Basket. More on the In-Basket can be found in Section 5.7.2 'The In Basket'.
- *Out-Basket*: Select this option to access the Out-Basket, the place where outgoing messages are stored temporarily. Refer to Section 5.7.1 'The Out-Basket', for detailed information.
- *Filing Cabinet*: This option is used to review and/or alter the contents of your WinCIM Filing Cabinet, the digital version of the Filing Cabinet in your room or office. The Filing

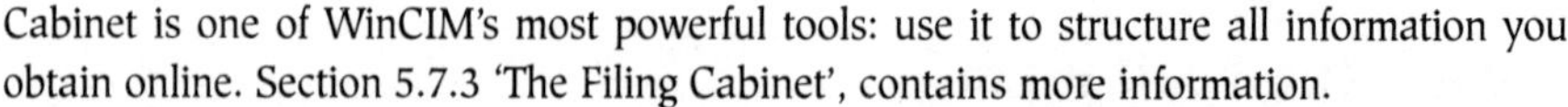

Cabinet is one of WinCIM's most powerful tools: use it to structure all information you obtain online. Section 5.7.3 'The Filing Cabinet', contains more information.

- *Address Book*: Select this option to access the WinCIM Address Book, a database in which you can store the e-mail addresses of people you exchange messages with. We deal with the WinCIM Address Book in Section 7.2.2.
- *Create Forum Message*: Use this option to start a new *forum thread*: a string with messages about a particular subject. For more about forum messages, threads and related subjects, refer to Section 8.7.
- *Member Directory*: Consult the online Member Directory if you are looking for a particular e-mail address. Every CompuServe member is listed in the Directory, except when he or she has specifically asked to be excluded. Section 7.2, contains more information about the Member Directory.

5.8.5 The Special menu

The options on the Special menu allow you to change the behaviour of WinCIM, or to alter your configuration. As you will see in the following list, most of the options on this menu are discussed in other sections.

- *Session Settings*: Select this option to specify or change information regarding your name and User ID, modem, and serial port configuration. The details of this very important window are discussed more extensively in Section 5.9, 'Configuring WinCIM'.
- *Connection Info*: This option displays information about the current and previous connections between WinCIM and CompuServe. Consult this information if you don't manage to get online with WinCIM. In some cases, CompuServe Customer Service will ask you for the information displayed in this window.
  Note that the Connection Info window also displays the total amount of connect time. If WinCIM is the only program you use to access CompuServe, you can reset this value at the beginning of each month, for example, to monitor the telephone costs.
- *Preferences*: Use this option to configure WinCIM to your needs. More information can be found in Section 5.9 'Configuring WinCIM'.
- *Terminal Emulation*: Most of the services that CompuServe provides, are easily accessible *via* WinCIM's user-friendly menus and options. However, there are also some facilities that aren't implemented (yet). To allow you to visit those services using WinCIM, a Terminal Emulation feature is provided. Once you get online using this option, you give CompuServe commands *via* the ASCII Interface.

Note that in some circumstances, WinCIM will invoke Terminal Emulation automatically. During Terminal Emulation, WinCIM maintains a special *buffer* in which the previously displayed lines are stored. You can change the size of this buffer as well as some other Terminal Emulation parameters.

- *Rebuild Cabinet Indexes*: The messages and articles that you save in the In-Basket, Out-Basket and Filing Cabinet are stored in a special database format. Occasionally, the internal WinCIM database structure can be damaged. If this happens, you will experience difficulties accessing these storage tools: messages that are listed won't show up, some messages are only partially shown, and so on. By selecting the `Rebuild Cabinet Indexes` option, you tell WinCIM to reconstruct the database index, thereby eliminating these errors. Don't delete Cabinet files yourself, unless you are specifically advised to do so.
- *Forum Database*: Every time you leave a forum, WinCIM will store information about that forum (like the message sections) in a special file. When you decide to write a forum message offline, WinCIM will use the information from that file to display a list of available forum sections.
  If, for some reason, you want to delete the information that WinCIM has stored for a particular forum, select the `Forum Database` option. Note however, that WinCIM will restore this information once you visit (or rather, leave) the forum again during a future online session.
- *Notices*: This option is available only when you are currently visiting a forum. When you select this option, WinCIM shows a list of notices: general messages about (parts of) the forum.
- *Forum Options*: Use this option to change your *forum name*. The name you use in a forum doesn't have to be the same as the name you used when you became a CompuServe member. Although most forums ask their members to use their first and last names, there are exceptions. The Gamers forum (`GO GAMERS`), for instance, allows the usage of so-called *handles* as forum names. When you visit such a forum, be prepared to see forum messages from senders like *Falcon*, *GameOver*, and so on.
  The Forum Options dialog also lets you specify the number of the last message you have read. For every forum that you visit, CompuServe maintains some important information, like your forum name and the number of the last message you have read. If, for some reason, you want to browse through *all* forum messages (as opposed to only the new messages in the forum), specify 1 as the Last Message number. (Next, leave the forum and enter it again to get access to those messages.) By checking the Permanent box, you instruct WinCIM to store your new forum name permanently as a part of your online forum information.

Sharing your account

If you share your account with someone else, your spouse for example, you can both use your own name while visiting a forum. This works best when both of you have your own range of forums you visit; one account cannot be a member of the same forum twice. In other words: when both of you visit the same forum, CompuServe will only show the new messages since the last visit of either one of you. But when either you or your spouse is the only one who visits a particular forum, you can select `Forum Options` on the Special menu to change your forum name.

Note that it is also possible to visit a forum together! Just enter both of your names in the User Name box. The HSX forums (`GO HSX100` and `GO HSX200`) have a lot of members that share an account this way.

- *Join Forum*: As a forum visitor, you don't have all the features at your disposal that regular forum members have. Therefore, if you didn't do so when you entered the forum for the first time, select this option to join the forum officially. That way, CompuServe will make an entry in the forum database for you, in which your name and some other personal information (like the number of the last message you have read) are stored. Apart from that, you get access to all public forum facilities like the message boards, the library, and the conference rooms.
- *Search Membership*: A lot of members use this option to search for another forum member (note that we are talking about *forum members* and not about *CompuServe members* here!) that shares the same interests, or simply to see if someone they know is also a member of the forum. You can search on user name (note that this doesn't necessarily has to be the same name as the 'official' name of the person you are looking for), User ID, or special interests. Although every forum member is listed in an internal 'forum directory', you will have to update your entry (that is, add information about your interests) to become visible to other members. To do this, select the `Change Member Entry` option on the Special menu.
- *Change Member Entry*: Select this option to add or modify your entry in the special forum directory. Only after you have added information to the Interests fields can other forum members find you when they use the `Search Membership` option.

Forum members and the Member Directory

Note that the 'member lists' that are maintained by forums have no resemblance to the Member Directory, which contains the names and e-mail addresses of CompuServe members. However, the forum member lists can be used for something that is not possible with the regular Member Directory: if you know the User ID of someone, but don't know his or her name, you can try your luck and search for this User ID in one or more forums. If the person is a member of a forum, his User ID and forum name (which doesn't have to be his or her real name, though) show up.

5.8.6 The Window menu

The Window menu contains options to organize the on-screen display of all WinCIM windows. The following options are available:

- *Cascade*: Choose this option to place all windows in such a way that they are all partly visible.
- *Tile*: Use this option to place the open windows next to each other. The current window will be placed on the leftmost side of the WinCIM program window.
- *Arrange Icons*: This option arranges the icons of all minimized windows.
- *Close All*: Select this option to close all open and minimized windows. If the window contains information that you have not saved yet (like a graphics file, for example), WinCIM will ask you whether or not you would like to save the contents on your hard disk.

The names of all windows are shown as entries on the Window menu. To bring a window to the foreground, just select the appropriate option on the Window menu.

5.8.7 The Help menu

Apart from the standard options that you find on almost every Help menu, this menu contains one special feature. The following options are available:

- *Contents*: This option shows the contents of the WinCIM help file.
- *Search for Help On*: Use this option when you need help on a particular WinCIM subject.
- *How to Use Help*: If you are new to the Windows environment, use this option to get acquainted with the Windows Help system
- *CompuServe Directory*: Use this option to get access to the CompuServe Directory, a Windows Help file that contains information about all services available on CompuServe. Note that this directory is not included with the version of WinCIM that comes with this book. However, updates can be obtained from the WinCIM download area: (GO WINCIM) the CompuServe Directory is included in the Support Files.
- *About CIM*: This option shows a dialog with copyright information, as well as the amount of free space on your hard disk.

5.8.8 The Messages menu

This menu, which is available only while you are visiting a forum, contains the following options:

- *Browse*: Use this option to browse through the message boards. When you select the `Browse` option, WinCIM displays a list of the names of all *sections* on the message board (see Figure 5.16). This list contains the following information:
  - As stated, the names of all forum sections. The maximum number of message sections is 24, although forums exist that use only one or two sections, depending on the actual need.
  - The total number of *topics* (message threads) for each section.
  - The total number of messages for each section.

  You can perform one or more of the following actions:
  - Review the contents of a section: double-click on the section name (or use the arrow keys and press Enter). WinCIM shows a list of topics in that section. You can either *get* a topic (read it online), or *mark* it for retrieval to your hard disk. For more information about reading forum messages (either online or offline), refer to Section 8.7.2.
  - Mark a complete section for retrieval to your hard disk. To do this, check the box in front of the section name. When you have marked all sections and/or messages you wish to read, select the `Retrieve Marked` option on the Message menu to actually retrieve the marked messages to your hard disk.

Background on forum messages

Note that WinCIM (or rather, CompuServe) only summarizes the new forum messages since the last time you used the Browse option. In other words: if you leave the forum after selecting the Browse option and enter the forum again right away, selecting the Browse option will, in most cases, result in an (almost) empty list of new messages. The reason for this is that CompuServe maintains internal information about the last message you have 'read' (or rather, 'scanned') on each forum. Next time you enter that forum, CompuServe assumes that you don't want to read old messages and won't show them to you. If you want to see them again, you can use either `Set Date` on the Messages menu or `Forum Options` on the Special menu.

- *Search*: Use this option if you are looking for forum messages sent by or to someone specific, or for messages about a particular topic (subject). When you select the `Search` option, the dialog shown in Figure 5.17 is displayed. This dialog contains the following fields:

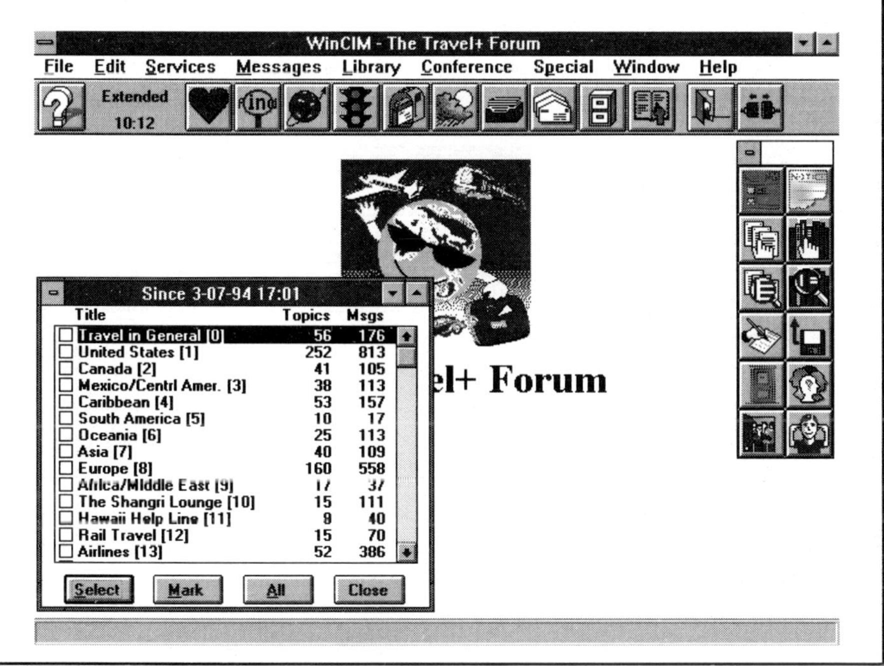

Figure 5.16 Browsing messages with WinCIM

- *In Sections*: Check the sections that you want to search in. By default, all sections are selected. You can check or uncheck sections manually, or you can press either the `All` or the `None` button to have WinCIM check or uncheck all sections at once.
- *Search For*: Select one of the option buttons to indicate the item you are looking for: Subject (the topic, or thread name), From (the person who sent the message), To (the person to whom the message was sent), or Message Number. Next, enter the search string in the text box.
- *Since*: If you want to search for older messages as well (that is, messages that you have scanned or read during a previous visit to the forum, and that are still available on the message board), you can enter the start date in this field. Note that this field normally contains the date of your last forum visit.
- *Mark Results*: WinCIM will show the results of the search in a special dialog, giving you the option of reading them online or retrieving them to your hard disk for offline processing. By selecting the Mark Results box, you ask WinCIM to mark all items found. That way, you can retrieve them to your hard disk by selecting the `Retrieve Marked` option on the `Messages` menu.
- *Search*: Press this button to start the actual search procedure. After a few moments, WinCIM will show the results in a dialog.

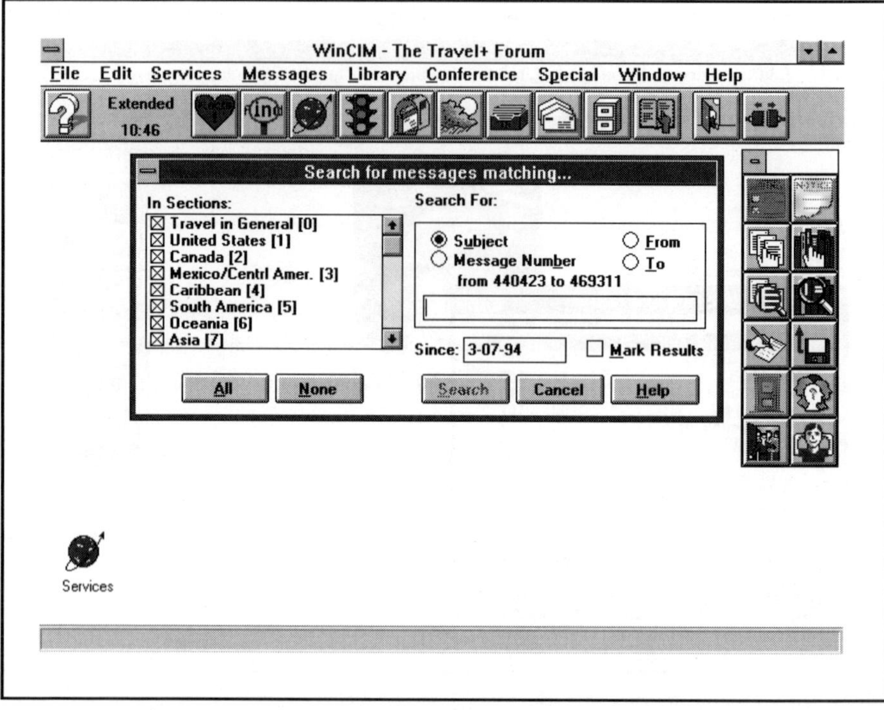

Figure 5.17 Searching for specific forum messages

- *Get Waiting*: If you are expecting personal messages, but don't have the time for an extensive message reading session, you can select this option. WinCIM will only retrieve the new messages sent to you. Because the internal information about the last message read or scanned by you will not be updated, all new messages are still available next time you visit the forum.
- *Retrieve Marked*: This option is available only if you have marked one or more messages, threads, or complete sections. Select this option to retrieve those marked items to your hard disk, for processing offline. WinCIM will place the retrieved items in a Filing Cabinet folder with the same name as the forum. To review the retrieved items, select the `Filing Cabinet` option on the `Mail` menu.

HINTS & TIPS

Can messages be downloaded?

Some forum members use the term 'downloading' when they are referring to the process of marking and retrieving messages. Actually, retrieving and downloading both relate to the same action: retrieving information from one computer and storing that information on another computer.

- *Set Date*: Use this option if you want to review 'older' forum messages: messages that were posted before the last time you visited the forum, and that haven't scrolled off yet. For each forum you are a member of, CompuServe maintains internal information. Part of that information is the date of your last visit to a particular forum, as well as the number of the last message you have read. Both of these items are updated automatically when you leave a particular forum, although you can modify them yourself as well: the date by selecting the `Set Date` option on the Messages menu, and the last message number by selecting `Forum Options` on the Special menu.
- *Freshen Messages*: When, during a particular session, you have spent a reasonably long time on a forum (for instance, because you have downloaded a large file), the chances are that new messages have been posted by other forum members who visit the forum at the same time as you do. Normally, you don't see those new messages until you visit the forum the next time. However, you can select the `Freshen Messages` option to see them right away. You can select this option as often as you like during your forum visit.
- *Create Message*: Select this option to create a new forum message. More information about writing forum messages can be found in Section 8.7.4.
- *In-Basket*: This option provides access to the In-Basket, one of WinCIM's powerful information management tools. Refer to Section 5.7, 'WinCIM Tools For Data Management', for more information about the In-Basket. When you are offline, the `In-Basket` option can be found on the Mail menu.
- *Out-Basket*: Select this option to open the Out-Basket, a WinCIM information management tool that stores all your outgoing messages that haven't been sent to CompuServe yet. More information about the Out-Basket can be found in Section 5.7, 'WinCIM Tools For Data Management'. When you are offline, you can review the Out-Basket by selecting the `Out-Basket` option on the Mail menu.
- *Filing Cabinet*: Selecting this option opens the Filing Cabinet, your storage medium for all messages and articles you have retrieved from CompuServe. Section 5.7, 'WinCIM Tools For Data Management', contains more information about the Filing Cabinet and the other information management tools that WinCIM provides. Offline, the `Filing Cabinet` option can be found on the Mail menu.
- *Address Book*: Use your WinCIM Address Book to store the e-mail addresses of people you exchange messages with. The Address Book is covered in more detail in Section 7.2.2.
- *Notice*: Selecting this option shows information about the usage of the message board on this forum.
- *Descriptions*: Select this option for a summary of the available message sections in this forum.

WinCIM and forum messages

If you want to practise reading, writing and replying to forum messages, `GO PRACTICE` to visit the free CompuServe Practice Forum. The Practice Forum has answers to all your forum-related questions as well. Another good place to talk about WinCIM is the free WinCIM Support Forum: `GO WCIMSUP`. (Note that communication surcharges still apply.)

5.8.9 The Library menu

The Library menu contains options related to downloading and uploading files to the forum library.

- *Browse*: Use this option to browse through the available forum library sections. WinCIM displays a list of available library sections. After you have selected a section, WinCIM shows the files in that section, beginning with the newest file. To review more information about the file, press the `Description` button. When you have found a file you would like to download, you can either mark it (by checking the box in front of the file name, or by pressing the Mark button) and retrieve it, together with other files, in one batch, or download it right away by pressing the `Retrieve` button. See the description of the Library Search dialog below for a more extensive description of the available options.
- *Search*: Select this option to search for library files that match a certain search specification, or to download a specific file whose name you know. The Search for Files dialog, which appears when you select this option, contains the following fields:
  - *In sections*: Check the sections you would like to search. By default, all sections are selected. You can either select or deselect sections manually, or use the `All` and `None` buttons.
  - *File Name*: If you know the name of the file to download, for example because someone pointed you to it, enter it in this field, select all sections and press the `Search` button.
  - *Contributor*: If you are looking for a file that is uploaded by someone specific, enter his or her User ID in this field. Note that this field doesn't accept names, only User Ids.
  - *Keywords*: When uploading ('contributing') a file, certain keywords are provided to make it easy to track the file down. If you are searching for files that deal with a specific topic, enter one or more possible keywords in this field (separate them with a space character). Note that only the files that match all keywords will be displayed. Therefore, start by specifying one keyword. If this delivers too many files, you can always specify a second one.
  - *Between*: By default, all files in the library will be searched, irrespective of age. However, you can specify start and end dates, in which case the search will be limited to the files that were uploaded between those dates.

When you press the `Search` button, CompuServe starts to search for files that match your specifications. If any files are found, they are listed in the Library Search dialog, shown in Figure 5.18. This dialog contains the following options:

- *Description*: Press this button to see a more extensive description of the file.
- *Mark*: If you press this button, the file is marked for later retrieval. This is useful if you want to download several files. After you have marked those files, select the `Retrieve Marked` option on the Library menu to initiate the download.
  After you have pressed the `Mark` button, WinCIM will ask for the name under which the file should be saved onto your hard disk. You can either accept the name that CompuServe proposes, or edit it. WinCIM will store the downloaded files into the `\CSERVE\DOWNLOAD` directory by default. If you want to assign another directory for downloaded files, select the `Preferences` option on the `Special` menu. A submenu appears: select the `General` option to display the General Preferences dialog. This dialog lists the default directories used by WinCIM.
- *Retrieve*: Press this button to download the file to your computer. This option is useful if you know beforehand that you are only going to download one file.
  Before starting the download, WinCIM will ask for the name under which it should save the file onto your hard disk. Unless you specify otherwise, the file will be stored in the `\CSERVE\DOWNLOAD` directory.
- *View*: Pressing this button displays the contents of the file on your screen. Note that not all file formats can be viewed. Version 1.3 of WinCIM supports online display of graphics files in GIF and JPEG format, and of regular ASCII text files.

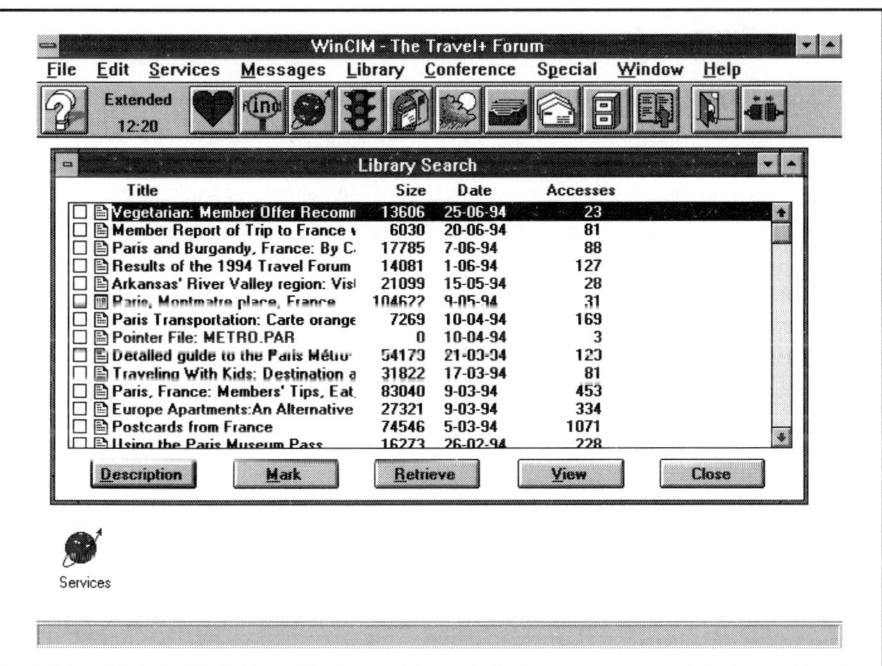

Figure 5.18 The Library Search dialog lists the files that match your search specifications

HINTS & TIPS

Powerful searching tools: the CompuServe File Finders

If you are looking for a specific file, but don't know in which forum you should search, consider using one of the CompuServe File Finders. The File Finders contain a summary of the files available in hundreds of popular CompuServe forums. As a WinCIM user, you can mark the files you are interested in and retrieve them all *via* one simple command. `GO PCFF` for the PC File Finder (MS-DOS compatible files), `GO GRAPHFF` for the Graphics File Finder (graphic files), `GO MACFF` for the Macintosh File Finder), `GO ATARIFF` for the Atari ST File Finder, or `GO AMIGAFF` for the Amiga File Finder. Note that the CompuServe File Finders are part of the extended services: you pay the same price as when visiting a forum. If you are a ZiffNet member, you have two more File Finders at your disposal: `GO ZNT:ZNTFF` for the ZiffNet Forum File Finder (MS-DOS files), or `GO ZNT:ZMAC` and follow the instructions for the Ziffnet Mac Forum File Finder (Macintosh Files).

The CompuServe File Finders are very easy to use, especially if you work with WinCIM. For additional information refer to Section 8.8.5.

- *Retrieve Marked*: This option is available only if you have selected one or more files to download. ('Retrieving' and 'Downloading' are two terms that pertain to the same action: transferring files from CompuServe to your computer.)

HINTS & TIPS

Busy downloading? Don't just sit there waiting!

Have you ever wondered what to do while WinCIM is busy downloading your files? You could visit a conference room, browse through the list looking for other files to download, or read some messages online! Although not every WinCIM user is aware of this, it is perfectly possible to carry out other forum activities while WinCIM is downloading. Although the download will slow down a little while you retrieve other kinds of information, it is a nice way to kill the time.

- *Contribute*: If you have a program, document, graphic, or some other interesting file that you would like to share with your fellow forum members, you can upload it to the forum by selecting this option. Note that uploading is free as far as connect charges are concerned, although communication surcharges still apply.
  After you select the `Contribute` option, WinCIM asks for the name and exact location of the file on your hard disk. Next, you have to specify the name that the file should be given once uploaded to CompuServe. You also have to provide information about the forum library to place the file in, a title (which will be shown as a description for the file), one or more keywords that members can use to search for your file and, finally, a description of the file.
  After you have uploaded the file, it will be checked by a forum sysop for possible viruses and other problems. If your file is 'released' (normally after no more than 24 hours), you will be notified and it will appear in the appropriate forum library.

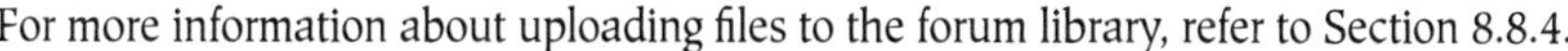

For more information about uploading files to the forum library, refer to Section 8.8.4.

- *Notice*: Selecting this option shows information and guidelines related to the forum library.
- *Descriptions*: Select this option to get a summary of the available forum library sections.

HINTS & TIPS

WinCIM and the forum library

If you want to practise downloading files with WinCIM, visit the free CompuServe Practice Forum: **GO PRACTICE**. (Note that communication surcharges still apply.) **GO WCIMSUP** for answers to all your questions about WinCIM; while you are there, don't forget to scan the library of the free WinCIM Support Forum for additional information. Another place that shouldn't be overlooked, is the free CompuServe Help Forum: **GO HELPFORUM**. Finally, Section 8.8 contains more information about downloading and uploading files using WinCIM.

5.8.10 The Conference menu

If money is of no concern to you, or if you have to spend some time in a forum, while downloading one or more files, you could visit one of the Conference Rooms that are available in almost all forums. Or you could invite (or be invited by) another forum member for what is called a 'chat': an interactive conversation online. Whatever you type on your keyboard appears on the screen of the person(s) you are 'typing to'.

More information about forum conferences can be found in Section 8.9. In the next section, the available WinCIM menu options are discussed briefly.

- *Enter Room*: When you select this option, WinCIM displays a list of available conference rooms. Some forums only have one room, while others have one room for each message section.
  When you select a room, the number of people who are currently present in that room is shown at the bottom of the Conference Rooms window. You enter the room by double-clicking on its name, or by pressing the `Enter` button. You can also decide not to participate in the conversation, but simply to listen to it (without being noticed): press the `Listen` button to do so.
  As soon as you enter a room, WinCIM displays the ongoing conversation (from the moment you enter; it is not possible to review the previous part of the conversation) in a separate window. To say something, simply type the text in the input field. As soon as you press the [Enter] key, your text is sent to CompuServe and, after a few moments, displayed in the main part of the window, visible for all participants and listeners. To leave the room, select the `Leave` option on the File menu, or press the appropriate button on the WinCIM Ribbon.

- *Who's Here*: Select this option to see a list of all the people present in either the forum, a particular conference room, or the group you are currently in.
- *Set Nickname*: As a forum member, you will use your full name most of the time when writing or replying to messages. In conferences however, you may prefer to use a 'handle' or forum nickname by selecting this option. Your nickname will be shown when other forum members select the `Who's Here` option to get a list of members currently present in the forum. You can change your nickname as often as you like.
- *Invite*: Select this option to invite one or more present forum members for a private conversation: a *group conference*. Matters discussed during this conference are only visible on the screens of forum members that were actually invited to this group conference. It is not possible for other forum members to join the conference without receiving an invitation, nor is it possible for them to 'eavesdrop' by means of the `Listen` option.
  After you have selected the `Invite` option, you can mark the names of one or more present forum members and invite them all at once.

HINTS & TIPS

Be polite and respectful

Avoid sending multiple invitations to the same forum member. If he or she doesn't respond to your first invitation, your request probably didn't suit him or her. Like almost every forum member, I too have at times been assailed by dozens of requests by some fanatic conferencing enthusiast, which made me very grateful that something like an `Ignore` option exists! Of course, there is always a possibility that the appropriate person is simply not able to respond, because he or she uses an auto-access program like CompuServe Navigator or TapCIS.

- *Ignore*: If, for any reason, you want to suppress all messages and invitations sent by one or more particular forum members, you can 'squelch' them by selecting this option. The sender will not be informed of your action; a perfect way to ignore obnoxious individuals.
- *Notice*: Select this option to review information about conferencing on this forum.
- *Descriptions*: This option provides information about the available conference rooms.

5.9 Configuring WinCIM

When you have been online a few times using WinCIM, you will want to configure the program to your own needs. Apart from the necessary modem settings, you can change some parts of the user interface, make configurations for more than one User ID, and set your preferences for things like e-mail and forum visits.

The key to changing the WinCIM settings is the Special menu, although you will find some options in other menus as well.

5.9.1 Providing WinCIM with vital information: session settings

Before you can get online for the first time, you must enter important information like your User ID, password (eventually), access telephone number, and your modem. To update this information, select the `Session Settings` option on the Special menu. This opens the Setup Session Settings window. This very important window contains the following fields:

- *Session*: You can configure WinCIM for more than one session. Don't confuse the word session with the process of going online, performing online actions and disconnecting: in WinCIM jargon, a session is a packet with information about the User ID, password, access telephone number, and so on. The ability to install several sessions is very useful when you have WinCIM installed on a notebook computer that you take with you on your travels. For every city that you visit, you can create a separate session, in which you enter the correct access telephone number and WinCIM script.
  To create a new session, press the `New` button. To delete the current session, press the Delete button. Refer to Section 5.9.3 for more information about configuring WinCIM for more sessions.
- *Alternate*: If you wish, you can specify a session that WinCIM should use if execution of the current session results in problems. If there are more access telephone numbers for your city, you could consider creating a new session with a second telephone number, and specifying that session as your alternate session.
- *Name*: The name you enter in this field will be used by default every time you send an e-mail message or join a forum.
- *User ID*: Enter your CompuServe User ID here: two numbers, separated by a comma.
- *Password*: If you want WinCIM to connect automatically, you can enter your password in this field. The password will not be displayed while you type it.

HINTS & TIPS

And you thought your password was safe

As you may know, personal information like your User ID and your password are stored in a special initialization file, called CIS.INI. As a weapon against overly curious peeks from fellow users on your computer, your password is stored in a special, scrambled format, a format so complicated that you have to call CompuServe if you ever lose your password and need it again.

So your password is securely stored, isn't it? **No way**. For everyone with a little persistence, your password is an easy target. Any curious user with some computer experience and a little persistence will need only a few seconds to get to it.

That's right: a few seconds. And no, I am not kidding about this. So if your computer is located in a public place (like an office), don't take any risks – store your password in the only safe place that exists: in your head. Delete it from the Settings window, WinCIM will ask for it every time you go online.

- *Phone*: Enter the access phone number here. Use a comma to insert a pause.

Need an access telephone number?

If you are planning to travel and want to get information about possible access telephone numbers for your destination(s): `GO PHONES` for information about phone numbers, networks, and so on.

- *Connector*: Select the COM port your modem is connected to on this list. If your computer is part of a network work group that has access to a common modem, you can select the `Int14` option.
- *Baud Rate*: Select the maximum speed that is supported by the access telephone number you are calling. If you need more information about available connect speeds for a particular access telephone number, `GO PHONES`.
- *Network*: Select the network that you have to use to get access to CompuServe. Although the number of direct nodes (access telephone numbers that connect you directly to CompuServe) is growing, the chances are that you have to use a so-called *external network*. WinCIM comes with a collection of scripts for most, if not all, available networks, for access all over the world. If you use a standard CompuServe telephone number, select the CompuServe option on the drop down menu.

  The scripts that WinCIM uses to get you connected can be found in the `\CSERVE\SCRIPTS` directory. Although it is normally not necessary to edit these scripts, you can do so by using a normal Windows editor like Notepad, or your regular word processing program. Note that you have to save the edited file in regular text format, without formatting codes.
- *Dial Type*: If you are connected to a modern telephone system that can work with tone dialling, select Tone. If not, select Pulse. The best way to discover whether or not tone dialling is supported is to try it: if WinCIM generates an error message, try using pulse dialling instead. Note that you can also select Manual, if your modem doesn't support auto dialling, or if you are calling from a credit card phone.
- *Redial Attempts*: If the line is busy, WinCIM will dial again for the number of times you have specified in this field. If the program still doesn't succeed in establishing a connection, it will try an alternate session. If that doesn't work either, or if you didn't specify an alternate session, the attempt will be cancelled.

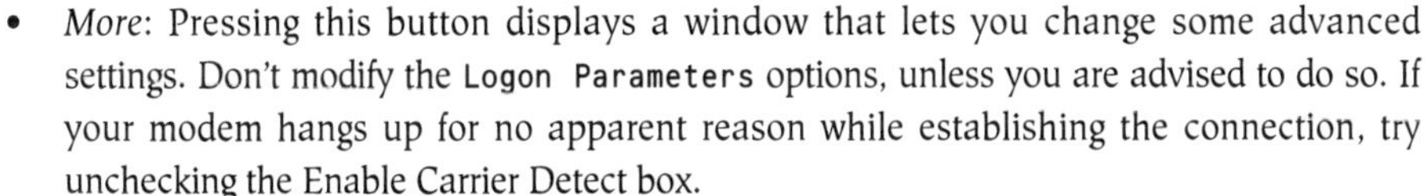

- *More*: Pressing this button displays a window that lets you change some advanced settings. Don't modify the `Logon Parameters` options, unless you are advised to do so. If your modem hangs up for no apparent reason while establishing the connection, try unchecking the Enable Carrier Detect box.

HINTS & TIPS

Attempting to resynchronize...

The HMI protocol can give some problems when you are accessing large databases using WinCIM. If you experience a lot of sudden disconnects because WinCIM could not resynchronize with CompuServe, it might help to increase the HMI count value, listed in the More dialog. However, note that increasing this value will mean that it takes WinCIM longer to detect that something has gone wrong, which could result in somewhat larger CompuServe and telephone bills.

- *Modem*: Press this button to display the Modem Control Strings dialog, shown in Figure 5.19. In most cases, WinCIM shouldn't have any problems detecting what kind of modem you have, and should adjust the settings in this window automatically. Consult your modem manual for information about specific commands for your modem.

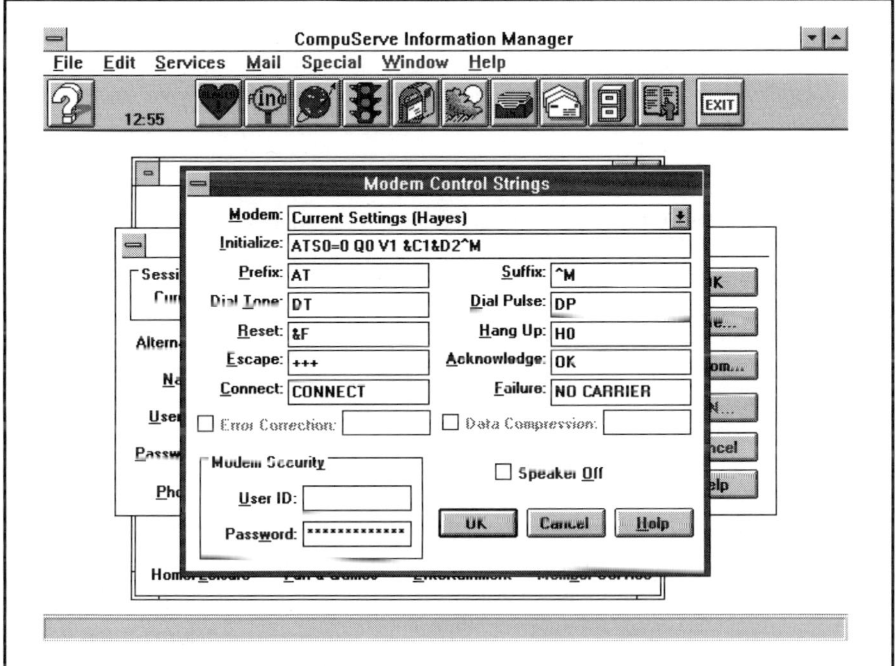

Figure 5.19 This dialog contains the modem settings

- *LAN*: This option, which is only available if you have informed WinCIM that you want to use a shared network modem (by selecting `Int14` in the Connector field), allows you to specify the connection port for that modem.

5.9.2 Your Favorite Places

After you have visited CompuServe a few times, you will find yourself returning to certain services more often. The time has come to collect these services into a special, personal toolkit: your Favorite Places. The Favorite Places feature of WinCIM allows you to make your own 'top ten' list (actually, the number of entries in the Favorite Places list is much higher) of favourite services. That way, you don't have to be afraid of missing something online: you just check your list of Favorite Places for services you haven't visited yet during a particular session. And because you can (and should) change the contents of the Favorite Places list as often as necessary, it is a very flexible tool.

To access the list of Favorite Places, do one of the following:

- Select the `Favorite Places` option on the Services menu.
- Press the special `Favorite Places` button on the WinCIM Ribbon.

When you start WinCIM for the very first time, the program will use a Favorite Places list that contains a few important services. You can either start adding your own services immediately, or you can have them added more or less automatically while you are online.

- *To add a service while you are offline*: Press the `Add` Button while the Favorite Places window is displayed. WinCIM will ask you for a description: this is the name that will appear in the Favorite Places list. Apart from that, WinCIM needs a *Service Name*: the `GO` word for that particular service. If you don't know the `GO` word, you can use the `CompuServe Directory` option on the `Help` menu to retrieve it.
- *To add a service while you are online*: While you are visiting the service, select the `Favorite Places` option on the Services menu, or press the special `Favorite Places` button on the WinCIM Ribbon. Press the `Add` button: WinCIM will retrieve the name and description of the service and place them in the right fields. Most of the time, all you have to do is to close the Add to Favorite Places dialog.
  Note that if you have used the `Find` option on the `Services` menu to get a list of all services that pertain to a certain topic, you can have one or more of those services added to your list of Favorite Places automatically.

- *To change the order in which the items are shown*: Select the `Preferences` option on the Special menu. A submenu appears: select the `General` option to display the General Preferences window. You will find three option buttons that allow you to choose the way the Favorite Places items should be sorted: by access (the service that you accessed last will be placed at the top of the list), alphabetic, or in the order in which you have added them.
- *To delete an item from the list*: Select the item you would like to delete from the list. Press the 'Delete' button.

5.9.3 Using WinCIM with more than one account

If you have several CompuServe accounts (one business and one private account, for instance), you can register both accounts with WinCIM. Once you have done that, you can easily select the account you would like to use as a separate *session*.

To provide WinCIM with information about an extra account, proceed as follows:

1. Select the `Session Settings` option on the Special menu. The Setup Session Settings window, shown in Figure 5.20, appears.
2. Press the `New` button, located in the Session box. WinCIM will ask you for the name of the new session. Most characters, including spaces, are allowed. Take time to think about a good, descriptive name: you won't be able to change it later. (Of course, you could create an entirely new session and delete the old one, but who wants to go through all that?)
3. When you have entered the name for the new session, the name appears in the Current field, in the Session box. The Current field is actually a drop down list, which contains all available sessions. The other parameters in the Setup Session Settings window all apply to the currently active session.
4. To add information about another account, you normally only have to change the User ID and Password fields, and the Name field. Once you have done that, you can select the account to use *via* the Current drop down list. Note that WinCIM remembers the active session and will use that session automatically from then on, until you select another session.

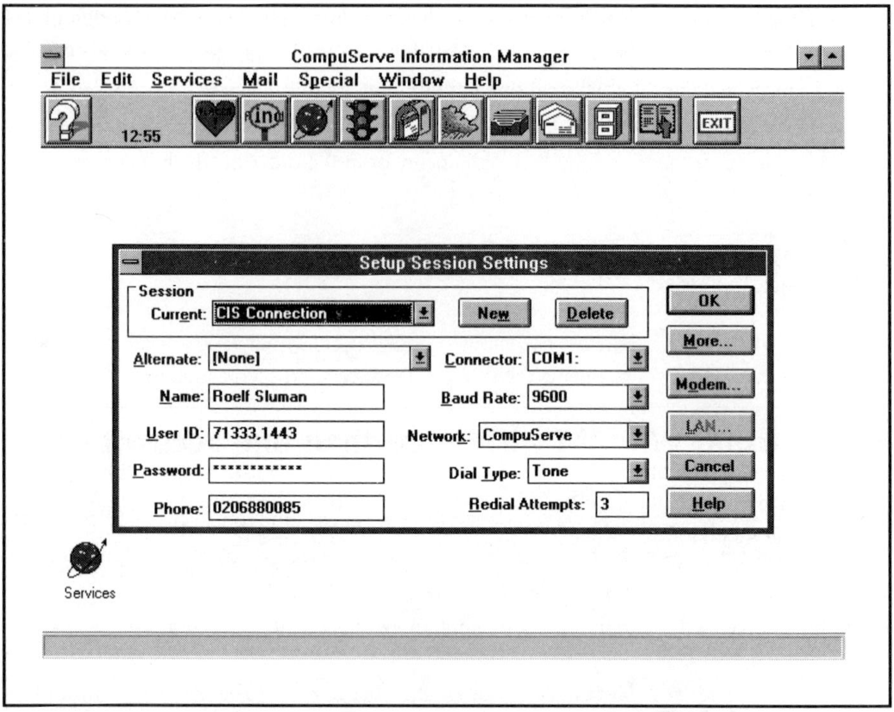

Figure 5.20 Use the Setup Session Settings window to add an account to the WinCIM configuration

Tip for travellers

Do you use WinCIM on your notebook computer? In that case, you might like to add several sessions for different locations. I have three sessions for the same account, for Amsterdam, London and Budapest: the User ID and password information are identical for each session, but the telephone numbers and network information differ. Instead of having to remember this information and change it every time I visit one of these places, I only need to select another item from the Current drop down list.

Changing to another account while you are online

Experienced CIS members sometimes use a trick to change to their other account, for instance to see if there is mail waiting for that account, without logging off. Although this officially cannot be done using WinCIM, there is a trick to accomplish this. When you have finished with the business for your current account, `GO ASCII` to enter the CompuServe ASCII Interface.

Next, type `login`: and press [Enter] CompuServe will end the current session and pretend that you have just logged in *via* Terminal Emulation. Enter your second User ID and password. You are now online with your second User ID, and you can use the CompuServe ASCII Interface to carry out commands. Finally, select the `Disconnect` option on the File menu, press [Ctrl]-[D], or use the `Disconnect` button on the WinCIM Ribbon.

5.9.4 Customizing the WinCIM Ribbon

If you use the mouse (and there are not many Windows users who don't), you can increase the efficiency of WinCIM by customizing the Ribbon. To do this, proceed as follows:

1. Select the `Preferences` option on the Special menu. A submenu appears: select the `Ribbon` option on that submenu. WinCIM displays the Customize Ribbon dialog, shown in Figure 5.21. This dialog consists of three parts. At the top, the actual contents of the Ribbon are displayed. At the bottom left, you choose the icon you would like to assign to the Ribbon. The Activities list, at the top right, contains all the WinCIM activities that can be assigned to the Ribbon.

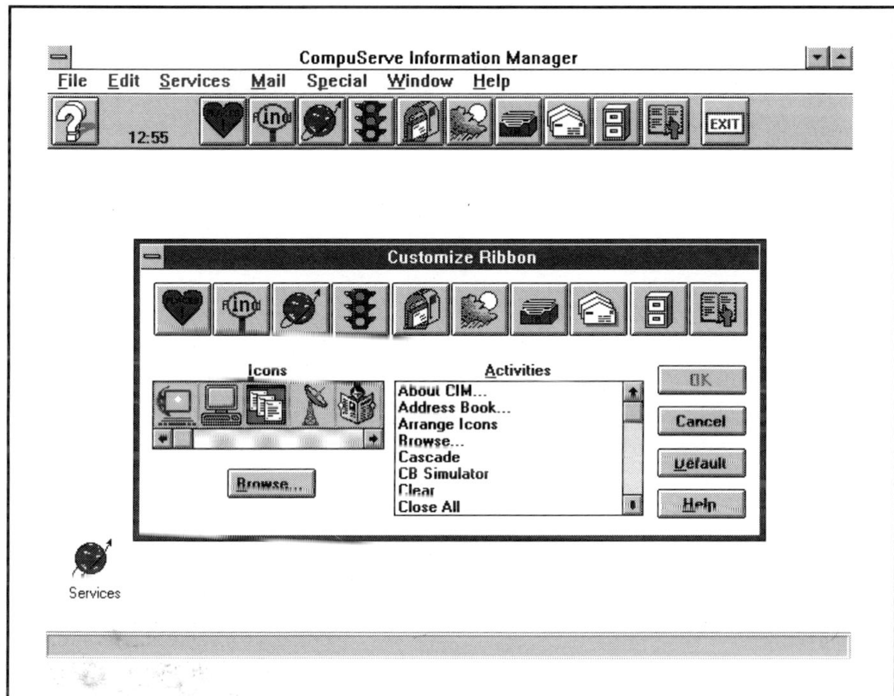

Figure 5.21 You can modify the WinCIM Ribbon with this dialog

2. Select an icon that you would like to place on the Ribbon. Apart from the built-in icons, you can use whatever Windows icon you choose. Press the Browse button and select the file from which to retrieve the icon.
3. Next, select the activity for that icon from the Activities list. It is not possible to assign the same activity more than once.
4. Finally, press the `Ribbon` button that you would like to replace with the new icon and action. The contents of the Ribbon will change.
5. If you want to make additional modifications, go back to step 2. If you are happy with the changes, press OK. You can also press `Cancel` to undo all changes you have made since you opened this dialog, or press `Default` to restore the WinCIM Ribbon to its original format.

The WinCIM Ribbon contains ten buttons. It is not possible to remove or add buttons.

Special Service Ribbons

Some CompuServe services have their own customized version of the WinCIM Ribbon, which can be smaller or larger that the original Ribbon. Also, there are services that make use of an additional Ribbon: the *Toolbar*. Examples of such services are all forums and ENS: the Executive News Service. If you use the mouse frequently, try to get used to these Toolbars as soon as possible. They contain most of the functionality needed to perform online actions for that service quickly.

Two famous CompuServe access programs

Two famous CompuServe access programs

Although CompuServe's CIM programs are ideal for real-time online access, they have one disadvantage, which is even more important for European users: they are *online* programs. In other words: when using CIM, you'll spend most of your time online, selecting messages to read, files to download and so on. All these activities could just as well be carried out offline. Some clever programmers hit upon the idea of further automating access to CompuServe, *via* so-called *automated access programs*. The first program that was released with the purpose of limiting the time spent online was *CompuServe Navigator for the Macintosh*. This program, an original CompuServe product, was soon followed by *TapCIS*, aimed at users of DOS computers. TapCIS is still very popular amongst a lot of CompuServe members, although the user interface is rather antique compared to competitive programs like *OzCIS* (a unique auto-access program that was originally distributed as freeware!), *WigWam*, a European product, and the new, revolutionary *CompuServe Navigator, Windows Edition*. Still, one fact applies to all auto-access programs: they can cut your CompuServe bill drastically.

Don't rob your own purse: use an auto-access program!

This is one remark that I can't make often enough. If you pay your own telephone bill and have to make an interlocal or even international telephone call to get access to CompuServe: make the switch to an auto-access program NOW! If you use one of the CIM packages, consider obtaining a version of CompuServe Navigator. Or, if you own a DOS computer, try out TapCIS, OzCIS or WigWam. Although you probably could do without the rather steep learning curve of these programs, they will help you cut costs dramatically. You can also look at them the other way: they act as a time saver, allowing you to do more online for the same amount of money.

All the programs mentioned have a large user base, and support for them can, of course, be found online. And to assist you further, or simply help you to make a purchase decision, this chapter contains a discussion of the most famous CompuServe access programs. After a brief look at the most important features, some examples are used to get you up and running as soon as possible.

Once you know your way around CompuServe using WinCIM, it might be time to make the switch to one of the special auto-access programs. These programs were written with just one purpose: doing as much as possible for a limited amount of money.

In this chapter, we focus on two very popular CompuServe auto-access programs. The first, CompuServe Navigator for Windows, is aimed at users of the popular Microsoft Windows operating system. The other, TapCIS, is still the favourite of many, DOS users.

6.1 CompuServe Navigator

CompuServe Navigator, also abbreviated to CSNav, is an auto-access program running under Windows. Because it shares a lot of facilities with WinCIM, it is easy to use both programs concurrently. For instance, you could use WinCIM from time to time to attend online conferences, go shopping, or do some research using the online databases, while you stick with CompuServe Navigator for carrying out your day-to-day activities, like reading forum messages, sending and receiving e-mail and downloading files.

The connection between CompuServe Navigator and WinCIM

CompuServe Navigator is aimed at members with at least some degree of experience online. Because CompuServe Navigator shares a lot of features with WinCIM, it is a good idea to get acquainted with WinCIM first. And because WinCIM is essentially free for CompuServe users (your CompuServe account is credited with the download charge you pay), it doesn't hurt your wallet to have a quick look at this program.

6.1.1 How to obtain CompuServe Navigator

There are two ways to obtain CompuServe Navigator. You can order it online (`GO ORDER`), or you can download it and start using it directly.

To download CompuServe Navigator, `GO CompuServe Navigator` and choose the `Download Navigator` option. CompuServe Navigator costs $30, but your account will be credited with $10. You don't pay connect charges during the download, but communication surcharges (as always) still apply.

HINTS & TIPS

Download failed? Try again, at no cost

If, for any reason, you didn't succeed in downloading the complete CompuServe Navigator files, you can try again for free. When you download CompuServe Navigator again within 30 days of the original download, you will not be charged, except for communication surcharges.

HINTS & TIPS

Downloading it takes some time...

The installation files for CompuServe Navigator are, in total, about 2.2 MB in size. Downloading both files (and you need them both to be able to run the program) will, at 9600 bps, take about 40 minutes. So, you might prefer to use the cheap hours for the download, thereby lowering your telephone charges and (depending where you live) your CompuServe communication surcharges.

6.1.2 How to get online support

Online support is available through a special forum. `GO CSNAVSUPPORT` to access this forum and seek answers for any questions you may have about CompuServe Navigator.

6.1.3 The main elements

As you can see from Figure 6.1, the CompuServe Navigator program window looks rather complicated. Basically, it consists of the following elements:

- A *Script Editor* window. This window contains the *script*; a script consists of *tasks* that CompuServe Navigator will perform online, in a so-called *session*. You can change the contents of a script (you can have as many scripts as you like), thereby tailoring the program to your requirements.

- A *Services* window, in which all CompuServe services that can be accessed with CompuServe Navigator are listed. By selecting an item from this window and moving it to the Script Editor window, it becomes a *task* that will be carried out by CompuServe Navigator. Because you can have as many scripts as you wish, you can schedule some services to be visited on a daily basis (or even more often), while visits to others (for instance, quieter forums with less message traffic) could be limited to once or twice a week.
- A *Session* window (not shown in Figure 6.1), which displays the result of an executed session.
- A *Ribbon* (the CompuServe term for a feature that you might know as the toolbar, toolbox, and so on.). This Ribbon, which cannot be customized, contains buttons for the most frequently used commands.

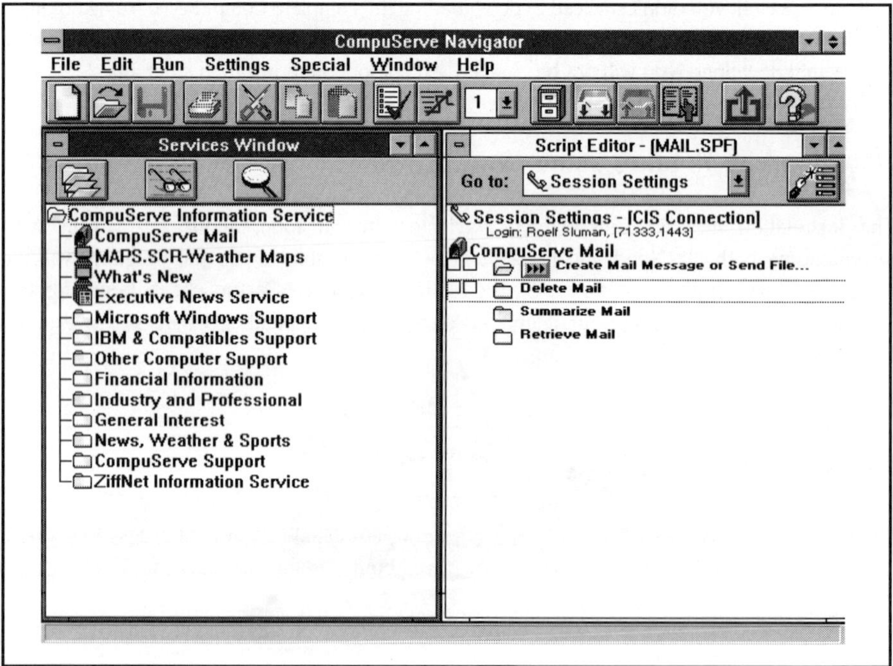

Figure 6.1 The CompuServe Navigator program window

6.1.4 The first step: installing CompuServe Navigator

The installation of CompuServe Navigator consists of three parts. You will probably have figured out the first two parts by yourself: after installing the actual program onto your hard disk, you enter your personal parameters (like your User ID, password, modem, and so on).

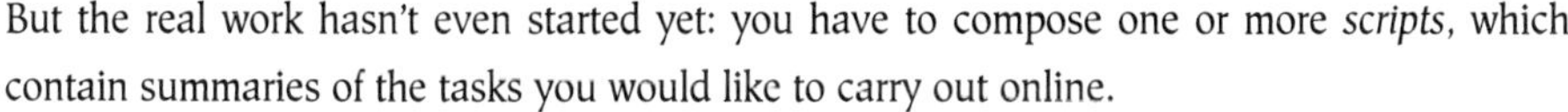

But the real work hasn't even started yet: you have to compose one or more *scripts*, which contain summaries of the tasks you would like to carry out online.
You will learn more about scripts in the next section. First, you learn how to install the program onto your hard disk, and how to configure it.

Installing CompuServe Navigator onto your hard disk

Installing CompuServe Navigator onto your hard disk is a pretty straightforward process. Proceed as follows:

- If you have obtained CompuServe Navigator on disks: insert the first program disk in your drive. Start the Setup program, either by double-clicking on its filename from within File Manager, or by selecting the `Run` option on the `File` menu in Program Manager. (Users of foreign-language Windows versions are advised to consult their manual for the appropriate commands.)
  The Setup program will ask you for the drive and directory where CompuServe Navigator should be installed. Normally, you will want to accept the proposed settings: that way, you are assured that the program will work together with WinCIM, by sharing address books, the In-Basket and Out-Basket, and so on. When Setup has finished, it will have created a new CompuServe program group with some icons, or added some icons to your existing CompuServe program group. You can start CompuServe Navigator by double-clicking on its icon, as you would do with any Windows program.
- If you have obtained the program by downloading it: copy both `EXE` files to a temporary directory (for instance, `C:\TEMP`), and decompress them by typing their names. (Both `DISK1.EXE` and `DISK2.EXE` are self-extracting archives.) You can do this from Windows (use the `Run` option on the `File` menu) or from DOS. After you have decompressed both `EXE` files, you can store them on floppy disks for backup purposes.
  To install CompuServe Navigator, you will have to start the Setup program which is now located in your temporary directory. You can do this from within File Manager or, again, by selecting the `Run` option on Program Manager's `File` menu.
  After asking you for the drive and directory where the program should be installed (in most cases, you don't need to change the proposed settings), the program will install itself. The result is a new program group, called 'CompuServe', with some icons in it; if you already had a CompuServe window, it will now contain some additional icons. To start CompuServe Navigator, double-click on the appropriate icon.

The interaction between CompuServe Navigator and the CIM packages

CompuServe Navigator shares its file structure with DOSCIM and WinCIM. If you use one of the CIM packages, you will most likely have a `\CSERVE` directory structure, which (amongst others) contains directories named `FCABINET`, `SUPPORT`, and `SCRIPTS`. By using this same directory structure, CompuServe Navigator can access your In-Basket, Out-Basket, Filing Cabinet, and even your personal information like your Address Book, User ID, password, and so on. Both programs work seamlessly together: a message stored in your In-Basket by CompuServe Navigator can also be accessed while using WinCIM. This allows you to choose which program you would like to use at any given moment, with optimal data interchange.

6.1.5 CompuServe Navigator – the basics

Basically, working with CompuServe Navigator involves a series of steps. Some of these steps need to be carried out only once, while others apply to every online session.

1. *Create a script*. First of all, you need to create a *script*: a series of commands called *tasks* that CompuServe Navigator will carry out once it gets online. To compose a script, you copy items from the *Services window* to a *Script Editor window*. The Services window contains an overview of all services available on CompuServe that can be accessed with CompuServe Navigator. The Script Editor window contains one or more *tasks*, which will be performed if you say so.
   CompuServe Navigator comes with a few example scripts: `MAIL.SPF` (a typical script to access your electronic mailbox) and `WHATSNEW.SPF`, which downloads the contents of the 'What's New This Week' menu and leaves you online afterwards. In this section, we will show you how to create your own scripts to access forums, one of the most powerful features of CompuServe Navigator.
   Creating scripts is usually something you only have to do once. Once you have a script for a particular service (or a group of services, such as several forums), you can use it as often as you like.

2. *Edit the script parameters*. In some cases, you will want to change some parameters before executing the script. For example, if you want to send some e-mail messages, you edit the appropriate script before running it, adding your messages, marking files to be sent, and so on. If you wish to upload a file to a forum, you edit the script to reflect that wish.

3. *Run the script and review the results in the Session window*. When you are ready to visit some forums, send or new e-mail, or do other things online, you run the appropriate script. CompuServe Navigator will go online, carry out all tasks assigned to it, store all information it receives, and disconnect, without the need for any human interaction.

Depending on the kind of activities you would like the program to carry out for you, it can be necessary to run a variation of the same script more than once. In CompuServe Navigator terminology, you have one or more script passes. In a typical forum script, pass one could consist of browsing message headers (topics), obtaining a list of new files in the library, and sending new forum messages that you have written. After carrying out all relevant tasks in the script, CompuServe Navigator will disconnect. Now it is your turn: you browse through the Session window to process the results of the first pass. Normally, this means that you will select the headers of messages you would like to read, mark one or more files for downloading, and reply to new forum messages that were addressed to you. Note that you do all these things *offline*, a major difference compared to WinCIM.

As soon as you have processed the results of the first pass, it's time to let CompuServe Navigator carry out pass two: it will read all the messages you have marked, and download the files. When CompuServe Navigator disconnects, it's your turn again: you read the messages that CompuServe Navigator has downloaded. If you choose to reply to some of them, you'll have one more pass to go: in pass three, CompuServe Navigator will upload your replies to the appropriate forum(s).

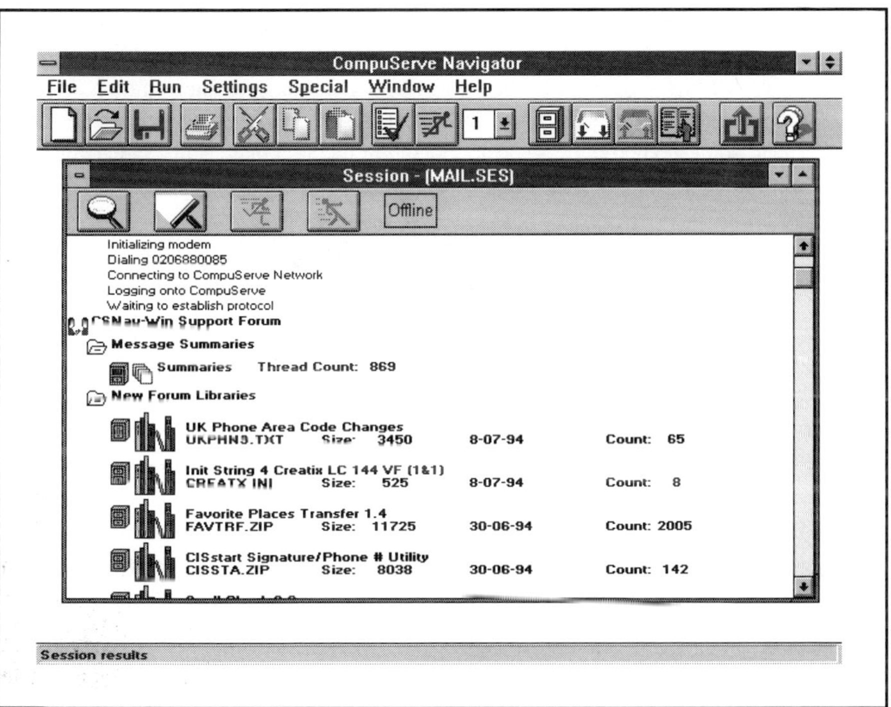

Figure 6.2 A typical Session window, after the first pass

HINTS & TIPS

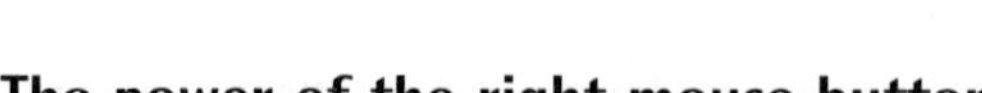

The power of the right mouse button

CompuServe Navigator provides support for the right mouse button. For example, to get help for an item in a Script Editor window, position the mouse pointer over it and press the right mouse button. CompuServe Navigator will show a pop-up menu, on which you will find a **`Help`** option. The right mouse button can also be used to delete a task from a script. Click on the task with the right mouse button, and select the **`Delete`** option on the pop-up menu.

6.1.6 Example one: sending and retrieving mail

If you have experience with WinCIM, the chances are that you have used the **`Send and Receive All Mail`** option to create your own automated session. CompuServe Navigator offers similar functionality, by means of a **`CompuServe Mail`** option in the Script Editor window.

The following example shows some important aspects of CompuServe Navigator. We will create a new Script Editor window, add a task, get online, and review the session information.

1. First, we make a new Script Editor window. To do this, choose the **`New`** option on the File menu. CompuServe Navigator will show the new, untitled window. It already has one task: Session Settings. This task is the only one that is obligatory: it contains vital information about your User ID, password, access telephone number, and so on. Session Settings should always be the first item in any Script Editor window.
   If your personal information (name and User ID) isn't shown under the Session Settings header, you can choose the **`Session`** option on the **`Settings`** menu. When you have verified that all entries are correct, select **`OK`** to close the Setup Session Settings window.

Tile your windows!

With a program like CompuServe Navigator, the Window menu is very important. Because you will constantly be copying items from the Services window to the Script Editor window, it is best to reserve all the space for those two windows. Close all other windows and choose the **`Tile Vertical`** option on the Window menu. The active window will appear on the left side of the screen, and the non-active window on the right.

2. The Services window contains a *tree* with a number of *branches*, which can be opened or closed. The first item in the tree, CompuServe Mail, is the item we are looking for. Copy this item to the Script Editor window. There are several ways to do this:
   - With the mouse: drag the item to the Script Editor window.

- With the mouse: double-click on the item and select the first option on the pop-up menu: `Add to Script Editor Window`.
- With the keyboard: select the item with the arrow keys, and press Enter. A pop-up menu will appear. Select the first option, `Add to Script Editor Window`, and press Enter.

3. In the Script Editor window, the CompuServe Mail header is displayed. Under this header, you see a number of folder symbols. Each symbol indicates one or more Mail *tasks*. It is up to you to select the tasks that you would like to be carried out, by checking the box in front of it. By default, none of the tasks are selected.

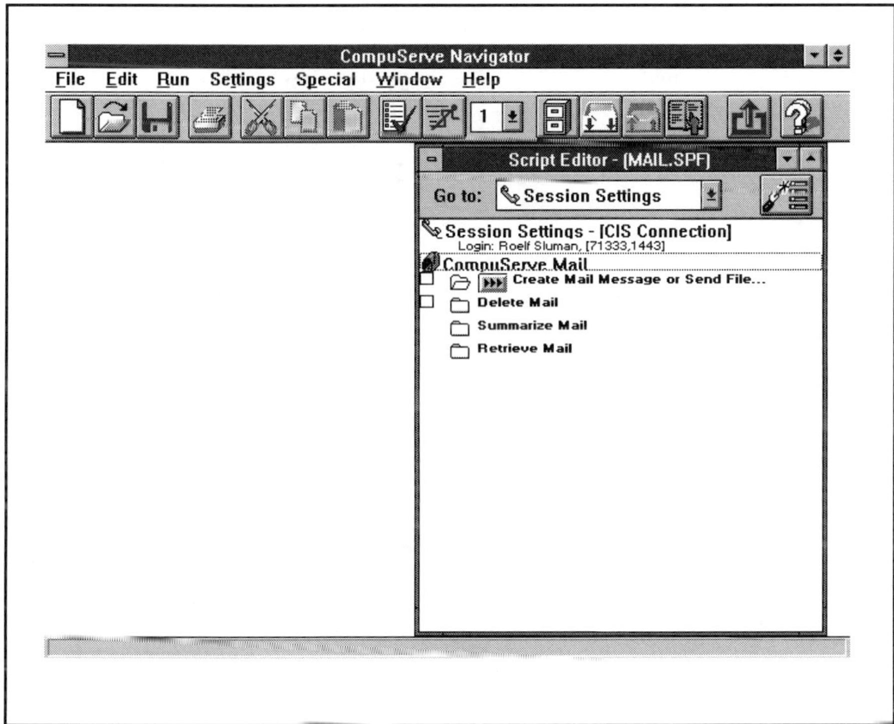

Figure 6.3 The basic Mail tasks

4. To demonstrate the possibilities of the basic Mail tasks, we will let CompuServe Navigator perform a simple task: go online and check for any waiting mail messages. There is a task for this: you will find it in the Retrieve Mail folder. Click on it to expand it:

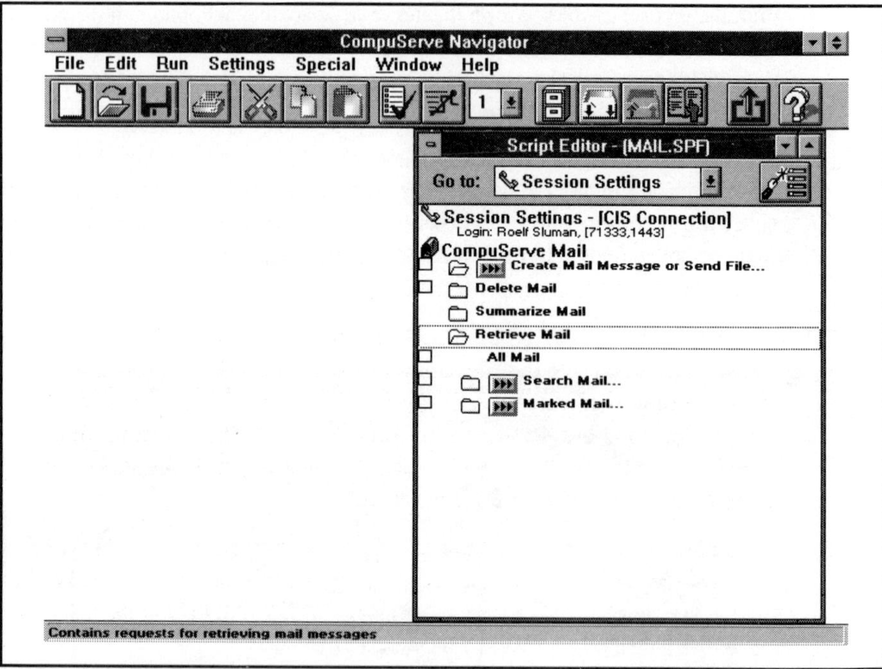

Figure 6.4 The available tasks for retrieving mail

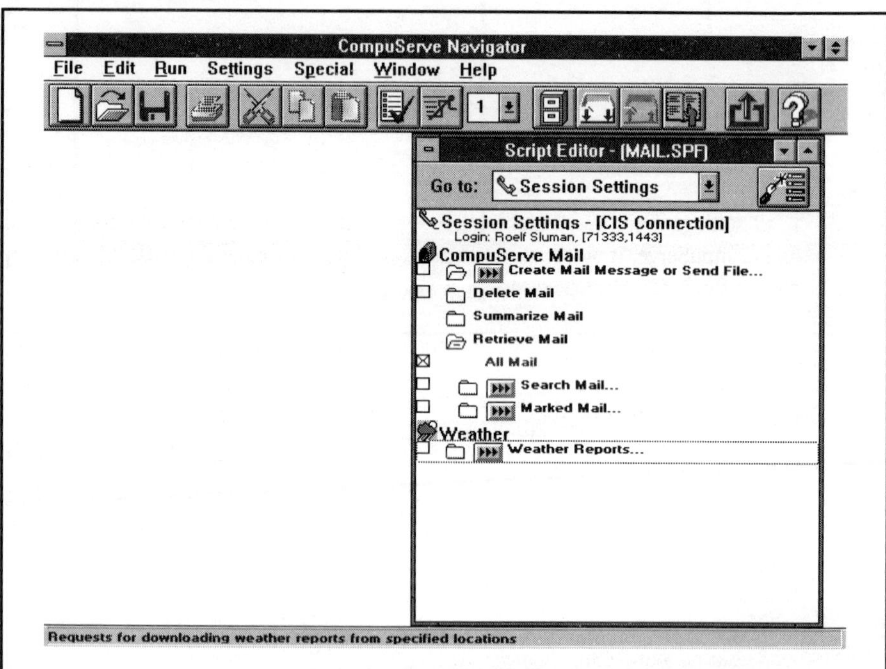

Figure 6.5 We have added a Weather task to our script

5. To let CompuServe Navigator read all mail available, check the `All Mail` option. The colour of this option changes to green, indicating that it is activated. You can close the Retrieve Mail folder: it will become green also, showing that one or more tasks are selected.

6. We are now ready to transfer control to CompuServe Navigator. But wait, we might as well extend the script a little bit, for example with a request for weather information. It is not too difficult to implement this request. In the Services window, open the folder named News, Weather & Sports. Now copy the first item in this folder, CompuServe Weather, to the Script Editor window. You can either put it before or after the CompuServe Mail header, whatever you prefer.

7. Although the weather task has been added to our script, it isn't active yet. To activate it, click on the button with the three arrows, or select the task and press Enter. A dialog appears, asking us for the location for which we would like to receive weather information. For now, leave the settings to Local Weather and choose `OK`. CompuServe Navigator will check the box before the Weather Reports task, indicating that this task will also be executed during the next online session.

8. We are now ready to run this script. There are several ways to do this. With the mouse, just click on the `Run` button, shown in Figure 6.6. When you use the keyboard, select the `Run Pass 1` option on the `Run` menu. (Don't worry about the text 'Pass 1' for now – we'll deal with that later.)

Figure 6.6 Press this button to run the current script

9. If all settings are correct, CompuServe Navigator will take over your computer and dial CompuServe. It opens a special *Session* window to show you what it is doing. The contents of that window are shown in Figure 6.7.

10. Just like a Script Editor window, the Session window contains items you can select to review their contents. The relevant items for this session are Mail Messages, which is empty, and Weather Information, which contains the local weather forecast. To see it, double-click on it, or select it with the arrow keys and press Enter. The results are shown in Figure 6.8.

11. When you are happy with the way this script works, you can save it for later use. Select the Script Editor window and choose the `Save As` option on the `File` menu. Enter a name for the script file (CompuServe Navigator will add the extension `.SPF` automatically). From now on, you can open this script whenever you would like to read your mail and check the weather.

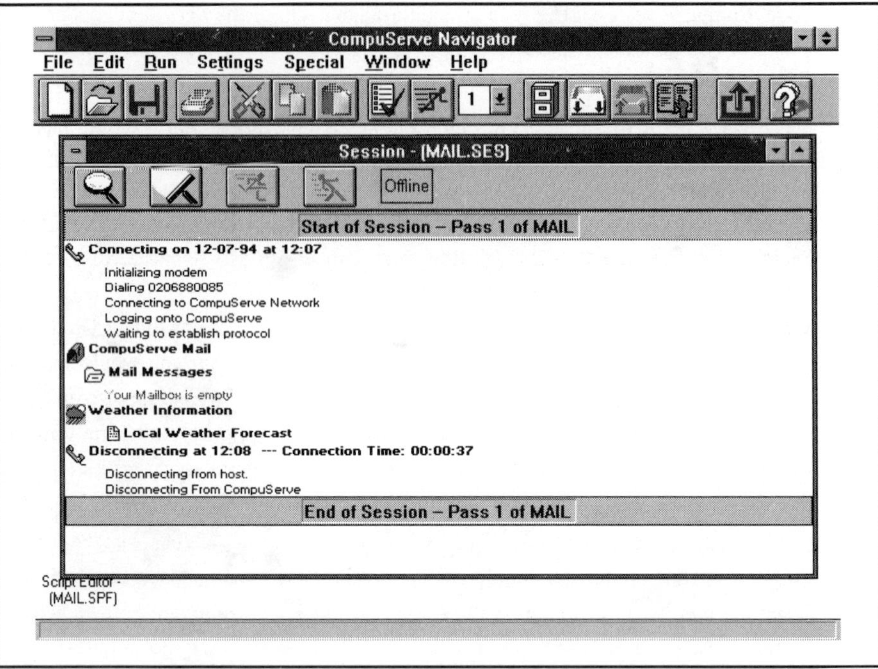

Figure 6.7 A typical Session window for our first script

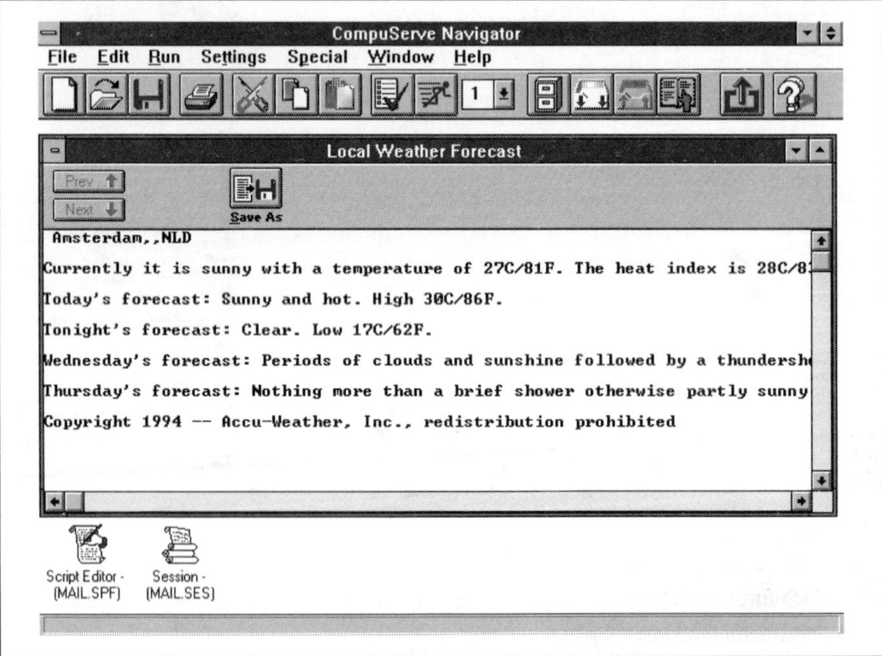

Figure 6.8 CompuServe Navigator has retrieved the local weather

6.1.7 Example two: visiting forums

Like all auto-access programs, CompuServe Navigator really shines when you start using it for your daily forum visits. By drastically cutting the time spent online, you will be able to do all the things you did before, but in a fraction of the time.

Don't expect your CompuServe bill to get lower, though. If you are like most users, you will invest your gained profit... online, visiting more forums, downloading more files, and getting more information for the same costs.

For every forum you want to visit, you enter a task in your Script Editor window. On a per-forum basis, you can select the sections you are interested in, the way you would like to download messages (all of them, or some of them, selected by message header), and so on. You can even make several scripts: one for forums you only visit once a week, another for forums that you stop by at least once a day... The possibilities are endless!

In this second example, we will visit two forums: the CSNav Support Forum and the CompuServe Help forum. In the first forum, we will have a look at all message headers in all sections, and decide which messages we would like to read. Next, we'll visit the CompuServe Help forum to have a look at the newest files in the library. You will see that this task, which could easily take a lot of time when using WinCIM, is carried out in only a few minutes!

Something that is new in this example, is CompuServe Navigator's ability to execute more than one *pass*. By dividing a script into several passes, you can carry out certain activities earlier than others. You will see that this option is very handy when it comes to forum visits!

Free forums!

Both the forums we are about to visit are free forums. That means that you don't incur any charges (except for communication surcharges) while you visit them. The fact that both these forums are free doesn't mean that they don't hold valuable information: I have them both on my list of frequently visited forums, and have obtained quite a number of handy tips from them!

1. To try out this example, create a new Script Editor window. We'll add two basic tasks to it: the names of the two forums we are going to visit. To do this, go to the Services window and open the CompuServe Support folder. As a result, all available free support forums are displayed (see Figure 6.9). Copy 'CSNav Support Forum' to the Script Editor window, followed by 'CompuServe Help Forum'.

2. Figure 6.10 shows the contents of our Script Editor window: two so-called *forum tasks*. Each forum is represented by three folders: Message Commands, Library Commands and Forum Options.

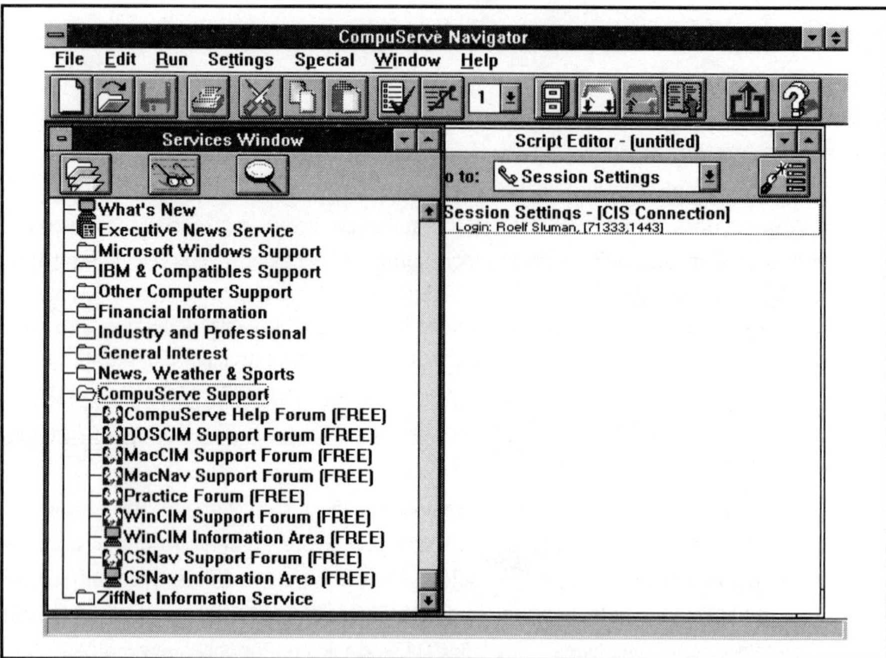

Figure 6.9 An important list: free support forums on CompuServe

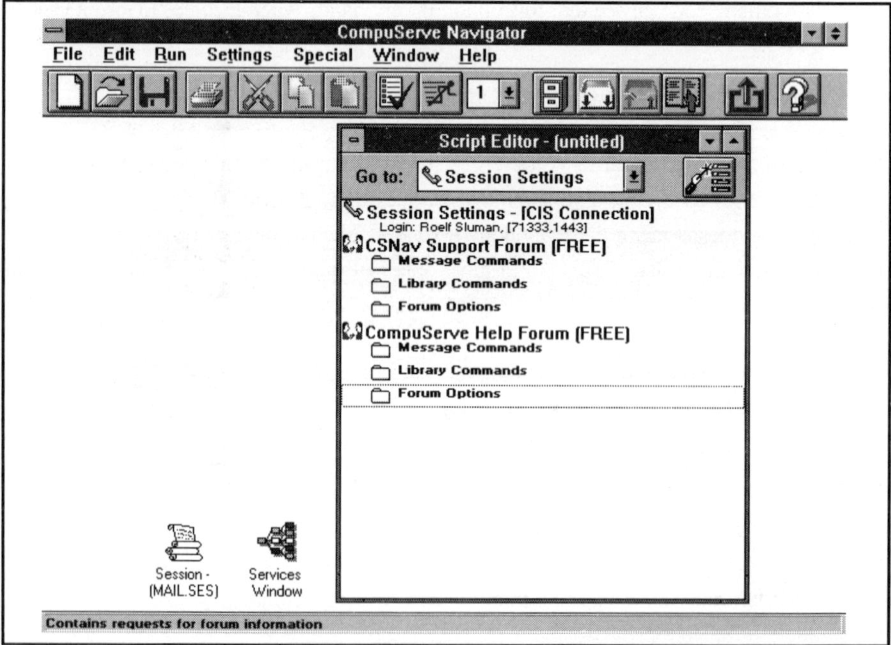

Figure 6.10 Our script, consisting of two forums

Joining forums with CompuServe Navigator

When using CompuServe Navigator, you don't have to worry about joining forums you haven't visited before; CompuServe Navigator does this automatically for you, unless you have indicated otherwise (by selecting the `Forums` option on the `Settings` menu).

3. As we stated before, we would like to get an overview of all message headers that currently exist in the CSNav Support Forum. To let CompuServe Navigator retrieve the information needed, click on the Message Commands folder (or select it and press Enter). Two new folders are displayed: 'Summarize Messages' and 'Retrieve Messages'. Click on the Summarize Message folder. As Figure 6.11 shows, the screen gets rather cluttered with of icons, buttons and check boxes. Matters aren't as complicated as they seem, however. We only have to deal with the two options that are related to Summarize Messages, namely:
   - *Waiting For Me*: If you check this option, CompuServe Navigator will only retrieve the headers of messages that are addressed to you. For now, leave this option unchecked.
   - *Since*: This is the option you will select most often. When you press the accompanying button, CompuServe Navigator will show a list of available sections and give you the opportunity to select the sections you are interested in. (In busy forums, with scroll rates of 500 messages per day, it helps when you deselect those sections that are of no interest to you.)

   After you press `OK`, you return to the Script Editor window.

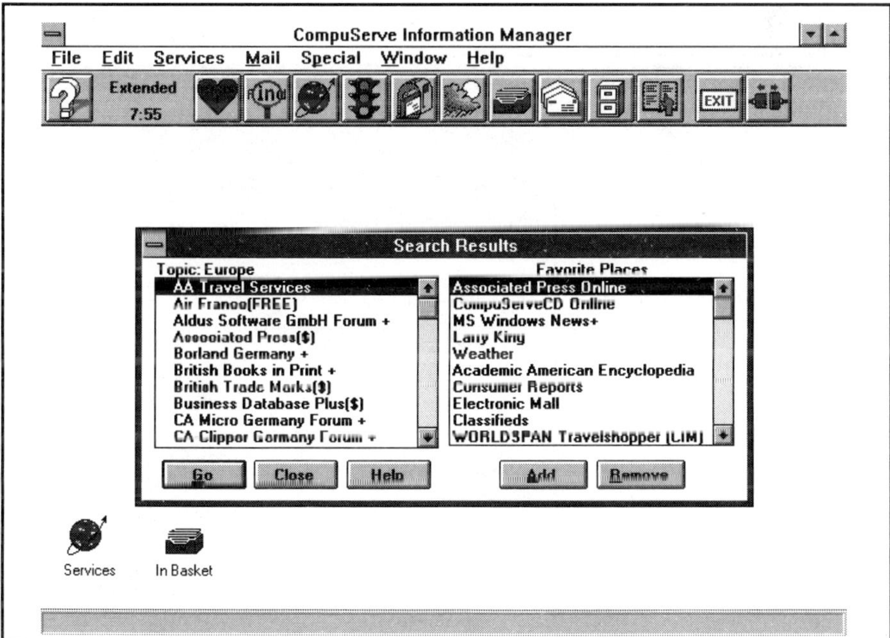

Figure 6.11 All tasks that have to do with summarizing messages

4. For now, we have finished with the CSNav Support Forum: we have indicated that we would like to see all (new) message headers. It's time to get on to the CompuServe Help Forum, because we would like to get a list of all files that have been uploaded during the past six months. Therefore, click on the Library Commands folder (or select it and press the Enter key). There are four tasks related to the file library:
   - *Summarize New Files*: This is the one we are looking for. Press the accompanying button and a dialog is displayed. You can check the library sections that you are interested in (note that you have to visit a forum at least once to have the section names appear in the list). For now, leave all sections checked. Select the `Search by Date Range` option button and change the `From` date to a date about six months earlier (or whatever date you choose).
     After you press `OK`, you return to the Script Editor window.
   - *Search Library*: Use this task when you are looking for a particular file. CompuServe Navigator allows you to specify wildcards, keywords, and /or the User ID of the person who uploaded the file. For now, don't select this task.
   - *Contribute Files*: This is the task to use when you want to upload your own files to one of the forum library sections. Uploading files is a terrific way to share your work with fellow members, to gain almost instant fame, to start a career as a shareware programmer, and so on. And best of all: it's free! Apart from telecommunication surcharges and telephone costs, you don't pay anything when you are uploading files.
   - *Retrieve Files*: We will use this one shortly, to download one or more files that we are interested in. For now, ignore this task.

5. Figure 6.12 shows the contents of our edited Script Editor window. Time to get online and see the results. Click on the `Run` button, or select the option `Run Pass 1` on the `Run` menu.

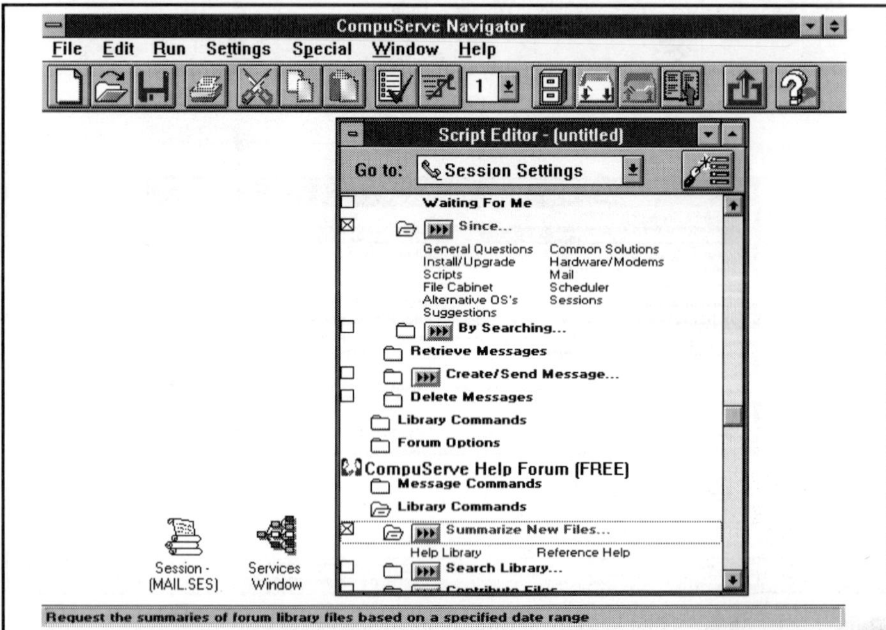

Figure 6.12 Our script is completed, and we can activate CompuServe Navigator

Stopping a script

If you want to cancel the execution of a script, you can do so by pressing the **Stop** button, shown in Figure 6.13, or by selecting the **Abort Script** option on the **Run** menu.

Figure 6.13 Press this button if you want to cancel the execution of a script.

Keyboard users can choose the **Abort Script** option on the **Run** menu.

6. The complete execution of this script shouldn't take more than a few minutes at 9600 bps. To make the process even quicker, you can minimize the Session window during the time that CompuServe Navigator is online.

   After CompuServe Navigator has done its work, you can review the contents of the Session window (see Figure 6.14). Various symbols indicate that information has been downloaded: to access that information, double-click on the symbol, or select it with the arrow keys and press [Enter].

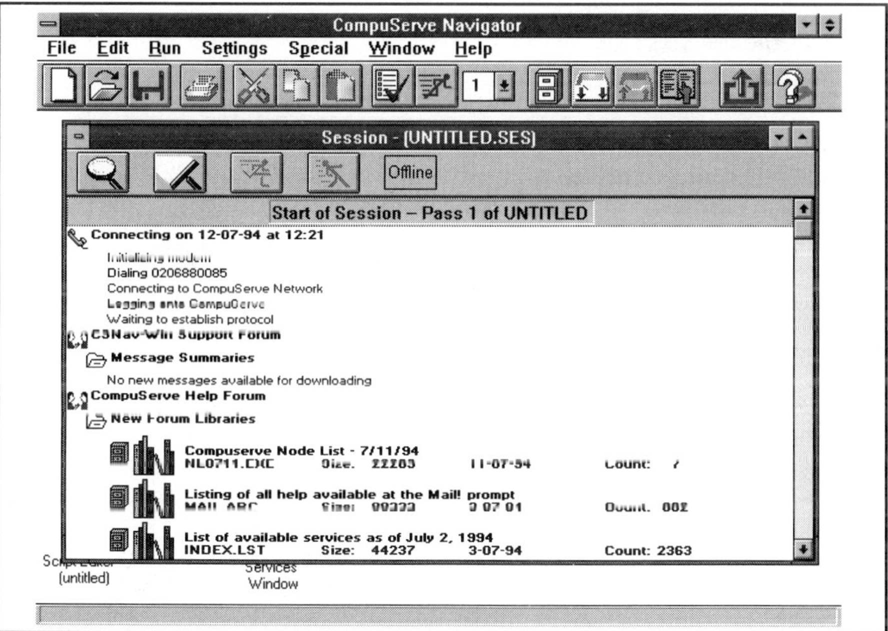

Figure 6.14 The contents of a typical Session window, after visiting a few forums

7. An example is shown in Figure 6.15. Normally, you would read this information online (or at least take a quick glance at it), something that costs valuable time online. By allowing you to read this message without occurring any more charges, CompuServe Navigator enables you to see information you otherwise might have missed.

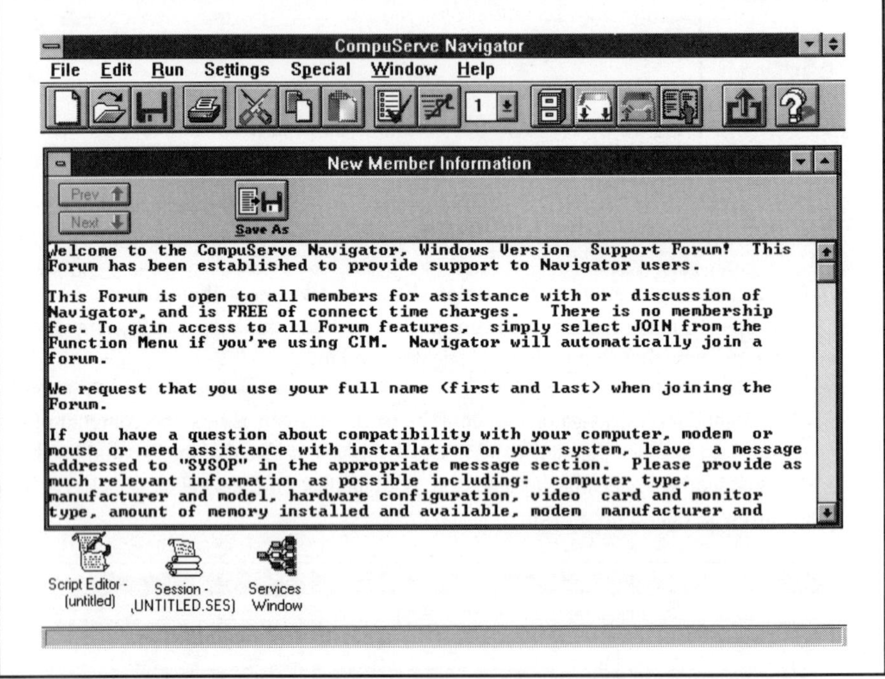

Figure 6.15 Double-clicking on the New Member Information item displays this information window. It shows the text you normally would have seen when entering the forum for the first time interactively.

8. Another look at the Session window shows some very interesting items. Let's start with Message Summaries. Double-clicking on the Thread Count line reveals a virtually endless list of message headers. Imagine scanning all these headers online! However, you can take your time selecting each message header at your own pace, pressing the following buttons for the messages you are interested in:
   - *New*: during the next session, CompuServe Navigator will download all new messages in this thread: messages that weren't available the last time you entered the forum.
   - *Single*: during the next session, CompuServe Navigator will download the last message in the selected thread.
   - *All*: during the next session, CompuServe Navigator will download all messages in the selected thread.
   - *Ignore*: during the next session, all messages in the selected thread will be ignored. This is the default setting for all downloaded message headers.

9. After pressing one of these buttons, you select the message headers that interest you by double-clicking on them, or by using the arrow keys and the Spacebar key. Calmly work your way through all the message headers: keep in mind that you are not online, and that all this costs you nothing extra.
   Special symbols are used to indicate the message headers you have selected; these symbols resemble the symbols on the `New`, `Single`, `All` and `Ignore` buttons. While selecting the various message headers, you can modify a choice at any time.

HINTS & TIPS

Lost Session windows

Don't worry if you accidentally close your Session window. CompuServe Navigator will save it automatically when you close it, for instance by pressing the Esc key. If you don't name the window, it will be saved as `UNTITLED.SES`. You can re-open it by selecting the `Open` option on the `File` menu.

10. Do you remember that we actually visited two forums? Apart from the message headers belonging to the CSNav Support Forum, we also requested a list of the latest files from the CompuServe Help Forum library. This list is added to our session window (see Figure 6.16). If you would like to know more about a file, just double-click on its entry, or select it and press the Enter key.

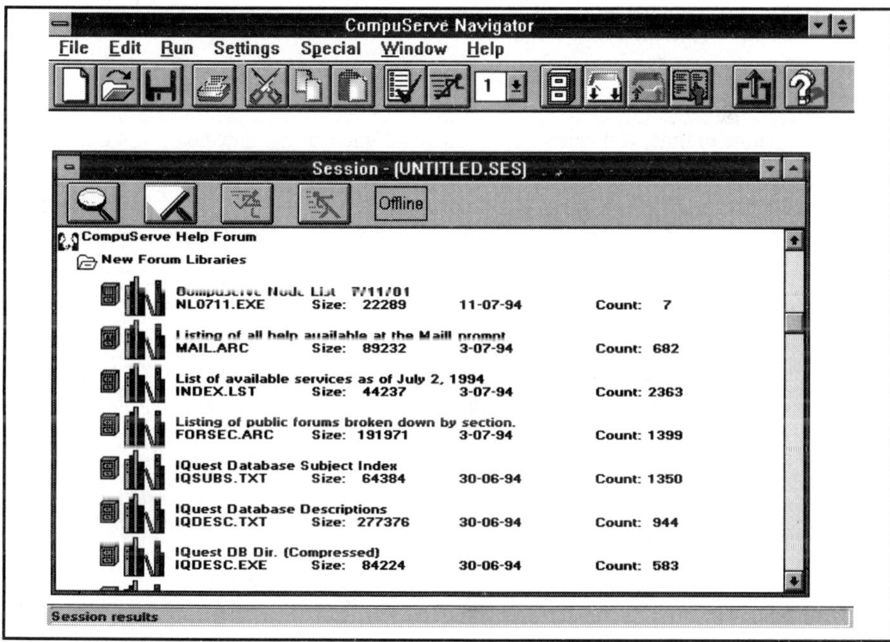

Figure 6.16 Information about available files in the forum library is also stored into the Session window

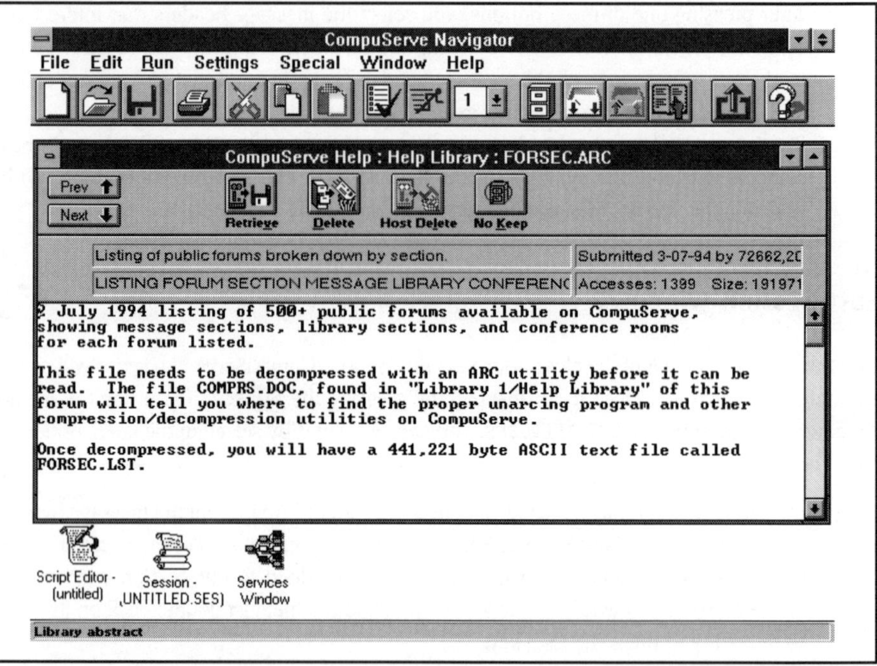

Figure 6.17 More detailed information about a particular file, found in one of the forum library sections

11. From time to time, you will discover a file that you want to download. To do that, you will have to give CompuServe Navigator a command to *retrieve* the file from CompuServe. Either double-click on the file specification as listed in the Session window, or select the file with the arrow keys and press Enter. CompuServe Navigator will display a more extensive file description, as shown in Figure 6.17. If you still want to download the file, press the `Retrieve` button.

12. You will probably be disappointed: it seems as if nothing has happened. CompuServe Navigator kindly shows a description of the next file, and that's about it. Things have changed, however. Close the file description window as well as the Session window, and take a closer look at the Library Commands for the CompuServe Help forum. As you can see in Figure 6.18, CompuServe Navigator has checked the box in front of the Retrieve Files task. Also, the words Retrieve Files are now displayed in green, indicating that a task is waiting to be performed.

13. At this time, you are probably tempted to give the `Run` command again. But let's wait a moment and take a closer look at the current Script Editor window. Apart from the

Retrieve File task, the original Summarize New Files is also checked. And so is one of the Summarize Messages tasks. However, we do not want to execute those tasks again – we are only interested in reading the marked messages and downloading the selected file. Therefore, we will have to uncheck the appropriate boxes, or use a second script. Or is there some other way?

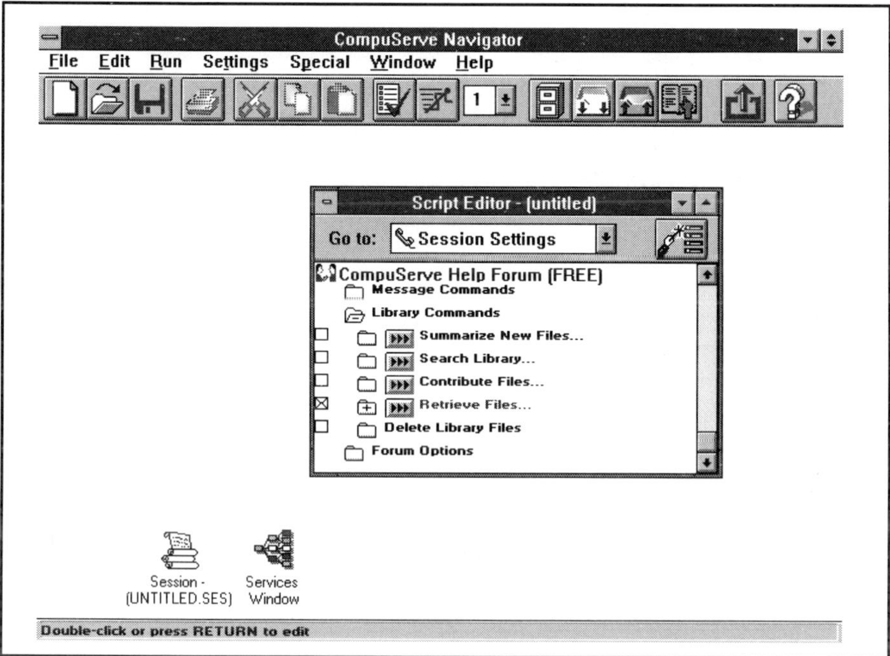

Figure 6.18 CompuServe Navigator is about to download one or more files: the box before the Retrieve Files task is checked

Fortunately, there is. The time has come to shine some light on one of the hidden powers of CompuServe Navigator: the possibility of running certain parts of a script as a separate pass. We have just executed pass one: we retrieved message headers and file descriptions. After selecting the messages we would like to read, and the file(s) we would like to download, it's time to execute pass two!

Do you remember the `Run Pass 1` option on the `Run` menu? This option hints that there is a possibility of dividing a script into several passes. This is actually very easy. The only thing you have to do is to select the `General` option on the Settings menu, and to press the Advanced button in the resulting General Preferences window. As a result of this, the Advanced Preferences dialog appears (see Figure 6.19).

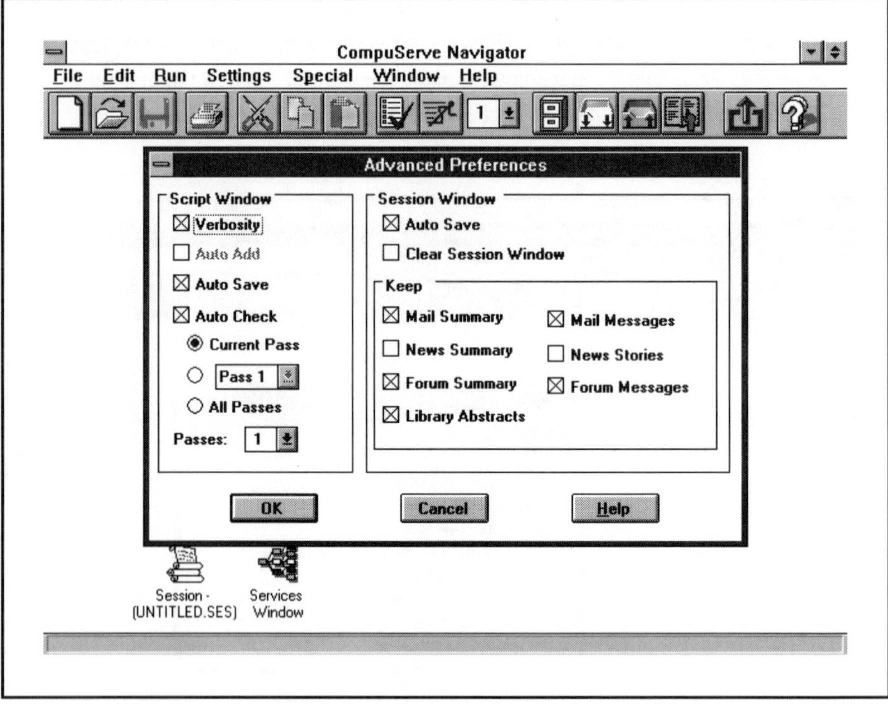

Figure 6.19 The Advanced Preferences dialog allows you to specify a number of passes for each script

14. The Advanced Preferences dialog contains an option called Passes. You can change the value in the accompanying combo box to 2, 3 or 4: for now, set it to 2 and close the dialog. Close the General Preferences dialog as well, and look at the results: every task in the Script Editor window is now preceded by *two* check boxes (see Figure 6.20).

15. You will probably get the idea. To indicate the tasks that you would like to be executed in the first pass, just check the *first* box in front of them. And to tell CompuServe Navigator which tasks should be carried out during the second pass, you check the *second* box.

    In our example, this means that we have to edit our script a little bit. First, select the Retrieve Messages task belonging to the CSNav Support Forum (it is displayed in green). Click on the folder to expand it. You will see that the first box before the Marked task is checked: check the second box instead, to indicate that this task should only be performed during the second pass. Look at the colour of the Marked task: it changes from green to blue, to indicate that it is part of another pass.

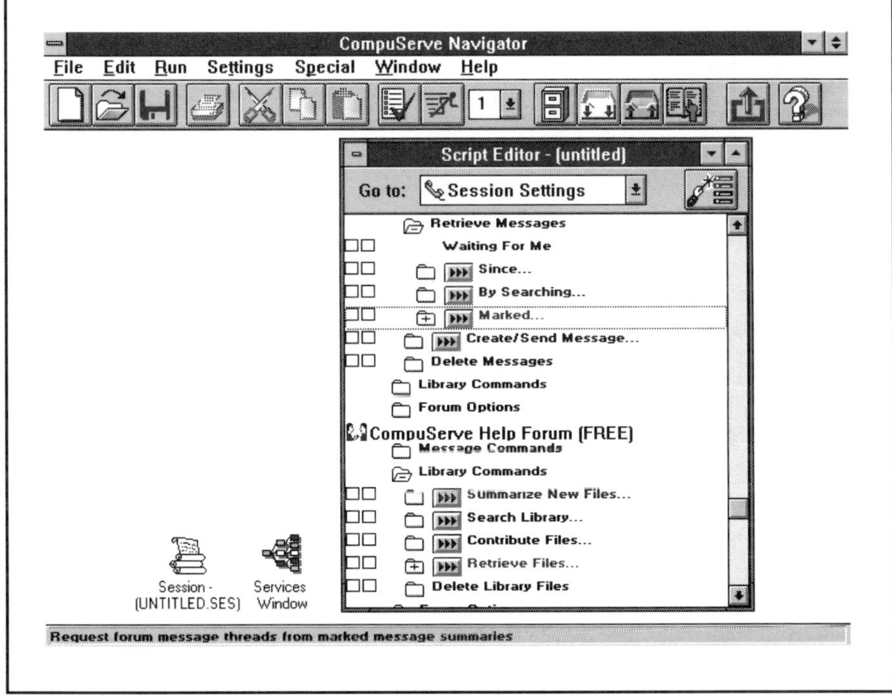

Figure 6.20 The two check boxes allow us to divide our tasks into two passes

Next, go to the tasks for the CompuServe Help Forum, and check the second box before the Retrieve Files task. As this is a task that should only be performed as a part of the second pass, uncheck the first box.

16. Now that we have indicated which tasks should be performed during the second pass, it is time to actually execute them. Select the `Run Pass 2` option on the `Run` menu. Mouse users can also select the value 2 from the combo box on the Ribbon, and press the `Run` button. Note that the blue tasks change to green, to indicate that they will be executed as a result of the next `Run` command.

Previewing your script

If you would like to preview the script you are about to execute, you can select the `Preview script` option on the `Run` menu. Mouse users can also click on the special `Preview` button, shown in Figure 6.21.

Figure 6.21 The Preview button on the Ribbon

17. If you have done everything correctly, CompuServe Navigator will go online and carry out the tasks for the second pass. As a result of this, it will first visit the CSNav Support Forum and retrieve all messages that you have marked in the Session window. (Watch the status bar for information about the message(s) being retrieved.) Next, it will visit the CompuServe Help Forum and download the file(s) you have marked for retrieval. As soon as CompuServe Navigator has carried out those tasks, it will disconnect, leaving you with a new or updated Session window. You can now start reading the messages, either by selecting them in the Session window, or by opening the CSNav-Win Support folder in the Filing Cabinet.
    Once you have finished reading the messages, you can take a look at the file(s) you have downloaded. Unless you have downloaded a graphics file (with the extension `.GIF` or `.JPG`), the downloaded files are put into the `\CSERVE\DOWNLOAD` directory. `GIF` graphic files are stored in the `\CSERVE\GIF` directory; similarly, downloaded `.JPG` graphic files can be found in the `\CSERVE\JPG` directory.

If you have worked through both examples, you should have a fairly good idea of what CompuServe Navigator is all about. It helps to understand that the ability to execute scripts in several passes is what gives CompuServe Navigator its strength. When you start building your own scripts for visiting forums, reading e-mail, and so on, you could use the following basic scheme, consisting of three passes:

1. In the first pass, you retrieve your e-mail, send your e-mail messages, retrieve message headers, and retrieve file catalogues.
2. When you have answered your e-mail messages and indicated which message threads you would like to read and which files you would like to download, you start the second pass. In most cases, the execution of this pass will consume most of your online time. Keep an eye on the status bar for any error messages. Although CompuServe Navigator works fairly intelligently, and can often decide that it has to go offline due to some error, it helps to watch its progress now and then, so that you can intervene if something goes wrong.
3. If you have replied to one or more forum messages, you have to execute a third pass to send your replies to CompuServe.

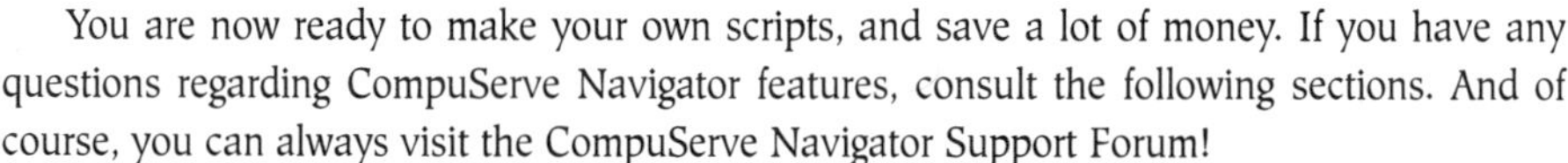

You are now ready to make your own scripts, and save a lot of money. If you have any questions regarding CompuServe Navigator features, consult the following sections. And of course, you can always visit the CompuServe Navigator Support Forum!

6.1.8 Overview of menus and options

In this section, you will find a brief overview of the most important menus and options in CompuServe Navigator.

The File menu

You use the options on this menu to open and close files, combine script files, print the contents of a window, and exit the program. The following options are available:

- *New*: Use this option to open a new Script Editor window. You can have as many open Script Editor windows as you wish; when you run a script, CompuServe Navigator will use the active window.
- *Open*: This option allows you to open a file that is stored on disk. You can open files in the following categories:
  - *Script files*: these contain a script that can be executed by CompuServe Navigator. They have the extension `.SPF`.
  - *Session files*, used to store logs of executed scripts. These files have the extension `.SES`.
  - *Services files*: these contain a list of CompuServe services that can be accessed from CompuServe Navigator. Although the program comes with its own, extensive Services file, `CISTREE.BRO`, it is also possible to use services files provided by others, or to create your own services files. Refer to 'The Services window' on page 149 for more information about maintaining Services files.
  - *Graphics files*: these contain graphic images in one of the two formats supported by CompuServe Navigator: GIF (files with the `.GIF` extension) and JPEG (files with the `.JPG` extension). When you open a graphic file, CompuServe Navigator shows the contents in a separate window.
  - *Text files*: these files, with the extension `.TXT`, can contain plain ANSI text that you can import into your e mail and forum messages. CompuServe Navigator also allows you to save a text fragment as a plain ANSI text file. This feature can come in handy when you want to use the contents of a message or other text in, for instance, a word processor document.

    When you answer a lot of e-mail messages about the same subject (for instance, when you work in a service department), it could help to create some text files with standard replies (like company telephone numbers, and so on) that you can import whenever necessary. Every time you need to insert the information in a message, you only have to open the appropriate text file and transfer the information (*via* the Windows Clipboard) to your message.

When you open a text file using this option, CompuServe Navigator starts the Notepad Windows application.

- *Save*: Use this option to save the contents of the current window. If you haven't yet supplied a filename for the window, CompuServe Navigator will ask you for one before saving the file.
- *Save As*: Select this option to save the contents of the current window in a different file, for instance for backup purposes.
- *Delete*: CompuServe Navigator allows you to delete any file from your disk with this option.
- *Services Window*: Use this option to re-open or restore the Services window, and to make it the current window.
- *Print*: this option allows you to print the contents of the current window. It doesn't work with every window, though. A good example is the Services window: as long as it is the current window, the Print option is greyed-out.
- *Print Setup*: Select this option to configure your printer.
- *Exit*: Exits the CompuServe Navigator program.

The names of the last four saved files are shown as entries on the File menu. To open such a file, you just have to select the appropriate option. This saves you the process of going to the items in the Open File window.

The Edit menu

CompuServe Navigator's Edit menu contains options to edit regular text in a window. Therefore, these options are not available in Script Editor windows, the Services window, or in other windows that don't contain regular text.

- *Undo*: This option cancels the effects of the last edit.
- *Cut*: Use this option to cut out the selected text to the Windows Clipboard. You can select text with the mouse (by dragging over it), with the cursor keys (press the arrow keys while holding down the Shift key), or by selecting the `Select All` option on the Edit menu (to select all text).
- *Copy*: This option copies the selected text to the Windows Clipboard, without deleting it from the current window.

- *Paste*: Select this option to paste the contents of the Clipboard to the current window. The `Paste` option is available only if the Clipboard contains text information. The text will be inserted at the cursor position. Because pasted text remains on the Clipboard, you can paste multiple copies of the same text, should you wish to do so.
- *Select All*: If you want to cut or copy the entire contents of a window to the Clipboard, you can choose this option to select all text in the window, instead of doing it by hand.
- *Paste From*: If you have experience of working with Windows programs that use OLE, you might be in for a surprise: CompuServe Navigator has its own `Paste From` option, which works quite differently than you might expect. Although this option doesn't allow you to link with other Windows applications, it is very powerful indeed. When you select this option, CompuServe Navigator displays the Paste From dialog, displayed in Figure 6.22. This dialog allows you to copy information from any of the archives created by CompuServe Navigator or WinCIM.

  The following options are only available when the Session window is the current window.
- *Add to Services*: This option allows you to add a new folder or service to the Services window. The new item will appear directly *after* the current item. With new forums and other facilities becoming available all the time, this option is necessary when you want to access a new service with CompuServe Navigator.
- *Insert in Services*: This option inserts a new folder or service in the Services window. It will become the first part of the current item.

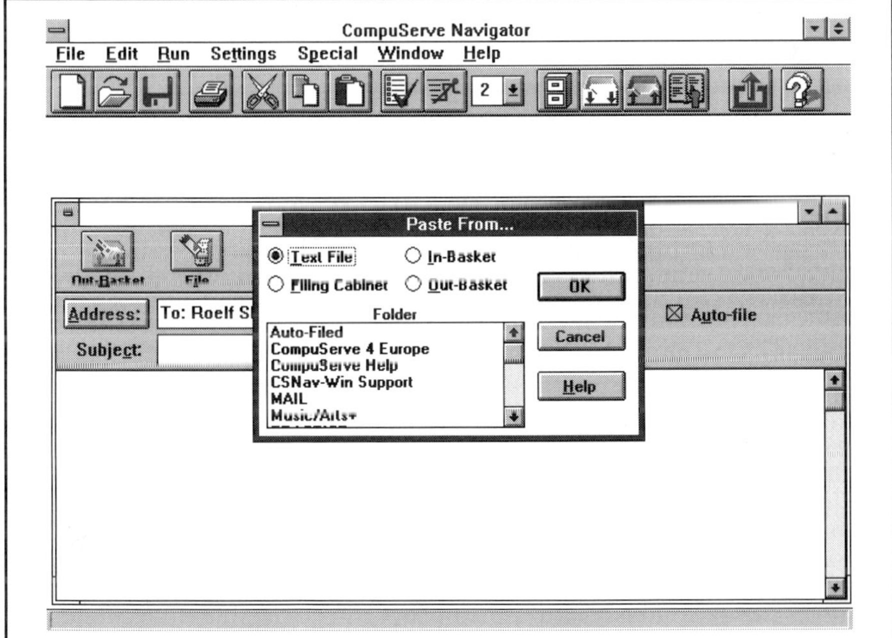

Figure 6.22 The Paste From dialog

- *Delete from Services*: Use this option to delete the selected item from the Services window.
- *View/Update in Services*: Use this option to review the information for the current item in the Services window. If the official CompuServe `GO` word for the item should change (which happens not too often), you can update the Services window to reflect those changes.
- *Search Services*: You can use this option whenever you are looking for particular services. After you specify the search string, CompuServe Navigator will search through the Services window and select the first item that matches your search criteria. You can then either close the Search Services Tree dialog, or search for the next item in the Services window.
- *Expand Branch in Services*: The hundreds of items listed in the Services window are divided into branches. For an optimal overview of the Services window, you can close one or more branches. Once you have found a branch that could contain services that you are interested in, you can expand it by double-clicking on it, or by selecting this option.

The Terminal menu

This menu is available only in Terminal Emulation mode. It contains the following options:

- *Capture Buffer*: Select this option to replace the contents of the terminal window (in which the last 'screen' received from CompuServe is displayed) by the current contents of the capture buffer (which contains the last hundred lines of screen information).
  Don't confuse this capture buffer with the *log file* facility. The contents of the capture buffer will eventually 'scroll off' and be overwritten by new data. Therefore, the capture buffer is a useful means to look up 'what happened on the previous screen'; if you want to store the information that was sent to your screen on your hard disk, use the `Log to File` option instead.
- *Terminal Window*: Select this option to switch off the display of the capture buffer, and to restore the terminal window.
- *Log to Printer*: When you select this option, WinCIM will send all retrieved information to the printer.
- *Log to File*: Select this option to create a *log file* (sometimes referred to as a *capture file*) in which all data that CompuServe sends to your screen will be stored. Log files can help you save considerable time online; after CompuServe Navigator has retrieved all needed information, disconnect from CompuServe and turn to your log file to process it.
- *Set Function Keys*: This option allows you to assign text strings or commands to the function keys. When, during Terminal Emulation, you press a function key while holding down the [Alt] key, the corresponding text string or command will be sent to CompuServe.

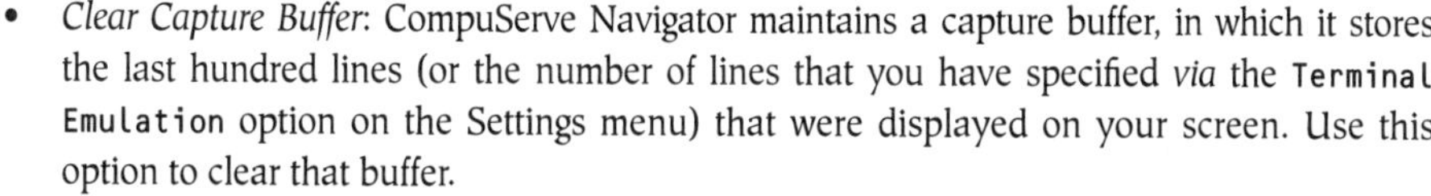

- *Clear Capture Buffer*: CompuServe Navigator maintains a capture buffer, in which it stores the last hundred lines (or the number of lines that you have specified *via* the `Terminal Emulation` option on the Settings menu) that were displayed on your screen. Use this option to clear that buffer.

The Run menu

The options on the Run menu all have to do with the execution of your CompuServe Navigator scripts. The following options are available:

- *Run Pass ...*: Depending on the number of passes you use, you select one of these options to run a part of your script. Only the tasks that have their respective boxes checked will be included in that pass. See 'Example two: visiting forums' on page 129 for a discussion on the benefits of passes.
- *Change Active Pass*: Use this option to change the current active pass. This option is only available if you use one or more passes. To specify the number of passes you want to use, select the `General` option on the Settings menu and press the `Advanced` button.
- *Preview Script*: You can use this option before actually executing a script. That way, you can see if all tasks that should be executed are actually included in the script. The `Preview Script` option is especially useful when your script consists of several passes. Because of the many check boxes in the Script Editor window, it can sometimes become difficult to check whether or not the right tasks are included. Previewing the script can help you track errors you wouldn't notice otherwise.
- *Abort Script*: When something goes wrong during the execution of a script, or when you simply want to cancel the execution, you can use the `Abort Script` option. CompuServe Navigator will finish its business as soon as possible and disconnect immediately afterwards. **Note:** always use the `Abort Script` option to cancel a script, and resist the temptation to disconnect manually. Because it can take CompuServe several minutes to notice that you aren't online any more, you could be charged too much, especially if the disconnection took place while you were visiting one of the extended services.
- *Next Script Task*: Choose this option when, while the script is being executed, you want to skip the current task

The Settings menu

You use the options on the Settings menu to configure CompuServe Navigator. The Settings menu contains the following options:

- *Session*: Selecting this option opens one of CompuServe Navigator's most important dialogs: Setup Session Settings. This is the place where you provide information about your User ID, password, the phone number your modem has to dial to reach CompuServe, the transmission speed, and so on.
  When you start either WinCIM or CompuServe Navigator for the first time, the program will present this dialog automatically.
  Note: to provide CompuServe Navigator with information about your modem (if the program didn't manage to get this information automatically), you press the `Modem` button.
- *General*: Use this option to adjust some general settings, like the automatic deletion and/or storage of your data files, the default script, and so on. The `Advanced` button deserves an honourable mention: this is the button that unleashes the real power of CompuServe Navigator, because it allows you to configure the program for the execution of multiple passes. Refer to 'Example two: visiting forums' on page 129 for additional information about passes.
- *Mail*: This option allows you to change the settings related to sending and receiving e-mail messages. If you share your CompuServe mailbox with other users, it could be a good idea to keep the e-mail messages available after you have read them, or to have them deleted only after a certain number of days have passed.
- *Forums*: Use this option to adjust the way CompuServe Navigator should behave when entering a forum you aren't a member of (that is, a forum that you haven't JOIN-ed before). You can also specify whether CompuServe Navigator should get News Flashes, and whether the messages you send should be stored into one of the Filing Cabinet drawers.
- *Terminal Emulation*: Although CompuServe Navigator can do a lot of things automatically, there are some services that aren't implemented (yet). To allow you to visit those services during the execution of a script, you can put a Terminal Emulation task into your Script Editor window. As soon as CompuServe Navigator reaches that task, it halts script execution and allows you to use the CompuServe ASCII Interface. When you have finished, select the `Next Script Task` option on the `Run` menu.
  During Terminal Emulation, you can use the special *buffer* that CompuServe Navigator maintains to scroll through the previously displayed lines. You can change the size of this buffer as well as some other Terminal Emulation parameters.
- *Script Template*: When you start composing your own scripts, you will find that you often adjust the same settings in the various forum and mail tasks. Therefore, it is often handy

to adjust the default layout of these tasks. That way, every time you copy these tasks to a Script Editor window, they already have the layout that you use most of the time, leaving it to you to make some small changes if necessary.
Use the `Script Template` option to change the initial specification of Forum and Mail tasks in the Script Editor window. You can open and close folders, as well as check boxes for one or more passes.

- *Directories*: Use this option to specify the directories where you want to store the various files that CompuServe Navigator uses or creates. Note that most of these files (with the exception of the files in the Data category) are also used by WinCIM. If you would like to share them between the two programs, you will have to change your WinCIM settings as well.

The Special menu

The options on the Special menu provide access to the places where CompuServe Navigator stores your data: the In-Basket and Out-Basket, the Filing Cabinet, and your Address Book. You will use one or more of the following options quite regularly:

- *Filing Cabinet*: Use this option to get access to your Filing Cabinet, a storage space for notes, e-mail messages, forum messages and so on. that you have retrieved using WinCIM or CompuServe Navigator. You can put these messages into separate folders (CompuServe Navigator will automatically do this for you when it retrieves messages from forums), move them to another folder, delete folders, and so on.
- *In-Basket*: All e-mail messages that CompuServe Navigator retrieves, as well as some system messages the program sends you to inform you about errors, e-mail costs and so on, are automatically put into your In-Basket. After reading those messages, you can decide what to do with them: leave them in your In-Basket, copy them to a folder in your Filing Cabinet, or delete them altogether.
- *Out-Basket*: CompuServe Navigator initially stores all e-mail and forum messages you create in the Out-Basket. Once online, it retrieves them from the Out-Basket, sends them to the appropriate recipients, and (eventually) moves them to an auto-storage folder.
  When, after composing your e-mail and forum messages, you have second thoughts about one or more of those messages, you only have to delete them from your Out-Basket to stop CompuServe Navigator from sending them.
  Note that the presence of one or more entries in the Out-Basket means that you have 'unfinished business'. It is therefore a good idea to check if your Out-Basket is empty (by looking at the Out-Basket symbol on the Ribbon, for instance) before exiting CompuServe Navigator.

- *Rebuild Indexes*: If you maintain a lot of data in your In-Basket and Filing Cabinet, it could happen that some of the index files get too large, making access to your information slow. By selecting the `Rebuild Indexes` option, you can let CompuServe Navigator re-index all your files for optimal speed. Note that, depending on the number of entries in your In-Basket and Filing Cabinet, it can take CompuServe Navigator from a few minutes to a few hours to rebuild the index list.
- *Address Book*: Use this option to maintain your CompuServe Navigator and WinCIM Address Book. Refer to Section 7.2.2 for more information.
- *Terminal Emulation*: If you would like to go online interactively, using the CompuServe ASCII interface, you can do so by selecting this option.
- *Search Libraries*: As you have seen in 'Example two: visiting forums' on page 129, CompuServe Navigator allows you to download file information from the various forum library sections. That way, you create your own, offline forum libraries. By using the `Search Libraries` option ('Search Library Sections' would have been a better name), you can search through one or more sections of a library for files that contain a certain keyword, have a certain extension, and so on. You can limit your search to only one section, or you can search them all. `The Search Libraries` option doesn't make CompuServe Navigator go online: you will therefore have to use a script to review the latest contents of a forum library.

The Window menu

The Window menu contains options to organize the on-screen display of the CompuServe Navigator windows. The following options are available:

- *Tile Vertical*: Use this option to put the open CompuServe Navigator windows next to each other. Note that the current window will be placed on the leftmost side of the CompuServe Navigator program window.
- *Tile Horizontal*: When you select this option, the open CompuServe Navigator windows will be put above each other. The current window will be placed on top of the CompuServe Navigator program window.
- *Cascade*: Choose this option to place all windows in such a way that they are all partly visible.
- *Arrange Icons*: This option arranges the icons of all minimized windows.

The names of all windows are shown as entries on the `Window` menu. To bring a window to the foreground, just select the appropriate option on the `Window` menu.

The Help menu

Apart from the standard options that you find on almost every Help menu, this menu contains some special features. The following options are available:

- *Contents*: This option shows the contents of the CompuServe Navigator help file.
- *Search for Help On*: Use this option when you need help about a particular CompuServe Navigator subject.
- *How to Use Help*: If you are new to the Windows environment, use this option to get acquainted with the Windows Help system.
- *Tutorial*: This option is your entry to a hands-on tutorial about CompuServe Navigator.
- *CompuServe Directory*: Use this option to get access to the CompuServe Directory, a Windows Help file that contains information about all services available on CompuServe. This is the same Directory that is included with WinCIM. Updates can be obtained from the WinCIM download area: the CompuServe Directory is included in the Support Files.
- *About CSNav*: This option shows a dialog with copyright information, as well as the amount of free space on your hard disk.

The Services window

The Services window contains a list of all the CompuServe services that can be included in a script. Besides copying an item to a Script Editor window, you have the following options, available *via* buttons at the top of the Services window (see Figure 6.23):

- *Expand* (the first button): When you press this button, the selected folder expands (opens), so that all underlying folders become visible. Press it again to close the folder. Note that you can do the same thing by double-clicking on the folder you want to expand, or by selecting the `Expand Branch in Services` option on the Edit menu.
- *View/Update* (the second button): Press this button to review the `GO` word for a listed service, or to update it. Note that you can perform the same action by selecting the `View/Update in Services` option on the `Edit` menu.
- *Search* (the third button): Pressing this button opens the Search Services Tree dialog, in which you can specify a search string in the Services window. Note that you can also do this by selecting the `Search Services` option on the `Edit` menu.

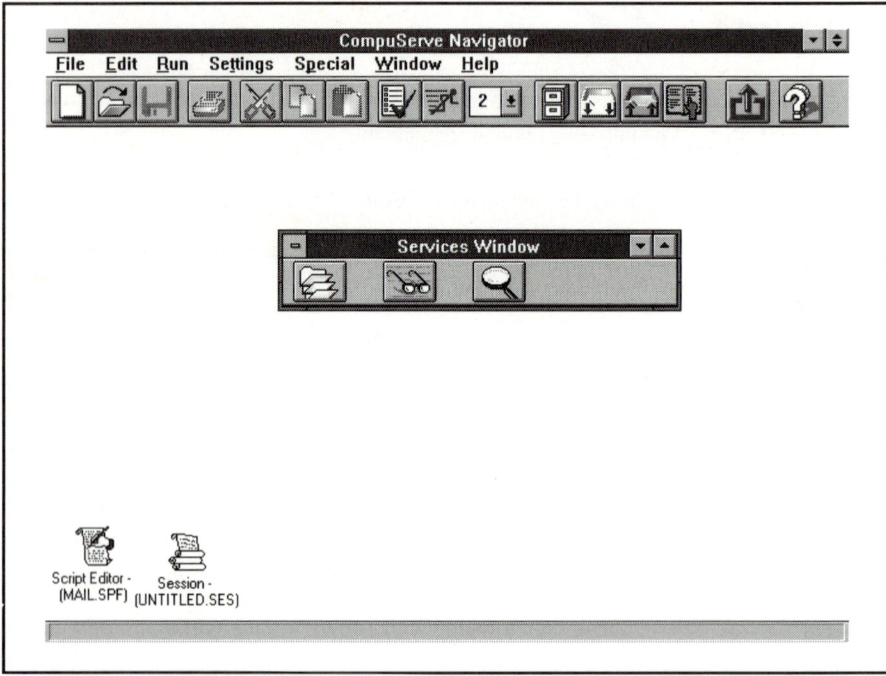

Figure 6.23 The buttons for the Services window

Tip for keyboard users

All mouse actions can be performed with the keyboard as well. After you have selected a service or folder, press the Spacebar key to display a pop-up menu. This pop-up menu contains all the options you need to maintain the Services window.

The Script Editor window

You use the Script Editor window to compose your *scripts*: series of *tasks* that CompuServe Navigator will carry out automatically once it gets online. Scripts can consist of multiple *passes*: by grouping the appropriate tasks in the same pass, and successively carrying out the several passes, you can completely automate the scanning and reading of forum messages, selecting and downloading of files, and so on.

Every item in the Script Editor window contains one or more check boxes (one for each available task: select the `General` option on the Settings menu and press the `Advanced` button to increase the number of passes). You will also encounter folder symbols and buttons. Folder symbols are used to expand a task into several subtasks. Buttons are used to indicate actions that you should to perform before going online, like writing e-mail or forum messages, selecting files to download, and so on.

Once you have finished composing the script, you do the following:

1. (If you haven't done this yet:) save the script by selecting the `Save` option on the File menu. If you want the script to be opened automatically every time you start CompuServe Navigator, select the `General` option on the Settings menu, and specify the script name in the Default Script field.
2. Select the *pass* you would like to execute. If you select pass 1, all items of whose first box is checked will be executed. With pass 2, all items with their second box checked will be executed, and so forth. In a typical CompuServe Navigator session, you will start with pass 1, review the results, execute pass 2, review the results again, and eventually execute pass 3.
3. Run the script.
4. Review the results in the Session window.
5. Eventually: go back to step 2.

6.1.9 Configuring CompuServe Navigator

Before you can start using CompuServe Navigator, you will have configure it. Depending on the presence of a CIM program, the chances are that you can limit the configuration to a quick visit to the Session Window, acknowledging the current settings. If you don't use WinCIM, you will have to change some settings yourself. Refer to Section 5.9.1 for more information.

6.1.10 The Scheduler

CompuServe Navigator comes with a special utility program, *CompuServe Scheduler*. You can use this program to have CompuServe Navigator execute a script automatically (or to execute any other Windows program). Beware that, although things don't go wrong very often, you could occur extra charges if, due to an error somewhere, the execution of the CompuServe Navigator script comes to a halt while still online.

6.2 TapCIS

TapCIS is undoubtedly one of the most famous auto-access programs available. Its incredible speed, in my opinion, more than makes up for its rather old-fashioned, and sometimes clumsy, user interface. There is not much that TapCIS can't do: the program contains a script facility that allows you to write your own procedures when a special feature is not supported by the program. Support is available *via* a special TapCIS forum (GO TAPCIS).

HINTS & TIPS

Note for new CompuServe members

TapCIS is not intended for novice users. If your CompuServe experience is limited, you are advised to spend some time online using programs like WinCIM before making the switch to TapCIS. Although TapCIS doesn't share its data structure with WinCIM, it is still possible to use both programs alternately.

6.2.1 How to obtain the program

To obtain a copy of TapCIS, GO TAPCIS. This brings you to thc TapCIS Forum. The files you should download can be found in section 1, TAPCIS (R): TAP.EXE (the program files) and TAPDOC.EXE (the documentation files).

HINTS & TIPS

Which version?

In this book, we discuss version 5.42 of TapCIS. This is the first version to support the Latin-1 character set, aimed especially at non-English speaking CompuServe members. For more information about new TapCIS versions, GO TAPCIS and browse through the forum library.

TapCIS is a shareware program: you get a 21-day trial period, starting from the day you first use the program. If you want to keep using the program after 21 days, you have to register it. The registration fee is $79. This is a very easy procedure: you just choose the appropriate option on the TapCIS welcome screen. TapCIS will generate an e-mail message to the TapCIS Registration Department. Within one or two weeks, you will receive a diskette version of the program, with a printed version of the manual, *via* regular mail.

HINTS & TIPS

Register, and become a power user!

Only registered TapCIS users can benefit from additional TapCIS tools, available in a special, closed section of the TapCIS forum. To get access to this closed section, you have to send a message to the TapCIS Registration Department. Additional information can be found in your TapCIS user manual.

6.2.2 How to get online support

To get online support for TapCIS, `GO TAPCIS` to visit the TapCIS Forum. This forum contains the following public sections:

1 TAPCIS Q & A

2 Scripts and Tools

3 Modems/HW/OS

4 Problem reports

5 Suggestion box

6 International

7 The TAProom

8 Section 8

14 Looking for...

16 TAPNews and Notices

17 The Parlor

Note that section 6, International, is aimed specifically at CompuServe members outside the United States.

6.2.3 The main elements

The TapCIS main menu is shown in Figure 6.24. Basically, it contains the following elements:

- A *Parameters* menu, where you configure TapCIS.
- A *Forums* menu, which lists all installed forums.
- An *ONLINE* menu, which contains activities that TapCIS should perform online.
- An *OFFLINE* menu, with activities to perform offline.

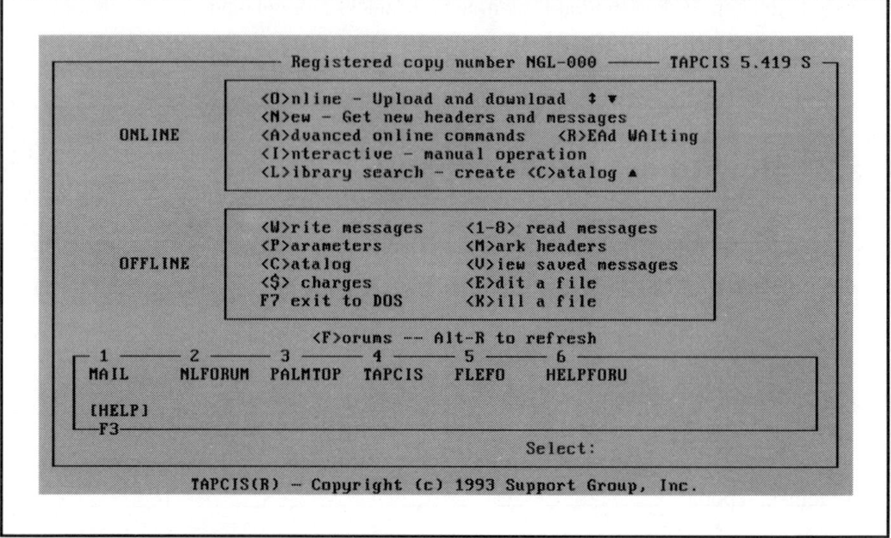

Figure 6.24 The TapCIS main menu

As a first-time user, you first change a few options on the Parameters menu. Once you have done that, a typical TapCIS session consists of the following activities:

1. First, you use the `<F>orums` command to select the forums you want to visit.
2. You select the `<N>` command: TapCIS will go online and check all selected forums for new messages and messages waiting for you. Depending on your settings, TapCIS will retrieve either all messages, or only the message headers. Depending on the number of forums selected, this will take anywhere from a few seconds to several minutes.
3. If TapCIS retrieved the message headers only, you give the `<M>ark headers` command to indicate which messages you would like TapCIS to retrieve. This is an offline process.
4. Next, you give the `<O>nline` command: TapCIS will go online again, and retrieve all selected messages. During this process, it will visit only those forums for which you have marked messages. Again, depending on the number of forums selected and messages marked, this process will take anywhere from a few seconds to several minutes.
5. Offline again, you press the appropriate forum key (either a digit for a forum located on the top row, or Shift plus a function key for a forum located on the bottom row) to read the forum messages and, eventually, reply to them.
6. Finally, you select the `<O>nline` command again: TapCIS will go online and send your replies to the appropriate forums.

As you can see, TapCIS spends as little time online as possible. That's why this program pays for itself in almost no time: you can cut your CompuServe bill very, very drastically. For example, I visit about 15 forums twice a day, and check my e-mail every three or four hours. Because TapCIS allows me to do almost all work offline, I rarely spend more than $1.50 per day for my regular e-mail and forum messages. When I used CIM to do the same amount of work, my bill ran as high as $15 per day!

6.2.4 Getting started with TapCIS

As with most computer programs, the key to an optimal and efficient usage of TapCIS is the installation. TapCIS takes a little more time to install than other programs, but once you have the program up and running, configuring it is very easy.

Step one: installing the program files

After you have downloaded `TAP.EXE` and `TAPDOC.EXE`, copy both files to a new directory. If you plan to use, or keep using, other CompuServe access programs as well, it might be a good idea to create a `CSERVE` directory (if a previous installation program hasn't already done this) and place a `TAPCIS` directory into that directory. For example, my hard disk contains the following directories:

- `\CSERVE`: This is the main CompuServe directory. It contains only a few files: some `INI` files (used by DOSCIM, WinCIM and CompuServe Navigator) and a large help file, `ALMANAC.HLP`, which contains the CompuServe Directory, used by WinCIM and CompuServe Navigator.
- `\CSERVE\CSNAV`: This directory contains the program files for CompuServe Navigator, the official CompuServe navigation program.
- `\CSERVE\DOSCIM`: This is the directory for the DOS CIM program files.
- `\CSERVE\DOWNLOAD`: All files downloaded by the various CompuServe access programs, are stored in this directory. That way, I don't have to remember what program I used to download a specific file: it will be saved into the `DOWNLOAD` directory automatically.
- `\CSERVE\FCABINET`: This directory contains additional files and directories to support the special data management tools present in WinCIM, DOSCIM and CompuServe Navigator.
- `\CSERVE\GIF`: This directory is used by WinCIM and DOSCIM to store graphic files that were viewed during an online session.

- \CSERVE\OZCIS: This is the directory for all OzCIS program and message files. In my case, files that OzCIS downloaded from the forum library are stored in the \CSERVE\DOWNLOAD directory.
- \CSERVE\SCRIPTS: This is the storage space for script files used by WinCIM, DOSCIM and CompuServe Navigator.
- \CSERVE\SUPPORT: This directory contains files needed and generated by WinCIM and DOSCIM. For example, all bitmap files that contain the forum logos, displayed by WinCIM, are saved in this directory.
- \CSERVE\TAPCIS: This is the TapCIS program directory. In my case, it contains all files needed and generated by TapCIS, except for files that were downloaded from the forum library. Because TapCIS uses fixed extensions for its message files, file catalogues, mark files, and so on, I have no problems with storing them all in just one directory. If you wish, however, you can instruct TapCIS to store all data files in a separate directory, for instance \CSERVE\DATA.
- \CSERVE\WINCIM: This directory contains the program files for WinCIM.

If you were to use this structure yourself, you would copy the TAP.EXE and TAPDOC.EXE files to the \CSERVE\TAPCIS directory.

Both TAP.EXE and TAPDOC.EXE are self-extracting files: they contain other files, stored in a compressed format to minimize the time needed to download them. TAP.EXE contains the program files needed to run TapCIS; TAPDOC.EXE contains the TapCIS documentation files, in plain ASCII format. You can import these files into your word processor, or you can 'copy' them to your printer by typing the following command after the DOS prompt:

```
copy filename prn
```

After you have decompressed the TAP.EXE file, you can delete it from the \CSERVE\TAPCIS directory. However, it doesn't hurt to keep a backup copy of the file on a diskette.

Step two: basic configuration

Next, you can start TapCIS for the very first time, by typing the TAPCIS command and pressing the Enter key. Because this is the first time you run TapCIS, the program will ask you for your name. This information will be stored into a special file: PARAMS.CIS. This so-called *parameter file* will later be used to store other important information, like your modem settings, installed forums, storage options, and so on.

When you have typed in your name and pressed the Enter key, the TapCIS main menu appears, shown in Figure 6.25.

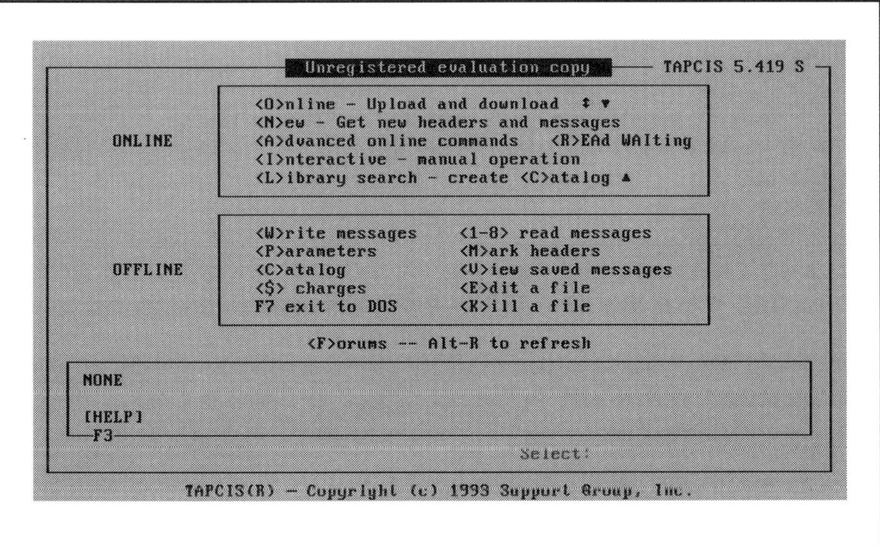

Figure 6.25 The TapCIS main menu

Before you can go online for the first time, you will have to perform a basic offline configuration. Press the [P] key to select the `<P>arameters` command. TapCIS will display the screen shown in Figure 6.26. This screen contains a range of options and fields. To select an option, press the capitalized letter placed between angle brackets:

- *<C>ommunications port*: Choose this option to select the communication port your modem is connected to. Every time you choose this option, TapCIS will show you (the status of) the next available port.
- *<I>nitialize modem*: This one is very, very important! It contains the string that is sent to your modem to initialize it. Unfortunately, there is no 'default string' that works with all modems. A typical initialization string could be as simple as `ATZ V1 DT`. You can consult your modem manual for more details, or you could copy the information from another program. Pay attention, WinCIM users: select the `Session Settings` option on the `Special` menu, and press the `Modem` button. The second field in the Modem Control Strings dialog contains the initialization string that WinCIM uses for your modem. Write this string down and copy it to your TapCIS configuration screen.

HINTS & TIPS

Important! Pulse dialling and tone dialling

Unlike programs like WinCIM and CompuServe Navigator, TapCIS doesn't have a separate field to indicate whether you want the program to 'pulse dial' or 'tone dial'. You have to specify this manually, by adding a modem command to the initialization string. Type `DT` if you want to use tone dialling, or `DP` if you prefer pulse dialling.

- *<O>nline report*: You normally shouldn't have to change this option. It contains the last four letters of the string your modem sends to your computer when a connection has been established.

Connecting when you dial the number yourself

If your modem cannot dial the number (some pay phones demand that you dial the number manually), set this option to `NONE`. In that case, TapCIS will assume that you are online the moment you select one of the appropriate menu commands.

- *<F>ail report*: Normally, you don't change this option. It contains the code HAYS, indicating that your modem supports the standard Hayes message set. When trying to establish a connection, TapCIS checks for either the CONNECT message or one of the Hayes status messages.
- *<R>eset modem*: Leave this field as is, unless you find that your modem has problems disconnecting. In that case, you could specify a command that disconnects your modem. The following command switches the modem into command mode, after pausing two seconds, and issues the `On Hook` command:

  ```
  ?2+++?2ATHO^M
  ```

- *<T>elephone numbers*: TapCIS allows you to store up to six telephone numbers and/or connection speeds. The number and/or speed that TapCIS currently uses is indicated by the * symbol. To have TapCIS use another telephone number, just press the numeric key in front of it.
  To change a telephone number, select it first (by pressing the numeric key in front of it). Next, press the [T] key and type the number. You can use a comma to specify a pause.
  After you have typed the telephone number, don't press [Enter] yet! TapCIS expects you to specify a *script code* for the network you will be accessing. A few examples: if you will be dialling a regular CompuServe node, you use the `CSERVE.SCR` script. If you dial *via* a European INFONET node, you use the `INFOEUR.SCR` script. TapCIS contains a lot of these scripts (they all have the extension `.SCR`), for almost all access networks. To specify a script, type an underscore, followed by its name without the extension. For example, if you live in London and use the regular CompuServe access number, you would specify `4908881_CSERVE`: 4908881 is the telephone number, `CSERVE.SCR` is the name of the TapCIS access script.
  After you have typed the telephone number and script, press [Enter]. This brings you to the modem speed field. Enter any valid modem speed, such as 300, 1200, 2400 or 9600.

TapCIS and 14 400 BPS

To indicate that you want to use the 14 400 bps connection speed (if the dial-in node supports this, of course), specify 19200.

When no script is available for your access network

If you use a network for which there is no TapCIS script available (like the Hungarian network, for example), you will have to get online to obtain it. Visit the International section of the TapCIS Forum for more details.

- *<U>ser ID*: Type your CompuServe User ID into this field: the two numbers, separated by a comma (for example `71333,1443`).
- *<P>assword*: This field can be used to store your password.

How safe is your password?

It isn't.

TapCIS stores your password in a *parameter file* (all files with the `.CIS` extension are parameter files). The password is actually encrypted, but in such a simplistic way that it can be 'cracked' in a matter of seconds. In other words: your password lies there for everyone who is interested in it. So if you are not the only one who has access to your computer, the Golden Rule applies: don't enter your password on the Parameters screen. TapCIS will ask for your password every time you start the program.

- *<S>torage disk path*: As you start using the program, TapCIS will make a large number of files to store e-mail and forum messages, forum catalogues and other important information. If you leave this field empty, these files will be stored in the TapCIS program directory. Because all these files have separate extensions, this normally doesn't cause any problems. However, you can specify another directory to place these files in. The most important file extensions are:
  - *.SEC*: Section files, with information about the names of the message and library sections of a particular forum. For every forum you install, a separate section file is created.
  - *.MSG*: Message files, which contain retrieved e-mail and forum messages. For every forum (e-mail is considered a forum as well), a separate file is created. The filename is identical to the first eight letters of the GO word to access that forum.
  - *.CAT*: Catalogue files which contain listings of forum libraries.

- *.MRK*: These are temporary files. They contain the numbers of the message threads that TapCIS should retrieve the next time it goes online. TapCIS generates a separate file for each forum. Normally, TapCIS will erase `.MRK` files after processing them.
- *.DOW*: Temporary files, which contain the names of files that TapCIS should download. The program generates a separate file for each forum. Normally, `.DOW` files will be erased as soon as they have been processed.
- *.SND*: Temporary files, which contain the messages and replies you have written offline. For every forum (TapCIS considers e-mail to be a forum as well), a separate `.SND` file is created.
- *.SAV*: Backup files that contain messages specifically saved by you, or auto-saved by TapCIS. For example, if you have indicated (*via* the `<K>eep outbox` file option) that you want TapCIS to save an offline copy of all e-mail messages you write, TapCIS will automatically create a file called `MAIL.SAV`.

- *<D>ownload file path*: Use this option to specify the directory where downloaded files should be stored. Note that we are talking only about actual *files*, downloaded from forum libraries, not about forum messages.

  To avoid 'cluttering' up your regular TapCIS directory, it is good practice to reserve a separate directory for your downloaded files. If you use WinCIM as well as TapCIS, it doesn't hurt to use the `\CSERVE\DOWNLOAD` directory for this. That way, you always know where your downloaded files are!

- *<L>og*: You can have TapCIS maintain a file called `XFER.LOG`, which contains extensive information about each and every file you have downloaded. Consider this file your 'offline retrieved file catalogue', and use it (you can import it into any word processor program) whenever you are looking for a particular file but have forgotten its name. To indicate that you want TapCIS to create and update this file, choose the `<L>og` option three times: it will read 'Time and transfers'.

- *<M>onitor colors*: This option lets you change the screen colours.

- *<A>ppend/overwrite msg files*: For every forum you visit, TapCIS maintains a separate `.MSG` file. If you want the contents of this file to be overwritten every time you retrieve new messages, leave this option set to `Overwrite`. If you want to keep the original messages and append the new ones to them, select `Append`.

  Note that the maximum number of messages that TapCIS supports for one file is 5000. Therefore, if you use the `Append` option, you are advised to start 'fresh' message files from time to time: either delete the original ones, rename them, or store them for backup purposes.

Archiving utilities for TapCIS message files

If your message bases start to grow, it can be handy to use one of the special tools that have been developed for maintaining those files, like Recon and TapOrder. Refer to page 189, under the heading 'Useful utility programs', for more information.

- *<K>eep outbox file*: Use this option to specify if you want TapCIS to save the messages you're write in special `.SAV` files.
- *<N>ame*: Type your name (first and last name) in this field; it will be used when sending e-mail and forum messages. Also, TapCIS will use this name when joining a forum.

```
<C>ommunications port              COM1:
<I>nitialize modem                 ATV1DT
<O>nline report (4 chars.)         NECT
<F>ail report (4 chars.)           HAYS
<R>eset modem                      ?3
<T>elephone numbers           <1>  555-1212                             *1200
                              <2>  555-1212                              1200
  Key digits 1-6 to           <3>  555-1212                              1200
  change selection            <4>  555-1212                              1200
  (* = selected)              <5>  555-1212                              1200
                              <6>  555-1212                              1200
<U>ser ID                          70000,1234
<P>assword                         [ blanked ]
<S>torage disk path
<D>ownload file path               .
<L>og                              None
<M>onitor colors                   Normal Hilite  Reverse  Prompt  Input
<A>ppend/overwrite msg files       Overwrite
<K>eep outbox file                 Never
<N>ame                             Roelf Sluman
            F7 Exit or Select:
                                                        Help=F3   Quit=ESC
```

Figure 6.26 The basic TapCIS Configuration Menu

An undocumented feature: the Twit Filter

When you are really, really annoyed by someone's messages, you can consider 'squelching' this person: TapCIS will hide all messages from this person from you. Although you can use this *Twit Filter* for only one User ID, there are occasions where it can come in very handy! From the Parameters menu, press the [B] key to activate the Twit Filter. To de-activate it: press the [B] key again and enter `NONE` as the User ID to squelch.

Once you have edited the basic configuration parameters, press [F7] to return to the main menu. You are now ready to get online with TapCIS for the first time.

HINTS & TIPS

You are a member, aren't you?

Don't try to perform the following procedure if you are not a CIS member yet. If necessary, sign up using WinCIM or a regular communication program.

From the main menu, press Alt-P. You don't have to install any forums yet: TapCIS will perform an extensive online configuration procedure that shouldn't take more than a few minutes. It will change a number of online options (your 'personal profile'), which allows it to perform optimally in the future.

Note that if you are planning to use TapCIS with different modem speeds, you will have to perform the 'Alt-P procedure' for every modem speed you have installed on the configuration screen, *via* the `<T>elephone numbers` option. As a global rule, perform an Alt-P procedure for every telephone number (and script) you have added to the configuration screen.

If TapCIS performed the Alt-P procedure without any problems, you are ready to proceed with the next section. If not, analyse the problem with the following checklist:

1. Is the modem connected, and does it work properly? Before TapCIS instructs the modem to dial, it initializes it by sending the string you entered on the configuration screen. Check if the modem responds with '`OK`'. If not, the chances are that there is a bad connection, or you have specified a command that your modem can't process. When in doubt, refer to your modem manual for a list of commands.
2. Does the modem dial? If you don't hear anything, insert the commands `M1 L0` in your modem initialization string. These commands cause the modem speaker to be switched on until the connection has been established, so you can monitor the dialling procedure. If you hear the dialling tones, but no response from the network you are trying to connect with, check if your telephone network supports tone dialling. The command `DT` at the end of your initialization string activates tone dialling; replace it by `DP` if you want to use the pulse dialling method instead.
3. So you can hear the phone ringing. But does the answering modem actually answer? You should hear a long high-pitched beep, followed by some noisy sounds. Next, the message `CONNECT` should appear on your screen.
4. The `CONNECT` message proves that TapCIS has established a connection. Next, it is up to the script to access CompuServe. Watch your screen for status messages. If necessary, go to the configuration screen and specify the script that should be used. Don't forget to put an underscore in front of the script name.

HINTS & TIPS

No luck? Try the most direct way: a direct CompuServe node

As you will understand, it is up to you to see that the first three steps are executed correctly. If you try to log in through a secondary network, and if you have reason to believe that the problem is related to a script, you could try to establish a direct CompuServe connection to begin with. Although this will probably increase your telephone bill a bit, you at least have the certainty that you are getting somewhere.

On the configuration screen, specify `_CSERVE` as the script. Once you have established a successful connection (and when TapCIS has performed the [Alt]-[P] procedure), you know that the problem must be somewhere in the script for your network. Check that you are using the right script for your network, and that you have the correct phone number (`GO PHONES` to verify this). When nothing seems to work, `GO TAPCIS` and ask for help in the International section of the TapCIS Forum.

Step three: Installing forum information

It worked: TapCIS can get online, and is almost ready to start cutting your CompuServe and phone bills! There is only one 'struggle' left: you have to tell TapCIS what forums you want to visit. This is done in the Forums menu. From the main menu, press the [F] key to get there.

The initial Forums menu is shown in Figure 6.27. First, we will summarize the most important commands available in this menu. Then, we go through the process of installing a forum.

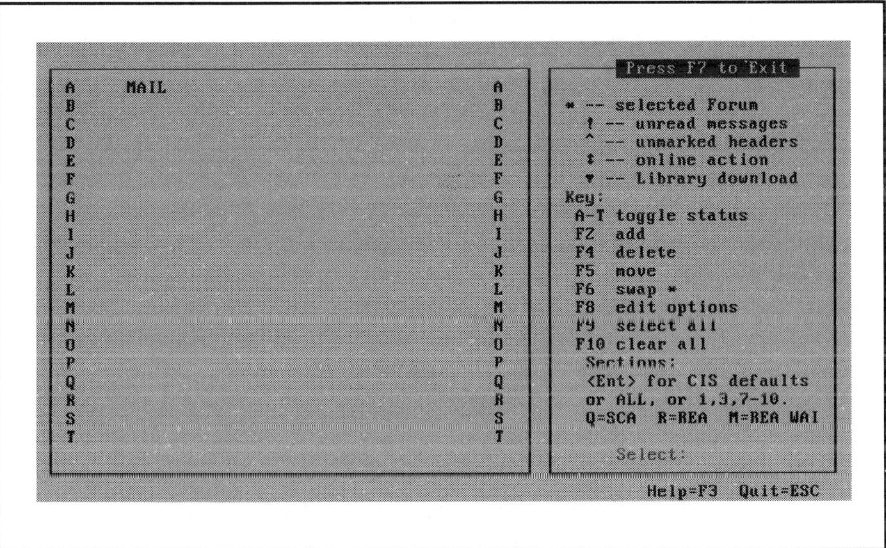

Figure 6.27 This is where you install forums: the Forums menu

The Forums menu contains the following options:

- *Toggle status*: As you can see, the main part of the Forums menu is taken up by a *list*. Initially, this list contains only one item: `MAIL`.

As you can see, there is space for 20 forums. Many users consider this a major limitation of TapCIS: the program cannot visit more than 20 forums during one single session. If there are more forums you would like to monitor, you have to create another list. (Press Alt-F to do this, or to select between lists. More on the ability to work with several forum lists can be found on page 177, under the heading 'Switch forums and parameters: Alt-F'.)

"Active" forums are indicated by the asterisk symbol after the forum letter. By pressing the appropriate letter key, you toggle the forum settings between active and not active. TapCIS will only visit forums that are marked as active.

Note that the TapCIS main menu provides space for only 15 forums. However, it will visit all active forums during `<N>ew` and `<O>nline` sessions, even the forums for which there isn't room on the TapCIS main menu.

HINTS & TIPS

What's ZiffNet?

ZiffNet is, in fact, an online information service, just like CompuServe, and is part of the Ziff-Davis Publishing Company, publisher of a large number of computer magazines.

Because both services use the same interface and are linked to each other *via* a gateway, CompuServe members can 'cross the bridge' and sign up to ZiffNet *via* a simple command: `GO ZIFFNET`. Similarly, ZiffNet members can `GO COMPUSERVE` and, after signing up, benefit from all CompuServe services. To visit a Ziffnet service, specify `ZNT:` before the actual `GO` word. A list of `GO` words for ZiffNet can be found in Section 9.6.3.

- *Add* (F2): Select this option to add a new forum to the list. The forum will be placed at the first available position.

  When you select the Add option, TapCIS asks for the forum name. Enter the first six to eight characters of the `GO` word for the forum you would like to add. A list of `GO` words can be found in Section 9.6.3.

  Next, TapCIS asks for the name of the *gateway* through which the forum can be accessed. For regular CompuServe forums, the gateway name is CIS; for ZiffNet forums, type `ZNT:` as the name of the gateway (don't forget the colon).

  As soon as you have typed the specifications for the forum and the gateway, TapCIS will look for a *sections file*: a special file that contains information about the message and library sections in the forum. Because this file is not present in the current directory, TapCIS will inform you that, once you have finished adding forums to the list, you have to press Alt-J from the main menu to 'join' this forum, even if you are already a member. This will give TapCIS the opportunity to collect the necessary information to create the sections file.

  When TapCIS asks for the *sections* you would like to monitor, press Enter to accept the default option: `ALL`. Next, the program asks what you would like it to do when it goes looking for new messages: *scan* them (retrieve the message headers), *read* them (all messages in the selected sections will be downloaded to your hard disk), or read only the *waiting* messages: messages addressed to you. Normally, you would press [Q] to select the `scan` option.

When you have completed this procedure, TapCIS will show the name of the new forum on the Forums menu, as shown in Figure 6.28.

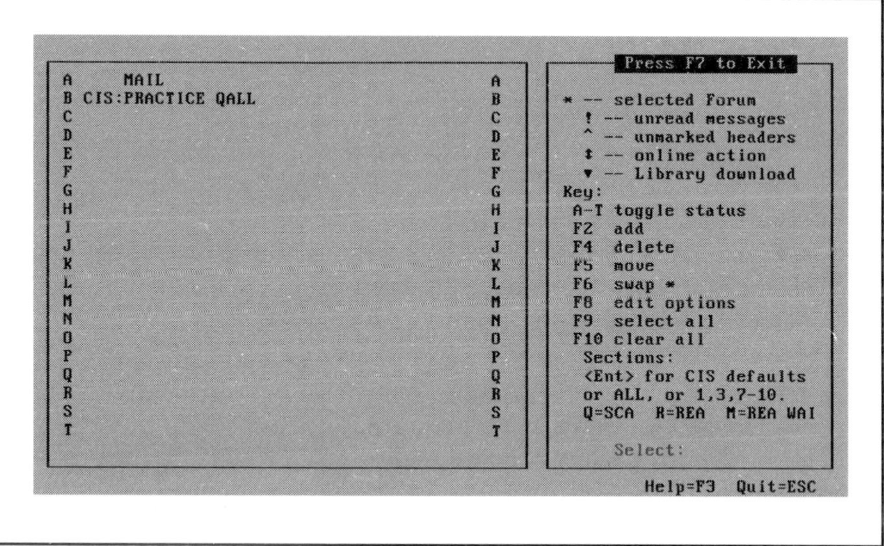

Figure 6.28 A new entry has been added to the Forums menu. Note the text QALL after the forum name, indicating that all sections will be scanned for new message headers.

- *Delete* ([F4]): Select this option to delete an item from the Forums menu. TapCIS will ask for the forum you would like to delete; press the appropriate letter key.
- *Move* ([F5]): Select this option to move a particular forum to another place on the Forums menu. Note that `MAIL`, if included, must always be the first option in the list.

  Yes, you can delete the `MAIL` entry, in which case TapCIS will not collect mail messages. Although it is probably not a good idea to remove the `MAIL` option from your first list of forums, it could be handy to do so when you maintain several of those lists. Refer to page 177, under the heading '**`Switch forums and parameters:`** [Alt]-[F]', for more information.

  When you press the [F5] key to select the `Move` option, TapCIS will ask for the forum you want to move. Press the appropriate letter key. Next, press the key that corresponds to the new place for the forum. If that place is currently occupied by another forum, the locations of both forums will be 'swapped'.

Some forums belong together

If you want to save money, use the **Move** option to keep those forums together that have to be accessed *via* the same gateway. Passing through the gateway takes up valuable time. Therefore it helps to group, for example, all ZiffNet forums. That way, you only have to pass through the gateway once.

- *Swap* * (F7): Select this option to de-activate all active forums, and vice versa. Note that active forums are indicated by an asterisk.
- *Edit options* (F8): This option is used to adjust the way TapCIS will process a forum during online sessions. After you have selected this option, press the letter for the forum you would like to edit. You now have two options:
  - *Mode*: You can specify whether you want TapCIS to retrieve only the new message headers of the forum (Q), or all new messages (R). If you want TapCIS to retrieve only the new messages addressed to you, press the M key.
  - *Secs*: When TapCIS has 'joined' the forum (because you pressed Alt-J from the main menu), it will have created a **.SEC** file for that forum. This file contains information about the message and library sections in that forum. Once this file is available, you can decide which sections you are interested in.
- *Select all* (F9): Choose this option to activate all forums. The next time you select the **<N>ew** option on the main menu, TapCIS will visit all those forums and check for new messages. Note that you can also select this option from the main menu: just press the F9 key. The Forums menu will be shown automatically, with all forums activated.
- *Clear all* (F10): Choose this option to de-activate all forums. Then, you can activate one or two forums easily. Note that you can select this option from the main menu as well, by pressing the F10 key. TapCIS will display the Forums menu, with all forums de-activated.

It is now a good time to start modifying your Forums menu. Let's install our first forum, the free Practice forum. The **GO** word for this forum is **PRACTICE**. Daredevils can do this entirely on their own, but if you aren't that confident yet, just proceed as follows:

1. In the main menu, press F to enter the **Forums** menu.
2. Press F2 to select the **Add** option. Type the **GO** word for the Practice forum: **PRACTICE**, and press the Enter key.
3. Press Enter to accept the default gateway for this forum, **CIS**:.
4. Press Enter again to accept the default sections to be scanned for this forum, **ALL**.
5. Press Enter once again to accept the default action that TapCIS should perform while visiting this forum: scanning for new messages.

6. If all went well, TapCIS will now have created an entry in the Forum menu. Press F10 to de-activate all forums. Next, press the letter that corresponds to the Practice forum, which is probably B.
7. Press F7 to return to the main menu. If you are lucky, the forums list on the main menu will show one item: `PRACTICE`. If not, go back to step one, and check again.

Step four: Testing one, two, three

HINTS & TIPS

Before you try this

You have configured TapCIS properly, haven't you? It is no use trying this example if you haven't performed an 'Alt-P procedure' to initialize TapCIS for the network you use to access CompuServe. When in doubt, go back to Section 6.2.4, 'Step two: basic configuration'.

Take a deep breath: we are almost ready for our first real online session. But first, we have to give TapCIS a chance to 'get to know' the Practice Forum. To do this, press Alt-J from the main menu. TapCIS will go online, join the forum, retrieve information about the message and library settings, and initialize some forum parameters that help to speed up consecutive accesses.

HINTS & TIPS

Joining again?

If you are already a forum member, TapCIS won't 'join' the forum again. It simply sees that you are already a forum member, and proceeds with the other activities necessary to improve performance. Using TapCIS, you can join a forum as often as you deem necessary. For example, if you know that the forum management has rearranged the sections, let TapCIS 'join' the forum again to update the `.SEC` file for that forum, so you can change your preferences accordingly.

HINTS & TIPS

Why not take it slow, and save some money!

Joining a forum doesn't take too much time, less than a minute at 2400 bps. If you normally use a higher transmission speed, consider switching to 2400 bps when you join a new forum that is part of the extended services. Because your total online time won't be more than a minute anyway, and because CompuServe always charges you in increments of one minute, you save some connect charges, and maybe even some communication surcharges, depending on the network you use to get access to CompuServe.

Now TapCIS has joined the forum, it knows everything it needs to know to get started. So we are ready to start our first interactive session. Press the H key to get a list of new message headers for the Practice Forum. TapCIS will go online and retrieve those headers into a special file. You can watch the headers scroll by while TapCIS retrieves them and stores them onto your hard disk. After a few moments (normally not more than a few minutes, depending on the modem speed you use to access CompuServe), TapCIS will disconnect: it has retrieved all message headers for further processing offline.

When TapCIS has finished its business, either wait 30 seconds or press a key to return to the main menu. When you look at the PRACTICE item in the list of forums, shown on the bottom of the screen, you see a ^ *status mark* next to the forum key (a number or function key). This status mark indicates that there are message headers waiting to be *marked* by you. Press the M key, for the `<M>ark headers` command. TapCIS will ask for which forum you want to mark messages: press the 1 key for the Practice Forum.

HINTS & TIPS

Selecting a forum from the TapCIS main menu

To access a forum from the TapCIS main menu, press the appropriate *forum key*. The keys 1 to 8 are reserved for the top eight forums; hold down Shift and press one of the function keys F2 to F8 to access one of the bottom seven forums.

The Thread Marking screen is displayed, as shown in Figure 6.29. For every thread, the following information is listed:

- The *thread number*, in the first column.
- The number of *replies*, in the second column. If there are no replies, this column is empty.
- The *subject* (topic) of the thread, in the fourth column.
- The *section* in which the thread was posted, in the fifth and last column.

```
409755         finding shareware        S 1 / From the Sysops
409756         Finding Forum            S 1 / From the Sysops       PRACTICE
409757 [ 1]    How's this work?         S 1 / From the Sysops
409758 [ 1]    How's this work          S 1 / From the Sysops       R>ead
409760         frustration              S 1 / From the Sysops       S>ection
409761         One more                 S 1 / From the Sysops       <Space>
409770         marked items             S 1 / From the Sysops       K>ill
409771 [ 1]    asking questions         S 1 / From the Sysops       Help=F3
409791 [ 1]    practicing on forum      S 1 / From the Sysops       Quit=ESC
409792         self report              S 1 / From the Sysops
409793         Following a thread       S 1 / From the Sysops
409794         Bill                     S 1 / From the Sysops
409799 [ 1]    PRACTICE MSGNG           S 1 / From the Sysops
409800         main forum menu          S 1 / From the Sysops
409801 [ 1]    Newcomer                 S 1 / From the Sysops
409810 [ 1]    Practice Forum 1         S 1 / From the Sysops
409812 [ 1]    Hello!                   S 1 / From the Sysops
409820 [ 1]    Elite Ultra Problems     S 1 / From the Sysops
409832         the I.D. is too long     S 1 / From the Sysops
409754 [ 1]    Test Flight              S 2 / Composing/Replying
409787         message threads          S 2 / Composing/Replying
409798         logging off              S 2 / Composing/Replying
409802         HELP                     S 2 / Composing/Replying
409803         CURRENT EVENTS           S 2 / Composing/Replying
409829         Learning                 S 2 / Composing/Replying
```

Figure 6.29 TapCIS shows the message headers it has retrieved for a forum

The third column is initially empty. You can now mark the thread(s) that you would like to read. First, use the arrow keys to select the appropriate thread. Next, use one of the following keys:

- *To read the thread*: press the [R] key. An R appears in the third column, and TapCIS selects the next thread.
- *To read an entire section*: press the [S] key. An R appears in front of all thread names in the current section.
- *To delete a 'Read' mark for a thread*: select the thread and press the [Spacebar] key. The R disappears, indicating that TapCIS will ignore the thread.

When you have finished marking threads, press [F7] to return to the main menu. A special status mark after the forum key shows that an online action is pending for the corresponding forum. You are now ready for the second part of the online session, which consists of retrieving the messages for all marked threads. Press [O] to give the <O>nline command. Depending on the number of threads you have marked, TapCIS will spend a few seconds to several minutes reading the thread messages. As it retrieves the messages and stores them onto your hard disk, you can watch the progress on the screen.

When TapCIS has read all messages, it logs off. Wait 30 seconds, or press the [Spacebar] key, to return to the main menu. The ! status mark, displayed after the forum key, indicates that there are messages waiting for you to read. To read those messages, simply press the forum key (in this case the [1] key). TapCIS displays the first of the forum messages read during the previous session, as shown in Figure 6.30.

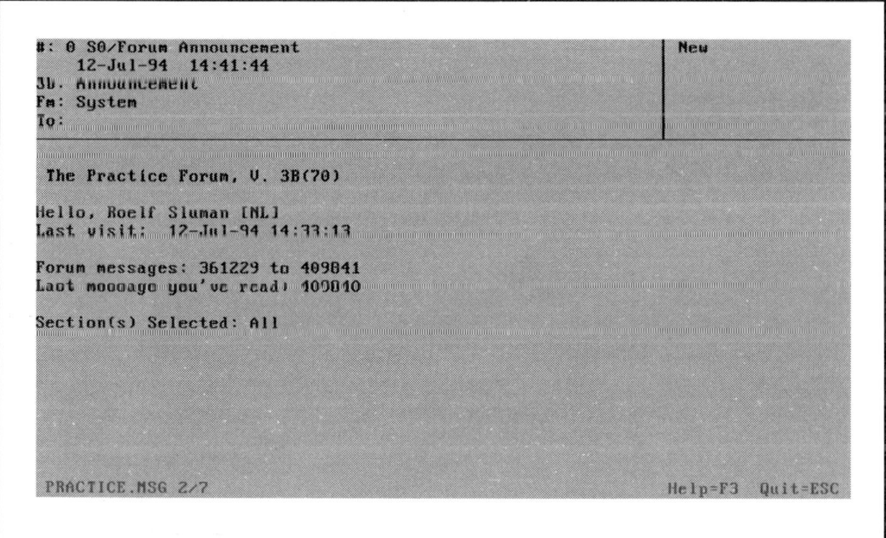

Figure 6.30 Reading messages with TapCIS

The top of the message screen contains information about the message that is being displayed, such as the forum message the message appeared in, the subject, the message sender, and the message recipient. On the top right, TapCIS shows some internal information about the message.

While reading the messages, you can give a large number of commands by pressing special keys. The most important keys are:

- [Spacebar] displays the next part of the current message. If you are currently looking at the last part of the current message, pressing Space shows the next message.
- [B] shows the previous part of the current message. If you are currently looking at the first part of the current message, pressing the [B] key shows the previous message.
- [A] lets you place add information about the sender, recipient, or both, in your TapCIS address book. Refer to Section 7.2.5 for more information about the address book.
- [R] lets you reply to the current message. Section 8.7.3 contains more information about replying to forum messages using TapCIS.
- [Tab] lets you forward the current message *via* CompuServe Mail.
- [X] *or* [Shift]-[F6] displays the first message of the next thread.
- [Ctrl]-[F6] displays the first message of the next section.
- [Shift]-[F5] goes to the previous thread.
- [Ctrl]-[F5] goes to the previous section.
- [F2] lets you search for a message that contains a certain text string. After you have used this option for the first time, you can press the [N] key to search for the next message that contains the same text string.

Need help? Press F3!

From most TapCIS menus and screens, you can press [F3] to obtain context-sensitive help.

6.2.5 The options on the main menu

The TapCIS main menu contains a number of listed and unlisted options, discussed in the following section. As with the other CompuServe access programs discussed in this book, most of the features of TapCIS are discussed more extensively in the appropriate sections. A few examples:

- Writing e-mail messages: Refer to Section 7.3.5.
- *Reading e-mail messages*: Refer to Section 7.3.5.
- *Reading forum messages*: Refer to Section 8.7.2.
- *Writing forum messages*: Refer to Section 8.7.4.
- *Downloading files*: Refer to Section 8.8.3.

<O>nline

When you select this option, TapCIS will go online and perform pending activities. To see if there are activities pending for any forum, look for special status marks in the forum list at the foot of the TapCIS screen. If there are no activities pending for the forums currently listed, TapCIS will ignore this option.

<O>nline and <N>ew

Use the `<O>nline` option to let TapCIS carry out specific instructions, like reading particular forum messages, downloading files you selected, and so on. Consider the `<O>nline` command as a 'follow-up' activity: normally, you will want to start with the `<N>ew` command, to get TapCIS to retrieve a list with new forum and e-mail messages. After you have processed this list, you give the `<O>nline` command to 'follow up' and have TapCIS retrieve the actual information.

<N>ew

Select this option to let TapCIS retrieve information about new e-mail and forum messages. Typically, TapCIS will retrieve the complete text for all e-mail and forum messages directed to you, and a summary of all other forum messages. After you have processed this summary (a list of *message headers*), you give the `<O>nline` command to have TapCIS retrieve the matching messages.

<A>dvanced online commands

From time to time, you will want to give a specific command for a particular forum. This option allows you to choose from a list of frequently used forum commands, or to write your own command strings. During the next online session (regardless of whether you select `<N>ew` or `<O>nline`), TapCIS will send those command strings to the appropriate forum.

When you select the `<A>dvanced` online commands option, TapCIS displays a menu with the following options:

- *<R>(Read CIS-marked messages)*: The next time you visit the forum, TapCIS will retrieve all new forum messages directed to you, regardless of the settings on the Forum menu. You have to select this option for every forum you want it to apply to.
- *<L> (Read messages addressed to ALL)*: The next time you visit the forum, TapCIS will retrieve all new messages directed to `ALL`. Members of support staffs often use this option to scan for new messages that could contain questions about the products they support. These people are normally not interested in discussions between forum members, in which case each message is directed at a particular User ID.
- *<T> and <B> (Read all messages To/By this User ID)*: The next time you visit the forum, TapCIS will retrieve all messages that are either sent by you, or directed to you. Note that this applies to both new and old messages.
- *<Z> (Delete (P) messages already read)*: If there are any private messages posted by you, or directed to you, use this option to delete them. It is good practice to delete private forum messages as soon as you have read them, thereby making room for other, non-private messages. Remember that each message that is posted results in another message, which could contain valuable information for other members, scrolling off the board. By removing your private message, a new message can be posted without the need for scrolling all other messages.
- *<U>* (User command): This is a very powerful option. It allows you to compose your own commands, using the CompuServe command set for forums. Advanced user commands can be used to read a particular forum message, to change your forum name, to read a number of messages again, and so on.
  When you select this option, TapCIS will ask you to choose the forum you want to apply the command to. Next, type the command and press the Enter key. The command will be stored into the `.ADV` file for the particular forum.

HINTS & TIPS

Tips for advanced user commands

If you would like to see a list of command examples, press F3 immediately after you select the `<A>dvanced` online commands option.

Cancelling commands before going online

All advanced commands that you give for a particular forum are stored in a `.ADV` file. For example, if you post an advanced command for the Practice forum, the command will be stored in a file named `PRACTICE.ADV`. If you want to cancel an advanced command, you have two options: delete the entire `PRACTICE.ADV` file (in which case all other advanced commands for that forum will be erased as well), or edit it using the built-in TapCIS editor. To delete a file, select the `<K>ill a file` option on the TapCIS main menu. To edit a file, select the `<E>dit a file` option, also on the TapCIS main menu.

<R>ead WAIting

Select this option if you want to do a quick check, on all active forums, for new messages directed to you. Forum sysops often use this option as an easy way to check for waiting messages. Note that the high message pointer will not be changed when you select this option: the next time you visit the forum, TapCIS will scan all messages posted since your last normal visit.

<I>nteractive

Although the power of TapCIS lies in its ability to carry out online commands automatically, there can be times when you want to go online interactively. One of the ways to do this is *via* the `<I>nteractive` command. TapCIS will ask for a forum; if you press one of the forum keys, TapCIS will transfer control to you after entering that forum. If you press the Enter key instead, TapCIS will transfer control to you as soon as it establishes the connection with CompuServe.

Go online interactively, and save money

The `<I>nteractive` option can come in handy when you want to check for a particular e-mail message, without downloading all other messages and files sent to you. I use this option quite often during the day, especially when I am expecting a rather large e-mail file. If I have no immediate need for that file, I prefer downloading it after business hours, when network surcharges as well as telephone charges are much lower. The `<I>nteractive` option allows me to `GO MAIL` manually, and to read important messages online.

<L>ibrary search

TapCIS can be used to download files from forum libraries. Normally, you first want to select the files to download from a *forum library catalogue*. TapCIS can help you with this: the program can download a list of files available in the library of a particular forum. Select the `<L>ibrary search` option to do this. First, TapCIS will ask for the forum for which it must create a library file. After you have chosen the forum from the list displayed on the TapCIS main menu, proceed as follows:

1. TapCIS asks for the *File(s) to find* and shows a provisional file specification (`*.*`), you can either press Enter to accept this proposal, or type another specification. For example, if you are looking for GIF files only, you could change the specification to `*.GIF`.
2. Next, TapCIS asks for one or more *keywords*. When someone uploads a file to a forum library, he or she will specify some keywords that describe the nature of the file as closely and, at the same time, as generally as possible. For example, if you upload a Windows utility that shows the time in the title bar, you could specify the keywords `WINDOWS`, `TIME` and `UTILITY`.
   If you want TapCIS to retrieve a list of all library files, simply press Enter. If you are looking for a fairly specific file, consider entering one or two keywords that the person who uploaded that file might have used.
3. The next part of the search criteria concerns the *AGE Range*: the minimum or maximum number of days that the file has to reside in the library. A few examples: if you enter 10 or minus 10, TapCIS will search the library for all files that were posted 10 or fewer than ten days ago. To search for all files that are between 10 and 20 days old, enter 10–20. To search for all files that are older than 20 days, enter 20 minus. Or you could simply press Enter to search for all files in the library, irrespective of their age.
   Note that TapCIS remembers the last time you used the `<L>ibrary` command for any forum. It will place a default value in the `AGE Range` field. Press Enter to accept this range.
4. There are two description methods available. *Short* descriptions are exactly one line long and contain brief information about the file. The advantage of using short descriptions is that it takes very little time to retrieve library information. *Long* descriptions are much more extensive, but take more time to retrieve. Since TapCIS allows you to do separate library searches for each forum, and even for one or more library sections, you can make the decision between short and long descriptions according to your needs.
5. Before TapCIS can start retrieving the library information, it needs to know what sections to search in. If TapCIS has 'join'-ed the forum, the available library sections are listed on the right side of the screen. If you want to select all sections, enter 1–24; TapCIS will ignore non-existent sections and simply retrieve information from all sections it can find.

Cancelling a library search command

To cancel a library search command before going online, simply delete the .DOW file for the relevant forum. From TapCIS, you can select the <K>ill a file option to do this. If you have specified more than one library search for that forum, you choose to edit the .DOW file instead: from the TapCIS main menu, press E to select the <E>dit a file option.

After TapCIS has retrieved the library information, choose the <C>atalog option to browse through the catalogue, and to select one or more files to download. TapCIS stores the retrieved library information in a file with the extension .CAT.

<W>rite messages

Select this option to write a forum or e-mail message. TapCIS will ask you to specify the forum for which the message is intended: select MAIL if you want to send the message *via* regular e-mail. More information about sending e-mail messages with TapCIS can be found in Section 8.7.4 for more information about sending forum messages with TapCIS.

<P>arameters

Choose this option to enter the TapCIS Parameters menu. This menu is covered in Section 6.2.4, 'Step two: basic configuration'.

<C>atalog

After TapCIS has retrieved the library information you have asked for with the <L>ibrary search command, you can use the <C>atalog option to browse through the list of files. When you see a file you would like to download, you can order TapCIS to do so by pressing the D key. TapCIS will download the program during the next online session.

Cancelling a download command

If you have second thoughts about a particular download, you can revoke the relevant command either by deleting the .DOW file for that forum (select the <K>ill a file option on the TapCIS main menu) or by editing it and deleting the respective line (select the <E>dit a file option).

<M>ark headers

When TapCIS has retrieved message headers during the first online session, choose the `<M>ark headers` option to select the messages you would actually like to read. More information about reading forum messages using TapCIS can be found in Section 8.7.2.

<V>iew saved messages

TapCIS stores the retrieved forum and e-mail messages in *message files* with the extension `.MSG`. The maximum number of message entries that TapCIS can process is 5000. Therefore, a lot of users occasionally delete their `.MSG` files, or use a utility program to do this. To preserve the information they really need, they let TapCIS save important messages in `.SAV` files. (When reading messages, press the [Ins] or [S] key to do this.) To review the contents of a `.SAV` file, select the `<V>iew saved messages` option.

<E>dit a file

You can use this option to edit an ASCII file. Apart from the special files that TapCIS maintains for the forums listed, which are all in ASCII format, you can also edit regular ASCII files like `AUTOEXEC.BAT` and `CONFIG.SYS`.

<K>ill a file

Select this option to delete one of the data files for a particular forum. After you have chosen a forum, TapCIS shows the possible file types:

- *.SND*: Contains messages written by you that TapCIS will send to the forum during its next visit. Normally, this file is deleted automatically when TapCIS has sent all the messages it contains.
- *.MSG*: Contains the messages that TapCIS retrieved from the forum.
- *.SAV*: Contains the messages that you have saved while reading them (by pressing the [Ins] or [S] key).
- *.DOW*: Contains downloading and library retrieval instructions for a particular forum. Normally, this file is deleted automatically when TapCIS has completed all the commands it contains.

- *.ADV*: Contains advanced commands and advanced user commands for a particular forum. Normally, this file is deleted automatically when TapCIS has performed all the commands it contains.
- *.MRK*: Contains the numbers of the messages that TapCIS will retrieve from the forum during its next visit: the so-called *marked messages*. Normally, this file is deleted automatically when TapCIS has retrieved all the marked messages.
- *.QSN*: Contains the numbers of the threads that contain new messages. When you select the `<M>ark headers` option on the TapCIS `main` menu, the program displays the information in this file. Normally, this file is deleted automatically when you have finished marking messages.

<$> charges

Select this option for an estimate of the charges you have incurred while using TapCIS. Because TapCIS doesn't differentiate between extended and basic services, this estimate is by no means accurate. Note that you should change the rates first (by selecting the `Rates` option) to reflect network surcharges.

<F>orums

Select this option to modify the list of forums, or to activate or de-activate one or more forums. More information about the Forums menu can be found in Section 6.2.4, 'Step three: Installing forum information'.

6.2.6 Unlisted options

TapCIS contains a number of commands that are not listed on the `main` menu. The most important of these are listed in this section.

Switch forums and parameters: Alt-F

The basic configuration parameters and information about the forums you want to visit are stored in a special *parameters* file: `PARAMS.CIS`. When you start TapCIS, it will look for this file and use the information from it. If you need more than one parameters file, for instance when you visit more than 20 forums on a regular basis, you can decide to make one or more additional parameters files. To do this, press [Alt]-[F] while the TapCIS main menu is displayed. TapCIS will show a list of available parameters files. The current parameters file is indicated by an asterisk. To make a copy of that file, press the [X] key. TapCIS will ask for a file extension for the new parameters file. Press the [Enter] key after you have typed the new extension. You will return to the TapCIS main menu; the program now uses your new parameters file. You can edit the contents of this file by selecting the `<P>arameters` and `<F>orum` options.

Refreshing status marks: Alt-R

Normally, TapCIS will add status marks to the forum list when certain actions are performed, and delete them if necessary. In some cases, for example when you use external utility programs to manage your TapCIS data files, it can be necessary to update the status mark by hand. Press [Alt]-[R] to do this. For all active forums, TapCIS will scan the data directory for available data files and update the status marks accordingly.

'Joining' a forum: Alt-J

Before you can use TapCIS for automatic access to a forum, you have to let TapCIS 'join' that forum, even if you are already an official forum member. Press [Alt]-[J] to do this: TapCIS will visit all active forums and update the .SEC files for those forums. It is advisable to 'join' a particular forum every time you hear that the message and/or library sections for that forum have changed. That way, you are certain that you see the correct information when you select either message sections to visit, or library sections from which you are about to retrieve catalogues.

Initializing TapCIS: Alt-P

Whenever you use a transmission speed or network for the first time, press [Alt]-[P]. TapCIS will go online and update the necessary CompuServe settings accordingly. If you experience difficulties while you are using TapCIS, try the [Alt]-[P] option first.

What Alt-P does

When you press [Alt]-[P], TapCIS goes online and executes the `PARAMS.SCR` script file. Check the contents of this script file if you would like to know which CompuServe settings are changed by TapCIS.

Starting the 'front-end' script: Alt-N

Once you are used to working with TapCIS for your regular e-mail and forum messages, it is time to unleash one of the most powerful resources of this program: the *script files*. You can write script files (or download them) for almost all available CompuServe services, like ENS (the Executive News Service), stock quotes, the weather, and so on.

More information about scripts, which are basically ASCII files containing so-called *script* commands, can be found on page 184, under the heading 'Writing TapCIS scripts'. Although scripts can have any valid DOS name, one name is reserved: FRONTEND.SCR. The script with this name will be executed automatically when you press [Alt]-[N] instead of [N]. After TapCIS has executed the script commands, it will perform a normal `<N>ew` command.

Shell to DOS: Ctrl-F1

If you need to perform a few DOS activities while you are using TapCIS, you can press [Ctrl]-[F1] to get access to a DOS shell. When you have finished, enter exit and press the [Enter] key to return to TapCIS.

6.2.7 Fine-tuning TapCIS

Once you start getting used to TapCIS, you might want to take a peek at the more advanced features of this program. There are quite a few things you can do to improve functionality even further:

- By editing the special configuration file **TAPCIS.CFG**, you can customize TapCIS for optimal use on your system.
- As delivered, TapCIS provides support for e-mail, as well as all CompuServe forums. But it doesn't stop there. You can use the powerful script feature to write your own scripts for services not currently supported by TapCIS.
- As TapCIS gained fame and popularity, a number of programs were written to make up for features originally missing from the program, like advanced thread management and library maintenance.

The TapCIS configuration file

Every time you start TapCIS, the program uses the settings specified in a special configuration file: `TAPCIS.CFG`. This file, which can be edited with a normal ASCII editor (and even within TapCIS), contains a number of *switches*. Initially, this file has the following contents:

```
; TAPCIS.CFG
;
; ANY CHANGES DO NOT TAKE EFFECT UNTIL YOU RESTART TAPCIS FROM DOS.
;
; This file contains all the command line options available in
; TAPCIS in a single file that is loaded, if found, each time
; TAPCIS starts. The options in this file are processed first
; and can be overridden by command line options. For example,
; /LOG=All here could be overridden by /LOG=N on the command line.
;
; Commands have been prefixed with a semicolon. Be sure to remove the
; semicolon so that the / is the first character of the line if you need to
; use those options.
;
; In BATch files, you should replace the equals (=) with a colon (:) as in
; /LOG:ALL instead of /LOG=ALL. The colon will work everywhere including here
; and on the command line.
;
; All settings here are the defaults.
;
; Parameter file selection; enter the file extension of the PARAMS.* you want
; to use.
;/PARAMS=CIS
;
; ONLINE.LOG settings: =ALL captures everything (old G), =LINES last 350 lines
; =APPEND is same as ALL plus append to file within a single TAPCIS execution,
; =N gives no logging at all
;/LOG=N
;
; Carrier Detect Checking (old C). =N no checking for modems with either
; no CD line or that have a defective or always ON CD line.
;/CHECKCD=N
```

```
;
; Fast drop-off from CompuServe (old D). =N use LOG to see CompuServe time
; record. If set to N, be sure that your reset string and DTR settings will
; disconnect the line. =Y is new default for 5.4.
;/FASTOFF=Y
;
; Intercharacter delay for initialization string in nn/10ths second. (Old Hnn)
;/MODEMDELAY=00
;
; Redial Delay (old Inn). Delay after busy or after disconnect.
;/DIALDELAY=30
;
; Skip ^U Line clearing (old U). Some networks don't like the line clearing
; at the beginning of each line. =Y Don't send send ^U's
;/SKIPCTRLU=N
;
; Change clear character from ^U to nn (old Vnn). Change ^U line clearing char.
;/CLEARCHAR=21
;
; Upload mail (old !). Send mail using B+ protocol for error free transmit.
; Not needed for error correcting modems.
;/UPLOADMAIL=N
;
; Save Mail instead of deleting from MAIL box. Will be downloaded
; each time you get new mail until you turn off this switch.
;/SAVEMAIL=N
;
; Big Cursor (old B). Useful on laptops where cursor is hard to see.
;/BIGCURSOR=N
;
; Disable S/D while reading and F9/F10 from main menu (old K).
; Some folks just don't like having those shortcut keys.
;/SAFEKEYS=N
;
; Quiet, no beeps (old Q)
;/QUIET=N
;
; Editor width (old Wnn). Limits are 40-76.
;/WIDTH=76
```

```
;
; Scan Waiting messages in Q Forums instead of Reading them.
;/SCANWAIT=N
;
; Supress various automatic actions. =1 Suppress Read Waiting (old S1),
; =2 Suppress Scan Waiting (old S2), =3 Suppress both (old S3).
;/SUPPRESS=0
;
; The NUMORDER option no longer has any effect on the order of messages
;/NUMORDER=N
;
; First commands. =N is New, =O for Online, =R is Read Waiting,
; =+ Alt-N (New+Frontend), =J is Alt-J (Join), =P is Alt-P (CompuServe Params).
;/CMD=
;
; Drop to DOS after first command (old X). Use =Y to drop to DOS.
;/DOS=N
;
;Time delayed execution (old Thh:mm). Time is in military time.
;/TIME=00:00
;
; B+ Packet size (old -n) as a multiplier of 128. Range is 1-8 (128-1024).
; You should not need to set this unless you have very noisy phone lines
; where =1 or =2 might give better performance.
;/PACKETSIZE=8
;
; Port speed (values 9600, 19200, 38400). Although there is little advantage
; to running at higher than the modem to modem speed, this option will let
; you set the computer to modem speed at a fixed, high speed. Note: unless
; you are using a FIFO buffered UART, you should not use high speeds.
;/PORTSPEED=19200
;
; No Header Lines in message reader. Some people prefer not to see the lines.
;/NOHDRLINES=N
;
; MsgBlanks for blank lines at the top of the message below the header line
;/MSGBLANKS=1
;
```

```
; Msgoverlap for lines of overlap between pages of the message
;/MSGOVERLAP=0
;
; Custom UART IRQ/Base address. Enter the IRQ in decimal and the Base address
; in hex. Note that you need only change the one that is different for the
; COM port selected within TAPCIS. CAUTION: do not set these choices without
; firm knowledge of their proper values. Doing otherwise can crash your system.
; Defaults (COMn/IRQ/BaseAddr): COM1/4/3F8, COM2/3/2F8, COM3/4/3E8, COM4/3/2E8,
; PS/2: COM1/COM2 same, COM3/3/3220, COM4/3/3228, COM5/3/$4220, COM6/3/$4228,
; COM7/3/$5220, COM8/3/$5228.
;/IRQ=
;/BASEADDR=
;
; XONXOFF flow control (software flow control) is available for computers and
; modems that do not support hardware flow control (using CTS/RTS). The modem
; must be set properly to use this option (most modems use CTS/RTS by default.
; For Hayes compatible modems, this is often &K4 for software, &K3 for CTS/RTS.
/XONXOFF=N
;
; FIFO buffering on 16550A UARTs. Option should normally be YES except on
; machines with defective FIFO buffers.
;/FIFO=Y
;
; Micro Interrogation (ESC I from CompuServe). This setting would allow you
; to disable the forcing of the MicroInt which TAPCIS does by putting /INT
; after the user ID on login. If you find this conflicts with your network,
; set =N. Default is =Y.
;/MICROINT=Y
;
; Up/Dn arrows in the message reader typically move by line. If you'd like
; them to move by page, set this to yes. If set yes, you must use F5/F6 to
; scroll by line.
;/ARROWPG=N
;
; Left/Right used to switch by forums. This is moved to F8/Sh-F8 but can be
; put back on the right/left with this command.
;/ARROWSW=N
;
; Forum maximum message size with the new (October 1992) CompuServe message
; software.
;/FORUMMAX=10000
;
```

```
; Support for Latin-1 Character Set
;/LATIN1=Y
;
; Screen Echo off
;/NOECHO
```

In this listing, all lines are preceded by a semicolon, the standard 'comment' character. Depending on the version of TapCIS you have downloaded, some semicolons in your file could be removed.

Most of the lines contain informative text, followed by a *switch*: a program command. Although you can specify switches from the command line as well (*tapcis /noecho /latin1=y* would be a valid way to start the program), it is often easier to modify the TAPCIS.CFG file, eliminating the need to specify those switches every time you start the program.

The last two options of the `TAPCIS.CFG` file are especially important for European users:

- */LATIN1=Y*: When you activate this switch (by removing the semicolon in front of it), TapCIS provides support for messages with 8-bit characters from the Latin-1 character set. This gives you the possibility of reading and writing messages that contain 'international' symbols like accents, cedillas, and so on. If the 'Latin-1' switch is not activated, CompuServe will show you the non-accented versions of those characters, which can make some messages fairly hard to read, depending on the language.
- */NOECHO*: This is a simple, yet very powerful switch. When you activate it, TapCIS will not display the text (such as e-mail and forum messages) it retrieves. As a result, it takes less time to store the text onto your hard disk, making your online sessions even shorter than they already are. You can still monitor the online action, because TapCIS shows you the commands it gives to CompuServe. A real money-saver!

Writing TapCIS scripts

If you are one of those curious types, the chances are that you have already browsed through the TapCIS directory and noticed all those files with the `.SCR` extension. Those files conceal the real power of TapCIS! By means of a simple but effective *script language*, you can visit almost every CompuServe service automatically. Furthermore, you can have TapCIS perform a script automatically when you start a new online session.

There are two possibilities for executing a TapCIS script:

- Go online in interactive mode. (Either use the `<I>nteractive` command on the main menu, or press Esc while you are online.) Next, press PgUp and specify the name of the script to be executed. Script files must have the extension `.SCR`, and must be stored in the default TapCIS directory.

- Press Alt-N from the main menu. TapCIS will go online and execute the script named `FRONTEND.SCR`.

TapCIS comes with two important script files:

- *PARAMS.SCR*: This script is executed when you press Alt-P from the TapCIS main menu. It changes a number of CompuServe settings to optimize speed.
- *FRONTEND.SCR*: This is an example script, which can be started by pressing Alt-N from the main menu. When you want to be able to execute your script by pressing Alt-N, simply rename it to `FRONTEND.SCR`.

The other .SCR files in your TapCIS directory

Actually, the TapCIS directory contains a lot more script files, used to establish the connection with CompuServe. (Do you remember that you specified the name of a script file on the TapCIS Parameters screen?) Although these files have another purpose, they use the same commands as script files that are to be executed once you are actually online.

To write your own scripts, use a plain ASCII editor. You can even write your scripts within TapCIS, by using the `<E>dit a file` command.

For an overview of the available script commands, we take a closer look at the contents of `FRONTEND.SCR`.

```
; FRONTEND.SCR Version 5.4 12/10/91
E FRONTEND.SCR - Sample Script for use with Alt-N from TAPCIS main menu
E                Output is captured to the MAIL.MSG file.
E                Captures WEAther & QUOtes and OLT-90.
E                Make changes for your city name and state and tickers.
E                Also shown in script is how to automate NEW
C N
; turn capture off
; lines starting with a semi-colon are ignored.  In this script,
; they document the previous command
S G CIS^M
; get a CompuServe top menu
W !
; wait for a system prompt
C Y
; turn capture on
```

```
S WEA Columbus,OH^M
; get local weather
W !
; wait for prompt
S QUO IBM,HRB,DJ 30^M
; get a quote on H&R Block stock
W !
; The next 9 lines demonstrate a way to read the entire offering of
; CompuServe's "What's New".  TAPCIS has a physical limit of 350 lines
; per mail message, so we've REMmed the WN commands in favor of the
; ones that follow, which get the daily news from Online Today.  You can
; reverse it by carefully deleting "; * " in each line where that sequence
; appears .......
; * S G NEW^M
; go to the "What's New" menu
; * W !
; * C Y
; * S ALL^M
; read everything
; * W age!
; wait for "last page!" message
; * C N
; ...... and deleting everything from this line down to (but not
; including)  S ^M below
S G OLT-90^M
;OLT-90 is the home of Online Today's daily edition ...
W !
S ALL^M
; ... read it
W Last
W age!
C N
S ^M
; outta here
W T-90
S ^M
; See news menu and make exit certain
; get back to a navigation prompt
W !
; return control, leaving TAPCIS at a navigation prompt
```

To understand this script, you need to know more about the available script commands. The following list contains a summary of commands that can be used in online script files:

- *; (Comment)*: Used to indicate commentary text. This text is ignored by the script.
- *C (Capture)*: Specifies a name for a capture file, and switches the capture mode on or off. This command has three forms:
  - *C filename*: Opens or creates the specified file: all captured data will be placed in this file. If you want to overwrite a previous file, use the *K(ILL)* command.
  - *C Y*: Activates the capture option: all retrieved data will be placed in the current capture file. You have to specify a filename first. There is one exception: if this command is part of the `FRONTEND.SCR` file, the output will be sent to the `MAIL.MSG` file by default.
  - *C N*: Deactivates the capture option.
- *E (Echo)*: Displays the following string on your computer screen.
- *I (Interactive)*: Switches on *interactive mode*: execution of the script is halted until you press the F7 key. In the meantime, anything you type will be sent to CompuServe.
- *K (Kill)*: Kills (deletes) the specified file.
- *S (Send)*: Sends the string that is specified after the `S` command to CompuServe. The `^M` symbol is used to indicate a simulated press on the Enter key. Similarly, use `^C` to simulate the Ctrl-C key.
  For example, the script command `S GO BASIC^M` has the same effect as typing `go basic` and pressing the Enter key.
- *W (Wait)*: Execution of the script is halted until the specified string (either one or four characters) is received. To pause until CompuServe shows a ! prompt, you would give the command `W !`
  Note that the WAIT script command accepts strings of either one or four characters long. Specifying any other string length can have unpredictable results.

One of the sections of the TapCIS Forum is devoted to scripts. Ask your questions there, or take a look at the scripts that other members have written. A few examples are listed below.

Filename: `BILLNG.SCR`
Bytes: 2682
Title: Script to capture current billing information.
Description: This script captures current billing information. Billing page will list information for the current week. `BILLNG.SCR` can be invoked by pressing `<PgUp>` while in Interactive mode, or can be copied to the filename `FRONTEND.SCR` and executed by logging on with the `<Alt-N>` command.
Upload/Author Thomas Harold [71750,3724]

Filename: CPHONE.SCR
Bytes: 2805
Title: Script to download CIS access node phone list
Description: A TAPCIS script to capture the ENTIRE CIS access node phone list. CPHONE.SCR can be invoked by pressing <PgUp> while in Intcractive mode, or can be copied to the filename FRONTEND.SCR and executed by logging on with the <Alt-N> command.
Upload/Author Thomas Harold [71750,3724]

Filename: EBERT.SCR
Bytes: 1675
Title: Script to capture Roger Ebert's Movie Reviews
Description: This script will capture ALL of Roger Ebert's current online movie reviews. EBERT.SCR can be invoked by pressing <PgUp> while in Interactive mode, or can be copied to the filename FRONTEND.SCR and executed by logging on with the <Alt-N> command. May require customization.
Upload/Author Thomas Harold [71750,3724]

Filename: ENR.ZIP
Bytes: 53519
Title: ENS Reader for TAPCIS
Description: This set of TAPCIS utilities provides a way of selecting and reading articles from CompuServe's Executive News Service. It works with TAPCIS and has the same design goals as TAPCIS: to automate most on-line activities, and to minimize your connect-time costs.
Written/uploaded by Masanobu Taniguchi [101015,2010]

Filename: EURMAP.SCR
Bytes: 2968
Title: Script for downloading non-US weather maps
Description: This script downloads weather maps for offline viewing with the .GIF viewer of your choice. EURMAP.SCR can be invoked by pressing <PgUp> while in Interactive mode, or can be copied to the filename FRONTEND.SCR and executed by logging on with the <Alt-N> command. See script comments for instructions on customizing EURMAP.SCR to download weather maps for Continental Europe, the United Kingdom/Ireland, and Japan/Far East.
Upl/auth Loren Jenkins

Filename: GETNUZ.SCR
Bytes: 925
Title: GETNUZ.SCR Script to capture AP Online News
Description: GETNUZ.SCR is a script which allows you to capture one or more of the hourly updates from AP Online to a file for viewing offline. This script demonstrates use of the "I" command in a script to allow for user input from a keyboard.
Upload by author Ed Truitt [76600,3336]

Filename: GETOLT.SCR

Bytes: 1741

Title: Script to capture Online Today stories

Description: This script captures Online Today stories. Stories are usually posted after 9 a.m. ET and are changed daily. GETOLT.SCR can be invoked by pressing <PgUp> while in Interactive mode, or can be copied to the filename FRONTEND.SCR and executed by logging on with the <Alt-N> command.

Upload/Author Thomas Harold [71750,3724]

Filename: MSKB.SCR

Bytes: 2482

Title: Script to capture Microsoft Knowledge Base Docs

Description: A TAPCIS script for downloading documents (by Document Number) from the Microsoft Knowledge Base. This script can be used either as an Interactive mode <PgUp> script, or as a front-end script. Refer to script file comments for instructions on customization and use. (See the file MSL.SCR, also in this library, for automating downloads from Microsoft Software Library.)

Upl/author Loren Jenkins

Filename: UKMAPS.SCR

Bytes: 3167

Title: Script to download UK weather maps

Description: A TAPCIS script to download United Kingdom weather maps. UKMAPS.SCR can be invoked by pressing <PgUp> while in Interactive mode, or can be copied to the filename FRONTEND.SCR and executed by logging on with the <Alt-N> command.

Upload/Author Thomas Harold [71750,3724]

Filename: WHATNW.SCR

Bytes: 1353

Title: Script to capture What's New news

Description: This script captures all What's New stories. WHATNW.SCR can be invoked by pressing <PgUp> while in Interactive mode, or can be copied to the filename FRONTEND.SCR and executed by logging on with the <Alt-N> command.

Upload/Author Thomas Harold [71750,3724]

Useful utility programs

Although TapCIS in itself is already a very powerful program, a number of utility programs has been written to extend its possibilities even further. A few of these programs even belong to the 'you can't do without it' category. If you want to become a TapCIS power user, take a look at the following files, available in the TapCIS Forum.

Filename: ADRBK.ZIP
Bytes: 168948
Title: Tapcis Address Book Manager 1.25
Description: A FREE program for managing TAPCIS-style address books. Useful for finding duplicates, editing, sorting. Features SAA style interface with mouse support. Allows searching for and marking of addresses with wildcards. Creates TAPCIS mailing lists. Uses XMS, EMS and disk as memory for thousands of addresses. Upgrade for TAPCIS 5.42 owners. See ADRBOOK.DOC for program history.
Uploaded by the author Michael Vesely.

Filename: CATSCN.EXE
Bytes: 83369
Title: v3.1d2 catalog manager/script writer for TAPCIS
Description: CatScan (v3.1d2) is a CompuServe data library catalog manager. This file plus CATDOC.EXE make up the entire package. CatScan maintains compressed catalogs, offering several ways to sort, view, search, delete, and print descriptions. It writes TAPCIS scripts to download files and to download and update catalogs. Shareware $30.
Upl/Author Don Strenczewilk, ASP member.

Filename: CIMTAP.ZIP
Bytes: 10788
Title: Converts CIM ADDRBOOK.DAT addresses to TAPCIS format
Description: This FREE program converts CIM address book entries (found in ADDRBOOK.DAT) to the TAPCIS format (found in USERID.CIS). MSC 5.1 source code included.
Uploaded by author Michael Vesely

Filename: DUPCAT.ZIP
Bytes: 97504
Title: CATDEDUP V1.6 De-dupes TAPCIS catalog entries
Description: A program that eliminates duplicate entries within individual (or all) forum *.CAT files downloaded by TAPCIS from CIS forum libraries. Run occasionally to reduce file size and remove needlessly repetitive duplicate entries. V. 1.6 fixes date bug, and adds selective string entry elimination. Source included. Free. Replaces all earlier versions.
Original author Stephen Haynes; modified and uploaded by Tim Godfrey [72617,2125]

Filename: PARMSX.EXE
Bytes: 40654
Title: Select forums from multiple TAPCIS PARAMS.* files
Description: PARMS (v7.3) is a TAPCIS add-on program that lets you choose forums to visit from a list of the forums in all of your PARAMS.* files. Unlike TAPCIS, it lets you choose from all PARAMS.* files at once, and puts your choices into a file named PARAMS.NOW. PARMSX.EXE is an LHA self- extracting file. ECOG donation is requested.
upl/auth Don Strenczewilk

Filename: RECON.ZIP

Bytes: 247534

Title: Message manager, reply editor, menu/batch/shell

Description: Recon v2.20. Message file manager, with pulldown menus & command line, message/reply EDITOR, now with import/export & cut/paste. Keeps MAIL & FORUM files trimmed and sorted into context. Menu SHELL organizes add-ons. SYSOP commands. Powerful file navigation/viewing, print, edit, delete, move or auto-age messages. Now with sticky UNREAD & N/REPLY flags, auto-signatures. Full documentation as ReconD.ZIP, update booklet as ReconU.ZIP. Shareware $38, upgrd $12.

upl/auth Orest Skrypuch, member ASP.

Filename: TAPORD.EXE

Bytes: 126196

Title: TAPORDER v1.4/TOTSR-TOLTSR v1.5 Thread Manager

Description: TAPORDER 1.4: Consolidate multiple TAPCIS online sessions into a single, properly threaded message collection. New unread messages are marked for easy scanning with TAPCIS' F2-Search. TSRs to delete/hold messages from within TAPCIS, set bookmark, and more. Remove and archive messages/threads of a specific age. Navigation aids, date checking, full control of defaults by file. Self-extracting file.

© 1992 Support Group, Inc.

Filename: TPT.EXE

Bytes: 198041

Title: TappeT(tm) Thread Marking Program & Docs Ver 1.52

Description: TappeT(tm) Thread Marking Program greatly improves message marking by tracking previous marking sessions and your section and keyword preferences. Supports mice, menus, huge QSN files, huge TMK files with ageing, and more. Download TAPPET.INF for a brief list of TappeT features. TPT.EXE is a self-extracting file. This file contains both the program and documentation which are also available in TAPPET.ZIP and TPTDOC.ZIP.

Copyright (c) 1992 Support Group, Inc.

Shareware $29, free use by Update Subscribers.

Important information for European CompuServe members

For European CompuServe members, the TapCIS forum library contains a number of interesting files. Check the International section regularly for updates. Some of the most important files are listed below.

Filename: INF04.ZIP

Bytes: 13492,

Title: INFONET NON-US Node Numbers as of 14 May 1994

Description: INF04.ZIP is a series of files captured from INFONET's IOL (INFONET OnLine) public database. (See INFODB.TXT re: IOL)

This one is: NETWORK ACCESS DIRECTORY - INTERNATIONAL. It's all INFONET nodes, with specifications, outside of the United States. New 14.4 nodes are being added all the time! Note that if the date of the file seems "old" it's just because there's been no recent changes, as I review the database once a week.

Captured & Uploaded by Jeff Gulliford – NL [71333,1375]

Filename: LOGIN.ZIP

Bytes: 50757

Title: The file you shouldn't leave home without

Description: From the common to the obscure, from the sublime to the ridiculous, it's all here. 53 files of scripts and other noises, with ALOGIN.TXT explaining the other 52. All known TAPCIS 5.42 login scripts (including two for use with phone charge cards), and text files concerning special circumstances.

Note: the login scripts are written for use by TAPCIS only! CISINTL.NOS updated, CHINA.SCR modified, MEXICO.SCR added.

All collected & some written by Jeff Gulliford – NL [71333,1375]

Filename: PHONE.PLG

Bytes: 7409

Title: Describes telephone plugs used around the world

Description: A text file which details the telephone plug used in most of the countries of the world with some additional hints for successful international communications.

Upload/Author Gordon Brown [100111,2713]

Filename: TELHOT.TXT

Bytes: 8020

Title: Hotel telephone questionnaire

Description: A questionnaire in ASCII format uploaded by Gordon Brown of TeleAdapt requesting information on telephone systems found in hotels worldwide.

Electronic mail

Electronic mail

As a member of CompuServe, you can benefit from the endless possibilities that electronic mail has to offer. CompuServe's advanced electronic mail (or e-mail, as it is often called) system makes it easy to send an electronic message to your neighbour next door, a colleague at the office, or a distant relative at the other side of the world. E-mail is simple to use, inexpensive and, above all, fast. Normally, it takes about three to five minutes for an e-mail to arrive at its destination, regardless whether it has been sent to London, New York or Sidney. A few examples where electronic mail can be useful:

- To keep in touch with the office, while you're on the road. Journalists send their articles *via* e-mail to their editor. Managers call meetings *via* e-mail. And writers are notified that the deadline is approaching rapidly...
- To do business! This book is a perfect example: my editor and I had exchanged a lot of e-mail messages before we actually met. And because e-mail is informal by nature, it's often not necessary to ponder for hours on end on the contents of your message, as you might do with a fax or with a regular letter.

- To keep in contact with friends. A letter containing only three lines of text looks silly, but e-mail messages don't suffer from that problem. E-mail is the perfect way to let someone know that you haven't forgotten about him or her, even if you don't have the time to write long epistles.

As you can gather from the preceding lines, e-mail has a lot of advantages. In fact, many CompuServe members use CIS almost exclusively for e-mail purposes and spend only a little of their time visiting forums, getting information online, and so on.

The main advantages of e-mail are:

- It's fast. A CompuServe e-mail message is normally delivered within a few minutes. And although CompuServe states that it can take as long as 20 minutes for a message to arrive, this is almost never the case.
- It's inexpensive. CIS charges $0.15 for a three-page message (containing up to 6000 bytes). Every 2000 bytes more cost another $0.05. Try to get a deal like that from your local post office! Distance doesn't apply: sending a message to someone in Budapest costs exacxtly the same as sending a message to someone at the front desk of your office building.
- It's informal. E-mail messages are almost always exchanged on a first-name basis. And it's friendly too. 'Flaming' is a rare phenomenon in e-mail messages.
- It can be 'to the point'. The best example of this is a reaction from a CompuServe manager: 'E-mail allows me to just say "yes" or "no". It takes away a lot of the formality that comes with letters and faxes. I get a lot more work done that way.'
- Time and place are of no account. Every CIS member has his or her own private mailbox: an amount of space on the large CompuServe computers in Columbus, Ohio. You can check your mailbox and read its contents any time of the day. And from any place in the world! CIS doesn't care where you are: as long as you have a computer and modem with you, and a telephone connection within reach, you can get access to your mailbox. Imagine going on a transatlantic journey: as soon as you arrive at your hotel, you hook up, dial and read the messages that your secretary has posted.
  This is a very important aspect when it comes to 'teleworking'. You're always within reach, even if you are far from home.

7.1 Electronic mail: fact box

- Every CompuServe member has his or her own mailbox, with room for a hundred messages.
- CompuServe keeps text messages sent to you for a period of 90 days. Binary messages (files) will be kept for a period of 30 days. When sending an e-mail message, you can specify the dispatch date. If a message isn't delivered, you'll be notified.
- To send an e-mail message, you have to provide three things: an address, a subject and the actual message text. CompuServe will not accept your message if one of those things is missing.
- E-mail messages are confidential. As long as you don't provide someone else with your password, no other CIS user has access to your personal mailbox.
- If you want to be absolutely sure that the addressee has seen your e-mail message (that is, he or she has either read or deleted it), you can use the `receipt acknowledge` option. In that case, you'll receive a message (*via* e-mail, of course) from CompuServe as soon as the addressee has accessed the message concerned.
- You can send text messages as well as binary files. The maximum size for a text message is 100 kilobytes. Binary files can be much larger, up to 2 megabytes. Therefore, you can use e-mail to send word processor documents, computer programs, or even complete disks. There's a drawback though: the price. If you sent the contents of an HD disk (1.44 megabytes) *via* e-mail, CompuServe would charge you 1440 times $0.25: a steep $36.00. But then, how much does a courier service charge to deliver a disk overnight to an overseas location?
- Although more and more people are joining CompuServe, and therefore more and more people have CIS e-mail addresses, it doesn't stop there. The CompuServe electronic mail system provides access to a growing number of addresses outside CIS, like the Internet and MCI Mail, to name just too. That expands the number of people that you can reach *via* e-mail to several tens of millions. To state it simply: if someone has an e-mail address at a large information system, it's almost certain that you can reach his or her mailbox from CompuServe.

7.2 Finding the right address

To send someone an electronic mail message, you need his or her electronic mail address. If the person concerned is a CompuServe member, the procedure to obtain his or her e-mail address is pretty straightforward: CompuServe maintains a *Member Directory* that lists the name, residential information and e-mail address of all members, providing they didn't ask to be excluded from this directory. (There are a *lot* of celebrities on CompuServe, and although some can be found in the member directory, most of them have chosen not to be listed.)

For privacy reasons (or rather, to avoid 'junk e-mail' on CompuServe), there are some restrictions that you will encounter while using the Membership directory. For starters, you are required to enter at least the first three letters of the last name. Also, there is a limit on the maximum number of entries shown: if there are too many matches for your search specification, you are requested to enter additional information, like the first name, city, and/or country of the person you are looking for.

Finding people near you

One of the most frequently asked questions about e-mail addresses is 'How can I get a list with e-mail addresses of CompuServe members who live in my neighbourhood?'

First the bad news: this is not possible *via* the Membership Directory. Because you have to enter at least the first three letters of a person's last name, you cannot do 'wildcard searches'.

But the good news is that there are several other ways to search for other CompuServe members in your city, country, and so on. The solution lies in the countless meeting places that CIS provides: the *forums*. Every forum has a list of *membership profiles*. Although it is not obligatory to fill out a membership profile, a number of forum members choose to do so, because it's one way to let the world online know that you are there in the first place!

Some forums to start with are the *Europe Forum* (**GO EURFORUM**), the *Foreign Language Forum* (**GO FLEFO**), and the *Travel Forum* (**GO TRAVSIG**). In Chapter 8 you will read more about visiting forums, browsing through membership profiles and filling out your own profile.

7.2.1 General guidelines

- To get access to the CompuServe Member Directory, **GO DIRECTORY**. The Member Directory is a free service, although communication surcharges still apply. Note that some access programs have special menu options that get you to the Member Directory.
- When using the Member Directory, you are required to enter some information. Only one piece of information is always obligatory: you'll have to enter at least the first three letters of the last name of the person you are looking for. If the number of 'hits' (information items found) is too high, you are required to enter more specific information, like first name, city, state (for American addresses) and/or country.
- The CompuServe Member Directory only lists e-mail addresses of actual CompuServe members. In other words: it's not possible to search for e-mail addresses for people who are, for instance, on the Internet or MCI Mail. Although you can send e-mail to them, you'll have to resort to other ways of getting their e-mail addresses.

- A nice way to try out the CompuServe Member Directory is to do a search on your own last name. Start by entering your last name only; add additional information like your city or country only if the search results in too large a number of hits.

  The chances are that you will not able to locate yourself in the Member Directory. The reason could be one of the following:
  - You have only been a member for a very short time. Normally, it takes about three weeks before the Member Directory is updated with your membership information.
  - When you became a member, you explicitly stated that you didn't want to be listed in the Member Directory. If you'd like to change that information: `GO DIRECTORY` and choose the option `'Include/exclude This User ID'`. Please note that it takes some time (usually about a week) for CompuServe to process your updated information. Therefore, your name will not immediately appear in the Member Directory.

7.2.2 WinCIM

WinCIM has a special menu option for finding entries in the Member Directory. In addition, you can have WinCIM add the information found to your Address Book, for future reference. Here's how it works:

Figure 7.1 The "Search Member Directory" dialog

1. (You don't have to be online for this.) Choose the `Member Directory` option from the `Mail` menu. As a result, the 'Search Member Directory' dialog appears (Figure 7.1).

2. Although the 'Search Member Directory' window contains quite a number of fields, you do not have to enter information into all of them. For instance, you can begin by specifying only the last name. The 'Last Name' field is the only one that is obligatory: you have to enter at least three characters.

3. If you have reason to expect that a search on only the last name will result in too many hits (in which case CompuServe will ask you to enter more specific information), you can enter information into one or more of the other fields as well.

4. After you have keyed in the search details, press 'Search'. WinCIM will go online and try to find the requested information in the Member Directory. If there are any matches, WinCIM will show them (Figure 7.2): proceed at step 5. If there are too many hits, you will have to go back to step 2 and enter more specific information. If the information you are looking for could not be found, you either go back to step 2 and try again (did you spell the name correctly?) or cancel the search. Whatever option you choose, note that you are still online. You might consider disconnecting first, when you think that you need some time to consider other search options.

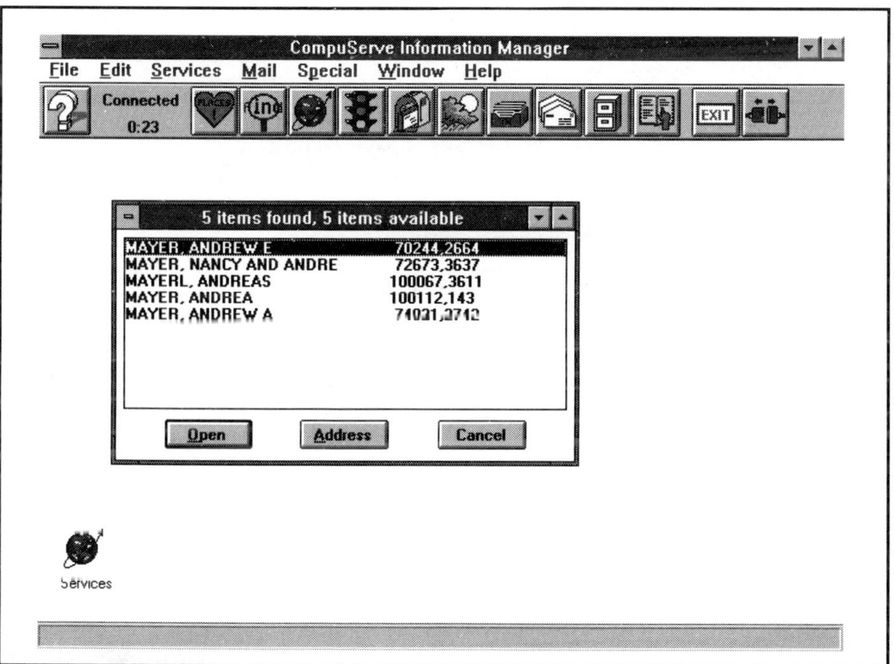

Figure 7.2 'Hits': entries located in the Member Directory

5. When a search action has resulted in one or more hits, WinCIM will list the records that were found. After you have selected an entry, you can press the **Open** button to get more information about it.
   If you wish, you can copy one or more entries to your WinCIM Address Book. To do this, select the appropriate entry and press the **Address** button. The WinCIM Address Book is actually a file, kept on your hard disk, which you can use whenever you write e-mail, compose forum messages, and so on. The WinCIM Address Book is a very powerful means of managing the online addresses of people you exchange e-mail with. See below for more information.

A powerful tool: the WinCIM Address Book

The **Address Book** option on the **Mail** menu provides access to a perfect means of managing your e-mail addresses and can be a real time saver. Once you have built a list of frequently used e-mail addresses, you can select the address you need *via* a simple mouse click. Also, you can make *groups* that contain, for instance, all the people that are involved in a certain project. That way, you can distribute important messages easily: once you have selected the group that something should be mailed to, WinCIM handles the process of actually addressing it to each and every group member.

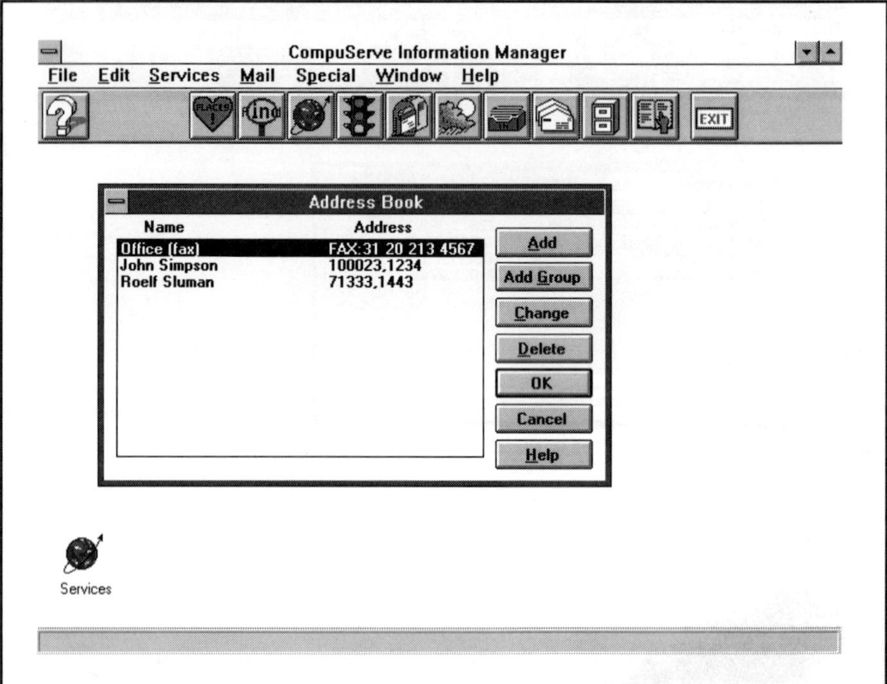

Figure 7.3 The WinCIM Address Book

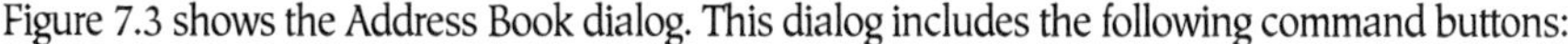

Figure 7.3 shows the Address Book dialog. This dialog includes the following command buttons:

- *Add:* Choose this option to add a new entry to the Address Book. Pressing the **Add** button has the same effect as choosing the **Address** option when you are reading e-mail and forum messages.

  The Add to Address Book dialog, shown in Figure 7.4, consists of three fields. The Name field contains the real name of the person you would like to insert: this is the name that will be shown under the Name header in your actual list of Address Book entries. All entries in the Address Book are sorted on the contents of the Name field. WinCIM uses an intelligent method to do this: it considers the last part of the name to be the actual last name of the person. Therefore, you don't have to use constructions like `'Doe, John'`; you can simply type `'John Doe'`.

  Next, the 'Address' field provides space for the actual CompuServe address. If you wish, you can use the 'Comments' field to enter additional information. Although this might seem redundant when it comes to your friends, colleagues and other people with whom you exchange e-mail on a regular basis, it can come in handy when you answer forum messages on a regular basis. From time to time I receive a 'thank you' message from someone I helped solve a problem. By putting his or her name in my Address Book, and adding a few comments, I save myself a lot of time when he or she contacts me again, sometimes months later.

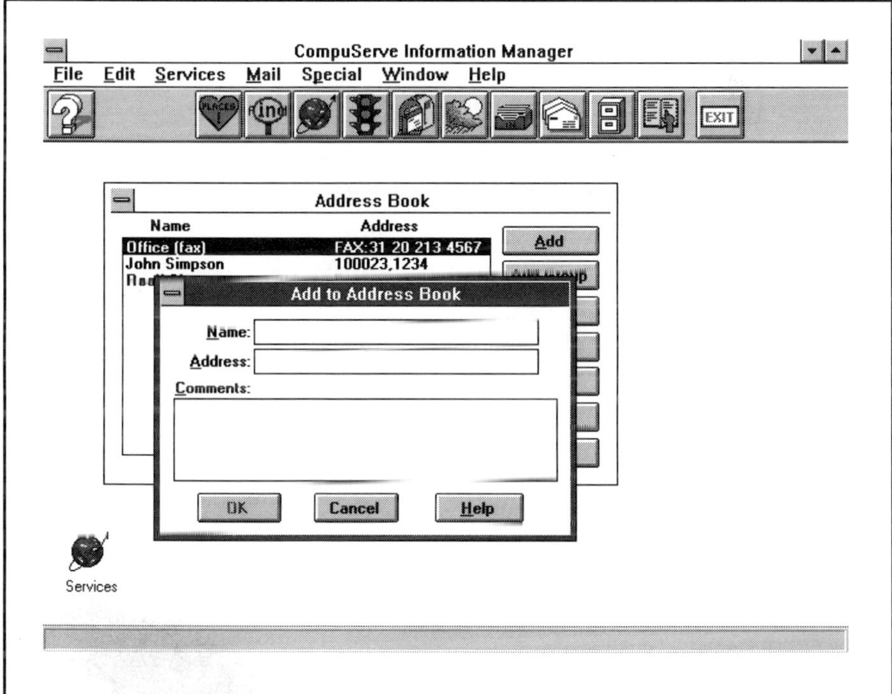

Figure 7.4 The 'Add to Address Book' dialog

- *Add Group:* When you regularly exchange e-mail with a fixed group of people, for instance when you are working on a team project, it can be wise to make a group entry for all team members. When you need to send a message to all members of the team, you can use the group name as an address, thereby assuring that every member of the team receives the message.
  When you press the `Add Group` button, the 'Add Group to Address Book' dialog is shown (Figure 7.5). In the 'Group Name' field, you type the name you would like to use as a general group address (for example, 'Project X'). Next, you can start adding names to the group: click on the `Add` button, after which you can select an entry from the Address Book. You are not restricted to names: it is also possible to nest groups inside another group. This makes the Group facility very suitable for matters like mailing lists, memos and so on.

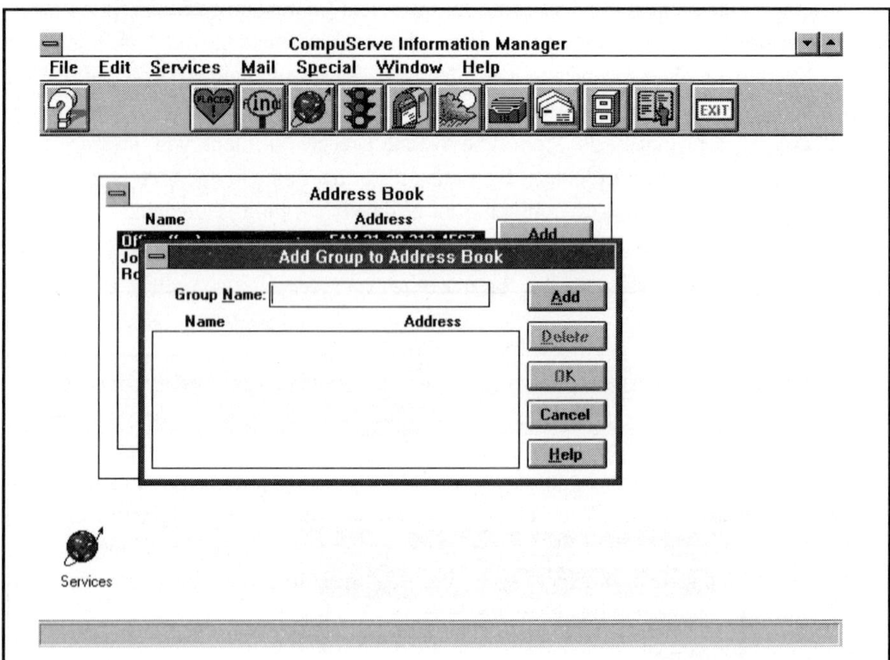

Figure 7.5 The 'Add Group to Address Book' dialog

- *Change:* Use this option when you want to change an existing group. You can change the group name as well as the entries it contains.
- *Delete:* When you find that you don't need a specific group any more, you can delete it and thereby release the space it occupied in the Address Book dialog. Deleting a group doesn't result in the deletion of the entries that were listed in it: these are still available as normal Address Book entries.

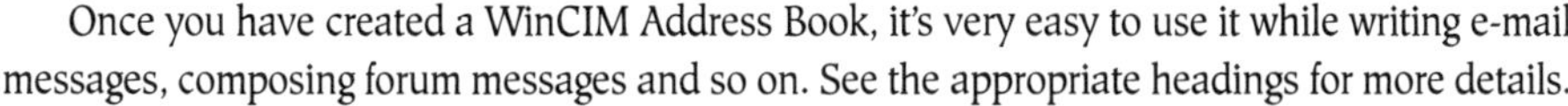

Once you have created a WinCIM Address Book, it's very easy to use it while writing e-mail messages, composing forum messages and so on. See the appropriate headings for more details.

7.2.3 Terminal mode

Once online, you can `GO DIRECTORY` to get access to the CompuServe Member Directory. `The Member Directory` Menu contains the following options:

1. *Explanation:* Gives you additional information about the CompuServe Member Directory.
2. *Member Directory Search:* This is the option you use to look up entries in the Member Directory.
3. *Include/Exclude This User ID:* Use this option if you would like your entry to be erased from the CompuServe Member Directory. After CIS have processed your request, your entry won't be visible any more: other CompuServe members will not be able to track you down *via* the Member Directory. This option can be handy when you have more than one CompuServe account.

As you will have guessed, option 2, `Member Directory Search`, helps you trace the CIS addresses of other members. CompuServe will ask you a few questions: after answering each question, you press the Enter key.

You start by entering the last name of the person you are looking for. If at this moment you change your mind and want to cancel the search, you can simply press the Enter key without typing anything at all. Otherwise, you enter at least three characters of the last name and press the Enter key. Next, CompuServe will ask you for the first name. You don't have to answer this question, but it helps to do so if you would like to narrow down the expected number of 'hits'.

After you have specified the name, CompuServe will try to obtain residential information: the city, country and state or province. Again, you don't have to specify this information, but you can narrow the number of hits if you do.

At any moment, you can type `/START` (and press the Enter key) to start a new search (and cancel the current one). If you'd like to log off quickly, you can enter `/OFF` at any prompt.

After you have specified the search information, CompuServe will begin scanning the Member Directory. The results (no, one or more hits) will be shown on your screen.

HINTS & TIPS

Save money!

Use the `capture file` option of your terminal program to record the information that CompuServe displays on your screen. That way, you can log off as soon as CIS has scanned the directory, and do the administrative work (like writing down and/or copying the entries) offline.

Filling in and editing the online address book

As part of the e-mail facility, you can use the CompuServe Address Book option. Every CIS member has his or her own online address book, which can be useful when you access CompuServe *via* a normal communication program. (Most specific CompuServe programs, like WinCIM, have built-in offline Address Book options). The CompuServe Address Book allows you to store up to 100 names and accompanying addresses. Once you have stored an address this way, it's much easier to send e-mail to it: you only have to enter the name, after which CompuServe will search for the matching address.

The first entry in the address book: you!

When you use the CompuServe terminal interface to send e-mail, and when you are the only one who uses a certain CompuServe account, it is a good idea to add your own name as the first entry in the address book. Every time you send an e-mail message, CompuServe derives the 'sender's name' from that first address book entry. This method saves you the work of keying in your name every time. This does not apply to users of access programs like WinCIM, which get the name of the sender from a configuration file.

It is not difficult to update the CompuServe Address Book. There is only one disadvantage: this is something that has to be done online. Proceed as follows:

1. `GO MAIL`, and select the `Address` option (or type `Address` at the `Mail!` prompt. The `Address!` prompt will be shown. All Address Book actions have to be carried out from this prompt.
2. To add an entry to the address book, choose the `Insert` option (or type `Insert` and press the Enter key). CompuServe will show you the number of the address you are about to insert (for example, 'Address 1', 'Address 2', and so on).
3. Type the name you would like to use in the future and press Enter.
4. Next, CompuServe will ask for the address. Enter the CompuServe address, or any valid e-mail address (see Section 7.7, 'Mail to and from other networks', for details about 'foreign' mail addresses).
5. After you have pressed Enter, CompuServe will ask you for the next address. If you have no more addresses to enter, simply press Enter to return to the `Address!` prompt.

There are a few other options/commands available from the `Address!` prompt:

- *Change:* This option enables you to change an Address Book entry.
- *Delete:* Use this option to delete an Address Book entry.
- *List* :This option shows you a numbered list of all entries in your Address Book.

- *Name:* When you have placed your own name and User ID in the CompuServe Address Book, CompuServe uses that information whenever you send an e-mail message. Using the Name option, you can change your name or delete it altogether.
- *Search:* When your CompuServe Address Book contains a lot of names (remember: the maximum number of entries is 100), you can use this option to search for all entries that contain a particular text.

Using commands? Abbreviate them to save time!

If you use the command mode, remember that all commands can be abbreviated to their first three characters. So instead of `Search`, you can type `sea`.

7.2.4 CompuServe Navigator

CompuServe Navigator doesn't have an option to automate the search for member addresses. Therefore, you have to resort to Terminal Emulation to find address information. If you don't have WinCIM installed, refer to Section 7.2.3, 'Terminal mode', for more directions on how to search using the online commands. However, if you are one of the many CompuServe members who use the powerful combination of WinCIM and CompuServe Navigator, you can use the search features of WinCIM to scan the Member Directory. See Section 7.2.2, 'WinCIM', for additional guidelines.

The CompuServe Navigator Address Book

CompuServe Navigator uses the same Address Book structure as WinCIM. Therefore, adding, deleting and editing address information works the same way. The `Address Book` option can be found on the `Special` menu of CompuServe Navigator. Refer to Section 7.2.2, 'A powerful tool: the WinCIM Address Book', for more details.

7.2.5 TapCIS

When reading e-mail and forum messages, you can press the [A] key to add an address to the TapCIS Address Book. This Address Book is actually an ASCII file with the name `USERID.CIS`, located in the TapCIS program directory.

Besides the actual name and address, you can key in a short description.

When writing e-mail and forum messages, you press the \ key, followed by an optional search string. The process is not as advanced as with the WinCIM Address Book, but it works surprisingly efficiently!

There is no built-in script to search for addresses online. Therefore, you will have to cope with the CompuServe Terminal Interface to get the address information you are looking for. There are two ways to do this:

- Go online `<I>nteractively`: choose the `I` command from the main menu. When asked for the forum to visit, just press Enter. After TapCIS has logged in, you are in the top menu. From there, proceed as described before, in Section 7.2.3, 'Terminal mode'.
- While TapCIS is busy executing automated commands, press the Esc key to signal that you want to stay online afterwards. When TapCIS has finished its business, you will hear a beep, signalling that you are now online interactively. From that moment on, you can proceed as described before, in Section 7.2.3, 'Terminal mode'.

Regardless of which way you use to get hold of address information, it all comes down to the file `USERID.CIS`, which contains the TapCIS Address Book. Because `USERID.CIS` is a no-frills, plain-text DOS file, you can edit it with any DOS editor, and even from within TapCIS *via* the `<E>dit` command. The pipe symbol (|) can be used to separate the name and address from the description. There are no built-in facilities to sort the Address Book, but feel free to do this yourself if you would like to.

7.3 Sending a mail message

The process of sending an e-mail message consists of three steps:

- Specifying the address of the person you want to send the message to.
- Writing the actual message.
- Sending the message.

The order in which these steps are executed depends on the software you use to access CompuServe. Of course, you save costs by doing as much as possible offline. In the following sections, we will show you ways to accomplish this.

7.3.1 General guidelines

A lot of tips that apply to forum messages (see Chapter 8) can be used for writing regular e-mail messages as well. Consult the following list for tips, techniques and general guidelines.

- Keep your messages short and simple. Don't use long paragraphs, and try to be brief and clear. And an important one: don't shout.
  That's right: you can actually shout while writing messages. But be assured: the addressee of your message will almost certainly give you a reprimand and tell you that shouting is not a nice thing to do.
  So how do you shout digitally? Well, in a very simple way: just write everything IN CAPITALS. BUT AS YOU CAN SEE FROM THIS TEXT, IT MAKES YOUR MESSAGE SIGNIFICANTLY HARDER TO READ, especially on computer screens. So do not shout.
- E-mail messages are composed and sent in plain ASCII, leaving no room for special characteristics like bold text, underlining, and so on. Therefore, you will have to resort to other means of accentuating your text. A few of the most often used methods are:
  - Use asterisks to surround your text, as is done with the *following* word. Experienced users of online services (and you will be one shortly!) know that the text is meant to be in *italics*.
  - In a similar way, you can <u>underline</u> your text by enclosing it between underscores, as is done with the with the _following_ word.
  - Another method you can use (but sparingly, for the above mentioned reason): put important text in CAPITALS.

  Whichever methods you use: take care not to 'clutter' your message by overusing these attributes.
- Be careful when making jokes! Don't forget that the recipient, when reading your message, doesn't see the expression on your face at the moment you wrote it. Something that you intended to be witty could come across as being too sarcastic, or even offensive. When in doubt, use special characters or abbreviations, like the so-called *emoticons*. Refer to Section 8.7.5 for more information and a list of commonly used symbols.
- Avoid 'flaming', a too-often used practice for 'punishing' people you do not agree with. Always picture yourself as the recipient of the e-mail message you are about to send. Would you yourself be offended by it? If you cannot help but answer that question with 'yes': back to the keyboard! See Section 8.7.5 when in doubt.

No-one to write to? Send a message to yourself – or to me!

If you are a newcomer to CompuServe, the chances are that you don't know anyone to whom you could send your first 'this is a test' message. In that case, you can send it to yourself! Just enter your name and CompuServe ID (the two numbers, separated by a comma) into your Address Book and make yourself the recipient.

However, if you would prefer writing to someone else, I really like receiving 'digital postcards' from all over the world! My CompuServe ID is 71333,1443, and there is plenty of room in my mailbox!

7.3.2 WinCIM

Thanks to a built-in facility called the *Out-Basket,* WinCIM allows you to do all the message writing offline. It is even possible to write more than one message, and send off the whole bunch in one online session.

When writing e-mail messages with WinCIM, you use one or more of the following elements:

- The WinCIM Address Book. This is a personal database, kept on disk, that contains e-mail addresses. It is very easy to maintain the WinCIM Address Book: see Section 7.2.2, 'A powerful tool: the WinCIM Address Book', for more information.
- The built-in WinCIM editor. This is a standard Windows editor, which has all the key commands that you find in edit boxes and in applications like Notepad. Because the WinCIM editor supports cutting and pasting of text *via* hot keys, it is actually possible to use your favourite word processing program to write e-mail messages: when you have finished, a simple copy-and-paste action is enough to transfer the message text to WinCIM.
- The WinCIM Out-Basket: an archive that contains all e-mail messages that you have written and that are waiting to be sent off. Because the Out-Basket can contain a virtually unlimited number of messages, you can write all messages offline before actually sending them. When you have finished, one command suffices to send and receive all your e-mail.

To write and send an e-mail message using WinCIM, you do the following:

1. Select the option `Create Mail` on the `Mail` menu. WinCIM shows the Recipient List dialog (Figure 7.6). This dialog allows you to specify the destination address, or addresses, for your e-mail message. Take some time to study the Recipient List dialog: there are several ways to fill in the respective fields. The `fields` and `command` buttons include the following:
   - *Name and Address:* In the Name field, you can type the name of the person you want to write to. The Name field and the Address field are linked to the contents of the Address Book: as soon as you type a few characters, WinCIM will scan through the Address Book for the entry that corresponds to the information you typed. If an appropriate entry is found, the Address field is updated automatically. If you want to specify a combination of a name and address that is not listed in the Address Book, you just type them in the respective Name and Address fields.
   - *Add:* Press this button to add a new name and address to the list of recipients of your message.
   - *Address Book:* In this box, the contents of your WinCIM Address Book are shown. After selecting an address (either with the keyboard or with the mouse), you can copy it to the Recipients box by double-clicking on it, or by choosing the `Copy` option.
   - *Recipients:* This box contains the future addressees of your e-mail message.

- *TO, CC and BC:* These option buttons refer to the status of the recipient of your message. If there is only one recipient, you do not have to bother with these options. But if you are about to send a message to several people at the same time, you could consider marking recipients for 'carbon copies' or 'blank copies', just as you would do when sending a company memo. There is a small difference between carbon copies and blank copies: addressees who receive a blank copy are not shown in the list of recipients.
- *Show Recipients:* This field determines whether or not all recipients of a message are shown in a special `Recipients` list, which is attached to each e-mail message to more than one addressee. When you do not want the addressee of your message to know who else received the same message, you can uncheck this option box.

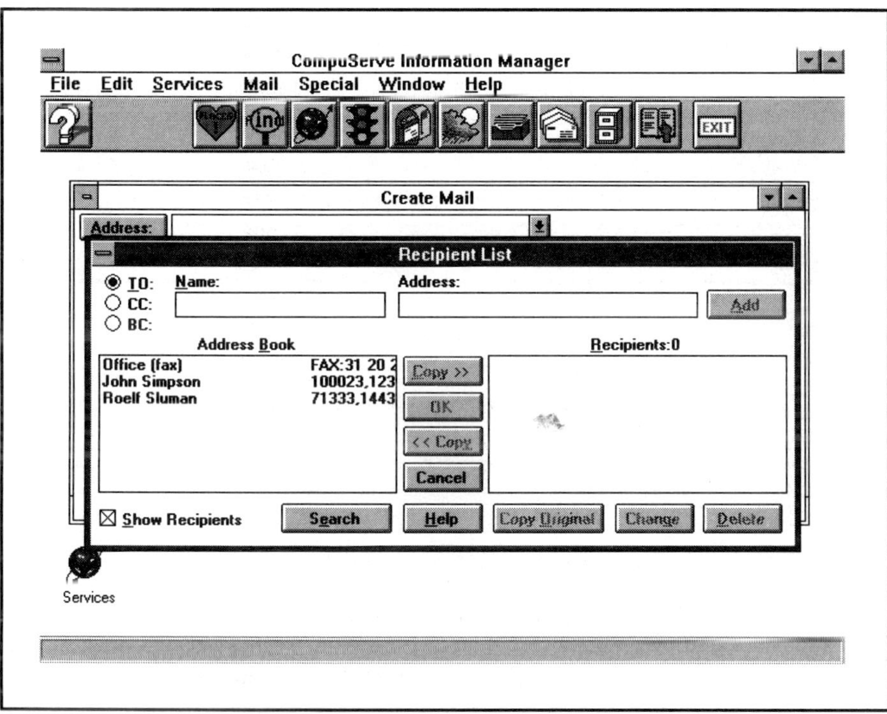

Figure 7.6 The 'Recipient List' dialog

2. After you have decided to whom you are going to send your message, it's time to actually start writing: press `OK` to display the Create Mail window. The name of the (first) recipient is displayed after the `Address` button (see Figure 7.7). As you might remember from Section 7.1, an e-mail message consist of three parts: an address, a subject and the actual message text. Now look again at Figure 7.7. Do you notice that both the `Out-Basket` and the `Send Now` buttons are greyed-out? The reason for this is that WinCIM detects that one or more of the obligatory parts is missing.

Write a small subject header that summarizes the contents of your message. When you have finished, enter the actual message text into the large text box. You will see that, as soon as you have typed the first character, both the `Out-Basket` and the `Send Now` buttons can be selected. WinCIM has noticed that your message meets all requirements.

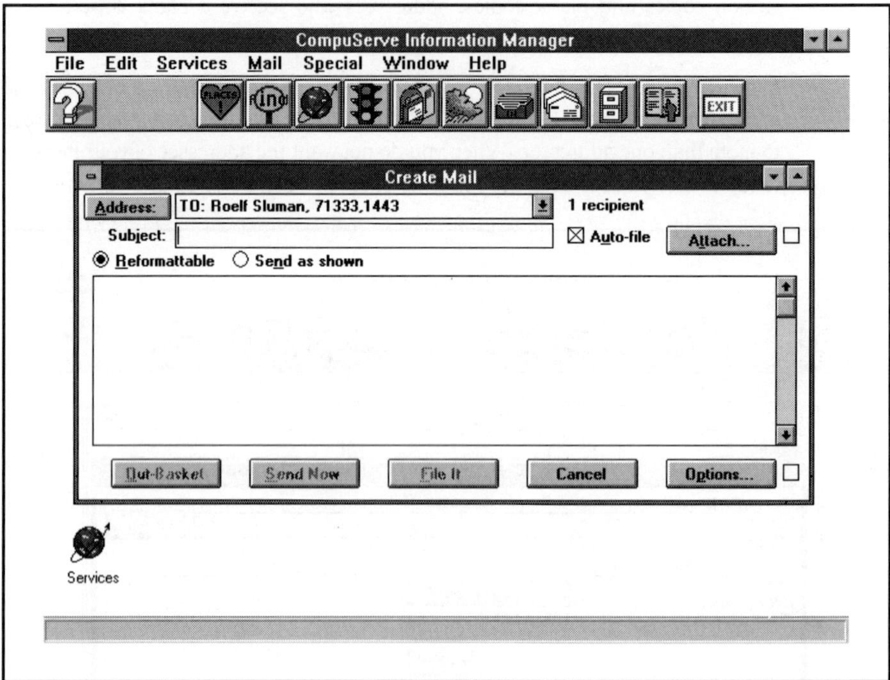

Figure 7.7 This is where you write your message: the 'Create Mail' dialog

3. When you have finished your e-mail message (see also Section 7.3.1, 'General guidelines'), you have two options:

   - You can put the message into your Out-Basket: a practical option when you want to compose more messages and send them all out in one session. Press the `Out-Basket` button. When you have finished writing all your messages, you can choose either the `Send/Receive All Mail` option (the e-mail contents of your Out-Basket will be sent, and your In-Basket will be filled with new e-mail messages sent to you), or the `Out-Basket` option. In the latter case, WinCIM shows a list of all the messages that are stored in your Out-Basket. See Section 5.7.1 for more information about the Out-Basket facility.
   - You can send it out right away by pressing the `Send Now` button. If you are offline, WinCIM will go online. Note that you have to disconnect manually after WinCIM has sent the message.

Tip: the WinCIM Ribbon

If you often create e-mail messages, you could consider changing the layout of the Ribbon. Once you have added a specific `Create Mail` button, you can start composing a new message by one simple mouse click. Refer to Section 5.9.4 for more information about the WinCIM Ribbon.

7.3.3 Terminal mode

Once online, you `GO MAIL` to enter the Mail Service.

CompuServe displays the `Mail!` prompt, as well as a status message reporting whether or not you have mail waiting:

```
CompuServe Mail
No messages pending
Mail!
```

To indicate that you want to write a new message, you use the `Compose` command and press the Enter key:

```
Mail! compose
Enter message. (/EXIT when done)
```

You can now enter the message text. This text will be placed into your *workspace*. Press Enter after each line. You can also insert empty lines, simply by pressing Enter more than once. Note that the editor does not support word wrapping. However, your text will be correctly formatted on the recipient's display, depending on the width of his or her screen. To indicate that you have finished the message, you type (on an empty line) `/exit`:.

```
Hi Roelf!
Too bad that I couldn't make it last night.
See you next week?
Regards,
John
```

```
/exit
```

After you have pressed the Enter key, CompuServe asks you for the addressee:

```
Send ($) to (Name or User ID):_
```

Enter the User ID, either with or without the name. If the recipient is listed in your CompuServe Address Book (see also Section 7.2.3, 'Terminal mode'), you only have to enter the name. A few examples are shown below:

```
Send ($) to (Name or User ID): Roelf Sluman 71333,1443
```

This is the standard way of doing things: the name of the addressee, followed by his or her User ID. An often-used variation is:

```
Send ($) to (Name or User ID): Roelf Sluman [71333,1443]
```

CompuServe ignores the brackets.
Another method: leave out the name of the addressee, as follows:

```
Send ($) to (Name or User ID): 71333,1443
```

And the last one, if the recipient is listed in your CompuServe Address Book:

```
Send ($) to (Name or User ID): Roelf Sluman
```

Next, CompuServe will ask you for a message subject:

```
Subject: _
```

This is where you type the topic of your e-mail message. The maximum length is 40 characters. An example:

```
Subject: Appointment
```

When you have finished, CompuServe lists a few details about the message that is about to be sent:

```
To:   71333,1443
From: John Brinkley
Subj: Appointment

Are your message and address correct? (Y or N)! _
```

You are almost there! As soon as you press [Y], followed by [Enter], your message is on its way:

```
Message sent to 71333,1443

Mail!
```

After completing an e-mail transaction like this, your screen would look more or less as follows:

```
CompuServe Mail

No messages pending

Mail! compose

Enter message. (/EXIT when done)

Hi Roelf!
Too bad that I couldn't make it last night.
See you next week!
Regards,

John
/exit

Send ($) to (Name or User ID): Roelf Sluman 71333,1443
Subject: Appointment

To:   71333,1443
From: John Brinkley
Subj: Test Message

Are your message and address correct? (Y or N)! Y

Message sent to 71333,1443

Mail!
```

Save money: prepare your message offline

Theoretically you could compose your entire message online (as was done in the previous example), but you would incur a lot of unnecessary charges doing so. Although the Mail service is free of connect charges, you would still have to pay communication surcharges, as well as your telephone bill. It is therefore good practice to write your actual message offline (using your favourite word processing program) and *upload* the message text to CompuServe. Real power users take advantage of a special message format to specify the recipient(s) and subject in the actual message body. That way, you spend only a very small time online.

The next message, a copy of the previous one, shows how this is done:

```
To: Roelf Sluman [71333,1443]
Subj: Appointment
Hi Roelf!
Too bad that I couldn't make it last night.
See you next week?
Regards,
John

/exit
```

You see that the first two lines of the message are different. These contain actual CompuServe directives, namely the addressee of the message (again, in any suitable format) and the message subject. These lines are followed by the actual message text. The last line contains the same *exit* command that you see in our first message.

Assuming that you used a normal text editor to write this message, and saved it on your hard disk, there are several methods to upload it to CompuServe. The first step, of course, is to get online and enter the Mail service:

```
!go mail

CompuServe Mail

No messages pending

Mail!_
```

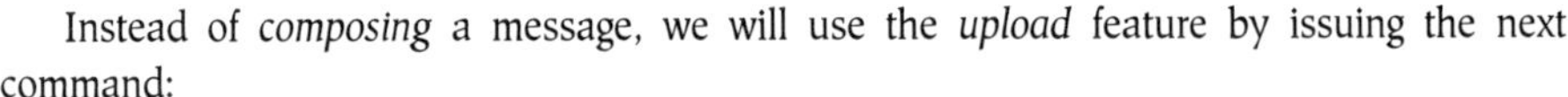

Instead of *composing* a message, we will use the *upload* feature by issuing the next command:

```
upload /pro:b /type:ascii mailtext.txt
```

(Yes, that's different stuff! But after all, you want to be a 'power user', don't you?)

Don't be scared by the seemingly complicated format of this command. It actually contains the following things:

- The actual command: *upload*.
- A so-called 'switch': `/pro` (the abbreviation of *protocol*). This switch specifies the upload protocol we are about to use: the b, following the colon. If we left out this switch, CompuServe would ask for the protocol anyway. But then, we want to get offline as soon as possible, don't we?
  When it comes to uploading and downloading files, CompuServe supports a number of protocols. The fastest one is the proprietary *CompuServe 'B' Protocol*, which is also supported by an increasing number of communication software packages. If your communication software does not support CompuServe 'B', consider switching to a program that does: you can use the much slower Xmodem protocol in the meantime. The CompuServe 'B' protocol is very fast, and has some excellent error-checking algorithms. And one last remark about Xmodem: the nature of this protocol (files are rounded to the next packet of 128 bytes) can result in problems when you try to send binary files (like MS-DOS programs).
- Another switch: */typ* (the abbreviation of *type*). You use this switch to specify the type of file to be uploaded. There are three possibilities:
  - Plain, seven-bit ASCII (as used in this example): `/typ:asc`. This is the fastest type, but you can only use it if your e-mail messages only contain regular ASCII characters.
  - Other text files, for instance files that contain foreign characters: `/typ:oth`. This is the one you should use for Latin 1 messages.
  - Binary files, like word processor documents and program files: `/typ:bin`. To learn more about sending binary files, refer to Section 7.4.3, 'Terminal mode'.
- The name of the file that you want to upload. Some communication programs can be 'polled' to start an upload and will use this information to send the correct file.

After you have pressed the Enter key, CompuServe will display the following message:

```
Uploading MAILTEST.TXT
```

If your communication program doesn't do so automatically, now is the time to start the upload procedure. As soon as your file has reached the CompuServe computers in Ohio, the next message appears:

```
*** File Transfer Completed ***

SEND! _
```

Next, you issue the actual command to send the message:

```
SEND! send
```

Normally, CompuServe would have asked you for the message subject and the address information. However, because this information is embedded in the message (remember the first two lines?), the correct information is displayed automatically:

```
To: [71333,1443]  Roelf Sluman
From: John Brinkley
Subj: Appointment

Are your message and address correct? <Y or N>! _
```

You're almost there. The only thing you have to do is press the Y key, followed by Enter. CompuServe will respond:

```
Message sent to [71333,1443]

Mail! _
```

That's it: you can log off, unless you have other online business to attend to:

```
Mail! Off
```

Uploading: your workspace

Beware: the previous contents of your workspace will be erased when you upload a file. In other words: it is not possible to compose some text online, add the contents of an uploaded file, and send off the result.

The main advantages of uploading messages instead of typing them are listed below:

- You save a lot of time online.
- You can use special symbols, like the characters in the Latin-1 Character Set. The Latin-1 symbols allow you to use accents, foreign characters and so on, a special feature for non-English speaking CompuServe users. These special symbols are not available when you type your message directly (*via* the **compose** command): you have to upload your messages to take advantage of this facility.
  Thanks to Latin-1, you can exchange messages in almost every language, without having to resort to tricks like 'artificial accents'. For example, German users can type 'schön' instead of 'schoen'. French users can type 'boîte' instead of 'boite', and Dutch users don't have to write 'kopieen' when they mean 'kopieën'.
  For MS-DOS users, the appearance of Latin-1 characters is actually related to the active code page. This gives you the additional benefit of being able to use characters that aren't even included in Latin-1. For example, two Hungarians who both use code page 852 can exchange messages with special Hungarian accents which are not available in other code pages. Although the characters involved would look different to someone who uses another code page, every user of code page 852 can see them.
  The same applies to messages in a language like Russian: just switch to the right code page to see them on your screen the way the sender wanted you to.
- You can use your own editor to compose your message text, without having to cope with the (rather primitive) CompuServe editor.

7.3.4 CompuServe Navigator

Writing and sending an e-mail message in CompuServe Navigator naturally bears a large resemblance to the same action in WinCIM. Proceed as follows:

1. In a Script Editor window, double-click on the `Create Mail Message or Send File` button. This opens the 'Recipient List' dialog, from which you can select one or more names you want to send the message to. Refer to page 211 for more information about this dialog.

2. After you have pressed the OK button, the 'Create CompuServe Mail' dialog appears (see Figure 7.8). In the 'Subject' field, you type a character string (maximum 40 characters) that specifies the subject of your message.

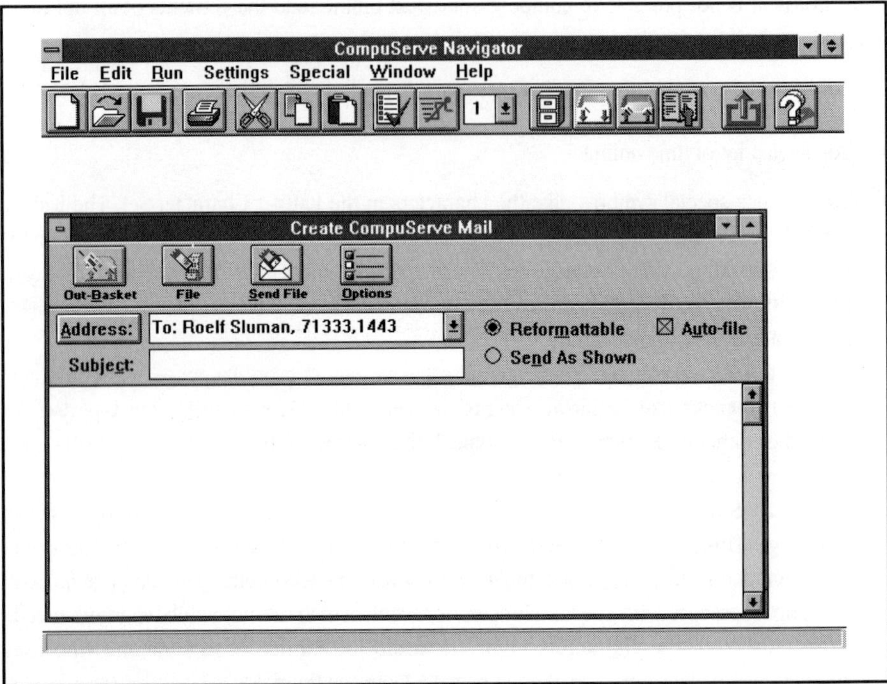

Figure 7.8 The Create CompuServe Mail dialog

3. Type your message text in the large text box. Because CompuServe Navigator is a Windows program, you can use standard Windows commands like `Paste` and `Paste From` (on the `Edit` menu) to paste text out of other Windows applications. This enables you to use your favourite Windows program to actually write the message: when you have finished, copy it to the Clipboard and paste it into the 'Create CompuServe Mail' dialog.

4. When you have finished typing and editing your message text, click on the `Out-Basket` button to put it in your Out-Basket. After that, you can either write some more messages or have the contents of your Out-Basket sent to CompuServe: run the script by pressing the `Run` button (see Figure 7.9).

Figure 7.9 Press this `Run` button to start the execution of a CSNav Script File

More on CompuServe Navigator

CompuServe Navigator is a powerful program, but can be quite confusing for new users. If you have problems, or if you would like to know more about the possibilities of this popular navigation tool, refer to Section 6.1 for a detailed explanation.

7.3.5 TapCIS

To send an e-mail message using TapCIS, proceed as follows:

1. Ensure that the Mail service is displayed in the `<F>orums` list. If that is not the case, press F to see the list of available forums, and activate forum A, `MAIL`.
2. In the main menu, choose the `<W>rite messages` option by pressing the W key. TapCIS will ask you for a forum: press the 1 key.
3. TapCIS asks for the address(es) to send this message to. You have two options:
   - Specify the address manually, for example `Roelf Sluman [71333,1443]`.
   - Select the address from your TapCIS address book. Press the Backslash key (\) followed by one or more letters of the name you are looking for. After you have pressed the Enter key, TapCIS will display all addresses that meet your search criteria. (For instance: to display all addresses that contain the string 'John', you press the Backslash key, type '`john`' (leave out the quotation marks) and press Enter.)
4. When you have specified an entry, press the Enter key. TapCIS will ask if you want to add another address (press the semicolon key); if you want to start composing the actual message, press Enter.
5. Next, TapCIS will ask for the message subject. Although CompuServe allows for subject headers with a maximum of 40 characters, TapCIS only lets you enter a maximum of 24 characters. See under 'Editing a completed message' on page 222 for a way to get round this limitation.
6. When you have entered the message subject, the edit screen is displayed. You can now type the actual text of your message.

Mailing lists

When you regularly send messages to the same group of people, you can consider making a *mailing list* of their addresses. This mailing list, a DOS text file, should contain the names and User IDs of every person in the group, separated by carriage returns, as follows:

```
John Brinkley  [100023,2743]
Roelf Sluman  [71333,1443]
Charles Wensell [100321,542]
```

Let's suppose you have saved this list (in your TapCIS directory), under the filename `WORK.LST`. When TapCIS asks you for the address(es), indicate that you want to use the list by specifying `=work.lst`.

Entering the message text: useful commands

When entering the actual message text, the following commands can come in quite handy:

- Reformatting the current paragraph: press Ctrl-B. This saves you the time of re-editing a paragraph when you have indented or deleted text.
- Inserting text from an ASCII file: press Shift-F10 or F9. This gives you the opportunity to prepare the message using your favourite word processor. Don't forget to save the text as an ASCII file!
- Import one or more lines from another (ASCII) file: press F2. TapCIS will ask for a search string. You can either enter search criteria (lines that match the criteria will be accentuated) or press Enter right away. After that, TapCIS will ask you for the filename or file type.
  For example, let's say that you send a message to someone who has asked you for the User ID of a mutual friend. Naturally, you have stored that User ID in your TapCIS address book. While you are writing the actual message, put the cursor on the spot where you want to insert the User ID and press F2. Type the first name of the person whose User ID you want to insert and press Enter, followed by V. TapCIS will now show you the first 20 lines of your address book, each one followed by a letter. To insert a line, press the appropriate letter. To see more lines, press PgDn.

Editing a completed message

When you compose one or e-mail messages, TapCIS stores them in a file called `MAIL.SND`. For last-minute modifications, you can edit this file directly, using an ASCII editor. It is also possible to use TapCIS for this purpose: press the E key to choose the `<E>dit a file` option. TapCIS will ask for a forum number: press 1 to select the Mail forum. Next, TapCIS asks what kind of file you want to edit. Press the S key to select the `SND` file. The contents of your

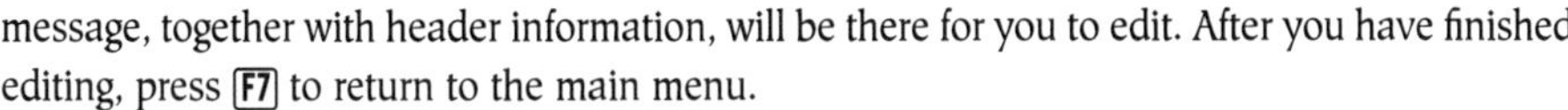

message, together with header information, will be there for you to edit. After you have finished editing, press [F7] to return to the main menu.

Work-around: longer subject headers

When you compose a message, TapCIS doesn't allow message headers that are longer than 24 characters. The official CompuServe limit, however, is 40 characters. If you definitely need those extra 16 characters, you can use the method described above to change the message header. But beware: when the message header is too long, CompuServe will not accept your message.

7.4 Sending a file

Besides regular messages, you can send complete files *via* CompuServe e-mail.

Do you send large files often? Save money while you can!

To calculate the price of sending a file *via* e-mail, multiply the file size (in kilobytes) by 0.025. Sending a file a hundred kilobytes long costs you $2.50. Sending a one-megabyte file costs you a steep $25.00! (Note that you get a $9 monthly mail allowance, so if you didn't send any other e-mail messages that month, CompuServe would charge you $16 instead of $25.) If you often have to send large files *via* e-mail, consider opening another account besides your normal one. By making this new one a 'pay-as-you-go' account (Alternate Pricing Plan) you pay for every minute you spend online. Let's say that you would like to send a one-megabyte file. When using your normal Standard Pricing Plan account, you would end up paying $25.00. Transmitting the file *via* your second account, at 9600 bps, would take about 20 minutes, which would result in a charge of about 20/60 times $22.80, which equals a little bit less than $8!

But beware. CompuServe knows about this 'loophole', so the chances are that they will take proper measures to close it. In the meantime however, use it to your advantage.

Etiquette online: announce your file

When sending a file to someone *via* e-mail, it is common practice to precede the 'file message' with a regular e-mail message, in which you announce that you are about to send a file. It doesn't hurt to include the filename: some communication programs use their own naming conventions when storing the file on the recipient's disk. Your very important WordPerfect document `CONTRACT.WPD` file could very well be stored under the name `MAIL1.BIN`, in which case the recipient of your file will have a hard time finding out what to do with it...

7.4.1 General guidelines

One of the most important tips when sending binary files: compress them! If you have used programs like PKZIP and ARJ before, you know what this is all about. If not: start saving a lot of money by reading the following section.

File compressing: a look behind the scenes

If you work with a DOS computer, the chances are that your computer uses a software compression schedule like Stacker or DoubleSpace to compress the data before storing it on your disk. Data compression is an intelligent method to make optimal use of disk space. Although you might expect differently, the methods of data compression are actually quite simple. The results, however, can be amazing: a good data compression algorithm can sometimes reduce the space needed for a file to no more then a few per cent of the actual size!

There are a lot of methods of compressing data. Which method is used depends on the structure of the file. Also important is the 'quality' of the data after being compressed and decompressed: the structure of some files (like some image types) allows for small losses, but when it comes to program files, even one missing bit can result in a complete system crash. Therefore, decisions about whether to compress *lossy* or *without loss* have to be made according to the purpose of the file.

HINTS & TIPS

Lossy compression online: JPEG

Have you had a chance to look at some of the weather maps that CompuServe provides? Or have you already paid a visit to the `NEWSPIX` forum? In that case, the chances are that you have already used one of the most impressive lossy compression schemes. The JPEG algorithm is gaining more and more popularity, because it allows for very small yet unexpectedly detailed files. WinCIM users can profit from the built-in JPEG decompressing facility to view the pictures on (amongst others) the `NEWSPIX` forum. Even the most detailed pictures, with hundreds of colours, are transferred to your screen within no more than a few seconds. And if you decide you need a better quality, you can always download the practically lossless GIF variant of the image, which is often much larger but offers an even better quality.

The first way, *Run Length Encoding*, is often used for files that contain a lot of consecutive, similar bytes, like images, tables, and so on. These files can be compressed easily by using a special *flag*, followed by a *count*.

Look at the following string:

```
abbaaaaaaceeeeeeed
```

As you can see, this string contains four different characters. First of all, we pick a character that we can use as a flag. In this case, we could use the character 'X'. In every case where a character repeats four or more times, we use our flag, followed by the character and a count. Our compressed string would look as follows:

```
a (the first character)
bb (the second and third characters)
X (the flag), a (the character that repeats), 6 (the number of
instances)
c (the tenth character)
X (the flag), e (the character that repeats), 7 (the number of
instances)
d (the last character)
```

The complete, compressed string would look as follows:

```
abbXa6cX7d
```

The result is impressive: we have limited the size of the original string (18 characters) to 10 characters: a compression of 55 per cent.

As you will understand, this is just a very rudimentary example. The actual compression algorithm is optimized to take advantage of several 'binary laws'. When it comes to saving space, programmers try to use every bit that is available! For example, when you have to compress a file that consists only of seven-bit characters, you could use the eight-bit as a flag, and the remaining seven bits as the actual counter. That way, you save a byte for every compressed string. Or you could use a combination of the Run Length Encoding technique and the *Huffman compression scheme*, discussed in the following paragraphs, to get an even larger amount of compression.

The Huffman compression method works quite differently. It is ideal for files that contain only a certain number of individual bytes, like most text files and word processor documents.

The principle of the Huffman algorithm is relatively simple. Yet, we will use an even less complex variation to illustrate the inner workings. We will compress the following example text:

```
Huffman is a very powerful algorithm to compress text files. It
compresses files by counting the individual characters.
```

First, we analyse this sentence by counting how often the various characters are used. In the following table, they are sorted according to frequency: the most frequently used character first, the least frequently used character last.

(space)	17	f	5	v	2
e	10	l	5	y	2
s	9	m	4	.	2
t	8	n	4	b	1
i	8	u	4	w	1
r	7	h	3	x	1
a	6	p	3	H	1
o	6	d	2	I	1
c	5	g	2		

As you can see, some characters appear (much) more often than others. As expected, the *space* character and the vowel *e* occur very frequently in our example text. On the other hand, characters like *x* and the capital letters are used rarely.

Now that we know the frequency with which the characters appear, we can start assigning unique codes to them. To do that, we will use groups of bits. Later, we will group these bits into a long string of bytes.

And here comes the key question. How can we separate one group from another? One way to do this is to use an exclusive combination that indicates the end of a bit group. In this example, we will use the combination '01'. As a result, the shortest bit group will have a length of two bits. Once again, look at our sorted list, which now has an extra column: the bit codes for the individual characters.

(space)	17	01	f	5	11101	v	2	1110001
e	10	001	l	5	000001	y	2	1111001
s	9	101	m	4	100001	.	2	1111101
t	8	0001	n	4	110001	b	1	00000001
i	8	1001	u	4	111001	w	1	10000001
r	7	1101	h	3	111101	x	1	11000001
a	6	00001	p	3	0000001	H	1	11100001
o	6	10001	d	2	1000001	I	1	11110001
c	5	11001	g	2	1100001			

As you can see, we have to take care that we never use the combination '01' somewhere in the middle of a group, for this would suggest the end of an encoded character, leading to unpredictable results.

Now that we have composed the codes for the individual characters, we can start compressing our text. The result in zeros and ones is shown below:

11100001 111001 11101 11101 100001 00001 110001 01	Huffman (space)
1001 101 01	is (space)
00001 01	a (space)
1110001 001 1101 1111001 01	very (space)
0000001 10001 10000001 001 11001 11101 111001 000001 01	powerful (space)
00001 000001 1100001 10001 1101 1001 0001 111101 100001 01	algorithm (space)
0001 10001 01	to (space)
11001 10001 100001 0000001 1101 001 101 101 01	compress (space)
0001 001 11000001 0001 01	text (space)
11101 1001 000001 001 101 1111101 01	files. (space)
11110001 0001 01	It (space)
11001 10001 100001 0000001 1101 001 101 101 001 101 01	compresses (space)
11101 1001 000001 001 101 01	files (space)
00000001 1111001 01	by (space)
11001 10001 111001 110001 0001 1001 110001 1100001 01	counting (space)
0001 111101 001 01	the (space)
1001 110001 1000001 110001 1110001 1001 1000001 110001 00001 000001 01	individual (space)
11001 111101 00001 1101 00001 11001 0001 001 1101 101 1111101	characters.

You will have to admit that the above looks quite impressive. However, it doesn't tell us anything yet about the actual size of the compressed text. One step is still missing: we will have to convert this code into regular bytes (every byte is eight bits long). We do this by placing all bits in succession, dividing them into bytes on the fly. The result is:

11100001	11100111	10111101	10000100	00111000	10110011	01010000	10111100
01001110	11111001	01000000	11000110	00000100	11100111	10111100	10000010
10000100	00011100	00110001	11011001	00011111	01100001	01000110	00101110
01100011	00001000	00011101	00110110	10100010	01110000	01000101	11101100
10000100	11011111	10101111	10001000	10111001	10001100	00100000	01110100
11011010	01101011	11011001	00000100	11010100	00000111	11001011	10011000
11110011	10001000	11001110	00111000	01010001	11110100	10110011	10001100
00011100	01111000	11001100	00011100	01000010	00001011	10011111	01000011
10100001	11001000	10011101	10111111	01			

That's it: we have compressed our text. The original length of our message was 102 characters. The number of bytes needed to compress it: 69. That comes down to a compression of 68 per cent. Not bad, but Huffman really shines with long texts, of several kilobytes or more. But you get the idea, and that was the purpose of this example.

I cheated!

If you have paid close attention to the preceding explanation, you will have noticed that something important was left out: the actual table of codes. Without such a table, no compression program would be able to derive the actual text. But as you will understand, when compressing a large(r) file, the actual compression table doesn't take up too much space. And apart from that, it is also possible to work with a fixed table, as some text compression programs do! That way, you don't have to 'hard-code' the table in the compression file.

This explanation should give you a very good idea of what compression is all about. Once again, please note that the examples shown are pretty basic. Skilled programmers have achieved real miracles and pushed compression to its limits. Also, new compression schemes are released constantly.

File compressing: the programs that you need

To be able to compress files yourself, you need one or more special programs, called *archivers* or *compression programs*. The names of the programs depend on the kind of computer (and operating system) you are using. Table 7.1 contains an overview of the most common compression programs. Naturally, you can download these programs from CompuServe: just visit the forum listed for the appropriate program. Refer to Section 8.8 for more information about downloading files from forum libraries.

Table 7.1 The most famous compression programs on CompuServe

Format: ARC	**Forum (GO word)**	**Library**	**Filename**
Commodore Amiga	Amiga User's Forum (GO AMIGAUSER)	Archivers/Crunchers	ARC.EXE
Apple Macintosh	Mac Communications Forum (GO MACCOMM)	Communication Progs/Utils	ARCPOP.BIN
Atari ST	Atari ST Prod. Forum (GO ATARIPRO)	Utility Programs	ARCLZH.PRG
MS-DOS	IBM Systems/Util. Forum (GO IBMSYS)	File Utilities	ARC602.EXE
OS/2	IBM Systems/Util. Forum (GO IBMSYS)	File Utilities	ARC2.EXE
Windows	MS Windows Shareware Forum (GO WINSHARE) (you need the DOS program PK204G.EXE to decompress this file)	File Utilities	WINZIP.ZIP

Format: ARJ	Forum (GO word)	Library	Filename
Atari ST	Atari ST Prod. Forum (GO ATARIPRO) (you need ARCLZH.PRG to decompress this file)	Utility Programs	STUNAR.ARC
MS-DOS	IBM Systems/Util. Forum (GO IBMSYS)	File Utilities	ARJ241.EXE
OS/2	IBM OS/2 Users Forum (GO OS2USER)	Tools	GNUARJ.EXE
Windows	MS Windows Shareware Forum (GO WINSHARE) (you need the DOS program PK204G.EXE to decompress this file)	File Utilities	WINZIP.ZIP

Formats: LHA, LZH	Forum (GO word)	Library	Filename
Commodore Amiga	Amiga User's Forum (GO AMIGAUSER)	Archivers/Crunchers	LHA138.RUN
Atari ST	Atari ST Prod. Forum (GO ATARIPRO)	Utility Programs	LHA232.TOS
MS-DOS	IBM Systems/Util. Forum (GO IBMSYS)	File Utilities	LHA213.EXE
OS/2	IBM OS/2 Users Forum (GO OS2USER) (you need the program PKZOS2.EXE to decompress this file)	Tools	LH2214.ZIP
Windows	MS Windows Shareware Forum (GO WINSHARE) (you need the DOS program PK204G.EXE to decompress this file)	File Utilities	WINZIP.ZIP

Format: SIT	Forum (GO word)	Library	Filename
Commodore Amiga	Amiga User's Forum (GO AMIGAUSER) (you need the program LHA138.RUN to decompress this file)	Archivers/Crunchers	UNSTUF.LHA
Atari ST	Atari ST Prod. Forum (GO ATARIPRO) (you need the program LHA232.TOS to decompress this file)	Utility Programs	UNSIT.LZH
MS-DOS	IBM Systems/Util. Forum (GO IBMSYS) (you need the program PK204G.EXE to decompress this file	File Utilities	UNSTUF.ZIP

Format: ZIP	Forum (GO word)	Library	Filename
Commodore Amiga	Amiga User's Forum (GO AMIGAUSER) (you need the program LHA138.RUN to decompress this file)	Archivers/Crunchers	UNZIP.LHA
Apple Macintosh	Mac Communications Forum (GO MACCOMM)	Communication Progs/Utils	ZIPIT.SEA
Atari ST	Atari ST Prod. Forum (GO ATARIPRO)	Utility Programs	ZIP25.TOS
MS-DOS	IBM Systems/Util. Forum (GO IBMSYS)	File Utilities	PK204G.EXE
OS/2	IBM Systems/Util. Forum (GO IBMSYS) (you need the program PKZOS2.EXE to decompress this file)	File Utilities	WINZIP.ZIP
Windows	MS Windows Shareware Forum (GO WINSHARE) (you need the DOS program PK204G.EXE to decompress this file)	File Utilities	WINZIP.ZIP

Format: ZOO	Forum (GO word)	Library	Filename
Commodore Amiga	Amiga User's Forum (GO AMIGAUSER)	Archivers/Crunchers	ZOO.EXE
Apple Macintosh	Mac Communications Forum (GO MACCOMM) (you need the program UNSTUF.SEA to decompress this file)	Communication Progs/Utils	BOOZ2.SIT
Atari ST	Atari ST Prod. Forum (GO ATARIPRO) (you need the program LHA232.TOS to decompress this file)	Utility Programs	ZOO214.LZH
MS-DOS	IBM Systems/Util. Forum (GO IBMSYS)	File Utilities	ZOO210.EXE
OS/2	IBM Systems/Util. Forum (GO IBMSYS) (you need the program PKZOS2.EXE to decompress this file)	File Utilities	ZOO201.ZIP

If you use another computer or operating system, consult Table 7.2 for a list of support forums.

Table 7.2 The most famous compression programs on CompuServe

Computer/operating system	Forum
Apple II models	Apple II Users Forum (GO APPUSER)
Apple IIgs	Apple II Users Forum (GO APPUSER)
Atari 400, 800, 800xl, 1200xl, 65xe, 130xe	Atari GAMING Forum (GO ATARIGAMING)
Commodore 64	Commodore Arts/Games Forum (GO CBMART) Commodore Applications Forum (GO CBMAPP)
Commodore 128	Commodore Applications Forum (GO CBMAPP)
NeXT	NeXT Forum (GO NEXTFORUM)
UNIX	UNIX Forum (GO UNIXFORUM)

7.4.2 WinCIM

Sending a file using WinCIM is not too different from sending a regular e-mail message. There is one major difference: you select the option `Send File` from the `Mail` menu, instead of `Create Mail`.

After you have selected the `Send File` option, the 'Recipient List' dialog appears. Please refer to Section 7.3.2, 'WinCIM', for an in-depth explanation of this dialog. When you close the dialog (after specifying one or more e-mail addresses), WinCIM displays the 'Send File Message' dialog (see Figure 7.10). This dialog contains the following fields:

- *Address*: The address of the person(s) you would like to send the message to. In most cases, you will have used the above mentioned 'Recipient List' dialog to enter this information. If you wish to add more recipients, or if you have other reasons to edit the list of addresses which send the file, you can do so by pressing this button.
- *Subject*: The subject of this message. That's right: CompuServe sees the file you are about to send as an e-mail message. Thus, you have to specify a subject, like you do when you are sending a normal e-mail message. The maximum length of the subject string is 40 characters.
- *File*: The name of the file you want to send. There are two ways to enter the file name. You can either type it (together with the disk and path where the file is stored) in the text box, or you can press the button. In the latter case, WinCIM will show a standard file selection dialog. When you have selected the file, press `OK`. The name of the file will be shown in the text box.

- *Additional information*: If you know that the recipient uses a CompuServe HMI program to read his or her e-mail, you can put some additional comments on this line. But beware: these comments cannot be read by people who use regular communication software or offline readers like TapCIS and OzCIS. As a general guideline, it is better not to put any important, not-to-be-missed information here.
- *Binary, Text, GIF and JPEG*: Use these option buttons to specify the file format. When sending normal binary files (like word processor documents, programs, and so on) you can leave the `Binary` button selected. If you plan to send a graphic file in one of the listed formats (`GIF` or `JPEG`), you can select the appropriate button. That way, the recipient of your message (when using the right communication software) can choose to have the image shown on his or her display while it is being received. If you are not sure which one to choose, just select `Binary`.
- *Options*: Click this button when you want the recipient to pay for the transmission, when you have agreed to split the charges, or when you have other preferences concerning this file message.

As with regular e-mail messages, you have the choice of either putting the file message into your Out-Basket or sending it off right away. Refer to Section 5.7 if you need more information about the Out-Basket and other WinCIM features.

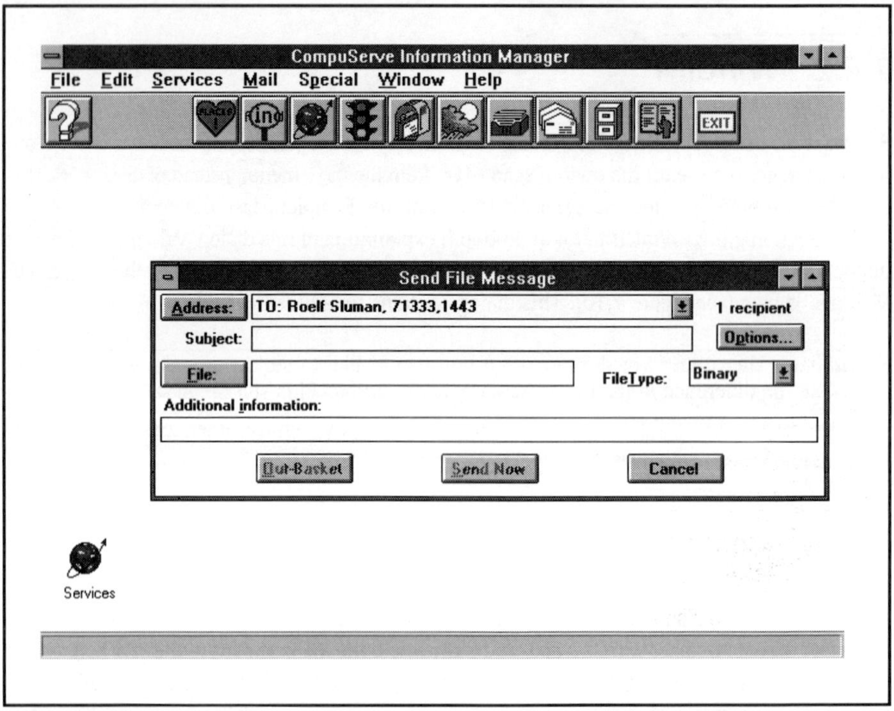

Figure 7.10 The Send File Message dialog

7.4.3 Terminal mode

If you have experience of uploading e-mail messages, you shouldn't have any problems with sending files. Because both procedures are practically identical, you can turn to page 216 and practise by uploading and sending a small e-mail message to yourself.

When sending a file instead of a regular e-mail message, the only difference is the file *type*. The following 'log' shows the online procedure to send a file called `TESTFILE.ZIP`.

```
CompuServe Mail

No messages pending

upload /pro:b /type:bin testfile.zip

Uploading TESTFILE.ZIP

Mail! Send

Send ($) to (Name or User ID): Roelf Sluman 71333,1443

Subject: File Transfer Demo


To:    71333,1443

From: John Brinkley

Subj: File Transfer Demo


Are your message and address correct? (Y or N)! Y

Message sent to 71333,1443
```

Note the difference in the `upload` command: the protocol is still the same, but the `type` is changed to `bin`, the abbreviation of `binary`.

7.4.4 CompuServe Navigator

Sending a file works almost exactly the same way as sending a regular e-mail message. That is, after you have selected or made a script that deals with the CompuServe Mail facility, you click on the `Create Mail` Message or `Send File` button. (See Section 7.3.4, 'CompuServe Navigator', for specific information about how to send e-mail messages with CompuServe Navigator.)

When you have entered the necessary address information and subject header, you click on the `Send File` button. CompuServe Navigator displays the 'Send File' dialog (see Figure 7.11). Specify the name of the file to be sent, either by typing it (don't forget the eventual disk and path name), or by selecting it from the 'File Select' dialog. Next, you place the file (or rather, the instructions that CompuServe Navigator needs to send it off) in your Out-Basket. Next time you run the appropriate script, the file will be sent to the recipient(s) you have specified.

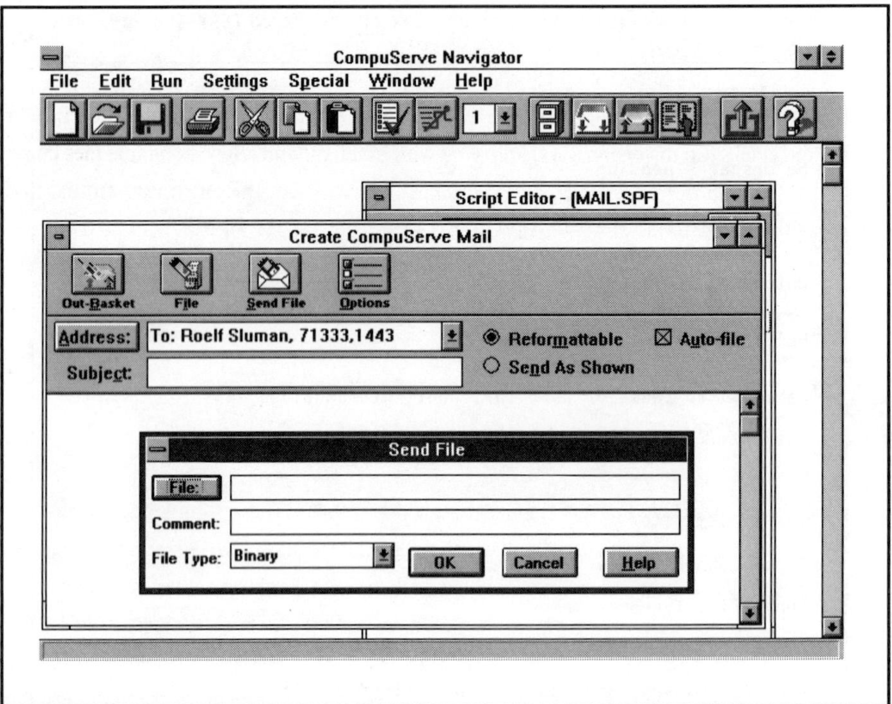

Figure 7.11 The CSNav Send File dialog

7.4.5 TapCIS

To send a file *via* e-mail, you take roughly the same steps as when sending a regular e-mail message. Therefore, refer to Section 7.3.5, 'TapCIS', for the necessary details.

New TapCIS users often get confused (I remember I did!) because there is no separate option to send a file instead of an e-mail message. The solution lies in the *message subject*. If you want to send a file instead of a normal message, enter at least one dot in the message header. (The name of the file you want to send almost always contains a dot.) TapCIS will ask you if you really wish to send a file (in which case you type the filename (don't forget the disk and path specification). If you intentionally used the dot, but don't want to send a file, press the Esc key.

When you have carried out all necessary actions, you can have TapCIS send the file as a part of its normal online actions, together with your e-mail messages, forum header request and so on.

Old TapCIS versions and the maximum file size

In former days, the size for files sent *via* CompuServe e-mail was limited to 512 kB. Old versions of TapCIS (up to version 5.41) still work with that limit and refuse to handle files larger than 512 kB. If you don't feel like upgrading to a newer version, there is a way around this limitation: specify the name of a smaller file (your `AUTOEXEC.BAT` file, for instance), and edit the `SND` file afterwards. Make sure that you specify the complete filename, including disk and path: once online, TapCIS will come to a halt if this information is incorrect.

7.5 Receiving a mail message

Receiving e-mail messages is even simpler than sending them. There is only one caveat: the costs of the message. In the old days, receiving regular CompuServe e-mail messages was free, because the sender paid for the charges. This has all changed, however. When you send an e-mail message, you can choose to pay the charges yourself, to split the charges, or to let the receiver pay in full. Message that have 'scrolled off' a forum's message board will be charged to the recipient as well; he or she will see a 'postage due' announcement for the mail message concerned.

Messages from the Internet

Sending as well as receiving Internet messages costs money; it's as easy as that. Per message, you pay $0.15 for the first six kB, and $0.05 for every two kB that follows. This can add up very rapidly, especially when you are a member of one or more Internet mailing lists.

If you use an auto-access program like TapCIS or OzCIS, go online interactively. Enter the `GO ASCIIMAIL` command and select option 6, `Set Options`. Use option 5, `Receive postage-due messages`, to indicate what CompuServe should do with messages for which postage is due. If you don't mind paying for them and just want to receive them as quickly as possible, set this option to `[YES]`.

HINTS & TIPS

You only pay once!

If you decide to read a certain postage-due message again, you won't incur any new postage-due charges.

7.5.1 General guidelines

If you use WinCIM to access CompuServe, check the Ribbon for waiting mail. On the right-hand side of the Ribbon there is a Mail icon; the status bar contains information about the number of messages waiting.

If you use a regular communication program, you will see the message You have mail waiting as soon as you have established the connection. The actual number of messages waiting in your mailbox will be shown when you enter the Mail service.

There are two ways to deal with the e-mail messages you receive: either you read them online, or you retrieve them to your hard disk and process them after you have disconnected. All the special CompuServe access programs discussed in this chapter have the ability to retrieve e-mail automatically.

After you have retrieved your messages, you can delete them from your CompuServe mailbox. If you don't delete them, CompuServe will keep them in your mailbox for 90 (regular messages) or 30 (binary files) days, reporting that you have new mail during all following online sessions. Your CompuServe mailbox provides room for 100 messages. If your mailbox is full, the sender of the next message is informed that there is no room in your mailbox.

7.5.2 WinCIM

There are two ways to retrieve your e-mail messages with WinCIM: manual and automatic.

Retrieving your e-mail automatically

Sending and retrieving your e-mail is actually one of the very few WinCIM activities that can be automated. In other words, you don't have to stay near your computer while WinCIM sends and retrieves your messages. When you select the option **Send/ Receive All Mail** on the **Mail** menu, WinCIM displays a dialog. Press the **OK** button to have the program send all e-mail messages from your Out-Basket, and to retrieve waiting e-mail messages into your In-Basket. If you check the Disconnect when Done box, WinCIM will even log off automatically.

WinCIM displays the number of messages it sent and retrieved on the status bar. If WinCIM has retrieved messages, they are waiting for you in the In-Basket; click on the special `In-Basket` button on the Ribbon, or select the `In-Basket` option on the `Mail` menu.

Retrieving your e-mail manually

Sometimes it can be better to check your mailbox manually, for instance if you expect some large files. It might be cheaper to retrieve those files during the evening hours, when the network and/or telephone charges are lower. If you retrieve your mail with the `Send/Receive All Mail` option, WinCIM will simply retrieve all mail waiting for you, including those large files. The manual method allows you to 'scan' your mailbox for urgent messages only.

HINTS & TIPS

Deleting unread messages

It is possible to delete a message without reading it: simply select the message and press the `Delete` button. Note that if the message was sent with a `receipt acknowledge` option, the sender of the message will be notified that you have seen the message. (The 'receipt acknowledge' facility sends a system e-mail message to the sender of a message as soon as the recipient has *seen* it. In other words: receiving a 'Message was retrieved' message does not tell you whether the recipient has read the message or just deleted it.)

To check if you have mail waiting, select the `Get New Mail` option on the `Mail` menu. WinCIM will go online and show the contents of your mailbox, if any. You can then open the messages randomly.

HINTS & TIPS

Erased or not erased...

If you use the `Send/ Receive All Mail` option to have WinCIM place any mail in the In-Basket, all mail messages will be deleted from your CompuServe mailbox. If you decide to read your mail manually, a particular message will be deleted from your mailbox only if you *retrieve* it in your In-Basket, or if you press the `Delete` button. Note that if you don't want WinCIM to delete any messages it has placed into your mailbox, you can select the `Preferences` option on the `Special` menu, followed by the `Mail` option. Uncheck the 'Delete Retrieved Messages' box in the 'Mail Preferences' window.

How WinCIM handles 'postage due' messages

By default, WinCIM will always retrieve any 'postage due' messages. To change this, select the `Preferences` option on the `Special` menu, followed by the `Mail` option. WinCIM will display the 'Mail Preferences' window, shown in Figure 7.12. This window contains the following options for postage-due messages:

- *Do not retrieve*: When you let WinCIM send and receive all mail automatically, it will leave any postage-due messages alone. These messages will stay in your mailbox; you will have to use the `Get New Mail` option either to retrieve them manually or to delete them.
- *Always retrieve*: This is the default option: postage-due messages will be retrieved with no questions asked.
- *Delete without retrieving*: This is a potentially dangerous option, as there is no way back: WinCIM deletes the messages without you ever seeing them. You could select this option temporarily if you have cancelled the subscription for your Internet news groups. That way, you won't incur any charges in the period until your cancellation becomes effective.

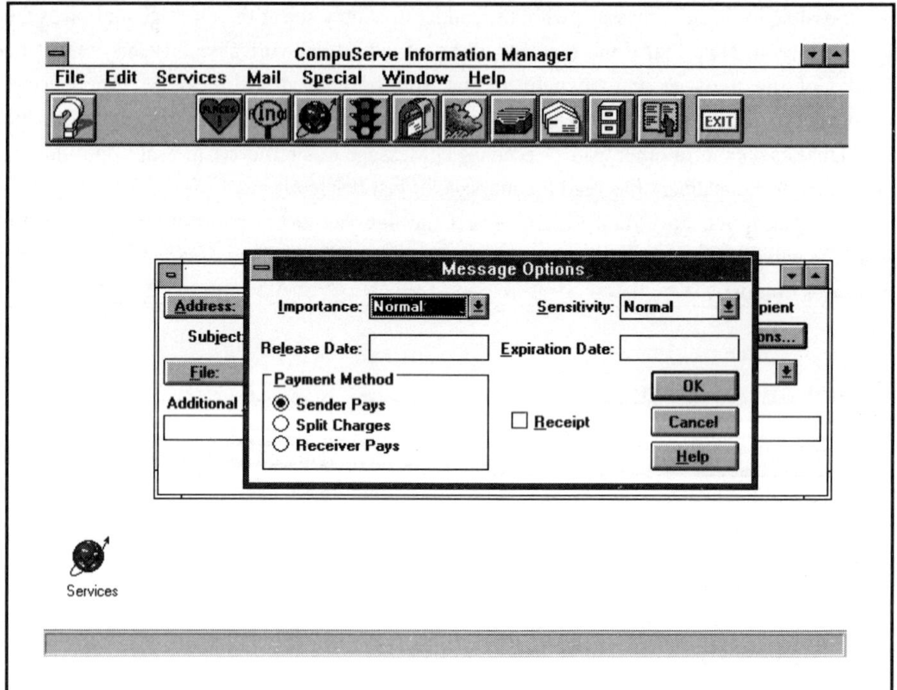

Figure 7.12 Change the default postage-due settings in this window

7.5.3 Terminal mode

In terminal mode, `GO MAIL` to enter the CompuServe Mail facility. CompuServe will tell you if there are any messages waiting. If so, use one of the following commands:

- *SCAN*: Shows a list of the subjects of all waiting e-mail messages. See below, under the heading "Checking your messages: the `SCAN` command", for additional information.
- *READ*: Displays a given message on your screen. This option is discussed under the heading 'Reading your messages: The `READ` command', on page 240.
- *DOWNLOAD*: Downloads a given message, or group of messages, to your computer. Use this command to download messages that contain binary text. More information can be found on page 240, under the heading 'Downloading messages and files: The `DOWNLOAD` command'.
- *DELETE*: Deletes a given message, or group of messages, from your CompuServe mailbox. If you don't delete the messages yourself, CompuServe will ask you whether it should delete them when you leave the Mail service.

Checking your messages: the SCAN command

When you have e-mail messages waiting, CompuServe shows the number of messages pending:

```
3 messages pending
```

Normally, you will want to check the origin of the messages first. To do this, use the `SCAN` command:

```
Mail! scan
```

CompuServe will show a list giving additional information about the messages:

```
1 Charles Wensell /contract.doc
   08-May-94 09:11 CEST 100321,542 Length 4575
    * Binary * Postage Due *
2 John Brinkley /Appointment
   08-May-94 10:42 CEST 100023,2743 Length 1129
3 Andrea Mayer /CALL ME!
   08-May-94 10:44 CEST 76004,3445 Length 101
    * RECEIPT notice pending *
```

The first message contains a binary file, with the name `CONTRACT.DOC`. Note the statement `* Binary *`; this file can not be read online, but has to be downloaded. Also, the statement `* Postage Due *` indicates that you will have to pay charges for downloading this file.

The second message is a regular e-mail message.

The third message has a receipt notice pending; as soon as you read or delete this message, CompuServe will inform the sender that you have seen the message.

Reading your messages: The READ command

Use the `READ` command to actually read the regular e-mail messages. It is not possible to 'read' binary files: you have to `DOWNLOAD` these to your computer before you can process them.

When you enter the `READ` command, you can either specify `ALL` or enter a range (for instance `READ 1–3` to read messages 1 through 3). After each message, CompuServe displays the `Action!` prompt. From this prompt, you can perform a number of actions. The most important are:

- *DELETE*: Use this command to delete the message from your CompuServe mailbox.
- *FORWARD*: This command lets you *forward* the message to someone else. CompuServe will ask for the address to forward the message to.
- *REREAD*: Use this command to read the message again.
- *REPLY*: Use this command to reply to the message. CompuServe will address the message to the sender, and use the same subject header.
- *DOWNLOAD*: This command can be used to download the current message to your mailbox. Use it if you get a `% Message is binary` error when you try to read a message.
- *ADDRESS*: Use this command to copy the sender's address to your CompuServe Address Book.
- *NEXT*: This command lets you proceed to the next message. Pressing the Enter key has the same effect.

Downloading messages and files: The DOWNLOAD command

Enter the `DOWNLOAD` command to download a message or file. CompuServe will ask for the protocol you want to use, as well as a filename. (See Section 7.3.3, 'Terminal mode', for more information about upload and download protocols). As with the `READ` command, you can specify a range of messages/files to download.

7.5.4 CompuServe Navigator

There are several possibilities for retrieving your electronic mail using CompuServe Navigator. In all cases, you will have to place a CompuServe Mail task into your 'Script Editor' window. More information about general features like the 'Script Editor' window can be found in Section 6.1.5.

- Click on the 'Retrieve Mail' folder and check the box in front of the `All Mail` option. The next time CompuServe Navigator goes online, it will retrieve all unread mail and place it in your In-Basket.
- Click on the 'Summarize Mail' folder and check the box in front of the `All Mail` option. When CompuServe Navigator goes online, it will retrieve the subject headers for all messages in your CompuServe mailbox. Next, click on the 'Retrieve Mail' folder. If you haven't yet marked the mail messages you would like CompuServe Navigator to retrieve, you can do so by double-clicking on the `Marked Mail` button. Finally, check the box in front of the 'Marked Mail' folder. Next time you execute the script, CompuServe Navigator will retrieve the marked messages and place them in your In-Basket.

7.5.5 TapCIS

To have TapCIS retrieve your e-mail automatically, select the `<N>ew` command while the `MAIL` forum is displayed in the forum list. If `MAIL` is not displayed, press the [F] key to display the Forums menu, followed by the [A] key to activate the `MAIL` option. When you press [F7] to return to the main menu, the `MAIL` option should be there.

TapCIS will retrieve all waiting e-mail messages, and delete them from your CompuServe mailbox. 'Postage due' messages will be retrieved as well; to leave them in your mailbox and retrieve them interactively, follow the procedure discussed in Section 7.5, 'Receiving a mail message'.

If there were any mail messages, TapCIS shows a `!` symbol after the `MAIL` label. Press the [1] key to read them.

7.6 Receiving a file

Receiving a file *via* e-mail is not too different from receiving a regular e-mail message. Apart from the *transfer protocol*, needed to get the message onto your hard disk undamaged, things work the same way.

7.6.1 General guidelines

When you have to retrieve one or more large files, it might be a good idea to wait until the evening hours, when network surcharges and telephone charges are usually lower than during daytime. The maximum size of a file that can be sent *via* CompuServe Mail is 2 MB. With a 9600 bps modem, it takes about 40 minutes to download a 2 MB file.

Naturally, things could go wrong when you retrieve files. Matters like bad connections and power surges could cause a download to be interrupted, leaving you with a file of whose last 200 bytes are missing...

Does that mean that you have to go through the whole download procedure again? Well, if you use one of the regular CompuServe access programs like WinCIM, CompuServe Navigator and TapCIS, you don't have to worry. These programs will detect the presence of (a part of) the file on your hard disk, and ask you if you want to continue the download, or if you want to overwrite the file. Most regular communication programs also support 'resumed downloading' check if this is the case for the program you use. Lack of a feature like this could be a good reason to consider the purchase of a communication program that does support resumed downloading. Believe me: it is not a nice feeling to have to go through the same download again (and, sometimes, again).

HINTS & TIPS

Is someone nice to you? You could do something back!

When someone does you a favour by sending some large file, you can show your gratitude in a graceful way. Simply notify the sender (before he or she sends the file) that you would like the charges to be split between the two of you. Note that only the sender of the message can decide to split the charges. It is important do this before the file is sent: there is no possibility of doing it afterwards.

7.6.2 WinCIM

Retrieving a file works more or less the same way as retrieving a regular e-mail message. The file will be stored in the `\CSERVE\DOWNLOAD` directory. After you have retrieved the file, check your In-Basket: it contains information that the sender of the file has specified.

7.6.3 Terminal mode

To retrieve a file that was sent *via* e-mail, you have to *download* it to your computer. To do this, you have to use the **DOWNLOAD** command instead of the **READ** command. More information can be found in Section 7.5.3, 'Downloading messages and files: The **DOWNLOAD** command'.

7.6.4 CompuServe Navigator

As with WinCIM, retrieving files works no differently from receiving regular e-mail messages. By default, the downloaded files will be placed in your `\CSERVE\DOWNLOAD` directory. To have CompuServe Navigator place them in another directory, select the `Directories` option on the `Settings` menu, and press the `Download` button.

7.6.5 TapCIS

TapCIS users are faced with a small problem when they retrieve files that were sent *via* e-mail. Although TapCIS downloads those files automatically, they lose their names. TapCIS will store them in the download directory, and name them `MAIL1.BIN`, `MAIL2.BIN`, and so on. It is up to you to rename the files. You can resort to the following methods to retrieve the original filename:

- Check the MAIL feature; TapCIS leaves a system message that contains additional information about the file. In some cases, the filename is included in the message comments.
- Check the special file that TapCIS uses to store download status information: `XFER.LOG`.

7.7 Mail to and from other networks

Sending e-mail to one of the millions of CompuServe members is easy. But it doesn't stop there! You can send mail to almost anyone with an e-mail address. And once you have stored his or her address in your Address Book, sending a message to that person isn't any more difficult than sending mail to a regular CompuServe member.

Of course, receiving e-mail from 'foreign networks' is possible as well. In this section, you will master the techniques necessary to benefit from this powerful feature.

Want to practise? Go ahead!

It is not always necessary to know someone on the network you try to mail to. In most cases, you can simply address the mail message to yourself. The message will sometimes travel a long way out of CompuServe, through unknown territories, and back into CompuServe, but it is possible!

Note that for sending e-mail to other networks, you pay the regular e-mail charges. However, receiving e-mail from those networks is not always free. When in doubt, `GO MAILRATES` for additional information.

7.7.1 Advantis

To send mail to an Advantis 400 address, use the following format:

```
X400:(C=country;A=IBMX400;P=private domain;S=surname;G=given name)
```

As a CompuServe member, you can be reached from any Advantis 400 address as follows:

- *Country*: US
- *Administrative mail domain (ADMD)*: COMPUSERVE
- *Private mail domain (PRMD)*: CSMAIL
- *Surname/domain-defined attribute (DDA) type*: ID
- *Given name/domain-defined attribute (DDA) value*: your User ID, with the comma replaced by a period.

7.7.2 America Online

To send mail to someone with an America Online address, use the following format:

```
INTERNET:address@aol.com
```

As a CompuServe member, you can be reached from America Online as follows:

```
id@compuserve.com
```

where *id* is your User ID, with the comma replaced by a period.
To send yourself an e-mail *via* this method, specify the following address, and replace 12345.6700 with your CompuServe User ID:

```
INTERNET:12345.6700@compuserve.com
```

Note that the gateway between CompuServe and America Online is actually an Internet gateway, which doesn't support binary e-mail messages. Also, you are charged not only for writing e-mail messages to the Internet, but for reading incoming Internet messages as well. See Section 7.7.14, 'The Internet', for additional information.

7.7.3 AT&T EasyLink

To send mail to someone with an AT&T EasyLink address, use the following format:

```
X400:(C=country;A=WESTERN UNION;P=private domain;S=surname;G=given
name;D=ELN:EasyLink number)
```

As a CompuServe member, you can be reached from any AT&T EasyLink address as follows:

- *Country*: US
- *Administrative mail domain (ADMD)*: COMPUSERVE
- *Private mail domain (PRMD)*: CSMAIL
- *Surname/domain-defined attribute (DDA) type*: ID
- *Given name/domain-defined attribute (DDA) value*: your User ID, with the comma replaced by a period.

To EasyLink via the Internet

It is also possible to send e-mail to an EasyLink member *via* the Internet. To send a message to someone with EasyLink number 62053511, the address would be `INTERNET: 62053511.@eln.attmail.com.` Note that you are charged not only for writing e-mail messages to the Internet, but for reading incoming Internet messages as well.

7.7.4 AT&T Mail

To send mail to someone with an AT&T Mail address, use one of the following formats:

```
X400:(C=country;A=ATTMAIL;D=ID:mail-id)
X400:(C=country;A=ATTMAIL;O=organization;S=surname;G=given name)
```

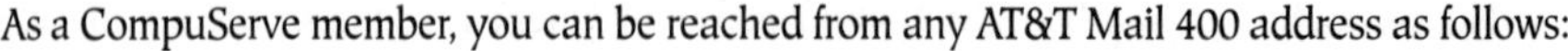

As a CompuServe member, you can be reached from any AT&T Mail 400 address as follows:

- *Country*: US
- *Administrative mail domain (ADMD)*: COMPUSERVE
- *Private mail domain (PRMD)*: CSMAIL
- *Surname/domain-defined attribute (DDA) type*: ID
- *Given name/domain-defined attribute (DDA) value*: your User ID, with the comma replaced by a period.

7.7.5 BIX

To send mail to someone on BIX, use the following format:

```
INTERNET:address@bix.com
```

As a CompuServe member, you can be reached from BIX as follows:

```
id@compuserve.com
```

where *id* is your User ID, with the comma replaced by a period.

To send yourself an e-mail *via* this method, specify the following address, and replace 12345.6700 with your CompuServe User ID:

```
INTERNET:12345.6700@compuserve.com
```

Note that the gateway between CompuServe and BIX is actually an Internet gateway, which doesn't support binary e-mail messages. Also, you are charged not only for writing e-mail messages to the Internet, but for reading incoming Internet messages as well. See Section 7.7.14, 'The Internet', for additional information.

7.7.6 British Telecom Messaging Service

To send mail to someone with a BT Messaging Service address, use the following format:

```
X400:(C=GB;A=BT;O=organization;S=surname;G=given name)
```

As a CompuServe member, you can be reached from any BT Messaging Service address as follows:

- *Country*: US
- *Administrative mail domain (ADMD)*: COMPUSERVE
- *Private mail domain (PRMD)*: CSMAIL
- *Surname/domain-defined attribute (DDA) type*: ID
- *Given name/domain-defined attribute (DDA) value*: your User ID, with the comma replaced by a period.

7.7.7 cc:Mail

To send a message to a cc:Mail user, the network to which that user belongs has to be registered at the CompuServe Mail Hub (GO MHS for more information). Once that is accomplished, use the following format:

```
CCMAIL:name at network
```

As a CompuServe member, you can be reached from any cc:Mail address (provided the network is registered at the Mail Hub) as follows:

```
id at CSERVE
```

where *id* is your CompuServe User ID.

To send yourself an e-mail *via* this method, specify the following address, and replace *12345,6700* with your CompuServe User ID:

```
CCMAIL:12345,6700 at CSERVE
```

7.7.8 CIX

To send mail to someone on CIX, use the following format:

```
INTERNET:address@cix.compulink.co.uk
```

As a CompuServe member, you can be reached from CIX as follows:

```
id@compuserve.com
```

where *id* is your User ID, with the comma replaced by a period.

To send yourself an e-mail *via* this method, specify the following address, and replace 12345.6700 with your CompuServe User ID:

```
INTERNET:12345.6700@compuserve.com
```

Note that the gateway between CompuServe and CIX is actually an Internet gateway, which doesn't support binary e-mail messages. You might be particularly confused when you receive your first 'binary' file from a CIX member *via* e-mail; CIX converts those files automatically into a special ASCII format, and splits them too. Section 7.7.14, 'The Internet', contains additional information.

7.7.9 Deutsche Bundespost

To send mail to someone with a Deutsche Bundespost address, use the following format:

```
X400:(C=DE;A=DBP;P=private domain;O=organization;S=surname;G=given
name)
```

As a CompuServe member, you can be reached from any Deutsche Bundespost address as follows:

- *Country*: US
- *Administrative mail domain (ADMD)*: COMPUSERVE
- *Private mail domain (PRMD)*: CSMAIL
- *Surname/domain-defined attribute (DDA) type*: ID

- *Given name/domain-defined attribute (DDA) value*: your User ID, with the comma replaced by a period.

7.7.10 FIDOnet

To send mail to someone with a FIDOnet address, use the following format:

```
INTERNET:first name.last name@ppoint.fnode.nnet.zzone
```

An example of a FIDOnet address would be:

```
INTERNET:john.simpson@p4.f3.n2.z1
```

As a CompuServe member, you can be reached from any FIDOnet address as follows:

```
id@compuserve.com ON 1:1/31
```

where *id* is your CompuServe User ID, with the comma replaced by a period.

Note that the gateway between CompuServe and FIDOnet is actually an Internet gateway, which doesn't support binary e-mail messages. Also, you are charged not only for writing e-mail messages to the Internet, but for reading incoming Internet messages as well. See Section 7.7.14, 'The Internet', for additional information.

7.7.11 GEnie

To send mail to someone with a GEnie address, use the following format:

```
INTERNET:address@genie.geis.com
```

As a CompuServe member, you can be reached from GEnie as follows:

```
id@compuserve.com
```

where *id* is your User ID, with the comma replaced by a period.

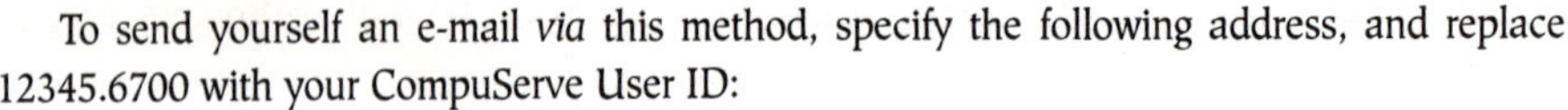

To send yourself an e-mail *via* this method, specify the following address, and replace 12345.6700 with your CompuServe User ID:

```
INTERNET:12345.6700@compuserve.com
```

Note that the gateway between CompuServe and GEnie is actually an Internet gateway, which doesn't support binary e-mail messages. Also, you are charged not only for writing e-mail messages to the Internet, but for reading incoming Internet messages as well. See Section 7.7.14, 'The Internet', for additional information.

7.7.12 INFONET

To send mail to someone with an INFONET address, use the following format:

```
X400:(C=country;A=INFONET;P=private
domain;O=organization;S=surname;G=given name)
```

As a CompuServe member, you can be reached from any INFONET address as follows:

- *Country*: US
- *Administrative mail domain (ADMD)*: COMPUSERVE
- *Private mail domain (PRMD)*: CSMAIL
- *Surname/domain-defined attribute (DDA) type*: ID
- *Given name/domain-defined attribute (DDA) value*: your User ID, with the comma replaced by a period.

7.7.13 Infoplex

To send mail to someone with an Infoplex (private CompuServe Mail) address, use the following format:

```
system-name:mail-id
```

As a CompuServe member, you only have to specify your User ID.

7.7.14 The Internet

To send mail to someone with an Internet address, use the following format:

```
INTERNET:address@domain
```

As a CompuServe member, you can be reached from any Internet address as follows:

```
id@compuserve.com
```

where *id* is your User ID, with the comma replaced by a period.

To send yourself an e-mail *via* this method, specify the following address, and replace 12345.6700 with your CompuServe User ID:

```
INTERNET:12345.6700@compuserve.com
```

Binary messages and the Internet

E-mail access to the Internet is limited to ASCII files only, with a maximum size of 50,000 bytes per message. Therefore, theoretically, it is not possible to send and receive binary messages to and from the Internet *via* e-mail.

But there is a solution for this problem. *Via* special utility programs that convert binary files into ASCII format and vice versa, you can 'encode' your file, split it into parts, and send it to someone 'on the net' who 'decodes' it. For more information about these programs, GO INETFORUM to visit the special Internet Forum. Or GO PCFF and search for files with the keyword UUENCODE. Don't let this scare you; encoding and decoding files is not as complicated as it seems.

Note that you incur charges for receiving e-mail messages from the Internet: a message costs $0.15 for the first 6 kB, and $.05 for every 2 kB thereafter.

7.7.15 MCI Mail

To send mail to someone with an MCI Mail address, use one of the following formats:

```
MCIMAIL:mail-id
```

where *mail-id* is the MCI Mail ID of the recipient.

```
MCIMAIL:name
```

where *name* is the registered name of the recipient.

As a CompuServe member, you can be reached from any MCI Mail address as follows:

- TO: *your name* [EMS]
- EMS: compuserve
- Mbx: *your CompuServe User ID*

7.7.16 NIFTY-Serve

To send mail to someone with a NIFTY-Serve address, use the following format:

```
NIFTY:mail-id
```

As a CompuServe member, you can be reached from any NIFTY-Serve address as follows:

```
CSERVE:mail-id
```

Replace *mail-id* with your User ID.

7.7.17 Prodigy

To send mail to someone with a Prodigy address, use the following format:

```
INTERNET:address@prodigy.com
```

As a CompuServe member, you can be reached from Prodigy as follows:

```
id@compuserve.com
```

where *id* is your User ID, with the comma replaced by a period.

To send yourself an e-mail *via* this method, specify the following address, and replace 12345.6700 with your CompuServe User ID:

```
INTERNET:12345.6700@compuserve.com
```

Note that the gateway between CompuServe and Prodigy is actually an Internet gateway, which doesn't support binary e-mail messages. Also, you are charged not only for writing e-mail messages to the Internet, but for reading incoming Internet messages as well. See Section 7.7.14, 'The Internet', for additional information.

7.7.18 SprintMail

To send mail to someone with a SprintMail address, use the following format:

```
X400:(C=country;A=TELEMAIL;P=private
domain;O=organization;S=surname;G=given name)
```

As a CompuServe member, you can be reached from any SprintMail address as follows:

- *Country*: US
- *Administrative mail domain (ADMD)*: COMPUSERVE
- *Private mail domain (PRMD)*: CSMAIL
- *Surname/domain-defined attribute (DDA) type*: ID
- *Given name/domain-defined attribute (DDA) value*: your User ID, with the comma replaced by a period.

7.7.19 Uniplus arCOM 400

To send mail to someone with a Uniplus arCOM 400 address, use the following format:

```
X400:(C=country;A=ARCOM;P=private domain;O=organization;S=surname;G=given name)
```

As a CompuServe member, you can be reached from any Uniplus arCOM address as follows:

- *Country*: US
- *Administrative mail domain (ADMD)*: COMPUSERVE
- *Private mail domain (PRMD)*: CSMAIL
- *Surname/domain-defined attribute (DDA) type*: ID
- *Given name/domain-defined attribute (DDA) value*: your User ID, with the comma replaced by a period.

7.8 Other mail facilities

As a CompuServe member, you can get your message across in ways other than e-mail only. CompuServe allows you to use the following methods as well:

- Fax messages, to almost any fax machine that is out there.
- Postal letters, to almost any valid mailing address in the world.
- Telex messages, to any valid telex number.

7.8.1 Sending fax messages with CompuServe

Even if you don't own a fax machine, you can send fax messages all over the world using your CompuServe account. Normally, the fax will be delivered within about 20 minutes after you have posted it. CompuServe will add a cover page to the fax message, consisting of information like the name of the recipient, the subject of the message, and the date and time the fax was sent. Your message may be any size, up to 50,000 characters.

It is not possible to receive faxes *via* CompuServe e-mail.

No graphics!

Note that it is not possible to send graphics or other binary information. The CompuServe fax service is text-only. Because the Latin-1 character set is supported, you can include accented letters in your message.

Sending a fax message works almost the same way as sending a regular e-mail message. The only difference, as you might have guessed, is the *address* you specify: instead of an e-mail address, you enter *FAX:*, followed by the fax number of the addressee. To send a fax to someone in London, you would provide an address like:

```
FAX:44717654321
```

or:

```
FAX:44-71-765-4321
```

(CompuServe will ignore any parentheses or dashes in the fax number.)
As you see, you supply the country code, the city code and the actual fax number.

You will be notified!

After you have sent a fax, watch your mailbox: CompuServe will inform you as soon as it has delivered the message. If for whatever reason the message couldn't be delivered, you will be informed as well.

The rates

All faxes that you send through CompuServe are transmitted from the United States. Therefore, sending faxes to Europe is slightly more expensive than 'staying close to home' and sending faxes to machines in the United States. Also, sending faxes to destinations like Asia and Japan can cost you a small fortune! The following list should give you a good indication. For additional information, `GO MAILRATES`.

- *Europe*: $0.90 per 1000 characters.
- *United States*: $0.75 for the first 1000 characters, $0.25 for each additional 1000 characters.
- *Brazil*: $3 for the first 1000 characters, $0.80 for each additional 1000 characters.
- *Africa*: Depending on the location: $3 to $6.20 for the first 1000 characters, $0.80 to $1.90 for each additional 1000 characters.
- *Japan*: $1.10 for the first 1000 characters, $0.90 for each additional 1000 characters.

Note that the charges you incur for sending fax messages will not be deducted from your monthly Mail allowance (if you are a member of the Standard Pricing Plan). You always have to pay for them in full.

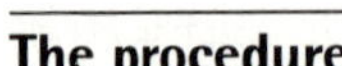

The procedure

If you use WinCIM or CompuServe Navigator: in the Recipient List window, enter the name of the recipient in the 'Name' field, and type the fax number in the 'Address' field, preceded by *FAX*: (don't forget the colon). Enter a subject, as you would do with a regular e-mail message. Next, type your fax message and press the **Send Now** button to send the fax immediately, or the **Out-Basket** button to place the fax in your Out-Basket.

If you use TapCIS: enter the name and fax number in the To field, as follows:

```
To: John Simpson >FAX:44-71-7654321
```

Next, enter a subject, just like you would do when writing a regular e-mail message. Write the fax text and store it as usual. The fax message will be sent to CompuServe when you select either the <N>ew or the <O>nline command.

If you use a regular communication program to access CompuServe, GO MAIL and proceed just as when you write a regular e-mail message. When prompted for the address to send the message to, enter the name and fax number, as follows:

```
John Simpson >FAX:44-71-7654321
```

Sending the same fax to several addresses

Just as with a regular e-mail message, you can have CompuServe send multiple copies of the fax to several fax machines. Just enter the fax numbers the same way as you would with e-mail addresses.

Designing your own cover sheets

CompuServe will add a cover page to the fax message, consisting of the following information:

- The text 'FACSIMILE COVER PAGE'.
- The text 'To:', followed by the name of the recipient.
- The text 'From:', followed by your name.
- The text 'Date:', followed by the date and time (in American format) CompuServe sent the fax.
- The text 'Subject:', followed by the text you typed in the 'Subject' field of the message.

Although the default cover pages used by CompuServe will be sufficient in most cases, you can actually 'design' your own cover page. This can be handy if you want the cover page to be in your own language, for instance. Also, custom cover pages allow for fax messages that consist of a cover page only, with the actual text included.

To design a cover page, you place a series of commands before the actual text for the fax message. The first line of your fax message should contain the following text only:

```
\CUSTOM\
```

To indicate the text for your new cover page, you use the following two commands:

```
\BEGIN COVER\
\END COVER\
```

Anything between those two commands will be interpreted as cover page information, up to a maximum of 50 lines. Note that text between the commands `\CUSTOM\` and `\BEGIN COVER\` is ignored.

If you wish, you can include special codes in your cover page; CompuServe will replace these codes by text. The available codes are:

- *\TO NAME*: When CompuServe sends the fax, it will replace this code by the name of the recipient. If, when sending a fax message, you have specified a fax number only, CompuServe will insert the text 'Recipient'.
  The `\TO NAME\` code can be abbreviated to `\TO\`.
- *\FROM NAME*: This code will be replaced by your name. You can abbreviate this code to `\FROM\`.
- *\SUBJECT*: This code will be replaced by the text you have entered in the Subject field of the message.
- *\DATE*: This code will be replaced by the time and date the fax message was sent by CompuServe. The format of this information cannot be changed.
- *\FAX PHONE*: This code will be replaced by the recipient's fax number. Note that you can abbreviate this code to `\PHONE\`.
- *\BANNER*: This code will be replaced by the text '`FACSIMILE COVER PAGE`', in a larger (24-point) font. It is not possible to alter this text.

A typical example of a cover page is:

```
\CUSTOM\
\BEGIN COVER\
F A X   M E S S A G E

To:        \TO NAME\
From:      \FROM NAME\
Subject:   \SUBJECT\
Date:      \DATE\

This cover page is sent through the CompuServe Fax service.
\END COVER\
```

If you need more information

For more help on sending faxes through CompuServe mail, `GO ASCIIMAIL` and enter `HELP FAX`. If you want more information about designing your own cover pages, `GO ASCIIMAIL` and enter `HELP FAX COVER_PAGE`.

7.8.2 Sending postal letters via CompuServe

You can use your CompuServe mailbox to send regular, 'snail-mail' postal letters. CompuServe will laser-print your message, put it in an envelope and send it to any regular postal address in the world.

The rates

Naturally, you are charged for this service:

- Postal letters to an address within the United States cost $1.50 for the first page and $0.20 for each additional page.
- Postal letters to any other address, including Europe, cost $2.50 for the first page and $0.20 for each additional page.

Note that the charges you incur for sending postal letters will not be deducted from your monthly Mail allowance (if you are a member of the Standard Pricing Plan). You always have to pay for them in full.

The procedure

There is one drawback to sending postal letters *via* CompuServe e-mail: you have to do it interactively, regardless of which access program you use. Normally, you would proceed as follows:

1. Compose the message text offline, using a general ASCII editor. Save the message as a plain ASCII file. Note that the maximum line length is 80 characters, and that your message may be no longer than 219 lines, which equals four pages. Use ASCII characters only; accented characters are not allowed and will be removed from your message.
   The last line of your message should contain the text **/EXIT**.

No graphics, please!

It is not possible to include graphics or other binary information in your message. You can include tabs, however, as well as Ctrl-L codes to have the following text start on a new page.

2. **Go ASCIIMAIL** interactively:
   - If you use WinCIM: **GO ASCIIMAIL**.
   - If you use a regular communication program: **GO MAIL**.
   - If you use CompuServe Navigator: either go online interactively and **GO ASCIIMAIL**, or place a terminal task into your script window
   - If you use TapCIS: give the **<I>nteractive** command and **GO MAIL**.
3. Here is where the fun starts: you have to upload the message that you prepared earlier. One way to do this is to type the command `upload /pro:b /type:ascii mailtext.txt`. You could also type `compose`, press the Enter key, and issue an ASCII upload from your communication program.
4. When CompuServe asks for the destination address ("Send to:"), enter **POSTAL** and press the Enter key. Next, CompuServe will ask for the following information:
   - *Recipient's name*: This is an easy one: type the name of the person you want to send the postal letter to.
   - *Title/Company*: This is an optional field; you can leave it blank if you wish.

- *Address Line 1*: If you need to include office, building or apartment information in the address, place it on this line. Otherwise type the regular address (street + number, or a postbox).
- *Address Line 2*: This is an optional field; you can leave it blank if you have specified the complete address on the previous line.
- *City*: The city. Don't place a postal code on this line.
- *State or Province*: If the letter is to be sent to an American address, you can either write the full name or use the standard abbreviation in this field. If you want to send the letter to a Canadian province, you can enter the name of that province. If the letter is to be sent to another address: enter the country name. CompuServe will detect that this is not a valid state name and show the next field.
- *Zip*: This field only appears when you have specified a valid state or province name. Enter the zip code.
- *Country*: The name of the country. This field will only appear if you have specified an invalid state or province name.
- *Postal code*: This is an optional field; you can leave it blank if there exists no postal code for the address.

5. After you have verified and confirmed the address information, CompuServe will ask for your return address. If you have entered your address information in the CompuServe Address Book, you will have to confirm that this information is still correct.

That's it: CompuServe will drop your message at the nearest post office and send you a confirmation message afterwards.

HINTS & TIPS

Use your CompuServe Address Book!

If you send postal messages regularly, you can save online time if you place the address information of your most important recipients in your CompuServe Address Book. That way, you only have to specify the name of the recipient when prompted. CompuServe will search your Address Book and use the information for that recipient automatically.

7.8.3 Sending telex messages via CompuServe

Although telex services are rapidly becoming obsolete, there are still countries that rely on them. It is nice to know that you can use your CompuServe mailbox to send and receive telexes to and from any Telex I or Telex II machine in the world.

Sending a telex message is no more difficult than sending a regular e-mail message. In the Address field, you enter the text `TELEX:`, followed by the country code and telex number.

The rates

You will be charged separately for sending telex messages:

- For destinations in the United States, you pay $1.15 for each 300 characters sent.
- For destinations in Europe, you pay from $1.15 to $2.80 for each 300 characters sent, depending on the location.
- For other destinations, expect to pay rates up to $5.50 for each 300 characters sent.

For actual rate information, `GO ASCIIMAIL` and type `HELP TELEX`.

Note that the charges you incur for sending telexes will not be deducted from your monthly Mail allowance (if you are a member of the Standard Pricing Plan). You always have to pay for them in full.

The procedure

If you use WinCIM or CompuServe Navigator: in the 'Recipient List' window, enter the name of the recipient in the 'Name' field, and type the three-digit country code and the telex number in the address field, preceded by `TELEX:` (don't forget the colon). Enter a subject, as you would do with a regular e-mail message. Next, type your telex message and press the `Send Now` button to send the telex immediately, or the `Out-Basket` button to place the telex in your Out-Basket. The maximum length of the message is 50,000 characters.

If you use TapCIS: enter the name and telex number in the To field, as follows:

```
To: John Simpson >TELEX:8507654321 answerback code
```

Although the answerback code can be omitted most of the time, you will have to send it in some cases. When in doubt, consult the recipient of your message.

Next, enter a subject, just like you would do when writing a regular e-mail message. Write the message text and store it as usual. The telex message will be sent to CompuServe when you select either the `<N>ew` or the `<O>nline` command.

If you use a regular communication program to access CompuServe, `GO MAIL` and proceed just as when you write a regular e-mail message. When prompted for the address to send the message to, enter the name, country code and telex number, as follows:

```
John Simpson >TELEX:8507654321 answerback code
```

Although the answerback code can be omitted most of the time, you will have to send it in some cases. When in doubt, consult the recipient of your message.

Sending the same message to several addresses

Just as with a regular e-mail message, you can have CompuServe send multiple copies of the message to several telex machines, and even to normal e-mail addresses. Just enter the telex numbers the same way you would do with e-mail addresses.

Receiving telex messages

It is a little-known fact that you can use your CompuServe mailbox to receive telex messages. The sender must do the following:

- The first line of the message must contain the text *TO:*, followed by your CompuServe User ID.
- If the sender wants to include a message subject, it should be placed on the second line, after the text *RE:*.
- The CompuServe telex number is 3762848. The answerback code is COMPUSERVE.

8 Forums

Forums

When it comes to meeting people, exchanging ideas, doing business, and getting the latest information as soon as it becomes available, forums are the route to follow. Twenty four hours a day members from all over the world meet in the several hundred forums that CompuServe offers. Every day, many thousands of forum messages are exchanged. Their contents vary: questions about a new word processing program, advice about Japanese restaurants in Amsterdam, heated discussions about political topics and an occasional flirtation between two members of the online community are only a few examples.

Thousands of CompuServe members visit one or more forums every day. Yet, not everybody is that confident. To a lot of people, forums seem like complicated services that are best avoided until a later time, when they have more experience on line.

Too bad. Although a lot of fun can be had while using facilities like e-mail, news and weather, and the online databases, the real thrill starts the moment you get involved in discussions between fellow members (or, for starters, just monitor them). I have met a lot of people online, most of them as a result of exchanging forum messages. Some of them I have even met for real: always an interesting experience! When it comes to a medium where looks, age – and sometimes even gender – are of secondary importance, you are in for some nice surprises when you actually get to meet someone you have known for a long time...

CompuServe forums all work the same way: when you have mastered the elementary techniques needed to post messages, download files and participate in an online conference, you can visit any forum without having to go through a learning curve again. But let's slow down a bit, lean back and take a closer look at a typical CompuServe forum.

8.1 The structure of a forum

Basically, a forum consists of three parts:

- *Message sections*: This is where the action is. Hundreds of discussions are going on in the message sections all simultaneously. Twenty four hours a day, forum members are busy reading the messages that others have posted, replying to them, or starting their own so-called 'message threads'. Forum messages are discussed in Section 8.7, 'Messages'.
- *File library*: Loaded with hundreds, sometimes thousands of files, the library is the place to turn to whenever you need in-depth information about a subject, when you are looking for updates of your favourite programs, or simply when you are in the mood for some new computer games! But it doesn't end there. Because you can contribute (upload) your own files as well, you have the possibility of sharing your pictures, sound effects, and even your latest piece of self-programmed master code with thousands of other forum members. More information about the file library can be found in Section 8.8, 'Files'.
- *Conference rooms*: Do you feel like chatting with a few forum visitors? Or would you like to attend the weekly 'Thank God It's Friday' meeting? In that case, hurry to one of the Conference rooms which are present in most of the forums. Although online chatting is not the most efficient way to spend your time online, it gives you plenty of opportunities to meet with fellow members. That is why quite a number of CompuServe members visit the Conference rooms from time to time. Section 8.9, 'Conferencing', contains more information about this fascinating feature.

It is not a hard-and-fast rule that a forum must contain all three features, although most forums do. Conference rooms for instance are normally not available in the free forums, and there are forums that provide only a file library and no message sections.

8.2 Finding the forum you're looking for

CompuServe contains hundreds and hundreds of forums, and new forums are added on a regular basis. It's quite logical that you feel 'lost in the dark'! But happily, there are ways of obtaining information about what forums are available, and how to reach them.

8.2.1 FIND...

The `FIND` feature is a very powerful way to get a list of services (not only forums, but other CompuServe services as well) that pertain to a certain *keyword*. The way to issue the `FIND` command depends on the access program you use.

The FIND feature is free: you don't incur any connect charges but communication surcharges still apply.

WinCIM

Select the Find option on the Services menu, or click on the Find button, located on the Ribbon. Enter a keyword in the dialog and press the Enter key, or click on the OK button. WinCIM will go online and retrieve a list of services that, in one way or another, cover the keyword you just typed. You can either GO to a service directly, or add one or more services to your list of Favorite Places.

HINTS & TIPS

Use the CompuServe Directory!

The complete version of WinCIM comes with a special file: the CompuServe Directory. This file, in Windows Help format, contains a comprehensive list of all CompuServe services, with additional information about each service; it should be the first resource you turn to. To consult the CompuServe Directory, select the CompuServe Directory option on the Help menu.

Terminal mode

GO INDEX. CompuServe displays the following menu:

```
CompuServe Index (FREE)  INDEX

FIND A TOPIC

 1 Search for Topics of Interest
 2 List ALL Indexed Topics
 3 Explanation of Index

Enter choice!
```

Press 1 to select the Search for Topics of Interest option. CompuServe responds as follows:

```
Enter topic (e.g. stock) :
```

Enter the topic you are interested in. After a few moments, CompuServe will show a list of forums and other services that pertain to the topic you entered. The official name of the service is displayed first, followed by the GO word for that service.

CompuServe Navigator

There are two ways to get a list of available services that deal with a particular keyword, only one of them requires you to go online.

- Select the CompuServe Directory option on the Help menu to access a large Windows help file with comprehensive information about the available CompuServe services.
- Go online in terminal mode and use the CompuServe Index. Refer to page 281, under the heading 'Terminal mode', for more information.

TapCIS

Go online interactively by selecting the <I>nteractive option on the TapCIS main menu, or by pressing the Esc key when TapCIS is performing an automated session (the program will remain online when it has finished its activities). GO INDEX and follow the procedures described on page 281, under the heading 'Terminal mode'.

8.2.2 The CompuServe Index

When you need a list of all available CompuServe services, turn to the CompuServe Index, an online reference that contains a list of GO words. In Section 9.6 you find a printed version of the index that should help you out in most situations. When you want to retrieve the latest version, GO INDEX is the route to follow.

WinCIM

Select the Go option on the Services menu, click on the GO button on the Ribbon, or press Ctrl-G. Enter INDEX and press the Enter key, or click on the OK button. WinCIM will go online, switch to Terminal Emulation mode, and display the following menu:

```
CompuServe Index (FREE)  INDEX

FIND A TOPIC

 1 Search for Topics of Interest
 2 List ALL Indexed Topics
 3 Explanation of Index

Enter choice!
```

Before you select the second option, `List ALL Indexed Topics`, be sure to open a *log file* that will store the index information. To do this, select the `Record in File` option on the Special menu, or double-click on the text `Off`, next to the `File Capture` text on the status bar. WinCIM will ask for the file in which the data should be stored: enter something like `INDEX.LOG` and press the `OK` button.

Next, select option 2, `List ALL Indexed Topics`. CompuServe will show the complete index on your screen; WinCIM will retrieve the data into the `INDEX.LOG` file. When all data have been retrieved, you can close the log file and process it offline.

Terminal mode

`GO INDEX` to access the CompuServe Index. The following menu will be displayed:

```
CompuServe Index (FREE)  INDEX

FIND A TOPIC

 1 Search for Topics of Interest
 2 List ALL Indexed Topics
 3 Explanation of Index

Enter choice!
```

Before you select the second option, be sure to open a *capture file* (some communication programs call these files *log files*) into which the index will be retrieved.

CompuServe Navigator

Go online interactively, either by selecting the `Terminal Emulation` option on the Special window, or by placing a Terminal Emulation task into your current script. Once online, **GO INDEX**. CompuServe will display the CompuServe `Index` menu.

Before you choose the second command on that menu, be sure to select the `Log to File` option on CompuServe `Navigator's Terminal` menu; the program will then store the index in a *log file* that you can process offline.

TapCIS

There are two ways to retrieve the index; manually or *via* a script. To do it manually, go online `<I>nteractively` and proceed as described under the heading 'Terminal mode' on page 269. Don't forget to open a capture file by pressing the PgDn key before you start retrieving the index.

The second way is much more interesting, though. By using the *script* facility that TapCIS provides, you can automate the procedure completely. The only thing you need is a script file that contains commands to retrieve the CompuServe Index. An example file is listed below:

```
; CISINDEX.SCR
; Use this file in <I>nteractive mode (press PgUp)
; or rename it to FRONTEND.SCR and start it with Alt-N

E This script retrieves the complete CompuServe Index
E to a file on your hard disk: CISINDEX.TXT.
E Note that the previous contents of your CISINDEX.TXT
E file will be overwritten.
E Written by Roelf Sluman

; We kill the old CISINDEX.TXT file first:
K CISINDEX.TXT
; GO INDEX (the GO command can be abbreviated):
S G CIS:INDEX^M
; Wait for "!":
W !
; Open the capture file (CISINDEX.TXT) for storage:
C CISINDEX.TXT
```

```
; Start capture
C Y
; Select "List ALL Indexed Topics" option:
S 2^M
; Wait for "Enter GO PAGE!":
W AGE!
; End capture
C N
E Index has been stored into CISINDEX.TXT.
```

Save this file in your TapCIS directory and name it `CISINDEX.SCR`. To retrieve the latest CompuServe Index using this file, proceed as follows:

1. Go online `<I>nteractively`.
2. Press PgDn.
3. Type *cisindex* and press Enter.

When execution of this script is completed, there will be a new file in your TapCIS directory: `CISINDEX.TXT`. This file contains the complete CompuServe index.

Fully automatic retrieval

You can automate the index retrieval even further, by renaming `CISINDEX.SCR` to `FRONTEND.SCR` (be sure to make a backup of your previous `FRONTEND.SCR` file). Next, activate the forums you want to visit and press Alt-N from the TapCIS main menu. TapCIS will connect and retrieve the index before visiting the forums.

8.2.3 The CompuServe Directory

If you use the WinCIM or CompuServe Navigator, you can browse through the CompuServe Directory, a Windows Help file that contains information about almost all CompuServe services, and about some ZiffNet services too. Select the `CompuServe Directory` option on the `Help` menu to access this useful file.

It is a little a known fact that the CompuServe Directory is available for users of other access programs as well. There is only one limitation: you need to have Windows installed. Just GO WINCIM to access the WinCIM download area; the newest version of the CompuServe Directory is listed as one of the free supplementary files.

8.2.4 The FORUMS.LST file

Although the CompuServe index provides the most up-to-date information about all available forums, there are a few files that could assist you in selecting the forums that deal with topics you are interested in. By far the most famous file is **FORUMS.LST**, which contains a comprehensive overview. For each forum, all message sections, library sections and conference rooms are listed. The **FORUMS.LST** file can be viewed and/or edited with any regular ASCII editor or word processor.

One of the places where the file is stored is the Help Library of the free Practice Forum. **GO PRACTICE** brings you to this forum. The filename you are looking for is **FORSEC.ARC**. For instructions about downloading the file, refer to Section 8.8.3, 'Downloading a file', and look under the heading for the access program you use.

To reduce download time, the **FORUMS.LST** file is *compressed* into the file **FORSEC.ARC**. (If that wasn't the case, it would take about three times longer to download it!)

To decompress this ARC file, you need a special utility program. The following list shows a few of the available ARC decompression programs for the various brands of computers:

- *MS-DOS*: **ARC-E.COM**, which can be found in the File Utilities library of the IBM Systems/Utilities Forum (**GO IBMSYS**).
- *UNIX*: **ARCSCO.TAZ**, which can be found in the Tools library of the Unix Forum (**GO UNIXFOR**).
- *Apple Macintosh*: **ARCPOP.BIN**, which can be found in the Communication Progs/Utils library of the Mac Communications Forum (**GO MACCOM**).
- *Commodore Amiga*: **ARC.EXE**, which can be found in the Archivers/Crunchers library of the Amiga Users forum (**GO AMIGAU**).
- *Atari ST*: ARC602.TTP, which can be found in the Utility Programs library of the Atari ST Productivity Forum (**GO ATARIPRO**).

For more information about downloading files from a forum library, refer to Section 8.8.3, 'Downloading a file', and look under the heading for the access program you use.

8.2.5 The CompuServe Help Forum

A good place to turn to if you need advice about appropriate forums that might be able to help you with a particular problem, is the CompuServe Help Forum (**GO HELPFORUM**). Leave a question in the 'Forum referrals' section - usually, one of the sysops will be back to you within no more than 24 hours.

HINTS & TIPS

Or GO NLFORUM, and ask us!

Although my own forum on CompuServe, the Netherlands Forum, is aimed especially at Dutch-speaking members, it has also libraries and message sections for English-speaking people. If you are stuck, just tell us! We will be happy to help you out. And while you are there, check out the contents of the 'General' library section as well. It contains files with news about CompuServe, announcements of new services, and additional help information. `GO NLFORUM` will take you there.

8.3 Joining a forum

Before you can use all the public features of a forum, you have to *join* it. Joining a forum doesn't cost you anything extra; it is simply an online formality. Although you can enter the forum as a 'visitor', that doesn't give you all the access rights that official forum members have. For instance, some forums don't allow visitors to do anything except read the *forum notices*, while other forums, for example, grant visitors the right to read forum messages. But to really benefit from all available forum facilities, you have to be a member. Don't give it a second thought: join as soon as possible.

Is joining a forum really free?

Some CompuServe members think that, as long as they haven't joined a particular forum, they don't pay connect charges for the time spent in that forum. Wrong: as soon as you leave Basic Services, the meter starts running, regardless of what you do. Forum visitors pay exactly the same as forum members, without having all the rights that regular members have. Therefore, joining as soon as possible is the most economic thing to do.

Joining a forum with WinCIM

Joining a forum with WinCIM is easy. As soon as you enter a forum of which you aren't a member, WinCIM displays the dialog shown in Figure 8.1. This dialog contains the following fields and options:

- *Name*: Enter the name you want to use in the forum. (This can be a name other than your own, for instance when you share an account with someone else.) Most forums demand that you use your real first name and last name; check the forum notices for details. If you need to change your forum name afterwards, you can do so by selecting `Forum Options` on the `Special` menu (while you are in the forum).

- *Interests*: If you wish, you can type a small description about yourself in this field. Other forum members can see this information when they browse through the 'forum directory'.
- *Join*: Press this button to join the forum. From that moment on, you are an official forum member, and you have access to all public features of the forum.
- *Leave*: Press this button if it is clear that you have entered the forum by mistake. You will return to the previous menu.
- *Visit*: Pressing this button makes you a 'forum visitor', with only limited access rights. (The actual rights are determined by the sysops of the forum.) If you choose this option, you can join the forum later on by selecting the `Join Forum` option on the `Special` menu.

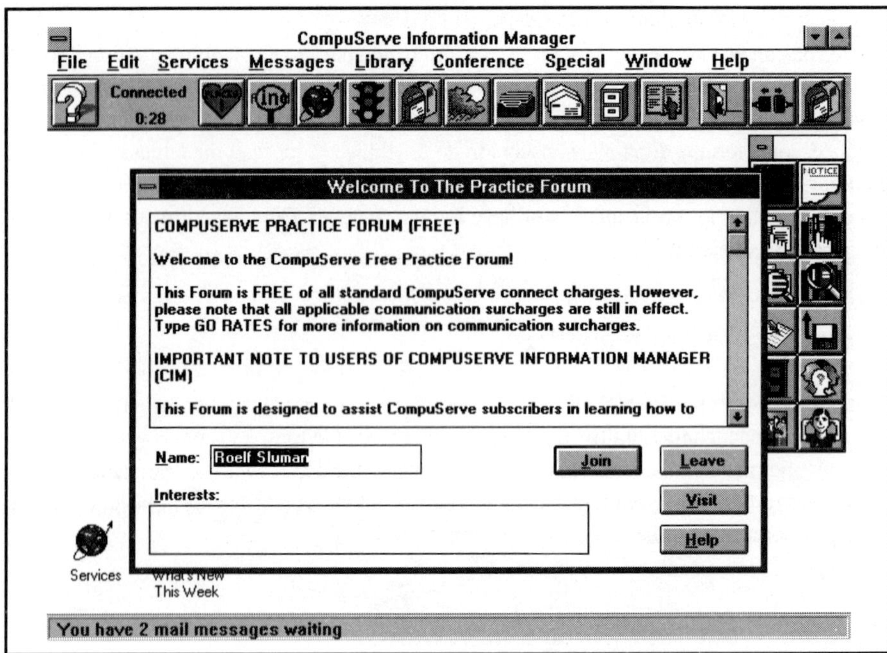

Figure 8.1 This dialog appears when you enter a forum for the first time

Joining a forum in terminal mode

When you enter a forum of which you aren't a member, you will see a welcome message, followed by the familiar ! prompt. If you want to join the forum, enter the `JOIN` command after the ! prompt

```
Forum !join

Please enter your name:
```

Type your name and press the Enter key to join the forum, and to get all the access rights that regular forum members have.

Changing your forum name afterwards

To change your forum name afterwards, enter the following command:
opt;name;your new name;p

Joining a forum with CompuServe Navigator

Normally, CompuServe Navigator will automatically join all forums of which you aren't a member yet. If you want to change this, select the `Forums` option on the `Settings` menu. CompuServe Navigator will display the 'Forum Preferences' window. Uncheck the Auto-Join box. Note that CompuServe Navigator will only perform the (script) actions that are allowed for a particular forum. In other words: if you aren't a forum member, CompuServe Navigator will almost never be able to read forum messages, download files, and so on.

When joining forums automatically, CompuServe Navigator will use the name that you have specified in the 'Setup Session Settings' dialog (select the `Session` option on the `Settings` menu).

Changing your forum name afterwards

Unfortunately, there is no CompuServe Navigator option (yet) to change your forum name: the name under which you are registered in the forum database. In other words, you will have to go on line manually. To do this, select the `Terminal Emulation` option on the `Special` menu and press the `Connect` button. CompuServe Navigator will go on line and display the Terminal Emulation screen. Next, `GO` to the forum and enter the following command:

```
opt;name;your new name;p
```

If you have typed this command correctly, CompuServe will show the ! prompt to indicate that it has accepted your command; your forum name is now changed. To log off, type `OFF` and press the Enter key, twice in a row.

Joining a forum with TapCIS

Joining forums with TapCIS is not only very easy, it is also essential to ensure that TapCIS will function properly.

First, enter the forums you want to join in the `<F>orum` menu. Next, press Alt-J from the TapCIS main menu. TapCIS will join *all* forums that are listed in the main menu; it will even 'rejoin' the forums of which you are already a member. During this procedure, TapCIS collects information about the message and library sections of those forums, and stores this information in the appropriate `.SEC` files. Because you will see this information whenever you retrieve updates of the contents of forum libraries and when you write forum messages, it can be a good idea to update these files regularly, by 'rejoining' forums from time to time.

When joining a forum, TapCIS will use the name you have entered in the `<P>arameters` menu. You can change your forum name afterwards very easily, using one of the advanced commands. Proceed as follows:

1. Choose the `<A>dvanced` command on the TapCIS main menu. Next, select the `<U>ser` command.
2. TapCIS will ask you to select the forum in which your name should be altered. Press one of the appropriate keys: digits for the first eight forums, Shift plus function keys for the other seven forums.
3. Next, you are asked to enter a command. TapCIS will place this command into an `.ADV` file for the selected forum. Next time the program accesses the forum, it will send the command. Enter the following line, replacing *your name* with the new name you want to use in the forum:

```
opt;name;your name;p
```

4. This is the abbreviated way of saying *Options, Name* and *Permanent*. Now, press Enter to return to the TapCIS main menu. The program will display an upload status mark next to the forum key.

8.3.2 Cancelling your forum membership

This paragraph can be brief: it is not possible to cancel a forum membership.

But then, it isn't necessary to do so: when you stop visiting a forum, your name will be erased from the forum records after a certain period of time. This period of time differs per forum: some forums keep records of members who pay a visit only once a year, while other forums remove from the list any member that hasn't stopped by for more than three months.

Don't take it as an offence when you find out that your membership has been cancelled. It is probably the result of an automated session; there is no forum sysop that 'picks' on members and removes them from the forum list as soon as possible. Feel free to join the forum again if you wish.

8.4 Reading the forum announcements

Forum announcements are an important, yet often neglected way to learn more about a specific forum and its purposes. Announcements, also called *notices*, tell you a lot about the people behind the forum, its intentions, and the way you should behave.

The following is a list of announcements normally available in every forum.

1. *News Flash*: This announcement contains the most recent information about the forum. When you enter the forum for the first time since this information was updated, it will appear automatically.
2. *General*: This announcement often contains information about the nature of the forum, as well as general guidelines for forum members. It is displayed automatically after you join the forum.
3. *Messages*: Contains information about the available message sections.
4. *Conference*: Contains information about the available conference rooms.
5. *Library*: Contains information about the forum library.
6. *Membership*: This announcement contains additional information about the forum, not found in the General announcement. Consult this announcement to see whether or not forum handles are allowed, and if there are extra features available.
7. *Sysop Roster*: Check this announcement for information about the people who run the forum: the *sysops* and *section leaders*.
8. *New Member*: This announcement is displayed automatically when you enter a forum of which you are not a member. It normally contains information about the nature of the forum, and an invitation to join it.

WinCIM and forum announcements

In WinCIM jargon, forum announcements are called *notices*. To read them, enter the forum and select the `Notices` option on the `Special` menu. WinCIM displays the available forum announcements in a dialog, as shown in Figure 8.2.

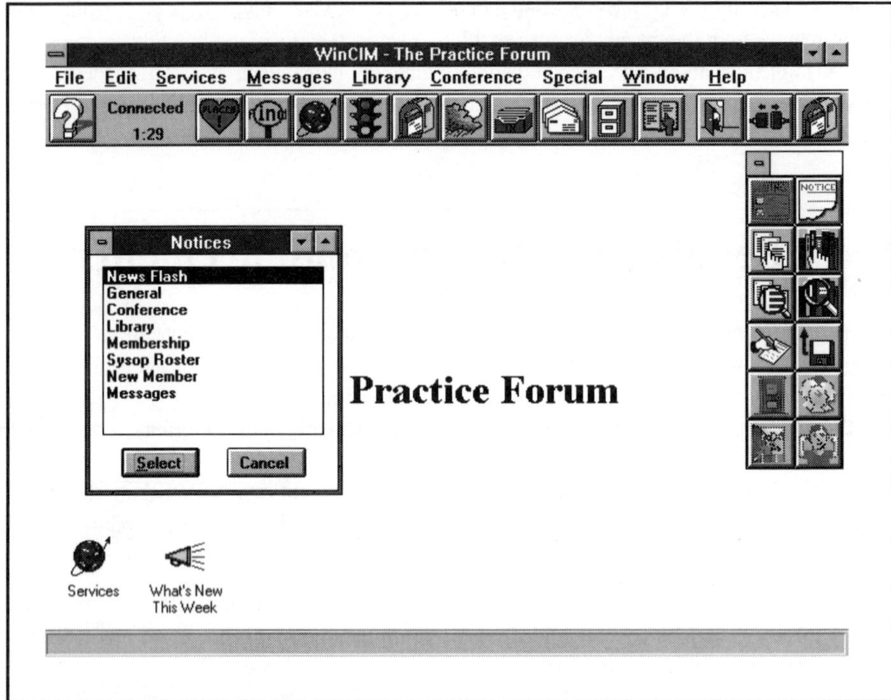

Figure 8.2 The available notices for the free Practice Forum

Reduce your online time!

Instead of reading the forum notices online, you could consider saving them to a file and reading them after you have disconnected. To do this, open the forum announcement you want to save. You will notice that the window that lists the announcement does not contain a `Filing Cabinet` button. Therefore, select the `Save` or `Save As` option on the `File` menu and enter a filename.

It is also possible to *append* information to a file. To store all forum announcements in a file, open the first one and select the `Save` option on the `File` menu. Type a filename, for instance `ANNOUNC.TXT`. Then, open the next announcement and select the `Save` option again. When asked for a filename, either type or click on `ANNOUNC.TXT`. WinCIM will report that this file already exists, and give you the opportunity to *append* the current announcement to it. Repeat this for all other announcements you are interested in.

After you have disconnected, open the **ANNOUNC.TXT** file by selecting the **Open** option on the **File** menu. This will launch a copy of the Windows Notepad application.

Reading forum announcements in terminal mode

To read the forum announcements in terminal mode, **GO** to the forum and enter the following command from any Forum ! prompt:

```
Forum ! announcements
```

This command, like all forum commands, can be abbreviated to:

```
Forum ! ann
```

CompuServe will display a list of available announcements. To read an announcement, just type its number and press the Enter key.

If you know beforehand what announcement you would like to read, enter the number after the command, like this:

```
Forum ! ann 1
```

Reading forum announcements with CompuServe Navigator

Reading the forum announcements can be automated in CompuServe Navigator. In the 'Script Editor' window, click on the Forum Options folder for the forum whose announcements you want to read (called *notices* in official WinCIM and CompuServe Navigator jargon). Next, click on the **Get Notices** button. CompuServe Navigator displays the 'Retrieve Notices' dialog, shown in Figure 8.3. After you have selected the announcements you would like to read, close the dialog. When the script is next executed, CompuServe Navigator will read the announcements and place them in your 'Session' window.

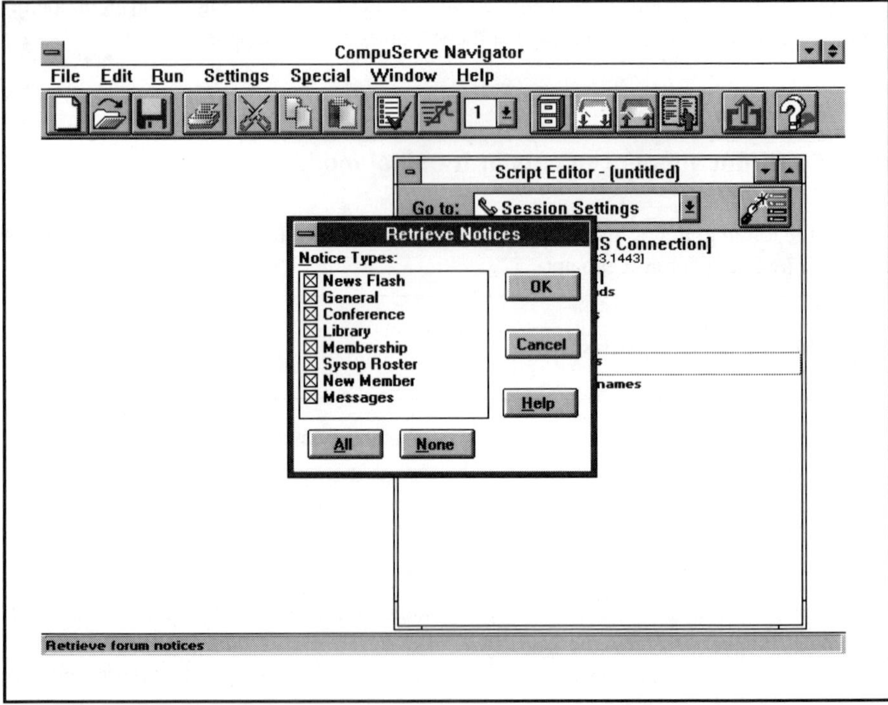

Figure 8.3 CompuServe Navigator can retrieve forum announcements automatically

TapCIS and forum announcements

By default, TapCIS will record the *News Flash*, an announcement that contains the latest news about a forum, in the **MSG** file for that forum. Therefore, you will see the news flash automatically when you read forum messages.

Although you could read the other forum announcements manually in terminal mode, it is more economic to use one of the **<A>dvanced** commands. Ensure that the forum for which you want to read the announcements is listed on the TapCIS main menu, and proceed as follows:

1. Choose the **<A>dvanced** command on the TapCIS main menu. Next, select the **<U>ser** command.

2. TapCIS will ask you to select the forum to which the command will apply. Press one of the appropriate keys: digits for the first eight forums, [Shift] plus function keys for the other seven forums.

3. You are now asked to enter a command. TapCIS will place this command in an `.ADV` file for the selected forum. Next time the program accesses the forum, it will send the command. Enter the following line, replacing `x` by the number of the announcement you want to read (as listed on page 277):

```
ann;x;t
```

4. Now, press Enter to return to the TapCIS main menu. The program will display an upload status mark next to the forum key. During the next forum visit, TapCIS will retrieve the announcement and place it in the `MSG` file for that forum.

8.5 Introduce yourself!

Now that you are a forum member, it is time to decide how to take advantage of your new membership. Is the forum library your first goal? Off to Section 8.8, 'Files', then, where you learn all you need to know about downloading lots of interesting stuff. Or maybe you are looking for a solution to a problem that has been bothering you for ages, in which case you will want to browse through the various message sections, discussed in Section 8.7, 'Messages'.

But maybe you have something to offer to the forum, or you are just looking for new friends. In that case, a good place to start is the Forum Member List, to which you can add a small *member profile* about who you are and what you do.

HINTS & TIPS

Posting 'I'm new' messages

A lot of forums welcome new members posting a message like 'Hello, I'm new' to introduce themselves. An example is the Working From Home Forum, which even has an entire section devoted to new forum members. Before posting such a message like that, it is a wise idea to see if it is really appropriate to do so in the forum you are visiting. Good places to check are the message sections and the forum announcements.

It must be said that not every forum member browses through the member profiles on a regular basis. But users of WinCIM are known to spend some time looking through them when they are downloading files. (WinCIM allows you to do other things in the forum while the program is downloading. In those situations, the list of member profiles is a nice place to visit.) Users of auto-access programs like CompuServe Navigator and TapCIS normally don't bother with it, though.

The chances are that when you joined the forum, you noticed the Interests field in the dialog that WinCIM displayed. If you entered some information about yourself in this field, you are already listed in the Forum Directory. If you left that field blank, or if you want to change the information you entered, GO to the forum and select the `Change Member Entry` option on WinCIM's `Special` menu.

8.6 Look for future friends

Most of the forums have a lot of members who are looking for 'online pen pals' with the same interests as they have. An excellent place to look for those people is the Forum Membership Directory, where members can leave their 'profile'. (See Section 8.5, 'Introduce yourself!', for information on how to do this.)

HINTS & TIPS

Watch your pocket!

Browsing the Forum Membership Directory like this can take up a lot of time, and it is not something that can be automated easily. To use your time online as efficiently as possible, access the Forum Membership Directory only when you are downloading a file; something that is currently only supported by the CIM packages. If you use another program to access CompuServe, it might be a good idea to use other means, like the message sections, to look for people who share your interests.

To browse through the Forum Membership Directory using WinCIM, GO to the forum and select the `Search Membership` option on the `Special` menu. You can search on user name (which can be a name other than the 'official' name of the person you are looking for), User ID or special interests. When WinCIM displays the names of members that match your search criteria, you can place them in your Address Book for future reference.

How about sending them an e-mail message?

Imagine getting letters, postcards, and so on from total strangers: an idea that doesn't appeal to many people. However, a lot of people don't mind getting their electronic mailbox cluttered with e-mail messages from all over the world. But there is a nicer way to approach future penpals that you found in the Forum Membership Directory: post a message on the forum. If the person is still an active forum member, he or she will get a 'messages waiting' notice upon entering the forum. And because most forums forward messages that 'scroll off' to someone's electronic mailbox anyway, you have a pretty good chance that your message will be read. And there is a bonus: because other forum members can read your forum message as well, you might get in touch with even more people!

8.7 Messages

The real fun starts when you begin reading, and maybe even replying to, forum messages.

Many CompuServe members find the concept of forum messaging complicated and difficult to comprehend. However, things aren't as bad as they seem. Once you know your way around in this world of topics and threads, it is actually quite simple and straightforward!

8.7.1 More on forum messages

The following terminology applies to each and every forum message.

- *Subject*: Just like e-mail messages, forum messages have subjects. Whenever you 'scan' forum messages, it is this subject that you see. Other words used in this context are 'topic' and 'message header'.
- *Thread*: A group of messages with the same subject is called a thread. In other words: all messages within a thread are, in one way or another, connected.
  Let's say that John starts a new thread, by posting a message on the forum. One hour later, Jane replies to that message, extending the thread to two messages. The next day, two people reply: Susan reacts to John's message, and Charles has something to say to Jane regarding her message to John. The thread now consists of four messages: the original one, two replies to John, and one reply to Jane. In this case, John's message is a *parent* of the messages that Jane and Susan have posted. Similarly, Jane's message is the parent of the message that she received from Charles. Jane's and Susan's messages are *siblings*: they both reply to John's message.
  As you will see later, there is a very important difference between *replying* to a current thread and *starting* a new one. Some members accidentally post 'loose messages' by starting a new thread, although their message is actually a reply to another message. More about this later.
- *Message number*: A unique number is assigned to every message that is posted. This number, the 'message number', can be used to read an individual message, thereby ignoring the thread to which the message belongs. Message numbers are assigned in chronological order: the next message that is posted after message 1001 gets number 1002 regardless of what thread the message belongs to. The forum maintains its threads by compiling lists of message numbers for each and every thread. In your personal forum record, a so-called *High Message Number* or *High Message Pointer* is kept: when you leave the forum (provided you have either read or scanned the messages, depending on the access program you use), this number is set to equal the last message plus one. So next time you visit the forum, you will only see the messages that were posted in the meantime.

A forum has storage space for only a limited number of messages. Under normal circumstances, that space is always filled (with the exception of brand-new forums). Every time a new forum message is posted, the oldest message scrolls off, and disappears into what is sometimes referred to as the 'binary bitbucket'. Depending on the forum's so-called 'scroll rate', messages stay 'on the board' for as long as two weeks, or not longer than twelve hours or so.

The software support forums illustrate this phenomenon. As soon as a new (version of a) program is released, the message load increases rapidly, to as many as 500 to 2000 messages a day! Once people get used to the new program, the number of newly posted messages decreases to a more normal number, say 100 to 150 per day. And after a few more months (depending on further product development, of course), the message traffic could get as low as about 20 to 50 messages a day.

To keep a forum as structured as possible (you don't really want to browse through hundreds of message headers a day, do you?), messages are kept in appropriate *sections*. By posting your message in the appropriate section, you have the greatest chance that people will answer it.

HINTS & TIPS

You have waiting messages – via e-mail!

By now, you know that a forum's message capacity is limited, and that messages eventually scroll off the forum. So what happens to messages addressed to you in a particular forum that you don't visit too often?

Thanks to a feature called *auto-forwarding*, you don't have to worry about missing such messages. Any messages directed to you that you haven't read yet will be forwarded to you as e-mail messages. Note that CompuServe will charge you for reading those messages: they are sent with *Postage Due*. Refer to Section 7.5.1 for more information about postage due messages.

8.7.2 Reading messages

The way you read forum messages depends largely on the access program you use. But all regular CompuServe access programs allow you to retrieve messages to your hard disk, so you can read them offline.

Reading messages with WinCIM

As soon as you enter a forum, the WinCIM menu structure changes. Three menus are added, one of which deals exclusively with reading, writing and replying to forum messages.
There are three ways to read forum messages:

- *Get waiting*: Use this method to read only the new messages addressed to you. If there are messages waiting for you when you enter the forum, you will be informed by a message on the status bar. Also, the `Get Waiting` button on the special Forum Toolbox will be active.
  Note that the High Message Number is not changed when you read your waiting message. So don't worry if you don't have the time to scan for other messages that may contain interesting information; the next time you visit the forum, you will still see all messages that were posted you haven't looked at before. With one exception, of course: if you wait too long before returning to the forum, the chances are that some (or all) unread messages will have scrolled off the forum.
  To read all messages in a particular forum, `GO` to that forum and press the `Get Waiting` button, or select the `Get Waiting` option on the `Messages` menu.

- *Get some*: This is the route that most CompuServe members follow. Although new CompuServe members are often tempted to read *all* messages in each and every forum, it takes only a short period of time to realize that this is simply impossible. Therefore, most members restrict themselves not only to a certain number of forums, but to a certain number of messages per forum as well.
  The best way to read forum messages selectively is to use a method called *scanning*. By *browsing* through the message topics and *marking* the messages that might contain something interesting, you collect a list that you can *retrieve* for offline processing. In WinCIM, this process works as follows:

1. First, you `GO` to the forum. When you have entered the forum, three menus will be added to the WinCIM menu bar.

2. You select the `Browse` option on the `Messages` menu, or you press the `Browse Messages` button on the special Forum Toolbox (the three documents with the pointing finger). WinCIM will display a dialog with information about the available message sections in the forum, as shown in Figure 8.4.

3. The dialog shows information for all message sections in the forum: the title of the section, the number of *topics* that contain new messages, and the actual number of new messages in that section.

4. If you want to read all new messages that in a particular section, check the box in front of that section. This method has both advantages and disadvantages. Eventually, there will be some forums that contain a few sections in which almost all messages interest you. In that case, it can be quicker simply to retrieve all the messages and disconnect, instead of going through the time-consuming process of selecting all the messages individually. But on the other hand, there will always be at least a few messages that don't contain anything useful at all. It is up to you to draw the line between 'get them all, I'll deal with them later' and 'let's be selective'.

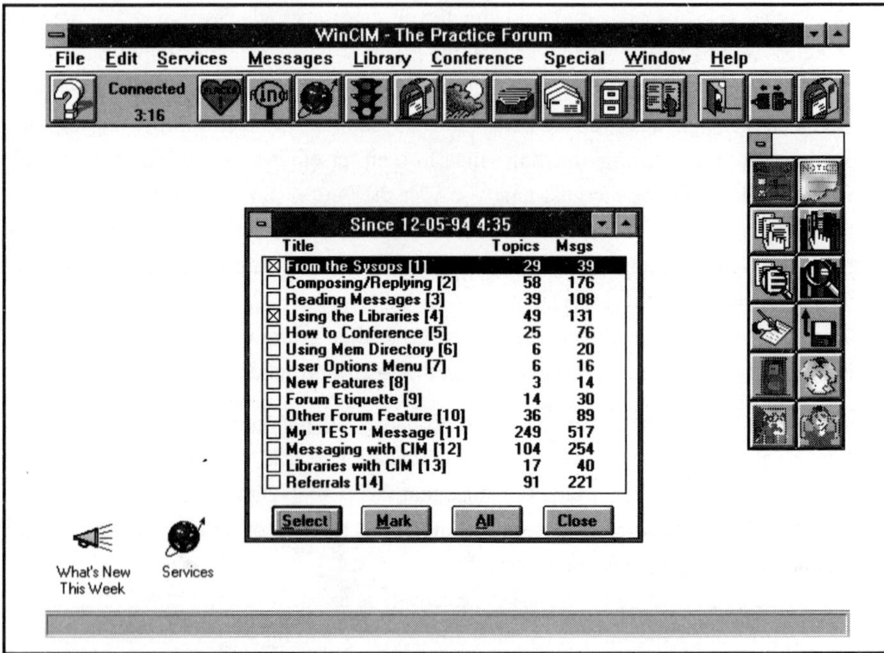

Figure 8.4 This dialog shows the available message sections in a forum, as well as the number of messages that have been posted since your last visit

Figure 8.5 This dialog lists all new messages in a particular section

5. If you want to review the contents of a section and mark only the messages that interest you, double-click on the section name, or use the arrow keys to select the section and press the Enter key. WinCIM will display another dialog, shown in Figure 8.5. Again, you can *mark* messages for later retrieval by checking the box in front of them. But if you don't care that the meter is running, you can read the new messages online by double-clicking on the topic name, or by selecting it and pressing the Enter key.

6. After you have marked all sections and/or messages that look interesting, it is time to let WinCIM do the work. Select the `Retrieve Marked` option on the `Messages` menu. WinCIM will display the `Retrieve Marked Message` dialog, shown in Figure 8.6. Press the `Get All` button to retrieve all messages listed in this dialog, or press the `Unmark` button if you have second thoughts about one or more messages. WinCIM will retrieve all marked messages and place them in a special Filing Cabinet folder with the same name as the forum to which the messages belong.

After WinCIM has retrieved all marked messages, you can either disconnect and start processing them, or visit another forum.

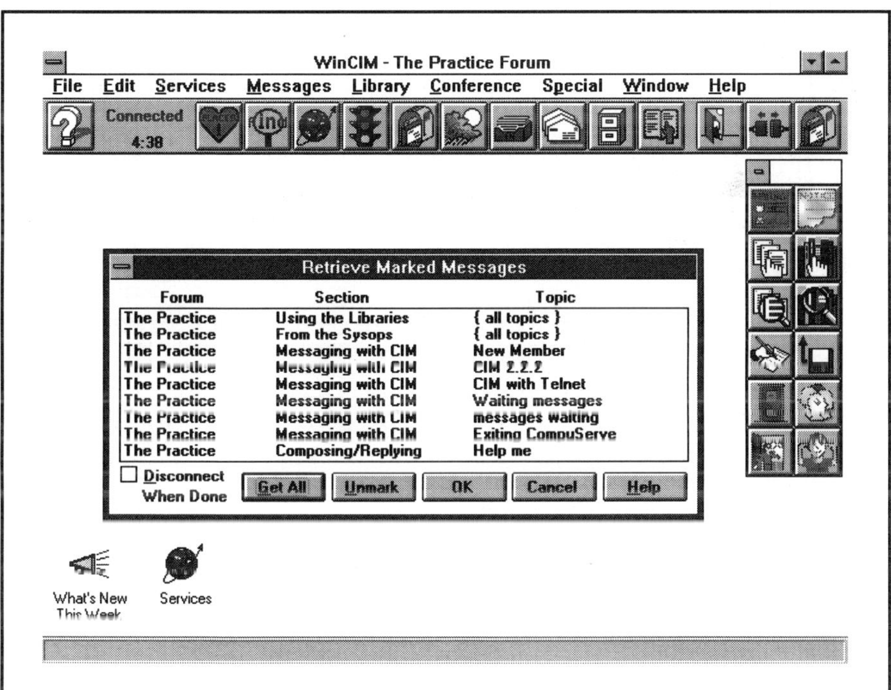

Figure 8.6 WinCIM is about to retrieve a series of marked messages

Make the most of your forum visit

If you use WinCIM to download files and retrieve forum messages, here's a useful tip: if you have files to download, first mark them and then retrieve them all at once using the `Retrieve Marked` option on the `Library` menu. While WinCIM retrieves the file(s), you can go to the message sections and start marking the sections and/or messages you are interested in. Although this will slow down the download a little, the overall time spent in the forum will be less than if you had just waited for the file download to finish.

Whether you read messages online or from your Filing Cabinet, you will use the dialog shown in Figure 8.7. This dialog contains a large amount of information, fields and options:

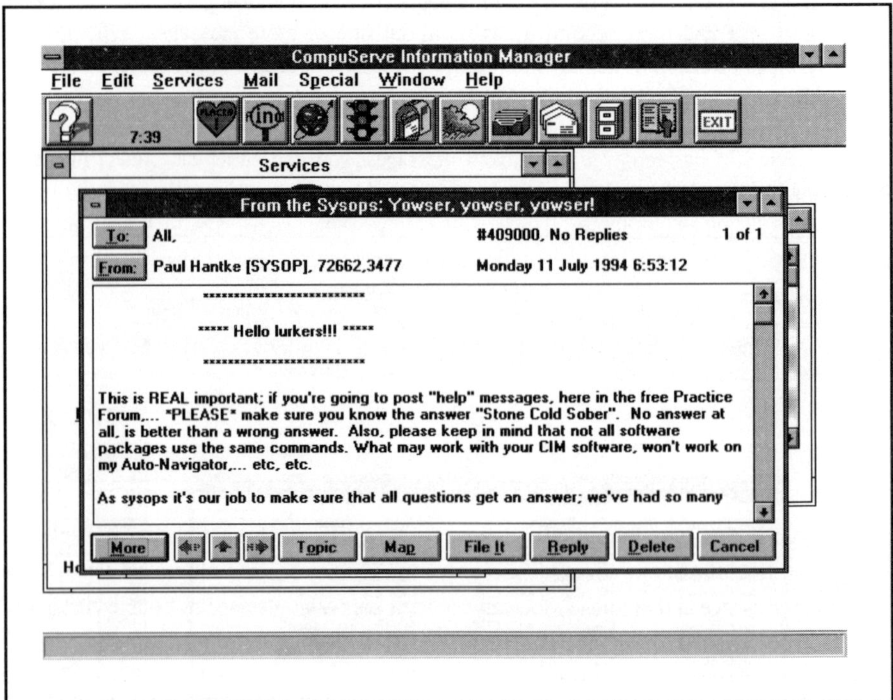

Figure 8.7 This dialog is used to read forum messages

- The title bar shows the name of the section in which the message was posted, as well as the message subject.
- The 'To' field contains the name and User ID of the person the message was addressed to. Forum messages can be directed to someone in particular, to `All`, to `Sysop`, or to `Sysop/All`. In the last three cases, it is not necessary to specify a User ID.

Note that you can easily include the addressee in your WinCIM Address Book; just press the `To` button.

- The 'From' field contains the name and User ID of the person who posted the message. You can add this information to your WinCIM Address Book by pressing the `From` button.
- On the right-hand side of the dialog, additional information is shown about the message: the message number, the number of replies, the date and time the message was posted, and the number of messages in this thread that are available for reading.
- The main part of the message dialog is reserved for the actual message text. Although you can't edit the message text, you can select some or all of it and copy it to your Windows Clipboard.
- Press the `More` button to see the next part of the current message. If you have reached the end of the message, WinCIM will display either the next message or the next thread, whichever is appropriate.
- Press the `Arrow Left` button to display the preceding message in the thread. Initially, the previous *sibling* will be shown; if there is no sibling, WinCIM displays the parent message. When you have reached the first of the available messages for that thread, the `Arrow Left` button is grey and cannot be pressed.
- Pressing the `Arrow Up` button displays the *parent* of the current message: the message to which the current message replied.
- Press the `Arrow Right` button to display the next message in the thread.
- You can press the `Topic` button to display the first available message for the next thread.
- The `Map` button (see Figure 8.7) is very useful for long message threads. It displays a graphic tree that shows the structure of the current thread, as well as the place of the current message in that thread. You can display a particular message by double-clicking on it, or you can select it with the arrow keys and press **Enter**.
- Press the `File It` button to store the message in the WinCIM Filing Cabinet. The Filing Cabinet is discussed in Section 5.7.3.
- To reply to the message, press the `Reply` button. More information about replying to forum messages can be found in Section 8.7.3, 'Replying to messages'.
- Press the `Delete` button to delete the message. Note that this button has two functions, depending on how you read the message. If you are online and read the message 'live', you can delete it from the forum, provided you were involved in it (that is, the message must have been either directed to you or posted by you). If you read the message offline, you can press this button to delete it from your WinCIM Filing Cabinet.

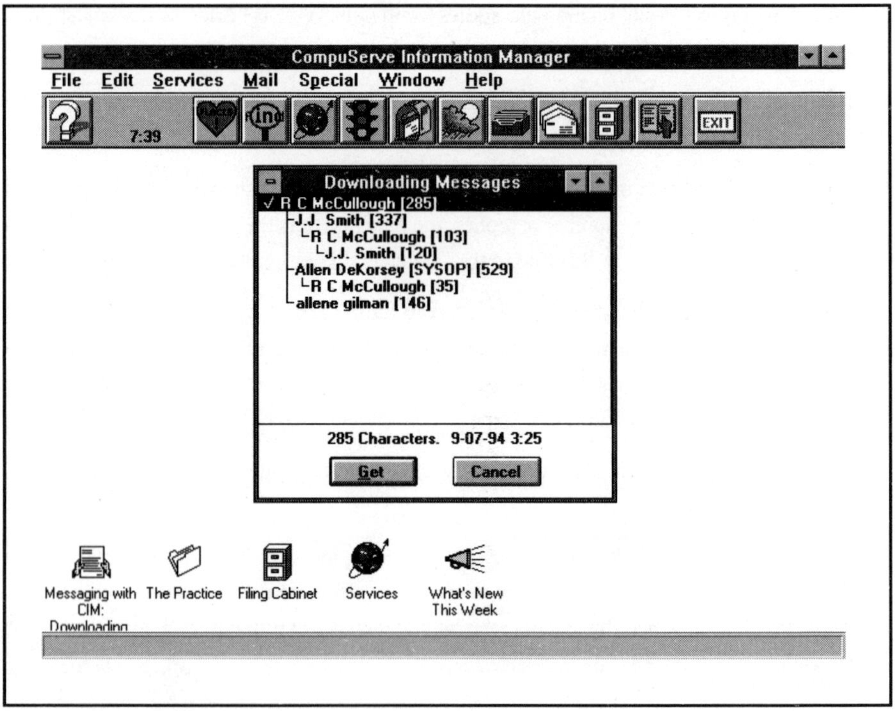

Figure 8.8 A typical 'thread map'

Reading messages in terminal mode

If you want to read forum messages as economically as possible, you typically will need to access CompuServe twice: once to get a list of new messages posted in the forum, and once to actually read the messages that you are interested in. Another possibility is to read all new messages that were posted in a particular forum, but it is normally only advisable to do so when message traffic isn't too high.

Once you have arrived in the forum, the first step is to access the message board. Enter the `MESSAGE` command (like all commands, this can be abbreviated to the first three letters) to do this:

```
Forum !mes
Messages !
```

Reading all new messages in the forum

To read all new messages that were posted in the forum since the last time you read or scanned messages, enter **READ THREAD NEW**. The messages will be displayed in thread order. To read the messages chronologically, enter **READ FORWARD NEW**.

Reading messages waiting for you

If you want to read all new messages that are addressed to you, use the **READ WAITING** command. Note that this command has no influence on the High Message Pointer. Therefore, CompuServe will show this message again the next time you enter the forum to scan for new messages. It won't be flagged as 'waiting', though,

First, open a file to capture the message headers. Consult the manual that came with your communication software if you don't know how to do this. Next, issue the following command:

```
Messages !scan quick new sec:1-24
```

If you want to limit the search to a particular range of sections, you can specify that range after the **SEC** subcommand. To scan for new messages in sections one and six only, you would enter:

```
Messages !scan quick new sec:1,6
```

CompuServe will display a list of information about threads that contain new messages. You get the following information for each thread:

- The number of the first new message in the thread.
- The thread subject.
- The section (number and name) in which the message was posted.

Once you have retrieved this list, you can close the capture file and disconnect. Next, you process the list, writing down the numbers of the threads that you want to retrieve. Go online again, open your capture file, and give the following command for each thread:

```
rea thr num:00000
```

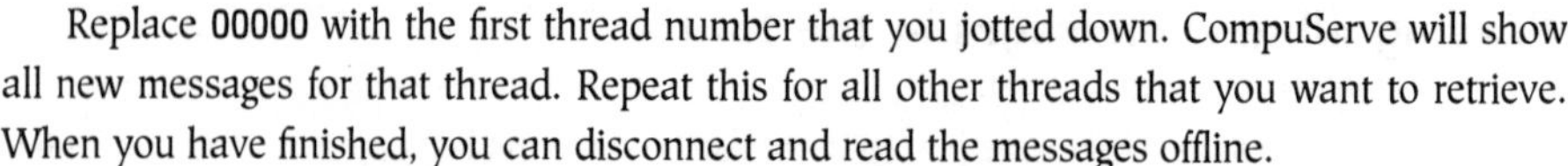

Replace 00000 with the first thread number that you jotted down. CompuServe will show all new messages for that thread. Repeat this for all other threads that you want to retrieve. When you have finished, you can disconnect and read the messages offline.

Reading messages with CompuServe Navigator

Reading forum messages with CompuServe Navigator typically consists of two or more sessions. During the first session, CompuServe Navigator will *summarize* messages. After you have marked the messages you would like to read, CompuServe Navigator *retrieves* them during a second session. Proceed as follows:

1. In the 'Script Editor' window, click on the Message Commands folder for the appropriate forum. This causes two folders to appear: Summarize Messages and Retrieve Messages.
2. Click on the Summarize Messages folder. Next, click on the Since button. You can now specify the sections from which you would like to read all new messages. Leave all other options unmodified. Press the OK button to return to the 'Script Editor' window.
3. Execute the script. When CompuServe Navigator has performed its duties, the 'Session' window will contain a Summaries icon. Double-click on it to see the summaries. If you have accidentally closed the 'Session' window without saving it, you can also open the forum's folder from the Filing Cabinet. You will find a Thread Summary item in it: double-click on it to review the message headers. In both cases, the 'Summaries' dialog appears, shown in Figure 8.9. This dialog contains an overview of all *threads*: groups of messages that have the same subject. Select a thread and press one of the following action buttons:
   - *New*: CompuServe Navigator will retrieve all new messages for this thread. That is, all messages that have been posted since the last time you retrieved a message summary for this forum.
   - *Single*: CompuServe Navigator will retrieve only the latest message posted in this thread since the last time you retrieved a summary for this forum.
   - *All*: CompuServe Navigator will retrieve all messages for this thread that are currently present on the message board. Note that this doesn't mean that you will actually get hold of the complete thread; in some cases, the beginning of the thread could already have scrolled off the forum.
   - *Ignore*: CompuServe Navigator won't download any messages belonging to this thread. Press this button if you want to cancel a previous command for this thread.
   - *Close*: Closes this dialog and returns you to the 'Session' window.

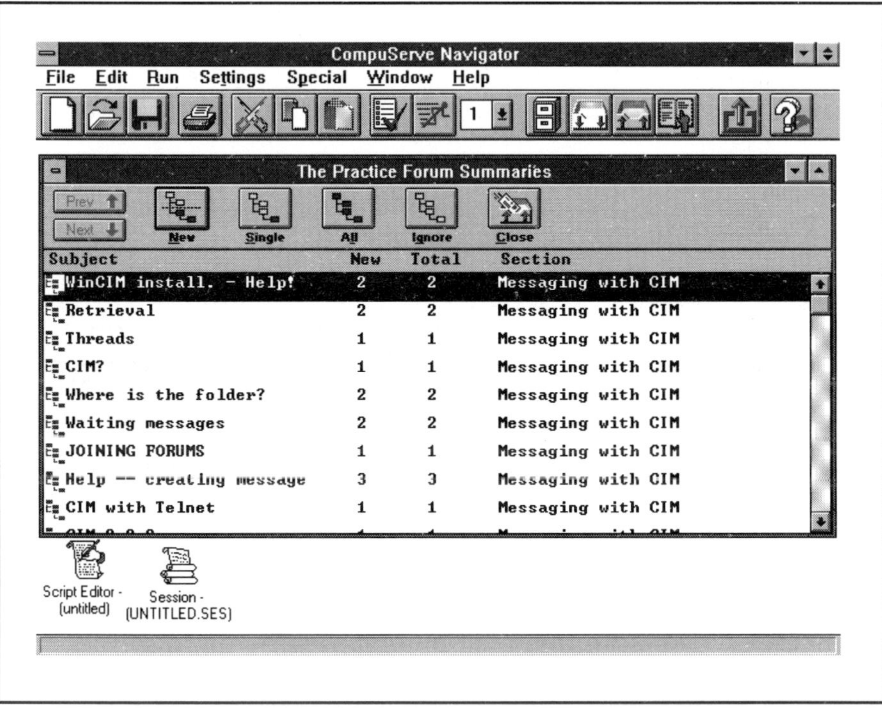

Figure 8.9 Use this dialog to mark the messages you want to read

4. You are now ready to have CompuServe Navigator retrieve the marked messages. If you use only one pass, uncheck the Summarize Messages task. Execute the script: CompuServe Navigator will go online and retrieve the messages into the forum's folder in your Filing Cabinet. They will be listed in the 'Session' window as well.

5. To read the messages, you use the dialog shown in Figure 8.10. This dialog contains a number of options. Whether or not a particular option is available depends on the message that is currently displayed.
   - *Prev [Arrow Up]*: Displays the first available message in the previous thread. This option is not available when you are currently reading the first thread in the list.
   - *Next [Arrow Down]*: Displays the first available message in the next thread. This option is not available when you are currently reading the last thread in the list.
   - *Msg [Arrow Up]*: Displays the previous message in this thread. If available, the parent of the current message will be displayed. If there is no parent available, the last message in the previous 'branch' of the 'thread tree' will be displayed.
   - *Msg [Arrow Dn]*: Displays the next message in this thread, in thread order. Replies to the current message will be displayed first. If there are no replies, eventually replies to the parent message will be displayed, and so on.

- *Map*: CompuServe Navigator displays a map of the current thread's structure.
- *File*: A copy of the current message will be placed in another folder of your Filing Cabinet.
- *Delete*: Select this option to delete the thread, or a part of it, from your Filing Cabinet.
- *Host Delete*: This option is available only for messages in which you were involved (that is, message that were either posted by you or directed to you). When you select it, CompuServe Navigator will delete the message from the forum during the next script execution.
- *Reply*: Select this option to reply to the current message. More information about replying to forum messages using CompuServe Navigator can be found in Section 8.7.3, 'Replying to messages'.

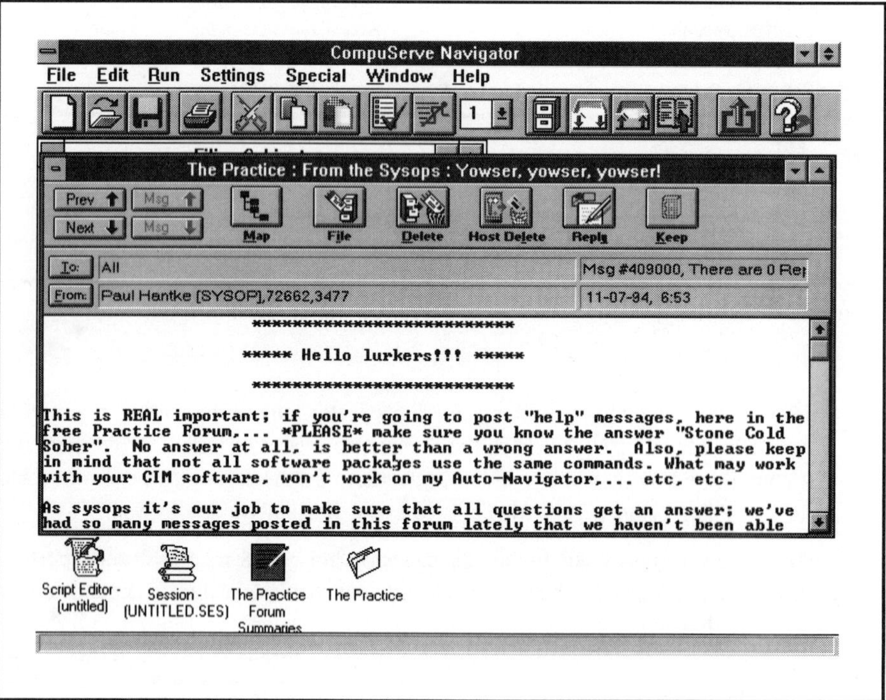

Figure 8.10 Reading messages with CompuServe Navigator

Using several passes

The real power of CompuServe Navigator will be unleashed once you start using more than one *pass*. During the first pass, you could let CompuServe Navigator summarize messages, as well as read all messages posted to you. When CompuServe Navigator has completed execution of the first pass, you mark the messages you would like to read, and read and answer your waiting messages. It is then time to invoke the second pass, in which CompuServe Navigator will retrieve the marked messages and send off your replies. Eventually, you could define a third pass, in which CompuServe Navigator will send off your replies to the forum messages that were retrieved during the second pass. To learn more about these advanced features of CompuServe Navigator, refer to Section 6.1.9.

Reading messages with TapCIS

Normally, you will initiate two or more sessions to read forum messages with TapCIS. The general procedure looks as follows:

1. Go to the `<F>orums` menu and select the forums for which you would like TapCIS to retrieve messages. TapCIS considers e-mail to be a forum as well: if you want to retrieve your e-mail, just select `MAIL` from the `Forums` menu as well.
2. Back in the TapCIS main menu, select `<N>`. TapCIS will go online and retrieve either complete messages or message headers, depending on the settings on the `Forums` menu.
3. When TapCIS disconnects, mark forum messages: review the message headers and decide which messages you would like to read. You can do this with TapCIS, but you can also use one of the special utility programs written to do this.
4. After you have marked all messages, select `<O>`. TapCIS will go online again and retrieve the marked messages.
5. When TapCIS disconnects, all forums that have new messages are indicated by a ! symbol. You can either start reading those messages, or use a special utility program (like Recon or TapOrder, both available for download in the TapCIS forum) to sort them into thread order, and to link them to earlier messages that belong to the same thread.

8.7.3 Replying to messages

As soon as you have received your permanent password, you can reply to forum messages. All regular CompuServe access programs allow you to write your replies offline, keeping your connect charges within limits.

Replying to forum messages is a fun method of getting to know new online friends. Feel free to 'jump into' discussions between two other forum members as well. If you wish, you could start your message with an abbreviation like PMFJI ('Pardon me for jumping in'), indicating that you would like to take part in the conversation.

HINTS & TIPS

Information for new CompuServe members

If you haven't received your permanent password yet, you can read current messages as well as post new ones. However, you can't reply to messages already on the forum.

Replying to forum messages effectively means that you add a message to an existing thread. The opposite action, *posting* a message, results in a completely new thread being created. From time to time, *broken threads* appear: while browsing through a message section, you see several threads with the same name. Those broken threads are caused by members who should have replied to a current message, but instead posted their reaction as the beginning of a new thread. To avoid creating broken threads, be sure that you know the difference between replying to a message and starting a new thread.

The thread drift phenomenon

Normally, someone has a question (or just something to say) and starts a new thread. Some people reply to that message, causing the thread to grow. Until to this point, the chances are pretty high that the messages in that thread all have something to do with the original thread subject.

But this can change rapidly. Often, members start their own 'mini-threads' inside the original thread: their messages wander off the thread topic.

There is nothing wrong with that. Actually, it's a normal thing, which happens in everyday conversations as well. The *thread drifting* phenomenon can, however, be frustrating to people who see the thread for the first time when the first three or four messages have already scrolled off the forum. They retrieved the thread that caught their interest, only to realize that the original subject has been abandoned.

Experienced CompuServe users recognize this problem and resolve it elegantly... They carry on the discussion in an entirely new thread, with a more appropriate subject. Don't hesitate to do this yourself, if you feel that you are up to it. You will earn the gratitude of your fellow forum members.

HINTS & TIPS

Forwarding messages to other forums, or via e-mail

If you wish, you can *forward* a message to someone else, or to another forum. To do this, select the `Forward` option in the access program that you are using. (Press the `Forward` button in programs like WinCIM and CompuServe Navigator, or press the [Tab] button while you read the message in TapCIS.)

WinCIM

To reply to a message using WinCIM, press the `Reply` button. WinCIM will create a dialog in which the necessary fields are already filled in (see Figure 8.11). All you have to do is write the message in the large edit box. You can use all the standard edit functions that Windows provides. It is even possible to prepare the reply with the word processing program you normally use and copy it *via* the Windows Clipboard to the 'Reply to Forum Message' dialog.

After you have composed the message, you have three choices:

- Discard it: press the `Cancel` button. Eventually, you can place a copy of the message in your Filing Cabinet, in case you want to have access to it later.
- Send it off immediately: press the `Send` button. WinCIM will connect to CompuServe and post the message in the right forum. Don't forget that you have to disconnect manually.
- Put it into your Out-Basket: press the `Out Basket` button. Use this method when you have other forum and/or e-mail messages to write. When you have finished, you can connect to CompuServe, visit all the appropriate forums and have WinCIM send all messages for that forum automatically. For more information, refer to Section 5.7.1.

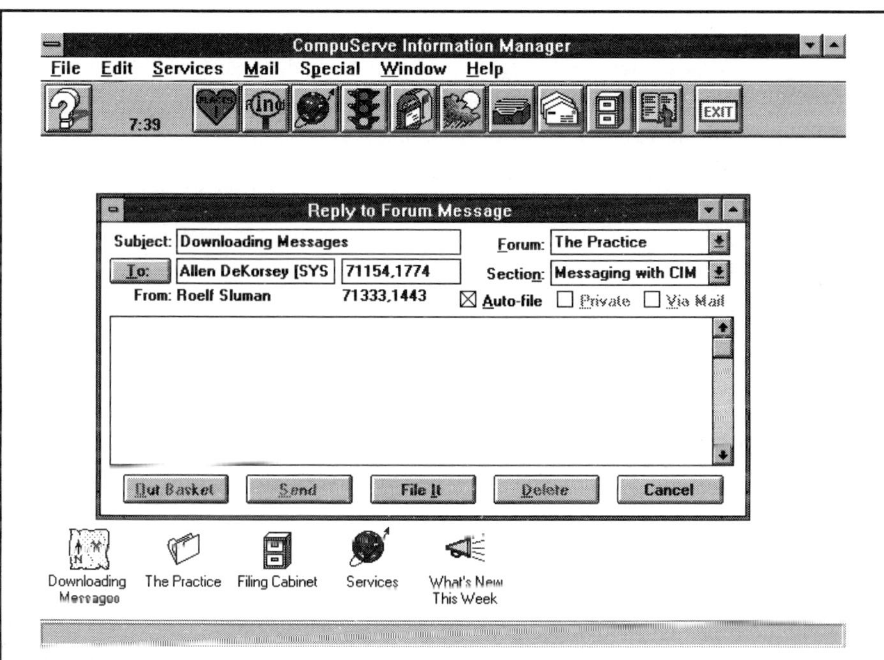

Figure 8.11 Replying to a forum message with WinCIM

Note that you can have the message sent *via* regular e-mail as well. Or you can mark it as *private*, in which case only the recipient can see it. Some forums don't allow private messages;

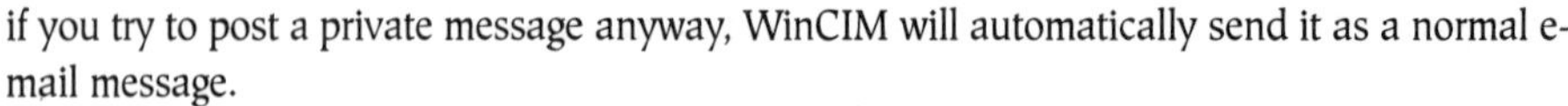

if you try to post a private message anyway, WinCIM will automatically send it as a normal e-mail message.

Terminal mode

To reply to a message, you have to know the message number. Next, enter the following command:

```
Forum !reply 00000
```

Replace 00000 with the number of the message you want to reply to. CompuServe will display the following text:

```
Enter reply. (/EXIT when done)
```

You can now type the text for the reply. When you are ready, press Enter to begin on a new line and type `/EXIT`. CompuServe will display the Post action ! prompt. Select one of the following options:

- *Post* the message. If you want the message to be private, add the `PRIVATE` parameter to the `POST` command.
- *Mail* the message. Use the `MAIL` command to do this.
- *Cancel* the message, by using the `CANCEL` command.

CompuServe Navigator

When you are reading a forum message that you want to reply to, press the `Reply` button. CompuServe Navigator displays the 'Reply' window, shown in Figure 8.12. You use the main part of the window to write your reply. In addition, you have the following options:

- *Out-Basket*: Press this button when you have finished. CompuServe Navigator will place the message in your Out-Basket, and send it off during the next script execution.
- *File*: Press this button to place a copy of the message in a Filing Cabinet folder.

- *Envelope*: Press this button to set special options for your reply. One of the most important options has to do with the way your message will be delivered: normally, privately (not possible in all forums), or *via* e-mail (not possible in free forums).
- *Auto-file*: When this option is selected, CompuServe Navigator will place a copy of your reply in the Filing Cabinet's Auto-Filed folder.

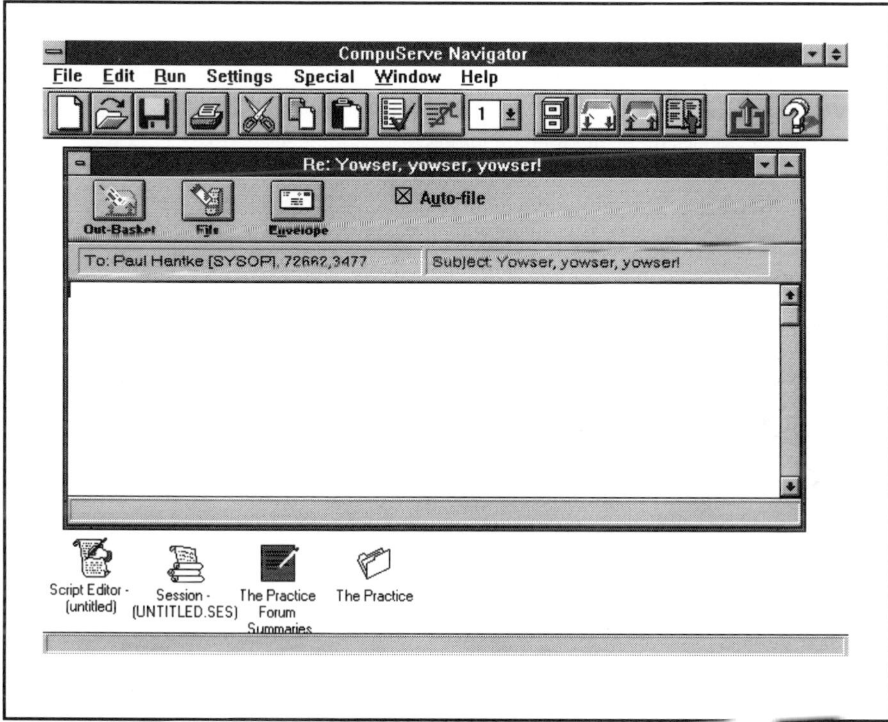

Figure 8.12 Replying to a forum message with CompuServe Navigator

TapCIS

While reading a message, press the [R] key to reply to it. After you have written the reply, press [F7] and select one of the available options. You can send the reply as a regular forum message, as a private message (not supported by all forums), or as a message that should be sent *via* e-mail (not supported by free forums).

HINTS & TIPS

The reformatting pitfall

Although your forum message might be formatted nicely on your screen, that's not necessarily the way other people are going to see it! When you read a forum message, CompuServe 'reformats' it for the screen size of the recipient. This can cause problems when you try to send the contents of files like `AUTOEXEC.BAT`, `WIN.INI`, and so on. as a forum message: CompuServe will neglect the carriage returns used to separate the lines, resulting in an almost unreadable message.

If it is important that the message arrives in exactly the same format as you composed it, send it 'unformatted'.

When you have replied to one or more messages, you have to go `<O>nline` again to have TapCIS post the replies to the appropriate forums.

A few additional tips:

- *To reformat a message*: Unlike other editors, TapCIS doesn't automatically reformat the text that you write. However, you don't have to reformat every paragraph yourself: just press Ctrl-B.
- *To review the message to which you reply*: Press F8 to switch between your reply and the original message.
- *To copy parts of the original message into your reply*: Press F8 to display the original message. Next, go to the first line that you want to copy and press Ctrl-K, followed by B. Go to the last line of the text to be copied and press Ctrl-K again, this time followed by K. The text will be selected. Press F8 to go back to your reply. After you have positioned the cursor, press Ctrl-K, followed by C to copy the message text into your reply.
- *To copy the entire message into your reply*: Press Shift+F9.
- *To forward messages*: Press the Tab key.

8.7.4 Starting a forum discussion

To create a message thread, all you have to do is post a forum message. As the replies to your message start coming in, and as other people react to those replies as well, your thread starts to develop into what might be a chain with tens or even hundreds of messages.

Of course, you want at least one, but maybe even lots of replies to your message. Therefore, consult the following guidelines before posting it:

- First, you have to select the forum in which to post the message. As you might have noticed already, it still happens that people post messages about word processing programs in the Travel forum! Don't think that this is a rare occasion: I saw at least ten mis-posted messages last week!

- After you know which forum would be appropriate for your message, you have to decide in which section to post it. This can be particularly important in forums where traffic is high, like in most software support forums. When in doubt, post your message in the 'General' section that most forums have (usually the first section).
- Next, you have to decide to whom you want to address your message. You have the following options:
  - Directing the message to `All` helps to get replies from different forum members. If you direct a message to a particular person, the chances are that other members will be reluctant to 'jump in', even if they know the answer. Note that you don't have to supply a User ID.
  - Direct a message to `Sysop` if you have a specific, forum-related question. The message will be flagged as 'waiting' for all forum sysops that log in, until one of them has read it. Note that although other members see the message as well, you are not likely to get a lot of reactions from them. As with messages directed to `All`, you don't have to supply a User ID.
  - If you want (and need) the best of both worlds, direct your message to `All/Sysop`. That way, you are sure that the sysop reads your message, while giving other forum members the opportunity to react as well.
  - Direct a message to `*Sysop` if you want only the 'chief sysop' (the *forum manager*, sometimes called the *wizop* of the forum) to be able to read your message. Again, you don't have to supply a User ID. Use this method only if you have a very specific, confidential question that only the wizop can answer. As nobody else will see this message, it is not advisable to use it to ask general questions.
- And here comes the key to getting the right answer as soon as possible: carefully think about the subject of your message. Too many members use subjects like 'Question', 'Help', or 'Problem'. Although forum sysops will likely read those messages and reply to them, the chances that other members will read them intentionally are small. Pick a subject that is short and to the point. In a modem support forum, don't use 'Modem problem'; instead, try 'CA-2000 won't dial' or something similar.

HINTS & TIPS

Private forum messages or e-mail?

If you have a message for someone specific that doesn't contain any information that could be of use to other forum members, consider using regular e-mail. For every forum message that you post, another message 'scrolls off' the forum. That could be the one with vital information that another forum member is looking for! Don't let this keep you from posting as many forum messages as you want, but keep in mind that people actually pay to visit the forum, and would like to get the most out of their money spent online, just like you!

Note that all except the free forums allow you to send a forum message *via* e-mail as well.

Watch out for the reformatting pitfall!

Even if your message looks nicely formatted on your computer screen, that doesn't necessarily mean that this is the case on the recipient's screen. Because CompuServe reformats messages by default, your message could actually look quite different from what you would expect. See page 300, under the heading 'The reformatting pitfall', for more details.

WinCIM

To post a forum message with WinCIM, select the `Create Forum Message` on the `Mail` menu (if you are offline), or the `Create Message` option on the `Messages` menu (if you are online, and currently visiting the forum). WinCIM displays the 'Create Forum Message' dialog, shown in Figure 8.13. First, you have to deal with the following fields and options:

- *Subject*: Type the subject (also known as the *topic*) of the message.
- *Forum*: Select the forum you want to post the message in. Note that WinCIM will only list the forums that you have actually visited. If you want to post a message in a forum of which you are not a yet member, you first have to join that forum.
- *Section*: Select the appropriate forum section for your message.
- *To*: Enter the name and User ID of the person to whom you want to direct the message, or use one of the keywords `All`, `Sysop`, `*Sysop` or `All/Sysop`. When you specify one of these keywords, no User ID is necessary.

You can now start writing the message. The maximum size is 10,000 characters. If you need more room, there is a trick: answer your own message. But note that very long messages won't make you too popular, unless they contain really valuable information.

When you have finished the message, you have the following options:

- Discard it: press the `Delete` button. If you think you might need the message text later, place a copy of it in your Filing Cabinet.
- Send it off immediately: press the `Send` button. WinCIM will connect to CompuServe and post the message in the right forum. Don't forget that you have to disconnect manually.
- Put it in your Out-Basket: press the `Out-Basket` button. Use this method when you have other forum and/or e-mail messages to write. When you have finished, you can connect to CompuServe, visit all the appropriate forums and have WinCIM send all messages for each forum automatically. For more information, refer to Section 5.7.1.

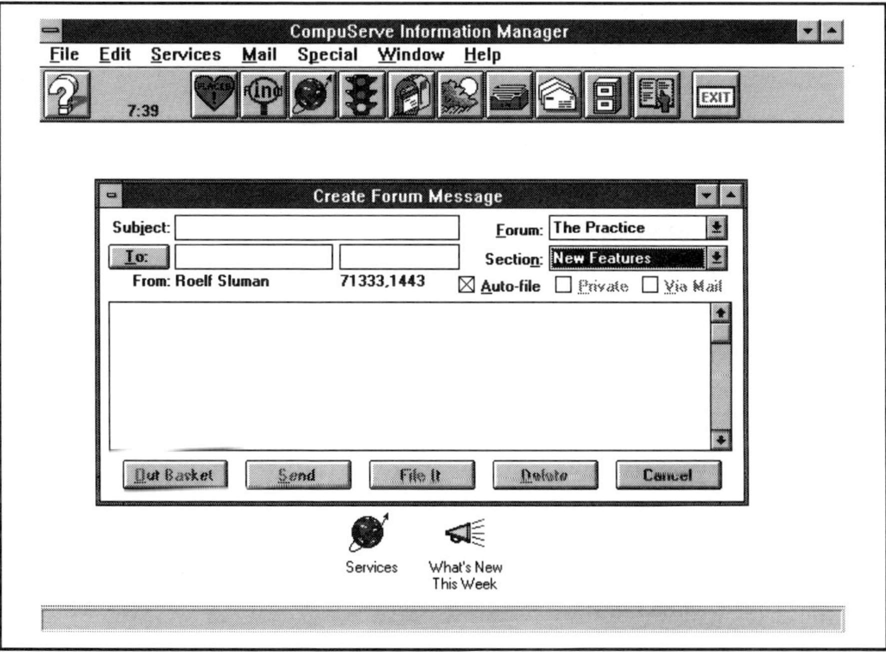

Figure 8.13 Use this dialog to post a forum message

So now you have posted your message. When will you get some answers? First of all: don't spend any time waiting in the forum for your message to be answered. Even if it is answered while you are online, you won't see any new messages posted unless you select the `Freshen Messages` option on the `Messages` menu. But there is more to it than that. Every minute of the day, people enter and leave forums. It is very likely that the person who has the answer to your message is not on the forum at the same time as you are. Typically, your message won't be answered for a couple of hours.

'You have removed my message!'

As a WinCIM user, you will almost certainly be confronted with the following problem sooner or later: when you visit a forum, you don't see the message you posted. Censorship? No, don't worry: CompuServe simply assumes that you are not interested in reading your own messages online. When you post your message, CompuServe assigns the current *High Message Number* to it and increases that number by one. When you leave the forum, the new High Message Number is recorded. Next time you visit the forum, you will only see the messages starting with that High Message Number: all messages posted *after* you left the forum! To see your own message, select the `Set Date` option on the `Messages` menu and change the date accordingly, or select `Forum Options` on the `Special` menu, change the last message number, and `GO` to the forum again.

HINTS & TIPS

Check for waiting messages quickly and easily: the WinCIM status bar

A lot of WinCIM users select the `Browse` command on the `Messages` menu to see if there are replies to their messages. This method has two drawbacks. First, it can take a considerable amount of online time before you either find your thread, or discover that it isn't there, meaning that there are new messages. Secondly, if you only check in this way to check for *personal* messages, you will miss all the other messages that might contain interesting information. If you use the `Browse` option, WinCIM will update the High Message Number as soon as you leave the forum, causing the current messages not to be visible when you enter the forum the next time.

The best and quickest way to check for new messages directed to youis to `GO` to the forum and watch the status bar. WinCIM will report if there are messages waiting. Only if that is the case, press the `Waiting` button on the special Forum Toolbox (the uppermost button on the left side) or select the `Get Waiting` option on the `Messages` menu.

Posting a message in terminal mode

To begin a new thread, issue the `COMPOSE` command from the `MESSAGES !` prompt. Write or upload the message, and enter `/EXIT` on an empty line. Next, you have to post the message; use the `POST` command to do this. An example of a valid syntax is:

```
Post action ! post section:1 to:Roelf Sluman [71333,1443] sub:Test
message
```

CompuServe will respond with something like:

```
Message # 12345 posted
```

HINTS & TIPS

Deleting a message

To delete a message in terminal mode, you use the `DEL` command from the `MESSAGES !` menu. Note that you can only delete messages that were posted to or by you.

CompuServe Navigator

In the 'Script Editor' window, click on the Message Commands folder for the forum in which you want to post a message. (If necessary, drag the forum service from the Services window into the 'Script Editor' window.) Next, click on the `Create/Send Message` button. CompuServe Navigator will display the 'Forum Message Envelope' dialog (see Figure 8.14). This dialog contains the following fields:

- *Forum*: This field contains the name of the forum in which your message will be posted.
- *Section*: Select the forum section in which to post the message from this field.
- *To*: Enter the name the recipient in this field. You can also press the `To` button to get access to your Address Book.
- *Addr*: Enter the User ID of the recipient in this field. If you have copied the address information from your Address Book, this field will already contain the necessary data. If you are sending a message to `Sysop` or to `All`, you can leave this field empty.
- *Subject*: Enter a subject for this message. Remember that this subject will be the *topic* of the message thread.
- *Send Options*: Decide how you want the message to be sent: normal (everyone on the forum can see the message), private (only the addressee can read the message), or *via* regular e-mail. Note that the Private and *Via* Mail options cannot be accessed from all forums. Typically, free forums don't support sending e-mail messages, while the private message facility is often disabled in forums with a lot of message traffic.

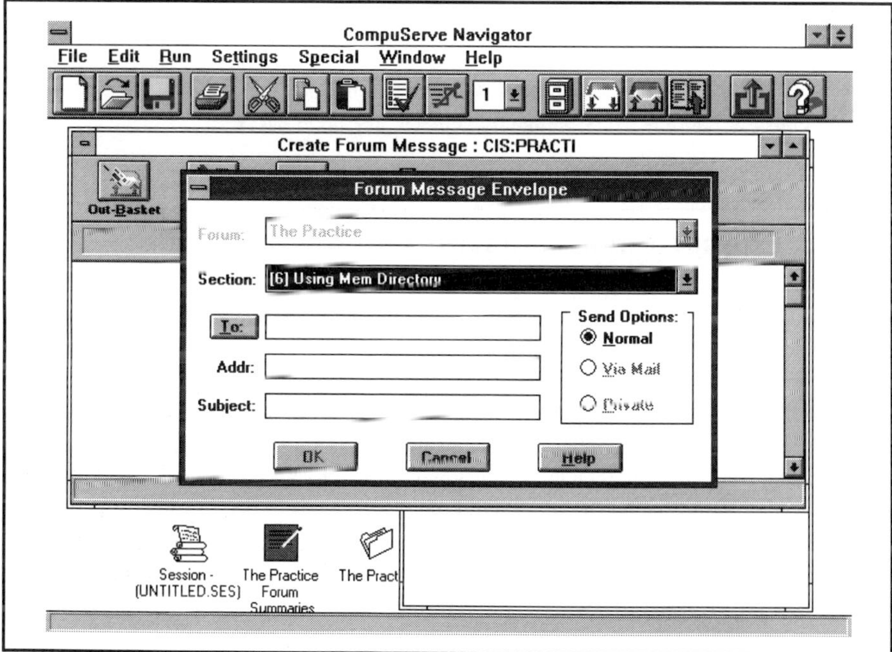

Figure 8.14 Use this dialog to specify addressing and other information

After you have closed the 'Forum Message Envelope' dialog by pressing **OK**, the Create 'Forum Message' dialog appears. The main part of this dialog is reserved for your message. Additionally, this dialog contains the following options:

- *Out-Basket*: Press this button when you have finished writing the message. CompuServe Navigator will place the message in your Out-Basket, and post it during the next script execution.
- *File*: Press this button to place a copy of your message in a Filing Cabinet folder.
- *Envelope*: Press this button to re-open the 'Envelope' dialog (see Figure 8.14).
- *Auto-file*: When this option is selected, CompuServe Navigator will place a copy of your message in the Filing Cabinet's Auto-Filed folder.

TapCIS

On the `<F>orums` menu, activate the forum in which you want to post the message. Next, on the TapCIS main menu, select <W>rite messages and choose the forum. You can now start composing the message. When you have finished, press F7 to have TapCIS store the message in a `.SND` file for that forum. Next time TapCIS goes online, it will post the message.

HINTS & TIPS

Reformatting your message text

Unlike other editors, TapCIS doesn't automatically reformat the text that you write. However, you don't have to reformat every paragraph yourself: just press Ctrl-B.

8.7.5 Etiquette and behaviour online

CompuServe members spend a lot of time writing messages, with results varying from sheer poetry to something that could best be described as 'unreadable trash'. Of course, anything between those two extremes can be found as well...

Naturally, you will want your forum messages to be read (something that applies to e-mail messages too). Nowadays, members of online services like CompuServe are confronted with loads of text, scrolling before their eyes. Don't expect them to read your message because *you* consider it important. But on the other hand, there is a lot you can do to make a message attractive to the eye, easy to read, and provocative enough to generate lots of replies.

I can imagine that you might find the guidelines in the following paragraphs a little restrictive, to say the least. In that case, just remember that these are the guidelines that I use, simply because they turned out to be effective. There is no 'one way solution' when it comes to writing electronic messages, so feel free to make your own rules.

By far the most important guideline: *check your spelling!* There are a lot of spelling checkers around these days, and some programs (like the revolutionary new NAVCIS program) even has one built in! Even if English isn't your native language, pay attention to this aspect, and be assured that your readers will be grateful to you. If you want to know why, just read a few messages posted by people who end their compositions with phrases like 'I typed this online, sorry about teh msitakes'. At first, reading such messages may be nothing more than annoying, but sooner or later you will find that you skip them without giving them a second thought. Now you don't want that to happen to your messages, do you?

Don't make your sentences too long, and avoid using complicated words or structures. Keep in mind that your fellow members don't necessarily speak English as well as you do. Keep it short and simple. If you really want the online audience to read all of your message, you could use the 'seven-seconds rule':

'If you can get them to keep reading for seven seconds, it is very likely that they will read it all.'

I heard that one at a seminar for editors, and I find it to be more than suitable when it comes to electronic messages.

Another useful tip: don't clutter your messages with unnecessary 'signatures' and 'headers'. These take time to download, and they often don't add anything substantial to the message. A lot of members get irritated by them, which could cause them not to respond to your message, even if they know the answer that you are looking for! If your program (OzCIS and NavCIS are good examples) supports these signatures: switch them off.

Next, the 'quote issue'. If you have BBS or USENET experience, the chances are that you have seen lots and lots of messages which seem to consist only of copies of previous messages, with short answers. In the next reply, the complete message (with all answers) is quoted in full again, making it almost impossible to read.

It is no wonder that forum sysops frown upon extensive quoting. First of all, it is superfluous. Because CompuServe's forum messages are based on a thread structure, every member can 'go back' and read the parent message, if necessary. (Most access programs support this feature extensively.) Secondly, it makes for dull writing. Skilled message writers almost never quote: they take up the challenge of composing their answers in such a way that they refer to the parent message in only a few words.

And finally, the most important one of all: be polite! Don't forget that the reader(s) of your message can't see your face at the moment you wrote it. Things that you wrote in jest can come across as sarcastic, or even downright painful. If necessary, use a special abbreviation or emoticon to indicate that you were only joking. Online, you will see plenty of examples. Don't use e-mail messages as a means to 'throw digital flames' at someone, a process that is known as *flaming*. If you are about to send a really angry message to someone, store it for a few more hours before you actually put it in the mail. Then, read it again and see if you still agree with everything you wrote. Always picture yourself as the receiver of that message. Would you be offended by it? In that case, it is likely that the recipient will be offended too.

Abbreviations

To keep messages short and to the point, and often out of habit, CompuServe members use a comprehensive range of abbreviations. Although some of these abbreviations are rather far-fetched, there are others that are hard to do without, once you are accustomed to using them.

The following list contains most of the abbreviations that you will encounter in forum messages. And if you should encounter an abbreviation that is not included in this list: don't hesitate to ask the sender what it means!

0.02	Throwing in your two cents' worth
AFAIK	As far as I know
AWHFY	Are we having fun yet?
B4	Before
B4N	Bye for Now
BAD	Broken as Designed
BBR	Burnt Beyond Repair
BBS	Bulletin Board System
BCNU	Be seein' you!
BFN	Bye For Now
BION	Believe it or not
BMTIPG	Brilliant minds think in parallel gutters
BRB	Be right back (during conferences, and on CB)
BRS	Big Red Switch
BTA	But then again
BTAIM	Be that as it may
BTOBD	Be there or be dead
BTSOOM	Beats the s**t out of me
BTW	By the way
BWQ	Buzz Word Quotient
CAD	Control-Alt-Delete
CADET	Can't add, doesn't even try
CIM	CompuServe Information Manager
CIS	Compuserve Information System
CI$	CompuServe Information System
CO	Conference
CU	See you
CUL8R	See you later
DIIK	Darn if I know
DL	Download
DOSCIM	CompuServe Information Manager for DOS
DTRT	Do the right thing
DWIMC	Do what I mean, correctly
ENS	Executive News Service (one of CompuServe's services)

FCFS	First come, first served
FISH	First in, still here
FOAF	Friend of a friend
FTF	Face to face
FUBAR	Fouled up beyond all recognition
FUD	Fear, uncertainty, and doubt
FWIW	For what it's worth
FYI	For your information
g,d&tr	grinning, ducking, and running
g,d&trf	grinning, ducking and running FAST!
g,d&trvvf	grinning, ducking and running VERY VERY FAST
GA	Go ahead
GDW	Grin, duck and weave
GIGO	Garbage in, garbage out
GLGH	Good luck and good hunting
GMTA	Great minds think alike
GOWI	Get on with it
GPF	General Protection Fault
GP,F	Go puke, fast!
HSIK	How should I know
IAAA	I am an accountant
IAAL	I am a lawyer
IANAA	I am not an accountant
IANAL	I am not a lawyer
IAC	In any case
IAE	In any event
IMO	In my opinion
IMHO	In my humble opinion
IMCO	In my considered opinion
IMAO	In my arrogant opinion
IME	In my experience
IMPOV	In my point of view
IOW	In other words
ITFA	In the final analysis
IWBNI	If would be nice if
IYFEG	Insert your favourite ethnic group
JAM	Just a moment
JAS	Just a second
JAWS	Just another Windows shell
JIC	Just in case
LMAO	Laughing my arm off
LOL	Laughing out loud
MOF	Matter of fact

MOTAS	Member of the appropriate sex
MOTOS	Member of the opposite sex
MOTSS	Member of the same sex
MOTM	Member of the month
NBD	No big deal
NFW	No f***ing way
NINO	Nothing in, nothing out
NOYB	None of your business
NQA	No questions asked
NTIM	Not that it matters
NTIMM	Not that it matters much
NUI	Network user identification
OBTW	Oh, by the way
OIC	Oh, I see
OTF	On the floor
OTL	Out to lunch
OTOH	On the other hand
OTTH	On the third hand
OTTOMH	Off the top of my head
PABG	Pack a big gun
PDN	Public data network
PITA	Pain in the anatomy
PLOKTA	Press lots of keys to abort
PMBI	Pardon my butting in
PMFBI	Pardon me for butting in
PMFJI	Pardon me for jumping in
POSSLQ	Person of opposite sex sharing living quarters
POV	Point of view
PPN	Programmer Project Number: old term for User-ID
RFD	Request for discussion
RHIP	Rank has its privileges
RLCO	Real Life Conference
RNA	Ring, no answer
ROFL	Rolling on floor, laughing
RPG	Role playing games
RSN	Real soon now (release date of software ...)
RTFM	Read the 'friendly' manual
SMOP	Small matter of programming
SNAFU	Situation normal, all 'fixed' up
SO	Significant other (cybertalk for 'partner')
SUFID	Screwing up face in disgust
SWMBO	She who must be obeyed
Sysop	System Operator

TAFN	Thats all for now
TANJ	There ain't no justice
TANSTAAFL	There ain't no such thing as a free lunch
TBYB	Try before you buy
TFTT	Thanks for the thought
TGIF	Thank God it's friday
TIA	Thanks in advance
TIC	Tongue in cheek
TM	Thread mangler
TPTB	The powers that be
TSR	Totally stupid rules
TTFN	Ta ta for now
TTL4N	That's the lot for now
UAE	Unrecoverable application error
UL or U/L	Upload
WAEF	When all else fails
WizOp	Wizard Sysop (the 'chief' sysop of a forum)
WOA	Work of art
WYSIWYG	What you see is what you get
WYSBYGI	What you see before you get it
WYGIWYPF	What you get is what you pay for
YADS	Yet another DOS shell
ZNT	ZiffNet

CompuServe sign language: emoticons

Remember the 'smileys' that people used to wear some years ago? For those of you who thought that you had seen the last of those creatures: they are back! The smileys of the digital age, called *emoticons*, have invaded information services like CompuServe, and can be spotted anywhere from online conferences to forum messages. By far the most popular one is :–). If you don't see what this symbol represents, just tilt your head to the left!

Smileys have come a long way on CompuServe. Take a look at the following list, which contains an overview of the creatures that might invade your messages too, sooner or later...

<table>
<tr><td>:-)</td><td>Smiling</td><td>:-r</td><td>Sticking tongue out</td></tr>
<tr><td>:-|</td><td>Grim</td><td>:-*</td><td>Oops!</td></tr>
<tr><td>:-(</td><td>Frowning</td><td>:-T</td><td>Keeping a straight face</td></tr>
<tr><td>:-c</td><td>Really unhappy</td><td>;-)</td><td>Sardonic incredulity</td></tr>
<tr><td>:-[</td><td>Pouting</td><td>:-D</td><td>Said with a smile</td></tr>
<tr><td>'-)</td><td>Wink</td><td>%-<I></td><td>Drunk with laughter</td></tr>
<tr><td>:-,</td><td>'Hmmmm '</td><td>:-x</td><td>Kiss kiss</td></tr>
<tr><td>:-o</td><td>Wow!</td><td>:-"</td><td>Pursing lips</td></tr>
<tr><td>:-C</td><td>Just totally unbelieving</td><td>:-#</td><td>My lips are sealed</td></tr>
<tr><td>:= |</td><td>Baboon</td><td>|-{</td><td>'Good Grief!'</td></tr>
<tr><td>:-B</td><td>Drooling</td><td>:-}</td><td>'Thish wine tashted</td></tr>
<tr><td>:-v</td><td>Speaking</td><td></td><td>pretty good'</td></tr>
<tr><td>:-,</td><td>Smirk</td><td>8-]</td><td>'wow, maaan'</td></tr>
<tr><td>:-V</td><td>Shout</td><td>:^D</td><td>'Great! I like it!'</td></tr>
<tr><td>:-||</td><td>Anger</td><td>B-D</td><td>'Serves you right,</td></tr>
<tr><td>:-w</td><td>Speak with forked tongue</td><td></td><td>dummy!!'</td></tr>
</table>

HINTS & TIPS

Not enough?

Do you want more smileys? `GO IBMFF` and search for files with the keyword `EMOTICON`.

8.8 Files

The hundreds of forum libraries on CompuServe are filled with programs, text files, pictures, videos, sounds, and lots of other interesting stuff, just waiting to be downloaded by you. As you will see, downloading files from CompuServe is very easy to do, especially if you use one of the special access programs.

If you are looking for a particular file, there are three ways to find out where it is:

- If you have a pretty good idea in which forum library the file can be found, you can *browse* through that library.
- If you know in which forum the file resides, and if you know the name of the file as well, you can *search* for it.
- If you haven't the vaguest idea where to look for the file, you can use one of the CompuServe File Finders.

8.8.1 Browsing the library

Browsing the library is a fun way to see what hidden treasures a particular forum contains. When you have stumbled across a file that you would like to obtain, you can download it to your own computer.

Browsing with WinCIM

To browse through the library of a forum with WinCIM, proceed as follows:

1. `GO` to the forum. When you arrive, press either the `Library Browse` button on the special Forum Toolbox (the book collection with the pointing hand), or select the `Browse` option on the `Library` menu.
2. WinCIM displays a list of available library sections. To browse through a section, double-click on it, or select it with the arrow keys and press Enter.
3. Next, WinCIM shows a list of files in the library, starting with the files most recently contributed. (See Figure 8.15.) After you have selected a file, you have the following options:
   - *Description*: Press this button to see a more extensive description of the file. If you want to save the description to review it online, select the `Save` option on the `File` menu. WinCIM will store the description in an ASCII file. To review the contents of this file, select the `Open` option on the `File` menu.
   - *Mark*: If you press this button, the file is *marked* for later retrieval. This is useful if you want to download several files. After you have marked those files, select the `Retrieve Marked` option on the `Library` menu to initiate the download.
     After you have pressed the `Mark` button, WinCIM will ask for the name under which the file should be saved onto your hard disk. You can either accept the name that CompuServe proposes, or edit it. WinCIM will store the download files in the `\CSERVE\DOWNLOAD` directory by default.
   - *Retrieve*: Press this button to download the file to your computer. This option is useful if you know beforehand that you are only going to download one file.
     Before starting the download, WinCIM will ask for the name under which it should save the file onto your hard disk. Unless you specify otherwise, the file will be stored in the `\CSERVE\DOWNLOAD` directory.
   - *View*: Pressing this button displays the contents of the file on your screen. Note that not all file formats can be viewed. Version 1.3 of WinCIM supports online display of graphics files in `GIF` and `JPEG` formats, and of regular ASCII text files.

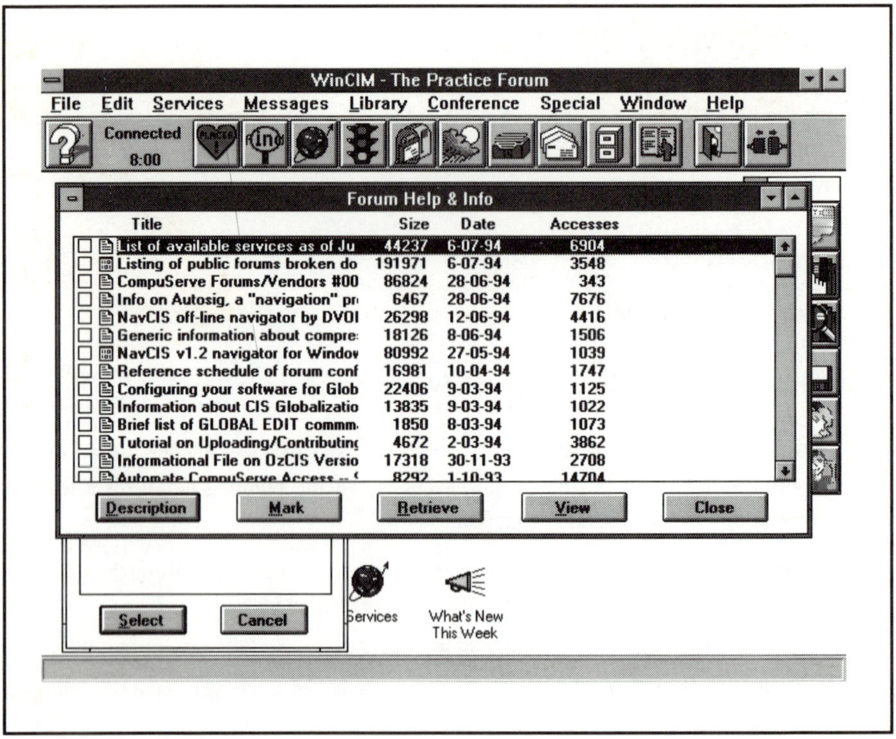

Figure 8.15 Free wealth on CompuServe: a sample of files in the Practice Forum

4. When you have marked one or more files for download, you can go back to step 2 and review the contents of another library (in the same forum).

HINTS & TIPS

Mark files and have WinCIM disconnect automatically

If you have marked one or more files and use the `Retrieve Marked` option on the `Library` menu to download them, you can check the 'Disconnect when Done' box. After downloading all files, WinCIM will disconnect automatically. This option is not available when you *retrieve* only one file.

Don't just sit there!

When WinCIM is busy retrieving files, you are free to do other things online, as long as you stay in the current forum. You could browse through other library sections, read some messages, or even participate in a conference. Because the download procedure takes precedence, you will notice that WinCIM functions a little more slowly than usual.

Browsing in terminal mode

To get access to the forum library, enter the LIBRARY command after any forum prompt:

```
Forum !library

Libraries Menu
...
...
Enter choice !
```

CompuServe shows a list of available library sections. Enter the number of the section that you want to use. You will see that, even if you are in a certain section, it is possible to retrieve information about files stored in other sections.

To get an overview of files available in one or more library sections, you use the SCAN command. It is useful to open a capture file before you do this, so that you can review the contents of the library section offline.

A typical example of the SCAN command is:

```
Enter choice !SCAN AGE:14 LIB:ALL SHORT
```

This will retrieve a summary of the files in all library sections that were uploaded during the past 14 days, with a short description for each file.

The next example would retrieve a complete list of long descriptions of all files in the forum library:

```
Enter choice !SCAN LIB:ALL DES
```

After you have retrieved one or more summaries, you can disconnect and review the results offline.

If you have all the time you need: the BROWSE command

If you don't mind staying online for a longer time, you can use the BROWSE command to browse through the library sections interactively. After showing the information for a file, CompuServe presents you with a menu of choices. You can either download the file, view it online, or go to the next file.

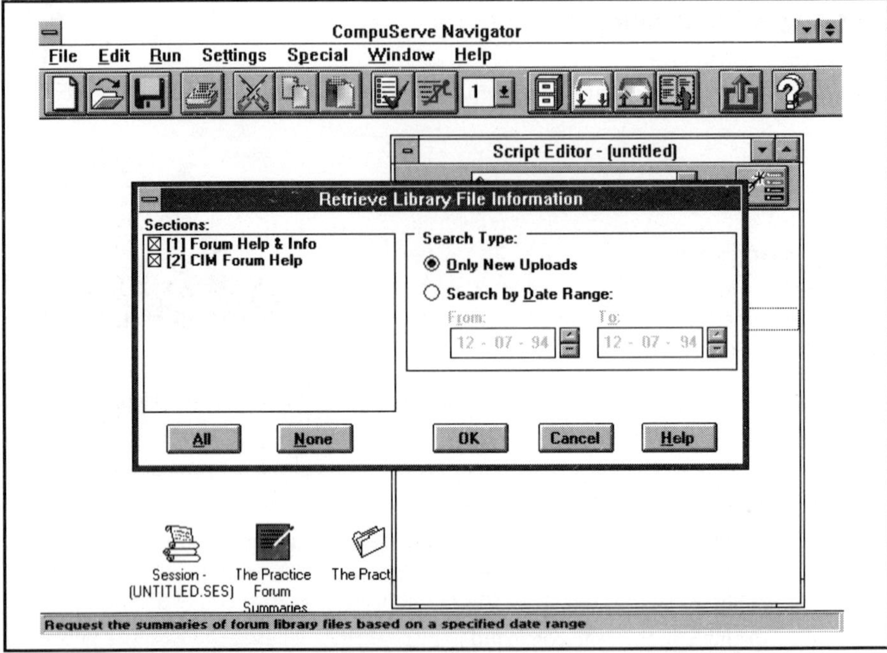

Figure 8.16 Retrieving library information with CompuServe Navigator

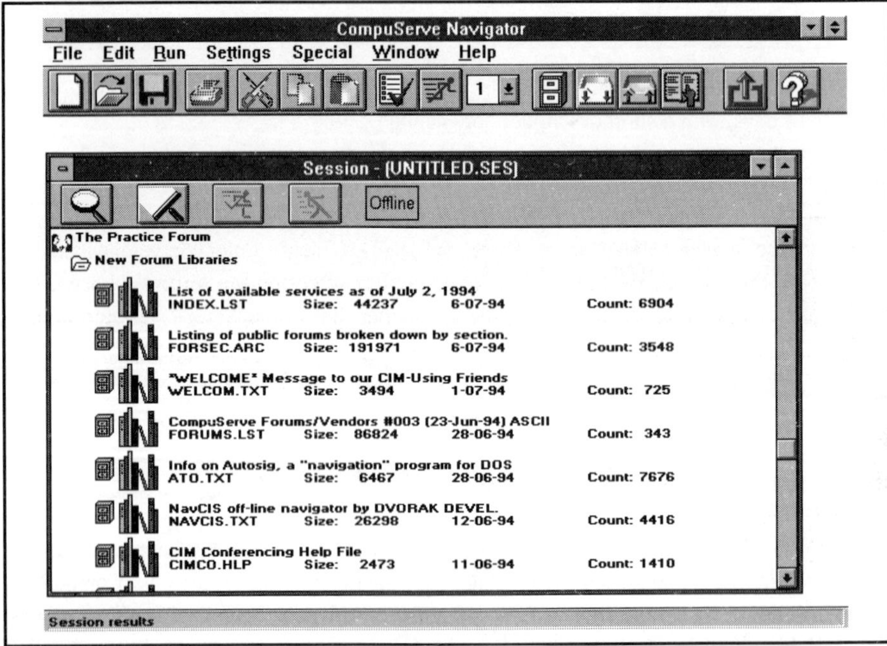

Figure 8.17 Browsing through the file entries

Browsing with CompuServe Navigator

CompuServe Navigator provides extensive facilities for browsing through forum libraries offline. It does so by collecting a *summary* into the Filing Cabinet. This summary contains a number of *file abstracts*: short, informative texts about the summarized files. When you review these abstracts offline, you can select the files you want to download and have CompuServe Navigator retrieve them automatically. Proceed as follows:

1. Go to the 'Script Editor' window, and click on the Library Commands folder for the appropriate forum to expand it. Four new tasks will appear, all related to library activities.
2. Click on the Summarize `New Files` button. A dialog appears (see Figure 8.16) that contains the following options:
   - *Sections*: Check the sections for which you would like to see a summary. By default, all sections are selected. You can select and deselect sections manually, or use the `All` and `None` buttons.
   - *Search Type*: When you select `Only New Uploads` (the default option), CompuServe Navigator will retrieve information for new files only (that is, files for which it hasn't yet retrieved a summary). If you wish, you can specify a date range to limit the search.

Once CompuServe Navigator has retrieved the summary, you will find the file descriptions in the 'Session' window. Figure 8.17 shows a list of files that reside in the free Practice Forum.

There are two ways to review a summary of files, depending on whether or not the 'Session' window is open:

- Double-click on the individual abstracts, listed in the 'Session' window.
- Select the `Search Libraries` option on the `Special` menu. CompuServe Navigator will display the 'Search Offline Library' dialog. After selecting the forums whose offline libraries you wish to review (that is, the summaries that CompuServe Navigator retrieved earlier), press the buttons `Add` and `Search`, respectively. CompuServe Navigator will display a list of entries: double-click on an entry to see its abstract.

Browsing with TapCIS

TapCIS provides facilities to browse through libraries offline, thereby reducing your costs substantially. To make this possible, TapCIS collects library information and stores it in *catalogue files*. Proceed as follows:

1. Go to the `<F>orums` menu and activate the forum for which you would like TapCIS to create a catalogue. You can activate as many forums as you wish.

2. On the TapCIS main menu, select the `<L>ibrary search` command. TapCIS will ask for the forum for which the command should be performed. Press the appropriate forum key: a number key for the forums on the first row, and Shift plus a function key for the forums on the second row.

3. TapCIS asks for the `File(s) to find` and shows a provisional file specification (`*.*`), you can either press Enter to accept this proposal, or type in another specification. For example, if you want to browse through all available `GIF` files only, change the specification to `*.GIF`.

4. Next, TapCIS asks for one or more *keywords*. Press Enter to browse through all files.

5. The next part of the search criteria concerns the *AGE Range*: the minimum or maximum number of days that the file has been residing in the library. A few examples: if you enter 10 or minus 10, TapCIS will search the library for all files that were posted 10 or less than 10 days ago. To search for all files that are between 10 and 20 days old, enter 10–20. To search for all files that are older than 20 days, enter 20 minus. Or you could simply press Enter to search for all files in the library, irrespective of their age.

   Note that TapCIS remembers the last time you used the `<L>ibrary` command for any forum. It will place a default value in the 'AGE Range' field. Press Enter to accept this range.

6. There are two description methods available. *Short* descriptions are exactly one line long and contain brief information about the file; they are the same descriptions that you see when you browse through a list of files displayed by WinCIM. The advantage of using short descriptions is that it takes very little time to retrieve library information. *Long* descriptions are much more extensive, but take more time to retrieve. They are identical to the text that you see when you press WinCIM's `Description` button. Since TapCIS allows you to do separate library searches for each forum, and even for one or more library sections, you can make the decision between short and long descriptions according to your needs.

7. Before TapCIS can start composing your catalogue, it needs to know what sections to search in. If TapCIS has 'join'-ed the forum, the available library sections are listed on the right-hand side of the screen. If you want to select all sections, enter 1–23; TapCIS will ignore non-existent sections and simply retrieve information from all sections it can find.

8. After TapCIS has retrieved the library information, choose the <C>atalog option to browse through the catalogue. When you see a file you like, press [D] to download the file, and to select one or more files to download.

8.8.2 Searching for a particular file

When you already know the name of the file, and in which forum that file is located, you can search for the library in which the file is stored. Additionally, you can search for all files in a particular forum that match one or more *keywords*. After you have found a file that matches your search criteria, you can download it to your computer.

Searching for files with WinCIM

Press the `Library Search` button on the Forum Toolbox (the book collection with the magnifying glass), or select the `Search` option on the `Library` menu. WinCIM will display the 'Search for Files' dialog (see Figure 8.18). This dialog contains the following options:

- *In sections*: Check the sections you would like to search. By default, all sections are selected. You can select or deselect sections manually, or use the `All` and `None` buttons. When you are not sure in which section the file you are looking for is stored, leave all sections set to 'on'.
- *File Name*: If you know the name of the file to download, for example because someone pointed you to it, enter it in this field, select all sections and press the `Search` button. Note that you can also enter a *wildcard specification*. For instance, if you want a list of all files with the extension `.TXT`, enter `*.TXT` in the 'File Name' field.
- *Contributor*: If you are looking for a file uploaded by someone specific, enter his or her User ID in this field. It is not possible to enter a name in this field: you have to know the User ID of the member that uploaded the file.
- *Keywords*: When someone uploads ('contributes') a file, he or she provides certain keywords that reflect the contents and purpose of the file. If you are searching for files that deal with a specific topic, enter one or more possible keywords in this field (separate them with a space character). Note that only the files that match all keywords will be displayed. Therefore, start by specifying one keyword. If this results in too many files, you can always specify a second keyword.
- *Between*: By default, all files in the library will be searched, irrespective of age. However, you can specify start and end dates, in which case the search will be limited to the files that were uploaded between those dates.

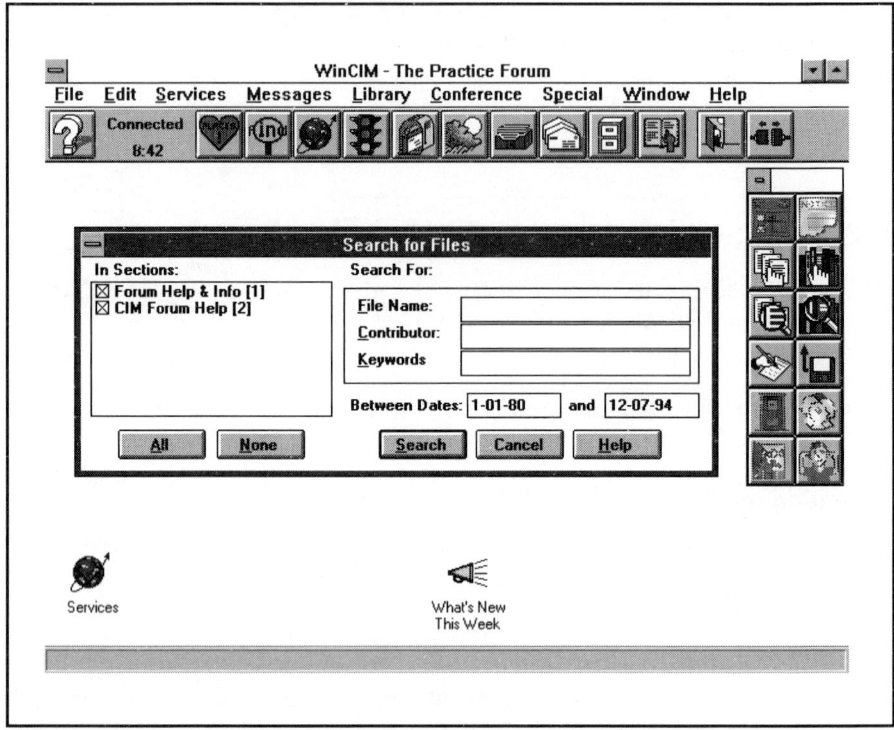

Figure 8.18 Use this dialog when you are looking for a specific file

Searching for files in terminal mode

You can ask CompuServe to display information for all files that match a *search specification*, or that were uploaded with one or more keywords. When you let your communication software store the search results in a capture file, you can review them offline.

Let's say that you are looking for all files that contain the keyword `WINDOWS`. In the forum, type `LIBRARY` to get to the library menu. Next, issue the following command:

```
Enter choice !scan keyword:windows lib:all des
```

This command retrieves a summary of all files that were uploaded with the `WINDOWS` keyword. For each file, the long description is displayed.

You can also use the **SCAN** command to look for files that match a certain specification. For instance, to search through all available sections for files with the extension **.GIF**, enter the following command:

```
Enter choice !scan *.GIF lib:all
```

For additional information about the possibilities of the **SCAN** command, see under the heading 'Browsing in terminal mode' on page 315.

Searching for files with CompuServe Navigator

When you order CompuServe Navigator to search for files, the application will collect a *summary* into the Filing Cabinet. This summary contains a number of *file abstracts*: short, informative texts about the summarized files. When you review those abstracts offline, you can select the files you want to download and have CompuServe Navigator retrieve them automatically. Proceed as follows:

1. Go to the 'Script Editor' window, and click on the Library Commands folder for the appropriate forum to expand it. Four new tasks will appear, all related to library activities.
2. Click on the **Search Library** button. A dialog appears (see Figure 8.19). This dialog contains the following fields and options:

- *Search sections*: Check the sections in which you would like CompuServe Navigator to search. By default, all sections are selected. You can select or deselect sections manually, or use the **All** and **None** buttons. When you are not sure in which section the file you are looking for is stored, leave all sections set to 'on'.
- *File Name*: If you know the name of the file to download, for example because someone pointed you to it, enter it in this field, select all sections and press the **OK** button. Note that you can also enter a *wildcard specification*. For instance, if you want a summary of all files with the extension **.TXT**, enter ***.TXT** in the File Name field.
- *Contributor*: If you are looking for a list of files uploaded by someone specific, enter his or her User ID in this field. It is not possible to enter a name: you have to know the User ID of the person that uploaded that file to CompuServe.
- *Keywords*: When someone uploads ('contributes') a file, he or she provides certain keywords that pertain to the contents and purpose of the file. If you are searching for files that deal with a specific topic, enter one or more possible keywords in this field (separate them with a space character). Note that only the files that match all keywords will be

displayed. Therefore, start by specifying one keyword. If this results in too many files, you can always specify a second one.

- *Date Range*: By default, all files in the library will be searched, irrespective of age. However, you can specify start and end dates, in which case the search will only produce files that were uploaded between those dates.

Do Not Delete After Processing: If you want to perform a one-time search only, uncheck this option. Leave it checked to create a search task that can be performed more often, for instance once every month.

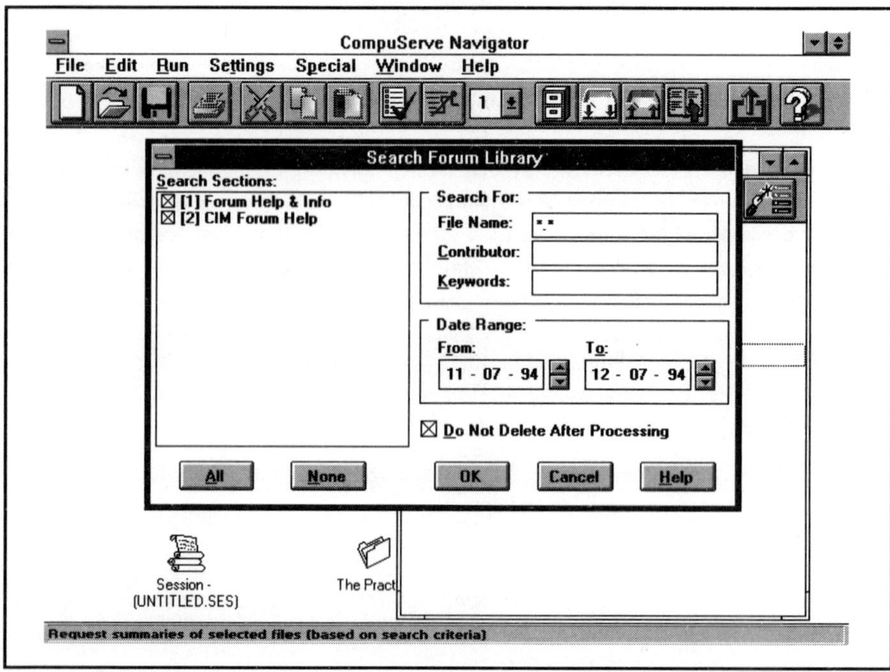

Figure 8.19 Searching for files with CompuServe Navigator

Searching for files with TapCIS

TapCIS helps you to prepare your search offline. It will use your search specifications to retrieve a *catalogue* that contains descriptions about all matching files. While browsing this catalogue, you can easily select the files to download by pressing the [D] key.

In TapCIS, there isn't much difference between searching for files and browsing through them. Therefore, refer to the heading 'Browsing with TapCIS' on page 317 for more information.

8.8.3 Downloading a file

The process of transferring a file from one computer to another is called *downloading*. During the download, both computers use a *protocol* to ensure that no data is lost on the way. When you use one of the popular CompuServe access programs, you can benefit from the built-in CompuServe B+ protocol. This protocol is not only very fast, it also allows for 'resumed downloads', in case something went wrong. Thanks to the ability to resume a download, you don't have to download a large file all over again if something untoward happened. Instead, only the missing part of the file has to be downloaded.

Downloading with WinCIM

To start downloading the file you have selected, press the `Retrieve` button. WinCIM will ask for the name under which it should store the file on your hard disk. The download commences as soon as you press the `OK` button. You don't have to worry about download protocols; WinCIM takes care of that. You can monitor the download process on-screen, if you wish.

If you have marked several files for download, select the `Retrieve Marked` option on the `Library` menu. WinCIM lists the files you are about to download, offering you the chance of removing one or more files if you have reconsidered in the meantime.

My download failed. Do I have to start all over again?

In most cases, you don't. Beginning with version 1.2, WinCIM supports *resumed downloads*. Just download the same file again; WinCIM will show a dialog to inform you that there is already a file with the same name present on your hard disk. Select `Resume` to have WinCIM download the remaining parts and add them to the file, or select `Overwrite` to replace the current file by the one that WinCIM is about to download.

Downloading in terminal mode

There are two ways to download a file in terminal mode. If you know the name of the file as well as the library section it's in, go to that section (use the `LID` command) and enter the `DOWNLOAD` command to download the file. You can use the Xmodem and Ymodem protocols, as well as Kermit and the regular CompuServe 'B' Protocol.

Another method uses the `BROWSE` command to locate the file. Let's say that you want to download the file `DEMO.EXE`, but you don't know in which section that file is stored. Enter the `BROWSE` command, as follows:

```
Enter choice !browse demo.exe lib:all
```

If CompuServe can locate the file in one of the library sections, it will display extensive information about it. To download the file, simply enter the **DOWNLOAD** command. If you want to download it using a special protocol, enter the protocol as a separate parameter. To download the file using the Xmodem protocol, enter:

```
Disposition!download proto:xmo
```

Downloading with CompuServe Navigator

Use one of the following methods to download a file:

- If you have retrieved a summary for the forum in which the file is stored (see under the heading 'Browsing with CompuServe Navigator' on page 317), select the **Search Libraries** option on the **Special** menu. Next, check the forum in the Libraries to Search section and press the buttons **Add** and **Search**, respectively. CompuServe Navigator will show the file summary; select the file to download and press the **Retrieve** button. After you close the dialog, the name of the file will appear in the 'Script Editor' window, as part of the Retrieve Files folder. Next time CompuServe Navigator executes the Retrieve Files task, it will download the file.
- If you know the name of the file, go to the 'Script Editor' window and click on the **Retrieve Files** button for the appropriate forum. Fill in the 'Retrieve Library File' dialog (you can omit the Submitter ID) and press **OK**. Next time CompuServe Navigator executes the Retrieve Files task, it will search for the file and download it, if found.

Cancelling a download

If you decide not to download a file after all, you can delete the instruction from the forum script. If necessary, open the Retrieve Files folder to display the names of the files that will be downloaded during the next script execution. Next, place the mouse pointer onto the filename and press the **right** mouse button. A pop-up menu appears; select the **Delete** option to delete the Retrieve task for that file from the 'Script Editor' window.

Downloading with TapCIS

TapCIS automates file downloading. When browsing through the library information (choose the `<C>atalog` option on the TapCIS main menu to do this), press the [D] key to mark the file for downloading. Next time TapCIS visits the forum, it will retrieve the file and store it in the download directory.

The destination of downloaded files

To specify where TapCIS should store the downloaded files, go to the `<P>arameters` screen and change the `<D>ownload` file path field. If TapCIS can't find the directory, it will store the files in the directory that contains the TapCIS program files.

In some occasions, you might prefer to go online `<I>nteractively` using TapCIS. Note that because the program supports automatic downloading in interactive mode as well, you can issue an online download command at any time. When CompuServe asks for a protocol, select `CompuServe B:` TapCIS will detect that a download is at hand and start it automatically.

Something went wrong during the download. Do I have to start all over again?

In most cases, you don't. Because TapCIS supports the advanced CompuServe B protocol, it can *resume* incomplete downloads. When TapCIS detects that a file is already (albeit partly) present on your hard disk, it will ask you whether you want to overwrite that file, or append data to it.

8.8.4 Uploading a file

If you have written a program that you would like to share with other forum members, or if you have any other file that you wish to contribute, you can upload it to one of the forums. Once your uploaded file is available on the forum, every member can download it. Lots of famous shareware authors started their careers by uploading a few programs to the right CompuServe forum!

Uploading a file to CompuServe is free of connect charges, although communication surcharges still apply (and don't forget your telephone bill, either). As soon as you enter the upload area, you are 'off the meter'.

Attention shareware writers!

If you earn your money writing shareware, you might consider allowing your users to register their software *via* CompuServe. `GO SWREG` for additional information.

After you have uploaded a file, one of the forum sysops will *evaluate* it (a procedure that normally involves a virus check as well) and, if he or she approves the file, make it accessible for the general public.

Watch your rights!

Please note that you have to own or have sufficient rights to the file(s) you are about to upload. CompuServe cannot be held responsible for any problems that arise as a result of copyright material unlawfully being uploaded to a forum, and will gladly direct the harmed party to you. But as long as you have the copyright to the file, or permission to upload it, you have nothing to worry about.

Uploading with WinCIM

To upload a file, press the special `Contribute` button on the Forum Toolbox (the disk with the arrow), or select the `Contribute` option on the `Library` menu. The 'Library Contribute' dialog is displayed, as seen in Figure 8.20. This dialog contains the following fields and options:

- *File Name*: Enter the filename in this field, or press the button to select it.
- *Destination Name*: Enter the name under which the file should appear in the forum library. There is one important limitation, which might disappear sometime in the future: the length of the filename may not exceed six characters. Extensions up to three characters are allowed as well; separate the name and the extension by a dot. Don't use the wildcard characters `*` and `?`. Examples of valid filenames are:

```
myfile.txt
demo.exe
beauty.gif
cs4eur.doc
```

- *File type*: Select the type of file you are about to upload. Be sure to select the right type, to enable forum members to view your file online, if they wish. The following file types are supported:
  - Text: Select this type if your file is in regular text format. Don't use it if you are about to upload a word processor document; in that case, use binary instead.
  - GIF: This is the type to select if you want to upload a picture file in GIF format.

- JPEG: Select this type if you are about to upload a JPEG graphics file.
- Binary: This is the type to use if you are uploading an executable file (programs), compressed file (ZIP, ARJ, etc.), word processor document, spreadsheet, or any other file that contains binary information.

- *Title*: Type the title you want to give to your file. This title, also called the short description, is displayed when people browse through the forum library. It is best to place a short descriptive text in this field.
- *Keys*: Type one or more keywords that describe the purpose of your file. Keep in mind that people often use these keywords when they are searching for a particular file. Therefore, be as creative and yet as general as you can.
- *Forum*: Select the forum you want to upload the file to. For the forum name to appear in this combo box, you need to have visited the forum at least once using WinCIM.
- *Library Section*: Select the library section into which the file should be placed. Note that the file becomes visible only after it has been approved by one of the forum sysops.
- *Description*: This is your 'advertisement space' for the file you are about to upload. You can enter a small descriptive text about the file, as well as some remarks as to its purpose. If you wish, you can include your name here, too. ('Uploaded by ...')

After you have filled in this dialog, press the OK button to return to the 'Script Editor' window. Next time you execute this script, the file will be uploaded.

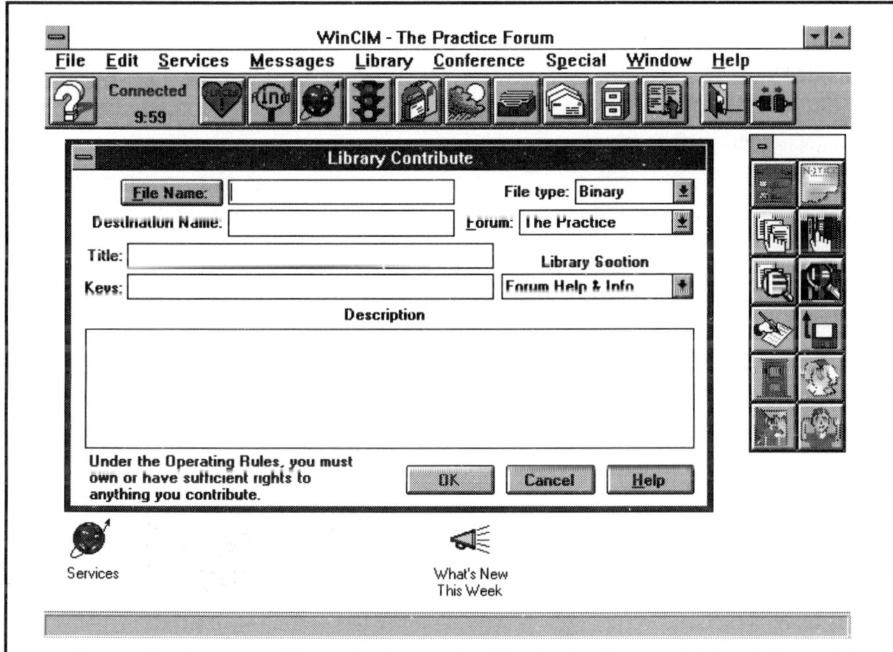

Figure 8.20 Fill in this dialog to upload a file

Uploading in terminal mode

After you have entered the forum to which you wish to upload a file, proceed as follows:

1. From the Forum! prompt, issue the `LIB` command. If you know the library section to upload the file to, type its number after the `LIB` command. If not, just type `LIB` and select the number from the menu.

```
Forum! lib 1
```

2. Next, issue the `upload` command, followed by the protocol that is supported by your access program. The following protocol options are available:
   - *PROTO:XMO*: Xmodem.
   - *PROTO:YMODEM*: Ymodem.
   - PROTO:B: CompuServe 'B'. This is the default protocol.
   - *PROTO:QB*: CompuServe Quick 'B'.
   - *PROTO:KER*: Kermit.

```
Lib 1! upload proto:xmo
```

3. CompuServe will inform you that you stop paying connect charges, and display some legal information. Also, it asks for the name under which the file should be stored in the forum:

```
Suspending connect charges...

Under our Agreement and Operating Rules,
you must own or have sufficient rights to
any information you place on the Service.
```

4. Type a filename of no more than six characters, and add an extension of three characters. Use a dot to separate the filename and the extension:

```
File name: mydoc.txt
```

5. CompuServe will show a list of available file types:

```
Transfer types available -

 1 Text (ANSI)
 2 Binary
 3 Image
 4 Graphic:RLE
 5 Graphic: NAPLPS
 6 Graphic: GIF
 7 Graphic: JPEG

Enter choice!
```

6. After you have selected one of these options, CompuServe will ask for the name under which this file is stored on your computer. Don't forget to enter the disk and directory specification as well.

```
File name for your computer: c:\docs\mydoc.txt
```

7. CompuServe will now retrieve the file from your computer, using the protocol you have specified.
8. When the upload is completed, CompuServe asks for a file description. This is the long description that members will see when they press the `Description` button using WinCIM or retrieve long descriptions in TapCIS catalogue files:

```
Enter File Description (up to 549 chars, or about seven 80-
character lines)
Type "/EXIT" when finished:
This is an example of a document, uploaded to
CompuServe.
/exit
```

9. Next, you have to provide one or more *keywords*. These should describe the purpose of your file. Keep in mind that people often use these keywords when they are searching for a particular file. Therefore, be as creative and yet as general as you can.

```
Enter Keywords ( or type "?" for HELP ): example document
```

10. The last question you have to answer pertains to the *title* of the file. This is the *short description* that will be shown when someone browses through the list of files.

```
Enter Title (up to 49 chars, <CR> when finished):
Title: Document example
```

11. Finally, CompuServe displays the information you have entered and asks you for confirmation:

```
Title   : Document example
Keywords: EXAMPLE DOCUMENT

This is an example of a  document, uploaded to
CompuServe.

Is this okay (Y or N)? y

Your request will be processed by the
Sysop as soon as possible.

Resuming connect charges.
```

Uploading with CompuServe Navigator

To upload a file to a forum, add that forum as a 'Service to the Script Editor' window. Proceed as follows:

1. Click on the Library Commands folder to expand it. Four new tasks will appear, all related to library activities.
2. Click on the `Contribute Files` button. CompuServe Navigator displays the dialog shown in Figure 8.21. This dialog contains the following fields:

- *File Name*: Enter the filename in this field, or press the button to select it from any directory and/or disk on your computer.
- *File Name for Library*: Enter the name under which the file should be appear in the forum library. The length of the filename may not exceed six characters. Extensions up to three characters are allowed as well; separate the name and the extension by a dot. Don't use the wildcard characters * and ?.
- *File type*: Select the type of file you are about to upload. Be sure to select the right type, to enable forum members to view your file online, if they wish.
- *Title*: Type the title you want to give to your file. This title, also called the *short description*, is displayed when people browse through the forum library. It is best to place a short descriptive text in this field.
- *Keys*: Type one or more keywords that describe the purpose of your file. Keep in mind that people often use these keywords when they are searching for a particular file. Therefore, be as creative and yet as general as you can.
- *Section*: Select the library section into which the file should be placed. Note that the file becomes visible only after it has been approved by one of the forum sysops.
- *Description*: This is your 'advertisement space' for the file you are about to upload. You can enter a small descriptive text about the file, as well as some remarks as to its purpose. If you wish, you can include your name here, too. ('`Uploaded by` ...')

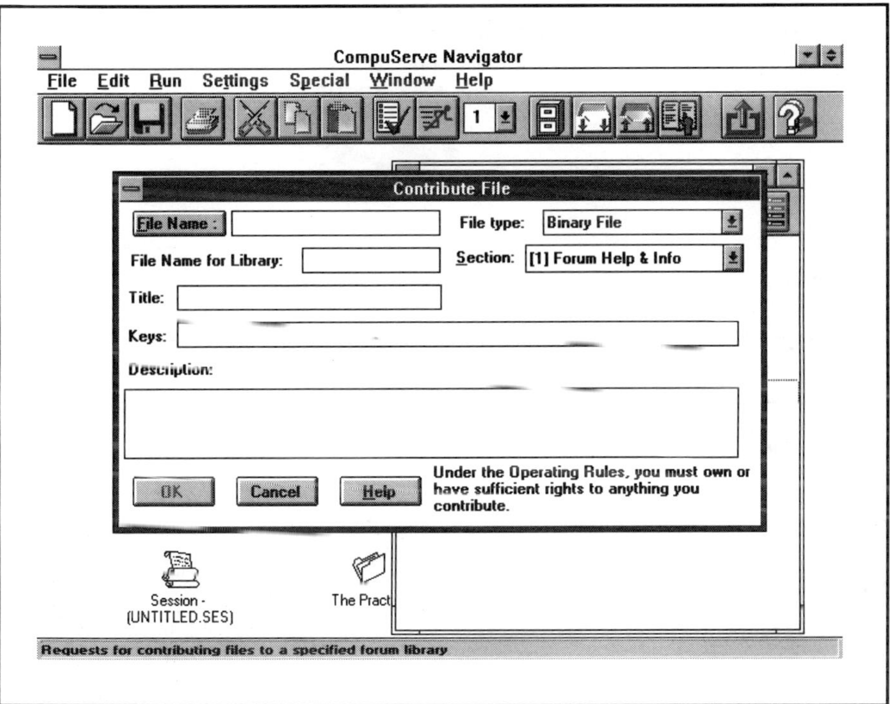

Figure 8.21 Contributing a file with CompuServe Navigator

Cancelling an upload

If you change your mind about uploading a particular file, you can delete it from the forum script. If necessary, open the Contribute Files folder to display brief information about the file to be uploaded. Next, place the mouse pointer onto the filename and press the **right** mouse button. A pop-up menu appears; select the `Delete` option to delete the Contribute task for that file from the 'Script Editor' window.

Uploading with TapCIS

There are two ways to upload a file using TapCIS. You can either do it `<I>nteractively`, or you can let a script do it for you.

Before you can upload a file to a forum, you have to know the library section in which the file should be stored. To find out what sections are available, use the `<L>ibrary` command on the TapCIS main menu, or to check the sections in the `<F>orums` menu. Write down the section number: you need it later.

After you have entered the forum to which you wish to upload a file, proceed as follows:

1. From the Forum! prompt, issue the `LIB` command, followed by the number of the library section. Next, issue the `UPLOAD` command and press Enter:

```
Forum! lib 1
Lib 1! upload
```

2. CompuServe will inform you that you stop paying connect charges, and display some legal information. Also, it asks for the name under which the file should be stored in the forum:

```
Suspending connect charges...

Under our Agreement and Operating Rules,
you must own or have sufficient rights to
any information you place on the Service.
```

3. Type a filename of no more than six characters, and add an extension of three characters. Use a dot to separate the filename and the extension:

```
File name: mydoc.txt
```

4. CompuServe will show a list of available file types:

```
Transfer types available -
 1 Text (ANSI)
 2 Binary
 3 Image
 4 Graphic:RLE
 5 Graphic: NAPLPS
 6 Graphic: GIF
 7 Graphic: JPEG
Enter choice!
```

5. After you have selected one of these options, CompuServe will ask for the name under which this file is stored on your computer. Don't forget to enter the disk and directory specification as well.

```
File name for your computer: c:\docs\mydoc.txt
```

6. CompuServe will now retrieve the file from your computer, using the CompuServe B protocol. Because TapCIS supports this protocol as well, this whole procedure is automated.

7 When the upload is completed, CompuServe asks for a file description. This is the long description that members will see when they press the `Description` button using WinCIM or retrieve long descriptions in TapCIS catalogue files:

```
Enter File Description (up to 549 chars, or about seven 80-
character lines)
Type "/EXIT" when finished.
This is an example of a document, uploaded to
CompuServe.
/exit
```

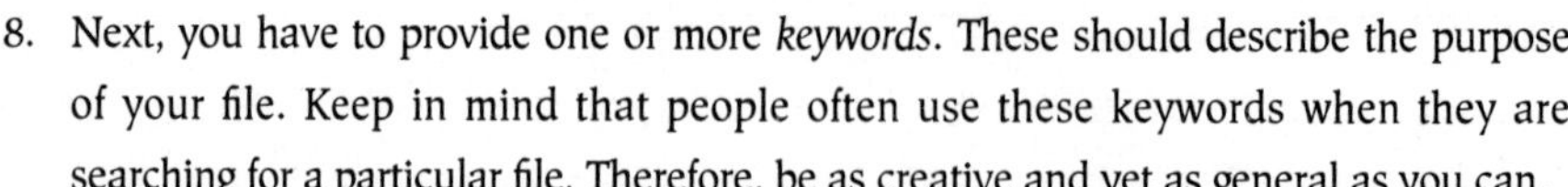

8. Next, you have to provide one or more *keywords*. These should describe the purpose of your file. Keep in mind that people often use these keywords when they are searching for a particular file. Therefore, be as creative and yet as general as you can.

```
Enter Keywords ( or type "?" for HELP ): example document
```

9. You are almost there. CompuServe asks you for the *title* of the file. This is the *short description* that will be shown when someone browses through the list of files.

```
Enter Title (up to 49 chars, <CR> when finished):
Title: Document example
```

10. And that's about it. CompuServe displays the information you have entered and asks you for confirmation:

```
Title   : Document example
Keywords: EXAMPLE DOCUMENT

This is an example of a document, uploaded to
CompuServe.

Is this okay (Y or N)? y

Your request will be processed by the
Sysop as soon as possible.

Resuming connect charges.
```

If you upload files on a frequent basis, these can be tedious steps to perform. Luckily, there is a script available that automates the uploading of files. To use this script, make a copy of it and change the contents to reflect the information for the file you are about to upload. You will find this script, naturally, in the TapCIS forum. Its description follows:

```
TAPCIS Forum, Library 2

[76702,1006]    Lib: 2
UPL.SCR/Text    Bytes:   1584, Count:  455, 27-Mar-90

Title   : Script for uploading files with TAPCIS
Keywords: UPLOAD SCRIPT UPL.SCR TAPCIS

In a circular sort of way, this is a file that was uploaded using
itself.
UPL.SCR will permit you to upload any file anywhere on CompuServe.
Edit it so that the Lib and Forums are correct and then go online
<I>nteractive selecting no Forum. At the first prompt, hit <PgUp> and
then enter UPL.
  Two rules   465 char max and no blank lines in this DES area.
```

8.8.5 The File Finders

Most of the time, you will have a pretty good idea of which forum to turn to when you are looking for a specific file. But sometimes you just don't know where to start searching, or you are simply interested in all files that match a certain keyword. Instead of visiting all available forums, consider using one of the File Finders that CompuServe provides. Updated regularly (at least once a month), File Finders are powerful indexes of the files available in most of the CompuServe forums. Currently, the following File Finders are available:

- *PC File Finder*: Contains an index of files for computers running the MS-DOS and/or Windows operating system. To get there, `GO PCMFF`.
- *Graphics File Finder*: Contains an index of graphic files, most of them in GIF and JPEG format. `GO GRAPHFF` to get there.
- *Macintosh File Finder*: Contains an index of files for Apple Macintosh computers. `GO MACFF` will take you there.
- *Atari ST File Finder*: Contains an index of files from the forums devoted to the Atari ST range of computers. `GO ATARIFF` to use this File Finder.

- *Amiga File Finder*: Contains an index of files for all Amiga computers. GO AMIGAFF to access this File Finder.

ZiffNet members (GO ZIFFNET for more information) have access to two additional File Finders:

- *ZiffNet Forum File Finder*: Contains an index of all MS-DOS and Windows files that can be found in the ZiffNet forums. To access this File Finder, GO ZNT:ZNTFF.
- *ZiffNet Mac Forum File Finder*: Contains an index of all files that can be found in the Macintosh forums on ZiffNet. GO ZNT:ZMAC and follow the instructions to access this File Finder.

The ZNT: extension is used to cross the gateway between CompuServe and ZiffNet. You don't need it if you are currently accessing another ZiffNet service. To get back to CompuServe, GO CIS:TOP.

HINTS & TIPS

No, they are not free!

The File Finders are part of CompuServe's extended services: you pay for every minute you use them. But this can be money well spent. Tracking a file using the File Finders is much quicker than visiting two or more forums for the same purpose.

Basically, a File Finder is nothing more than an index. To retrieve a file, you still have to visit the forum in which that file resides. However, WinCIM users have an advantage: they can retrieve the file directly from the File Finder. Refer to the heading 'WinCIM', below, for more information.

The Multimedia solution: CompuServe CD

If your computer is equipped with a CD-ROM player, you can either order or subscribe to one of CompuServe's multimedia projects: CompuServe CD. Updated bi-monthly, CompuServe CD contains a large number of interesting files, sound and video clips, as well as actual information about its online features. One of the most useful parts of CompuServe is the File Finder, which allows you to browse through the libraries offline, at your own pace. After you have selected one or more files, connect to CompuServe and download them to your computer. GO CCD for more information about this revolutionary product.

When you search for files using the File Finder, you will have to enter information in one or more of the following fields:

- *Keyword*: Select this field to enter one, two or three keywords. These keywords have to match those that were entered by the person who uploaded the file to one of the forums. Unfortunately, there is no fixed list of keywords. If you don't know where to start, begin with a fairly general keyword and review the results. It is best to 'narrow down' a search (that is, to start with a large number of retrieved items and decrease that number gradually).
- *Submission Date*: If you enter a date in this field, the File Finder will only display information for those files that were uploaded on or after that date. Note that you have to specify the date in MM/DD/YY format.
- *Forum Name*: If you want the search to be limited to one forum, choose this option to select the name of that forum. Note that not all forum libraries are included in the File Finder catalogue. When you want to know whether or not a particular forum is included, select this option.
- *File Type*: If you are looking for a specific type of file, you can select this option to narrow your search to ASCII, Binary, Image, Graphics or JPEG format.
- *File Extension*: If you are looking for files with a specific extension, enter it in this field. Don't include the dot that is normally used to separate filenames from extensions. Note that you can do a *wildcard search* using the 'File Name' field as well.
- *File Name*: If you are looking for a file with a specific name, you can enter that name in this field. Extensions are allowed, and so are wildcards. `TEST.DOC`, `TEST.*`, and `*.DOC` are all valid specifications.
- *File Submitter*: If you want the search to be limited to all files contributed by one member, enter his or her User ID in this field.
- *Display Selected Titles*: Select this option to see the list of titles that the 'File Finder' has retrieved, according to your search specifications.
- *Begin a New Search*: Select this option to reset all search criteria and to start an entirely new search.

WinCIM

When you access one of CompuServe's File Finders from WinCIM, you see the dialog shown in Figure 8.22. This dialog contains the fields and options discussed in the previous section. On top of the dialog, the 'Current' selection field shows the number of files that match your search criteria. If you have just entered the File Finder, the number of available files is shown.

Figure 8.22 WinCIM's File Finder dialog

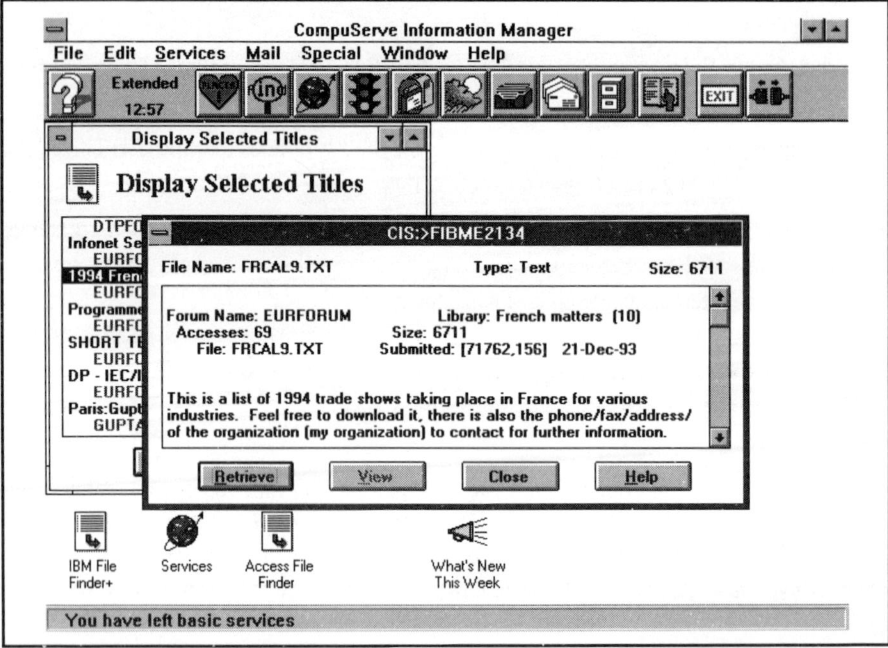

Figure 8.23 Additional information about the selected file

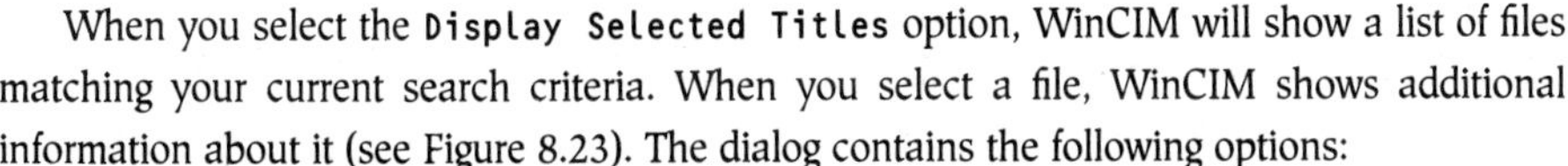

When you select the `Display Selected Titles` option, WinCIM will show a list of files matching your current search criteria. When you select a file, WinCIM shows additional information about it (see Figure 8.23). The dialog contains the following options:

- *Retrieve*: Press this button to download the file to your computer. The File Finder will retrieve the file from the actual forum library. Note that you don't have to be a forum member to do this. After WinCIM has downloaded the file, you return to the File Finder main menu.
- *View*: When you review the information for a file in one of the graphic formats that WinCIM supports, you can select this option to view the graphic.
- *Close*: This closes the file description dialog and returns you to the list of matching files.

8.9 Conferencing

Conferencing is a nice, albeit expensive, feature that is supported in almost all forums that are part of CompuServe's extended services. During a conference, anything you type can be seen by anyone attending.

"I just spoke to your son, and he wants you to know that he's all right"

In times of crisis, conferences sometimes prove to be very helpful. During the Los Angeles earthquake in early 1994, hundreds of CompuServe members from all over the world visited the California forum, offering moral support and sometimes even assistance. Foreign CompuServe members reached out a helping hand to members in the troubled areas, who couldn't make international telephone calls any more.

In the hours after the fatal crash of Formula One driver Ayrton Senna, in May 1994, fans joined in a spontaneous online conference in the Motor Sports Forum, reading the reports of European members. And those are just two examples of how powerful forum conferences can be.

There are two types of forum conference. *Scheduled* conferences are announced by the forum staff and include participation by at least one forum sysop. These conferences can be very popular. An example is the 'Friday Night' meeting in the Modem Games forum (`GO MODEMGAMES`), aimed especially at those who are new to conferencing. There is one drawback though, for us Europeans: this conference takes place at 9:00 p.m. USA Eastern Standard Time. If you want to attend this conference, be prepared for a late-nighter: it starts at 3:00 a.m. Central European Time...

There's no such thing as a free conference...

On free forums, conferencing is one of the disabled features. You can imagine why, can't you?

Most of the time, scheduled conferences are announced in the forum's News bulletin. You can check the announcements as well. Feel free to contact a forum sysop if you would like to organize your own conference, or just try to start a *spontaneous* conference. Invite one or more forum members that are in the forum the same time as you. Although some forums lend themselves to such spontaneous conferences better than others, you wouldn't be the first who succeeded in organizing an online media event this way!

Conferencing and your access program

Although auto-access programs often support basic forms of conferencing, they are normally not the kind of programs you would use for such a purpose. In this book, we only deal with online conferencing using WinCIM.

8.9.1 Any more visitors?

Before you can attend a conference, you have to know whether there are other members currently present in the forum. Press the special `Who's Here` button on the Forum Toolbox (the head with the question mark inside it), or select the `Who's Here` option on the Conference menu. WinCIM displays the 'Who's Here' dialog, shown in Figure 8.24. This forum contains the following options:

- *Name*: Select this option button to see the *nicknames* of everyone currently visiting the forum.
- *User ID*: If you want to see the User IDs instead of the names of everyone currently in the forum, select this option button.
- *All*: Select this button if you want to see a list of everyone in the forum, as opposed to everyone in a specific forum room, or in a discussion group.
- *Room*: Select this option and enter a room number to see a list of people currently present in that room.
- *Group*: Select this option to see a list of everyone currently in the same discussion group as you are. You can either start a new group (by inviting people using the Invite option on the Conference menu), or be invited into an existing one.

- *Profile*: If you want to learn more about the CompuServe member currently selected in the list displayed, press this button. If that member has entered some 'profile information' about him- or herself, WinCIM will display it.
- *Talk*: When you press this button, WinCIM opens a window that is split into two parts. Everything you type will be displayed at the bottom of the window. As soon as you press the Enter key, WinCIM will send it to the person selected in the 'Who's Here' window. When he or she types something back, it will be displayed at the top of the 'Talk' window.
- *Freeze*: When visiting a popular forum, members enter and leave all the time, causing the Who's Here list to be updated continually. If you don't want this to happen, just 'freeze' the list by selecting this option. New members entering will not be included in the list, but the entry forsomeone that has left the forum will be greyed-out.

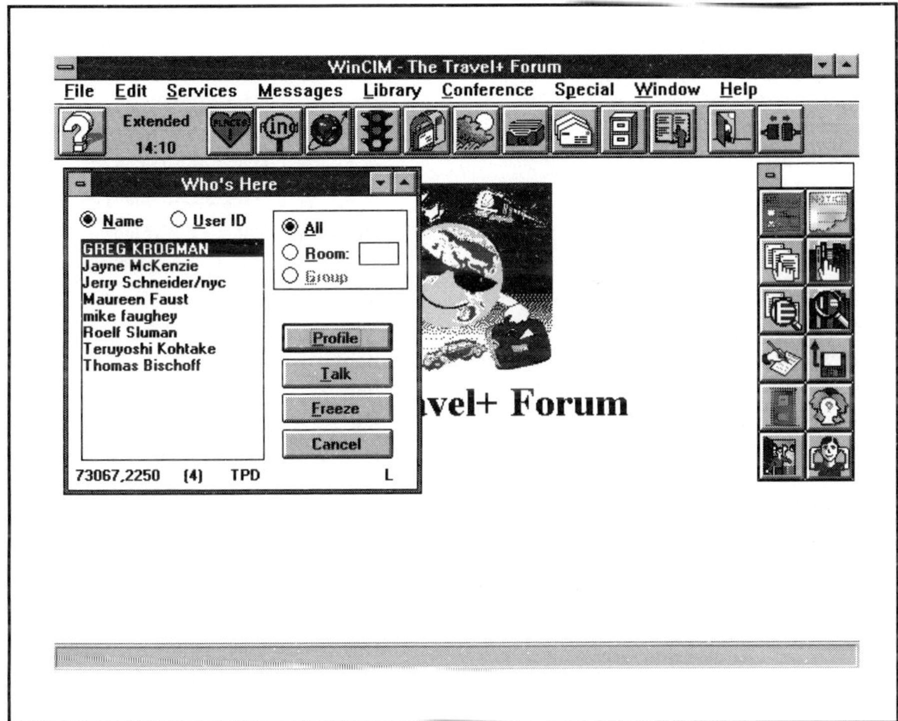

Figure 8.24 Checking who's visiting a forum with WinCIM

Many CompuServe members wonder what the abbreviations are displayed next to the User ID mean. They are *node numbers*: they indicate the node through which that member accesses CompuServe. The following list contains the codes for the most important European nodes:

AMR	Amsterdam, the Netherlands	FKA	Frankfurt, Germany
AMS	Amsterdam, the Netherlands	FKB	Frankfurt, Germany
AMU	Amsterdam, the Netherlands	FKC	Frankfurt, Germany
AMV	Amsterdam, the Netherlands	FKD	Frankfurt, Germany
AMW	Amsterdam, the Netherlands	FKE	Frankfurt, Germany
AMY	Amsterdam, the Netherlands	FKF	Frankfurt, Germany
BBC	Brussels, Belgium	FKG	Frankfurt, Germany
BBD	Brussels, Belgium	FKH	Frankfurt, Germany
BBE	Brussels, Belgium	FKI	Frankfurt, Germany
BBF	Brussels, Belgium	FKJ	Frankfurt, Germany
BBG	Brussels, Belgium	FKK	Frankfurt, Germany
BCL	Barcelona, Spain	FKR	Frankfurt, Germany
BCM	Barcelona, Spain	FKS	Frankfurt, Germany
BCN	Barcelona, Spain	FKT	Frankfurt, Germany
BDB	Budapest, Hungary	FKU	Frankfurt, Germany
BEO	Berlin, Germany	FKV	Frankfurt, Germany
BEP	Berlin, Germany	FKW	Frankfurt, Germany
BEQ	Berlin, Germany	FKX	Frankfurt, Germany
BER	Berlin, Germany	FKZ	Frankfurt, Germany
BGK	Birmingham, United Kingdom	FPC	Frankfurt, Germany
BGL	Birmingham, United Kingdom	HBA	Hanover, Germany
BGM	Birmingham, United Kingdom	HBG	Hamburg, Germany
BIR	Bristol, United Kingdom	HBH	Hamburg, Germany
BIS	Bristol, United Kingdom	HBI	Hamburg, Germany
BIT	Bristol, United Kingdom	LDA	London, United Kingdom
BIU	Bristol, United Kingdom	LDB	London, United Kingdom
BIX	Bristol, United Kingdom	LDC	London, United Kingdom
DGA	Dusseldorf, Germany	LDD	London, United Kingdom
DGC	Dusseldorf, Germany	LDJ	London, United Kingdom
DGD	Dusseldorf, Germany	LDK	London, United Kingdom
DGE	Dusseldorf, Germany	LDN	London, United Kingdom
DGF	Dusseldorf, Germany	LDO	London, United Kingdom
EDW	Edinburgh, United Kingdom	LDS	London, United Kingdom
EDX	Edinburgh, United Kingdom	LDV	London, United Kingdom
EDY	Edinburgh, United Kingdom	LDW	London, United Kingdom
EUA	Hamburg, Germany	LDX	London, United Kingdom
EUD	Paris, France	LDY	London, United Kingdom
EUF	Reading, United Kingdom	LNA	London, United Kingdom
EUO	Munich, Germany	LNB	London, United Kingdom

LNJ	London, United Kingdom
LXA	London, United Kingdom
LXB	London, United Kingdom
LXC	London, United Kingdom
LXD	London, United Kingdom
LXE	London, United Kingdom
LXF	London, United Kingdom
LXG	London, United Kingdom
LXH	London, United Kingdom
LXI	London, United Kingdom
LXJ	London, United Kingdom
LXK	London, United Kingdom
LXL	London, United Kingdom
LXM	London, United Kingdom
LXN	London, United Kingdom
LXO	London, United Kingdom
LXP	London, United Kingdom
LXQ	London, United Kingdom
LXR	London, United Kingdom
LXS	London, United Kingdom
LXT	London, United Kingdom
LXU	London, United Kingdom
LXV	London, United Kingdom
LXW	London, United Kingdom
LXX	London, United Kingdom
LXY	London, United Kingdom
LXZ	London, United Kingdom
MRA	Manchester, United Kingdom
MRB	Manchester, United Kingdom
MRC	Manchester, United Kingdom
MRD	Madrid, Spain
MRE	Madrid, Spain
MRF	Madrid, Spain
MUA	Munich, Germany
MUB	Munich, Germany
MUC	Munich, Germany
MUD	Munich, Germany
MUE	Munich, Germany
MUF	Munich, Germany
MUG	Munich, Germany
MUH	Munich, Germany
MUI	Munich, Germany
MUJ	Munich, Germany
MUK	Munich, Germany
MUL	Munich, Germany
MUM	Munich, Germany
MUO	Munich, Germany
PAH	Paris, France
PAL	Paris, France
PAM	Paris, France
PAN	Paris, France
PAO	Paris, France
PAR	Paris, France
PAS	Paris, France
PAT	Paris, France
PAU	Paris, France
PAV	Paris, France
PAW	Paris, France
PAX	Paris, France
PAY	Paris, France
PAZ	Paris, France
SXT	Stockholm, Sweden
SXU	Stockholm, Sweden
SXW	Stockholm, Sweden
SXX	Stockholm, Sweden
SXZ	Stockholm, Sweden
SZV	Stuttgart, Germany
SZW	Stuttgart, Germany
SZX	Stuttgart, Germany
SZY	Stuttgart, Germany
SZZ	Stuttgart, Germany
VNN	Vienna, Austria
VNO	Vienna, Austria
VNP	Vienna, Austria
VNQ	Vienna, Austria
ZUR	Zurich, Switzerland
ZUS	Zurich, Switzerland
ZUT	Zurich, Switzerland
ZUU	Zurich, Switzerland
ZUV	Zurich, Switzerland
ZUW	Zurich, Switzerland
ZUY	Zurich, Switzerland
ZUZ	Zurich, Switzerland

8.9.2 Talking to someone personally

If you want to send someone an online message that only he or she will see, press the `Talk` button on the 'Who's Here' dialog. WinCIM opens a window that is split into two parts. Everything you type will be displayed in the bottom of the window. As soon as you press the Enter key, WinCIM will send it to the person selected in the 'Who's Here' window. When he or she types something back, it will be displayed at the top of the 'Talk' window.

8.9.3 The conference rooms

Most forums (except for the forums that are free) consist of at least one conference room. To get an overview of the rooms that are available, select the `Enter Room` option on the `Conference` menu. WinCIM will display the available conference rooms in a separate dialog, shown in Figure 8.25.

To see how many people are currently in a certain room, select that room and look at the information shown at the bottom of the window. To enter a room, select it and press the Enter button. Once you have entered a room, WinCIM opens a window, consisting of two parts. All the text that you type will appear in the bottom part first. As soon as you press the Enter key, WinCIM sends it to CompuServe and it will appear in the top part. This text can be read by anyone currently visiting (or *monitoring*, we will come to that in a moment) the forum.

Figure 8.25 A list of available conference rooms

To leave a room, close the room window. Don't select the `Leave` option on the `File` menu, unless you want not only to leave the room but the entire forum as well.

Apart from attending a forum conference (with the possibility of actually talking to the other people), you might prefer to *listen* to a discussion that is currently going on in one of the rooms. WinCIM allows you to listen to the conversation in one room, while you actually take part in a discussion being held in another.

8.9.4 Joining a discussion

There are two types of conference discussion. Discussions that take place in *conference rooms* can be attended by all members of the forum. Discussions that are held in *groups* can only be attended if you receive an invitation. As a forum member, you can invite other members to your own group discussion: press the Invite button on the 'Who's Here' window to do this.

8.10 Additional information

Once you understand the principles of dealing with messages, libraries and conferences, you have mastered all the techniques that you need for your day-to-day forum visits. This section deals with some topics that you might find useful to know.

8.10.1 The forum staff

CompuServe maintains the software necessary to 'drive' a forum, but it stops there in most cases. Almost all forums are manned by an independent *contractor* called the *forum manager*, also known as the *wizop* (from *wizard sysop*, because of the almost magical powers that he or she has to maintain the forum), one or more *assistant sysops*, and sometimes one or more *section leaders*. Most of these people access CompuServe from their homes and offices, just like you do. But when it comes to the forum they work for, they can do things that regular forum members can't, such as opening and closing certain sections to other members, approving uploaded files, (re)moving messages to another section, and so on.

It is this group of people that determines the 'look and feel' of a forum. Although all forums have the same basic appearance, each forum has its own atmosphere, from 'clean and professional' to 'sociable and sometimes chaotic'. While some sysops participate in almost every message thread, others merely guide the message traffic, re-ordering threads and helping out new members on the way. Being a sysop has its advantages: you belong to a small group with a certain online status, and often have free access to one or more CompuServe facilities. But in return, sysops spend a considerable amount of their time online, doing a lot of work to keep 'their' forum running as smoothly as possible. Most sysops would describe their work on the forum as 'demanding, but rewarding'.

In a typical forum, the forum staff consists of the following members:

- A *wizop*: the chief sysop of the forum. The wizop is the person who has signed an agreement with CompuServe, and is fully responsible for everything that pertains to his or her forum.
- One or more *sysops*, who assist the wizop in performing the daily duties.
- One or more *section leaders*, especially for large forums that cover a broad range of subjects.

9 Popular services on CompuServe

Popular services on CompuServe

One of the nicest things about CompuServe is that there is so very much to explore. Members find themselves travelling CompuServe's freeways all the time, visiting forums, reading news, playing games, browsing references – the list goes on and on!

However, for new CompuServe members, all this information is sometimes overwhelming. Where to start? What can I expect? What does it cost?

In this chapter, we discuss some of the most popular CompuServe products. Some of them are free or part of Basic Services, most of them are part of Extended Services, and others carry an additional surcharge. But they all have one thing in common: they are at your disposal, 24 hours a day.

As CompuServe develops, new services are added every day. Therefore, a chapter like this is already outdated the day after it is written! Even when I was writing this chapter, I discovered that new, competitive services were added almost weekly.

If you would like to know more about new and updated CompuServe services, refer to the last section of Chapter 4. It contains a list of ways to find out what's new and changed on CompuServe.

WinCIM

In most cases, the services are described from the WinCIM user's point of view. For some services however, you will find some additional guidelines for use in Terminal Emulation mode.

9.1 News online

I have heard people say that, since they have become a CompuServe member, they don't watch television as often as they used to, and they have limited the number of newspapers and magazines they read.

This is not too hard to understand. Often, information is available on CompuServe long before you find it in your favourite magazines or newspapers. More and more members browse through some news services in the morning, download the articles they are interested in, and transfer them to their notebook or palmtop computer. (And you thought all those yuppie types in trains and aeroplanes were doing serious business work, didn't you?)

In this section, we focus on some of the major news services available on CompuServe. You will see which routes to follow to get weather information, daily news, stock prices and the latest computer and software news, to name just a few.

9.1.1 But first: a look at the weather (GO WEATHER)

To find information about the weather in your local area, or in any place in the world, `GO WEATHER`. If you use WinCIM, you can also select the `Weather` option on the `Services` menu, or press the special `Weather` button on the WinCIM Ribbon. After a few moments, the dialog displayed in Figure 9.1 appears.

If you press `OK` immediately, you will see information about the current and expected weather in your local area. However, you can select a range of other areas as well. If you know the official weather station name, you can enter it in the 'Station' field.

A particularly interesting option is `Maps`. When you press the `Maps` button, you can select from a range of graphical weather maps. An example is shown in Figure 9.2.

CompuServe Weather is part of Basic Services.

9.1.2 News and sports

The latest information about news and sports events is available 24 hours aday. You can use your CompuServe membership to read news from all around the world, get up-to-date information about the latest stock prices, or receive updates on new computer and software developments. There are a lot of news services available. The most famous ones, as well as the services that apply to European members, are discussed in this section.

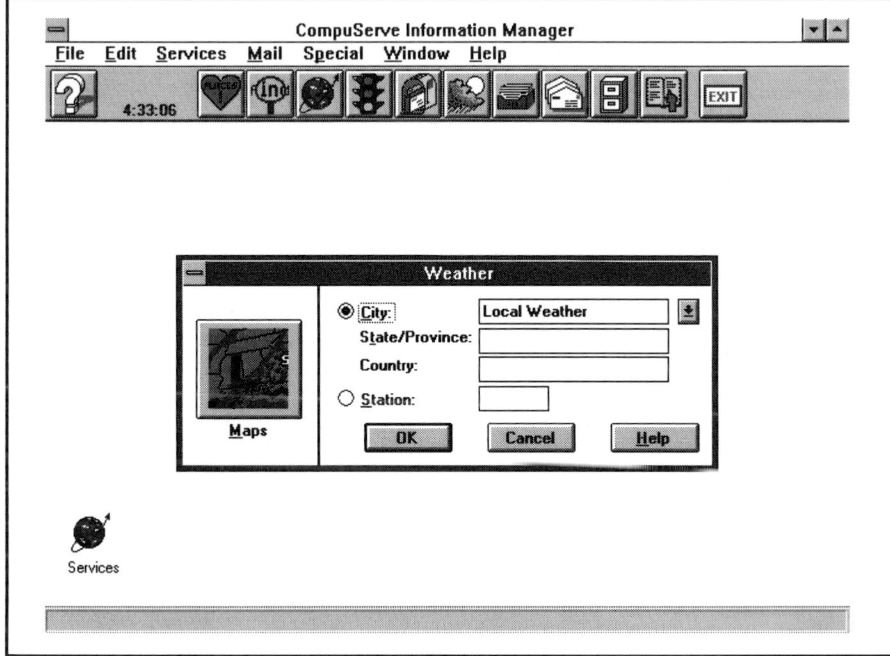

Figure 9.1 Weather information on CompuServe

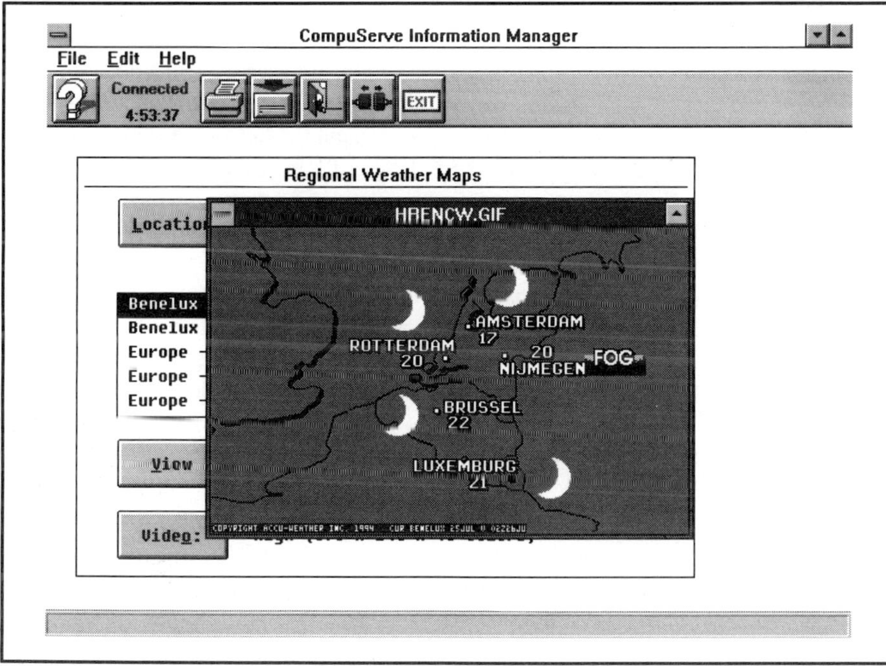

Figure 9.2 It only takes seconds to retrieve a weather map like this

Associated Press Online (GO APO)

One of CompuServe's most popular Basic Services. Visit AP Online to get the latest news on a variety of subjects. Apart from the latest news updated hourly (or sometimes more frequently, if need arises), there are sections like Sports, National, World, Entertainment, Business News and Science & Health.

While you there, don't forget to pay a visit to the Feature News/Today in the History section.

Associated Press Online is part of Basic Services.

The Executive News Service (GO ENS)

If you need to the first to know the latest news, you can't do without a subscription to the Executive News Service. However, there is a price tag involved. Not only is ENS part of Extended Services, it also carries a $15 per hour surcharge. But you get something in return: you can compose your own *clipping folders*, which will be automatically filled with news articles about topics you are interested in. For instance, I have a clipping folder called 'ONLINESERV', which is updated as soon as a news item pertaining to online services is posted. Very useful!

HINTS & TIPS

ENS and your CompuServe membership

To be able to benefit from the additional clipping facility of ENS, you need to select the Executive Option. Members who select the Executive Option will be charged a minimum of $10 per month, regardless of their actual usage that month. But because your Standard Pricing Plan charges add up to that minimum, you basically get the Executive Option for free if you spend more than $1.05 online during the current month. More information about the Executive Option can be found in Section 1.3.6. If you wish to select the Executive Option, GO CHOICES.

WinCIM users can enter the Executive News Service by selecting the corresponding option on the Services menu. After a few moments, the main ENS screen is displayed (see Figure 9.3).

As you can see, there are four folders. Three of them, the *public folders*, are available to all ENS users. One of them, ONLINESERV, is a personal clipping folder. Every time an article becomes available, CompuServe checks whether it matches the search specifications for that clipping folder. If it does, the article will be placed in the folder for a period of two weeks.

To read articles placed in public folders, proceed as follows:

1. Open the folder, by selecting it and pressing the Search button. After a few moments, the dialog shown in Figure 9.4 appears.
2. Select one or more press agencies by checking the boxes in front of their names. The list of press agencies is updated continual, so there might very well be an agency for your country, too.

Figure 9.3 The Executive News Service. The map consists of four folders: three public folders and one personal folder

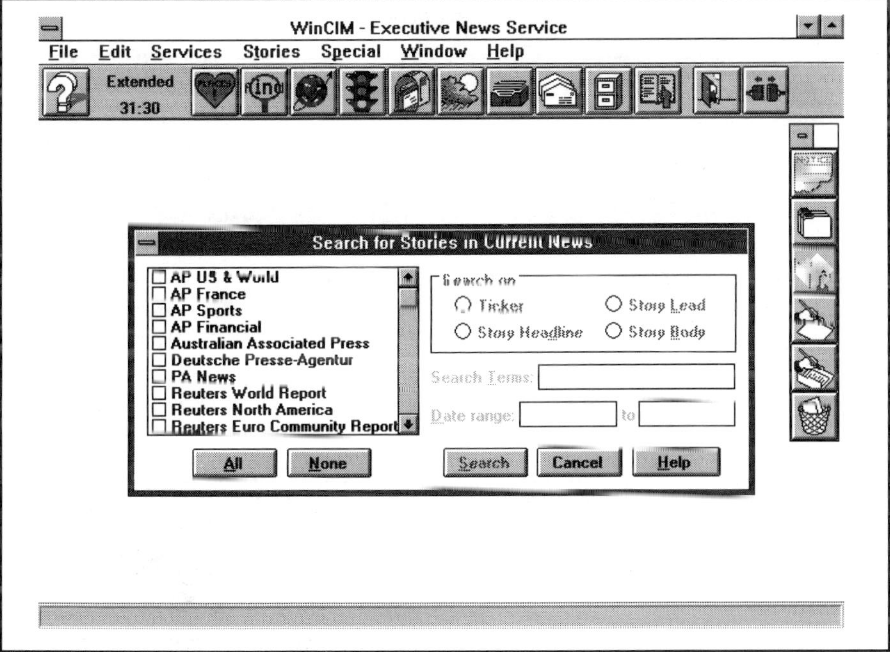

Figure 9.4 Use this dialog to select the press agencies

3. As soon as you have selected at least one agency, the **Search** button becomes active. Press it to see a list of articles posted by the selected agencies.
4. Now, select an article that you would like to read. To read it online (something that isn't too wise, because you are using a surcharged service), press the **Get** button. To mark it for later retrieval, press the **Mark** button. Select as many articles as you like.
5. When you have marked all the articles that you are interested in, select **Retrieve Marked Stories** on the **Stories** menu. The 'Retrieve Marked Stories' dialog appears; select **Get All** to retrieve the articles to your hard disk. You can now disconnect, or at least leave ENS.
6. To read the articles, open your Filing Cabinet and select the CURRENTNEWS folder. This folder will contain all the downloaded articles.

If you are interested in news updates about specific topics, you might consider one or more *personal clipping folders*. When you create a folder, you are asked to specify search information. As soon as an article is posted that matches your search specification, it will be placed in your clipping folder automatically. After you have created a clipping folder, you can browse through its contents, or get articles and mark them, just as you would do with public folders.

To create a personal clipping folder, proceed as follows:

1. Select the **Create Folder** option on the **Stories** menu. After a few moments, the 'Create Folder' dialog appears (see Figure 9.5).

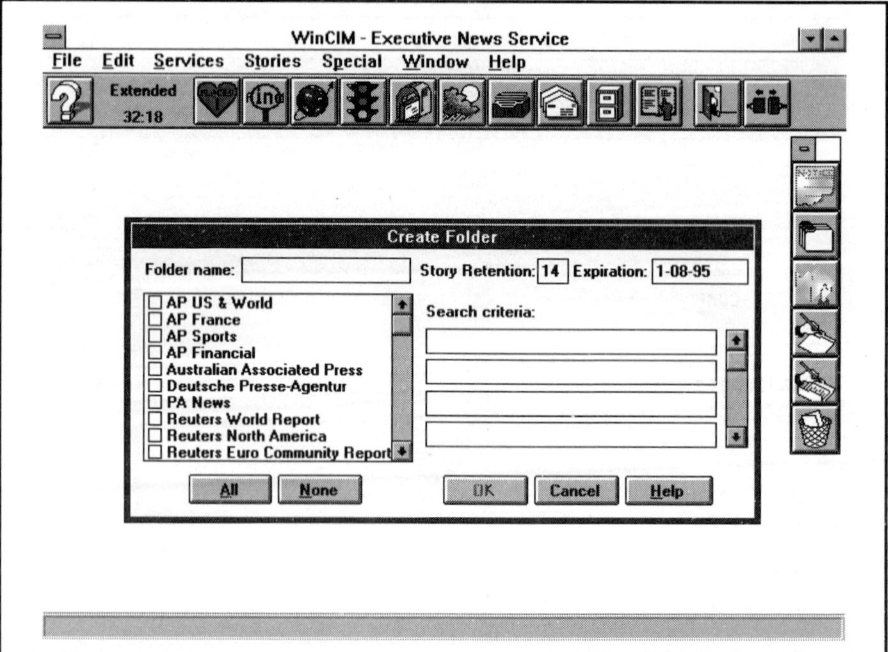

Figure 9.5 Use this dialog to create your own personal clipping folder

2. First, specify a name for your folder. Use letters and digits only; spaces and other symbols are not allowed.
3. Next, check the boxes in front of the press agencies that you are interested in. You need to select at least one agency, but you are free to select more, or even all of them.
4. Now, it's time to specify your *search criteria*. Do this carefully: the quality of your search criteria determines how appropriate the articles are that CompuServe places in your personal clipping folder. If you use search criteria that are too broad, the chances are that your clipping folder will be filled with articles that you aren't interested in. However, if your search criteria are too narrow, you will miss out on interesting articles. More on search criteria follows.
5. CompuServe maintains a personal clipping folder for a period of one year. However, you can 'renew' it by altering the 'Expiration' field. (This can also be done at a later time, by selecting the `Update Folder` option on the `Stories` menu.)
6. Typically, stories will remain in your clipping folder for two weeks, unless you delete them earlier. However, you can change this by entering another value in the Story Retention field.
7. After you have completed the 'Create Folder' dialog, press `OK` to close it. The new clipping folder will now be added to your list of personal folders. There won't be any articles in it, though. But that won't take long; CompuServe will now start adding articles to the folder automatically, even if you aren't connected. The next time you visit the Executive News Services, new articles will be waiting for you.

When specifying search criteria, the following rules apply:

- If you specify only one keyword, all articles that contain the keyword will be placed in your folder.
- If you specify several keywords, but all of them are single entries in separate fields, all articles that contain one or more of those keywords will be placed in your folder.
- If you specify keywords in one field and separate them with a plus sign (for instance, `COMPUTER+COMPUSERVE`), only those articles that contain both keywords will be placed in your folder.
- If you specify keywords in one field an separate them with a minus sign (for instance, `COMPUSERVE minus INTERNET`), only those articles that contain the first keyword but not the second one will be placed in your folder.
- If you specify keywords in one field but use the [I] sign to separate them, articles that contain any of those keywords will be placed into your folder.
- Normally, only articles that contain the exact keyword will be found. However, you can add the asterisk (*) to a keyword. In that case, all articles that contain either the keyword or a word in which the keyword is included will be placed in your folder. For example, `COM*` will retrieve all articles that contain the words *computer*, *communications*, *combo* and *command*.

Save money!

With a $15 surcharge, ENS is an expensive service. However, if you are willing to deal with CompuServe's ASCII Interface (that is, if you don't mind using Terminal Emulation), you can have CompuServe send the articles to your mailbox. In Terminal Emulation, `GO ENS` to visit the Executive News Service. When you see a summary of articles in your folder, you can use the `SEND` command to send them to any CompuServe User ID. (If you press Enter, CompuServe assumes that you want to send the articles to your own User ID.) This takes only a few seconds. Once you get the hang of it, you will see that you don't need much more than one minute to select all the articles you are interested in.

ENS is a surcharged service. You pay the normal Extended Services charges, plus a $15 per hour surcharge.

PA News Online (UK) (`GO NWS-1`)

If you live in the United Kingdom, or if you are interested in British news, you can use this service to keep you updated. There are a number of topics, such as General News, Financial News and even TV and radio listings. There is a lot of information here, but it is updated a little bit less frequently than AP Online.

Like AP Online, PA News Online (UK) is part of Extended Services.

Reuter News Pictures Forum (`GO NEWSPIX`)

This forum contains hundreds, if not thousands, of photos of news events. You can either view those illustrations online or download them to your computer.

The News Pictures Forum is actually a forum just like all the others, except that the message board is disabled. The photos can be found in its libraries, so you can use all the regular commands to browse the libraries, search for a particular keyword, and so on.

Note that the photos are stored in two compression formats. Both formats can be read by WinCIM. If you need a high-quality photo, download the GIF version. If you are only browsing, or if the quality isn't too important, go for the JPG version, which is much smaller and takes considerably less time to download.

The Reuter News Pictures Forum is part of Extended Services.

U.S. News & World Report Magazine (`GO USNEWS`)

This one of the first electronic versions of a general magazine to appear on an online service. The CompuServe edition of U.S. News & World Report Magazine, and its accompanying forum, contain all the main articles in the current edition of the 'paper version', complete with illustrations, as well as 'micro-documentaries': small, multimedia-media video clips. The forum gives you the possibility of exchanging thoughts with the editors and writers of the magazine.

The electronic edition of U.S. News & World Report Magazine is the first to use the new CompuServe graphical interface. The nice-looking graphical buttons and the new menu structure make you forget that you are actually accessing an online system!

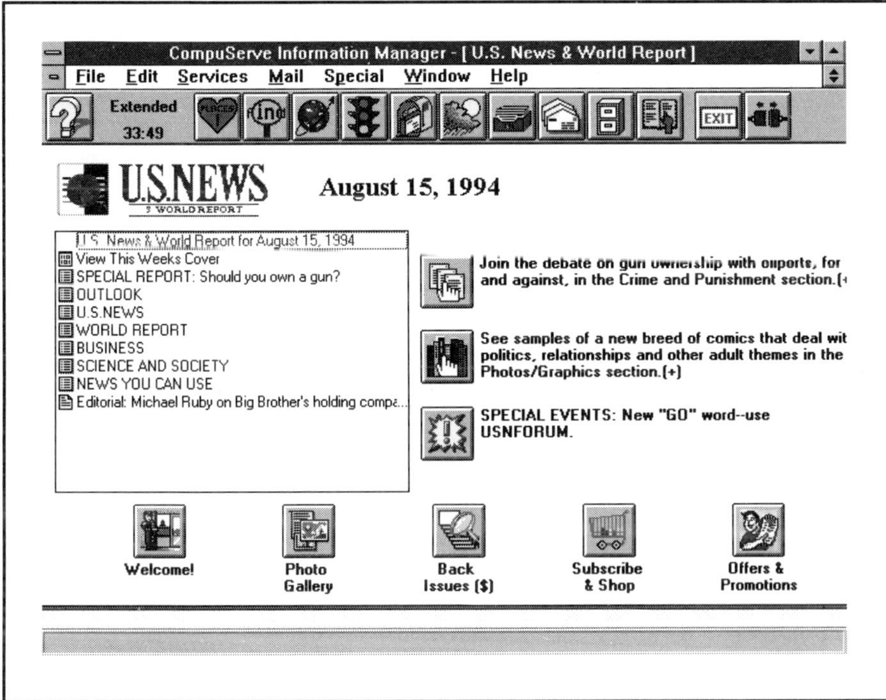

Figure 9.6 An attractive aspect of CompuServe: the U.S. News & World Report Magazine online

The U.S. News & World Report Magazine is part of Basic Services. The accompanying forum (U.S. News Forum), however, is part of Extended Services. To get to the forum directly, `GO USNFOR`.

The Business Wire (`GO TBW`)

The Business Wire contains the latest press releases and news articles from a broad range of companies. When you enter the Business Wire, you will see a menu that lists all the available articles. You can either read an article online or store it on your hard disk. To do this, either press the `File It` button to store it in your WinCIM Filing Cabinet, or select `Save` on the `File` menu when the article is displayed. The article will then be saved as a text file, in your default download directory.

The Business Wire is part of Extended Services.

Deutsche Press Agentur (GO DPA)

German CompuServe members and those who speak German can read news pertaining to Germany and the rest of the world in the German language. Deutsche Press Agentur offers news updates on a range of subjects, including politics, sports and cultural events.

If you wish to read an article offline, press the special `Save` button on the WinCIM Ribbon. It is not possible to store articles in your Filing Cabinet.

Deutsche Press Agentur is part of Basic Services.

AP France en Ligne (GO APFRANCE)

French members can obtain the latest news in their language directly from CompuServe. AP France en Ligne offers the latest economic, cultural and sports news, national as well as international.

AP France en Ligne is part of Basic Services.

AIDS Information (GO AIDS)

This is your entry point to a series of services pertaining to the disease AIDS. The services listed include:

- *HealthNet* (GO HNT): A reference library containing articles about topics such as disorders and diseases, drugs, home care and First Aid. Because HealthNet is part of Basic Services, this would normally be the first place to look.
- *AIDS News Clips* (GO AIDSNEWS): A series of articles posted by international news agencies, updated daily. AIDS News Clips is part of Extended Services.
- *CCML AIDS Articles* (GO CCMLAIDS): An online database that contains articles from medical sources. CCML AIDS Articles is a surcharged service: you pay standard connect charges, plus a surcharge. For more information about the surcharge, select the `Pricing` option.
- *Health Database Plus* (GO HLTDB): Another online database, with articles on all fields of medical science. Health Database Plus is a surcharged service: you pay standard connect charges, plus a surcharge. For more information about that surcharge, select the `Pricing` option.

Sports

If you are interested in sports news, there are number of services at your disposal. To display a menu where all services are listed, GO SPORTS. A summary:

- *Associated Press Sports Wire* (GO APSPORTS): This service contains news clips about sporting events. This is a surcharged service: apart from connection charges you pay a $15 per hour surcharge to use it.
- *Sports Images* (GO NEWSPIX): The Reuter News Pictures Forum contains hundreds, if not thousands, of photos about news events. You can either view those illustrations online or download them to your computer. As its name implies, the Reuter News Pictures Forum is actually a forum just like all the others, except that the message board is disabled. It contains a separate Sports library that contains up-to-date photos ofthe latest sports events.
  Note that the photos are stored in two compression formats. Both formats can be read by WinCIM. If you need a high-quality photo, download the GIF version. If you are only browsing, or if the quality isn't too important, go for the JPG version, which is much smaller and takes considerably less time to download. The Reuter News Pictures Forum is part of Extended Services.
- *Lanier Golf Database* (GO GOLF): This database contains information about more than 15,000 golf courses worldwide. The Lanier Golf Database is part of Basic Services.

Roger Ebert's Reviews & Features (GO EBERT)

Roger Ebert is one of America's leading movie critics. Lots of movie reviews, celebrity interviews and other news items from his pen can be found on CompuServe. GO EBERT brings you to a special menu, called Roger Ebert Movie Reviews. This menu, part of Basic Services, contains options like 'Most Recent Movie Reviews', 'Ebert's 10 Best Films of the Year' and 'Video Alert: New on Tape & Disc'. Apart from that, Roger Ebert has his own section in the Show Business/Media Forum (GO SHOWBIZ). This forum is part of Extended Services.

Online Today (GO OLT)

This is, in my opinion, one of the most underestimated services on CompuServe. If you are interested in computers and software, you might find yourself returning to it often: it keeps you up to date with what's going on in this fast-paced world.

Basically, Online Today consists of a series of articles on the following topics:

- *Monitor News* (GO OLT-160): News about developments in the world of computers, software and online services. New articles are uploaded every day, but you can also read articles that were posted during the past week.
- *Behind the Screens* (GO OLT-130): The 'electronic column' of journalist and CompuServe Magazine writer John Edwards. Edwards gives his opinion on all the 'world online'.
- *Book Reviews/Product Announcements* (GO OLT-200): Consult this section for regular updates about new software and hardware products, as well as reviews of books. Articles stay on this board for three months after they are posted.
- *CompuServe Magazine Specials*: From time to time, additional information about CompuServe Magazine features can be found on Online Today.

Online Today is part of Basic Services.

Computer and Software News (ZiffNet)

If you are interested in the latest news about computers and software, you might consider subscribing to a 'subservice' of CompuServe: ZiffNet. ZiffNet is actually another online service, which can be reached from CompuServe. (Likewise, ZiffNet members can access CompuServe if they wish.) Just like CompuServe, ZiffNet provides forums (mainly dealing with hardware and software topics), a File Finder, and a range of other products.

To be able to use ZiffNet, you have to subscribe to it. For a monthly fee of $2.95, you get access to a number of ZiffNet forums, as well as some special ZiffNet services:

- *PC News Weekly* (GO PCNEWS): This service contains articles from two of America's most famous weekly computer magazines: *PC News Weekly* and *Mac News Weekly*. And because the articles are posted the Friday before the actual editions hit the shelves, you are actually the first to read the latest computer news. ZiffNet gives you the option to download the articles or to read them online (and store them in your Filing Cabinet, for instance). PC News Weekly is free for ZiffNet Members. However, communication surcharges still apply.
- *Newsbytes* (GO NEWSBYTES): With daily updates (on workdays) on the latest computer and software news, Newsbytes is a very valuable service. It is the opinion of a lot of CompuServe members that Newsbytes alone more than justifies a ZiffNet membership!
  You can either download all Newsbytes or read them online: for the current day, for a particular day during the past week, or about a particular subject.

9.1.3 Financial services

If you need the latest financial information, you can turn to CompuServe. There are numerous financial services on CompuServe: to get an overview, select the `Find` command on the `Services` menu and enter the keyword *financial*. Amongst them, you find the following products:

- *Basic Quotes* (`GO BASICQUOTES`): This option shows you the most recent stock market quotes for one or more securities you have specified. After you have entered one or more securities (you can enter ticker symbols as well as CUSIP numbers), the available reports for those securities are displayed.
  If you need information about the available ticker symbols, `GO SYMBOLS` or `GO LOOKUP`. Basic Quotes is part of CompuServe's Basic Services.
- *Citibank's Global Report* (`GO GLOREP`): This service provides investors and business professionals with comprehensive news and financial data from sources around the world, including:
  - *AFX News*: extensive financial and business information, covering topics such as equities, foreign exchange rates, major banks, governments statistics, bonds, commodities, political news, companies and industrial sectors.
  - *Business International*: in-depth information about currency, exchange controls and taxes for a range of countries.
  - *Citibank*: (throughout business days) information about current rates on major currencies in New York and Tokyo, as well as market commentary.
  - *Comtex*: news updates from a large range of American and international sources.
  - *Financial Times Business Information*: daily updates and weekly analysis of foreign exchange and money markets, currency hedging advice and foreign exchange recommendations, plus comments on the international stock markets.
  - *Il Sole 24 Ore*: daily updates about developments on the Italian market, as well as company, economic and general business news pertaining to Italy.
  - *Standard & Poor's*: in-depth profiles of more than 10,000 American companies, including information on management, lines of business, operating results and securities ratings.

  Citibank's Global Report is a surcharged service, with a $60 surcharge on weekdays and a $30 surcharge at weekends.

How to find financial services

To get an overview of all available services pertaining to financial and business news, `GO MONEY`.

9.2 Reference online

In many cases, you can get answers to any questions you might have about a particular subject by visiting one or more of the *forums* on CompuServe. However, in some cases you may wish to use the *databases* that CompuServe provides. Some of them are free, others are part of Extended Services, still others are surcharged services, but they all have one thing in common: they provide you with access to information that is hard to get at otherwise.

There are a lot of online databases on CompuServe, and their number is growing. If you don't know where to start, `GO REFERENCE`. CompuServe will list all available reference products on the Reference menu, displayed in Figure 9.7. To learn more about a particular reference product, click on its name, or select it with the arrow keys and press the Enter key.

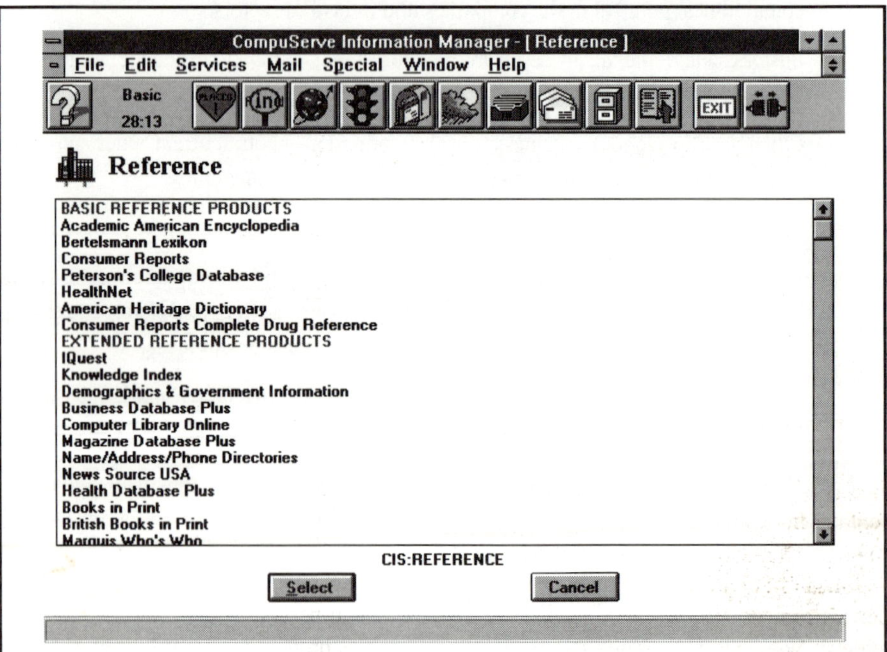

Figure 9.7 A part of the CompuServe Reference menu

All databases contain comprehensive online instructions. Most of the time, you don't incur any charges (except communication surcharges) for reading these instructions. Therefore, you are strongly advised to read them before you actually start using the database. Because most databases carry special surcharges, you can save a lot of money if you do a little preparation beforehand!

Use a log file!

Because most databases are surcharged services, don't forget that the meter is running! To reduce your online time, use log files whenever possible. Resist the temptation to read articles online; some services carry steep surcharges that make your online minutes very, very expensive.

9.2.1 General information

Consumer Reports (GO CONSUMER)

This service contains reviews of a large number of home products. Although some of these products are available on the American market only, most of them can be bought in Europe as well.

The Consumer Reports product is part of Basic Services.

The American Academic Encyclopedia (GO ENCYCLOPEDIA)

This is the online version of one of America's most popular encyclopaedias. Refer to Section 4.4 for a description of its use.

The American Academic Encyclopedia is part of Basic Services.

Magill's Survey of Cinema (GO MAGILL)

This is a very comprehensive database with information on movies released since 1902. It contains in-depth reviews, script summaries, biographies of actors, actresses and directors, and so on.

Magill's Survey of Cinema is a surcharged service; in addition to the normal Extended Service charges, you pay surcharges for every search you perform and for every article you retrieve. Note that movie buffs also have a Basic Services product at their disposal: GO EBERT will take you to the Roger Ebert's Movie Reviews service.

9.2.2 Business information

Business Database Plus (GO BUSDB)

This service contains articles from hundreds of business magazines, trade journals and business newspapers, as well as a comprehensive collection of last year's articles from hundreds of specialized business news letters. For a list of publications, GO ZIFFHELP to access the free ZiffNet Support Forum (you have to be a ZiffNet member to do this) and download the file BDPPUB.TXT from the BusinessDB Plus library.

Business Database Plus is a surcharged service; in addition to the normal Extended Service charges, you pay a $15 per hour connect time surcharge. Also, you pay a charge for every article you retrieve.

Marketing/Management Research Center (GO MGMTRC)

This online database contains (references to) articles published in leading American and other business, management and technical magazines, as well as references to market and industry research reports and market studies. Also, a series of company news releases is available.

The Marketing/Management Research Center is a surcharged service; in addition to the normal Extended Service charges, you pay surcharges for every search you perform and for every article you retrieve.

9.2.3 Computer and software information

Computer Database Plus (GO COMPDB)

This online database, one of the most popular databases on CompuServe, contains articles and references to articles from hundreds of computer magazines, newspapers and journals. For a list of publications covered in Computer Database Plus, GO ZIFFHELP to access the free ZiffNet Support Forum (you have to be a ZiffNet member to do this) and download the file CDPPUB.TXT from the ComputerDB Plus library.

Computer Database Plus is a surcharged service; in addition to the normal Extended Service charges, you pay a $15 per hour connect time surcharge. Also, you pay a charge for every article or abstract that you retrieve.

Data-Processing Newsletters (GO DPNEWS)

This is an online database that contains articles from a number of leading newsletters pertaining to computers, electronics and telecommunications. In most cases, the complete article text is available, as well as reference information.

Data-Processing Newsletters is a surcharged service; in addition to the normal Extended Service charges, you pay surcharges for every search you perform and for every article that you retrieve.

9.2.4 Books, magazines and newspapers

Magazine Database Plus (GO MAGDB)

Magazine Database Plus contains articles and references to articles from a large number of general-interest magazines, newspapers and journals. For a list of publications covered in Computer Database Plus, `GO ZIFFHELP` to access the free ZiffNet Support Forum (you have to be a ZiffNet member to do this) and download the file `MDPPUB.TXT` from the MagazineDB Plus library.

Magazine Database Plus is a surcharged service; in addition to the normal Extended Services charges, you pay a surcharge for every article that you retrieve.

Newspaper Archives (GO NEWSARCHIVE)

Newspaper Archives is an online library that contains articles from dozens of American and English newspapers. Except for classifieds and advertisements, almost all articles are available. Newspaper Archives is a surcharged service; in addition to the normal Extended Services charges, you pay a surcharge for every article that you retrieve.

UK Newspaper Library (GO UKPAPERS)

The UK Newspaper Library contains selected articles from a number of leading UK newspapers, such as The Daily Telegraph, The European, The Financial Times, The Times and The Independent. In most cases, you can search for articles that were published during the past year.

The UK Newspaper Library is a surcharged service; in addition to the normal Extended Services charges, you pay a surcharge for every search that you perform as well as for every article that you retrieve.

Book Review Digest (GO BOOKREVIEW)

Book Review Digest contains summaries of reviews of English-language books that have been published since 1983, as well as bibliographic references.

Book Review Digest is a surcharged service; in addition to the normal Extended Services charges, you pay a surcharge for every article that you retrieve.

Books in Print (GO BOOKS)

Books in Print is an online database that includes references to books that are either available in the United States or will be available shortly (within the next six months). Also, all books that went out of stock during the past two years are included. For every book, information about the author, title, publisher, publication date, edition, list price and subject is available.

Books in Print is a surcharged service; in addition to the normal Extended Services charges, you pay a surcharge for every search that you perform, as well as for every article that you retrieve.

9.2.5 Medical information

Health Database Plus (GO HLTDB)

Health Database Plus contains articles and references to articles from a large number of consumer and professional magazines, newspapers and journals pertaining to health care. For a list of publications covered in Computer Database Plus, **GO ZIFFHELP** to access the free ZiffNet Support Forum (you have to be a ZiffNet member to do this) and download the file **HDPPUB.TXT** from the HealthDB Plus library.

You don't pay any connect charges for using Health Database Plus, although communication surcharges still apply. However, you pay for every article or abstract that you retrieve.

PaperChase-MEDLINE (GO PAPERCHASE)

PaperChase-MEDLINE is aimed at physicians, nurses, dentists and other health care providers. It is an online database that provides access to one of the largest biomedical databases in the world: MEDLINE. It contains millions of references to articles in thousands of medical journals. Every week, more than 8,000 references are added.

PaperChase-MEDLINE is a surcharged service; in addition to Extended Services charges, you pay a surcharge.

Rare Disease Database (GO NORD)

The Rare Disease Database contains information maintained by the National Organization for Rare Disorders (NORD), an American voluntary health agency. As the name implies, the database focuses on rare diseases and disorders. The Rare Disease Database is part of Extended Services.

9.2.6 Special databases

Knowledge Index (GO KI)

The Knowledge Index is one of the most comprehensive databases available on CompuServe. It contains information derived from more than 100 full-text and bibliographic databases, and covers more than 50,000 journals. Actually, the Knowledge Index doesn't reside on CompuServe: it is maintained by Dialog Information Services Inc., an American database provider. In evening hours and at weekends (American time), CompuServe provides a direct link to this service.

Because the Knowledge Index is not a CompuServe product, it has an entirely different interface from the one that you are used to. There are two ways to use the Knowledge Index: *via* the available menu structure, or with keyed in commands. Naturally, it is possible to switch from menu mode to command mode and vice versa. Comprehensive user information is available online.

The Knowledge Index contains three types of information:

- *Full-text databases*: these contain complete articles.
- *Bibliographic databases*: these contain references to articles, including the publication name, title, author and the date of publication. If you wish, you can order the complete text of a particular article online, in which case it will be mailed to you. Note that this will cost extra.
- *Directory databases*: these are online versions of reference books. Because the information in directory databases is updated regularly, it is often more up to date than the corresponding reference book.

Informative files about the Knowledge Index

If you wish to know more about the Knowledge Index before you start using this service, `GO HELPFORUM` to visit the free CompuServe Help Forum (as always, communication surcharges still apply). The Reference Help library contains several files with lists of available databases, usage instructions and additional information.

The Knowledge Index is a surcharged service; although you don't pay regular connection charges (communication surcharges still apply), there is a $24 per hour surcharge. Also, note that the Knowledge Index is only available during evenings and weekends.

IQuest (GO IQUEST)

IQuest is by far the most comprehensive information resource available on CompuServe. It is also the most expensive, but it can be a real time saver if you are looking for specific information. It offers access to no fewer than 800 databases on every possible subject. Because of its complexity, there is extensive online help available: whenever you need someone to help you compose a search key, or when you feel that you are lost completely, just type `SOS` to call an IQuest Information Specialist: a live person who will assist you online.

Although IQuest is available on CompuServe, it is not a CompuServe product. It is maintained by an American company called Telebase Systems, Inc. and contains databases from a number of information providers including BRS Online Products, Data-Star, Dialog Information Services, FT Profile and NewsNet.

Because of its structure, IQuest is not intended for 'doing some casual browsing'. Instead, you have to decide what kind of information you are looking for before you instruct IQuest to retrieve that information.

One of the most powerful features of IQuest is the SmartSCAN: an extensive search command that searches a group of databases selected by you for information about a certain topic. A SmartSCAN will return results in the form of a series of references to database articles or extracts. If the information you need is listed in those references, you can either read it online if available, or have IQuest send it to you *via* regular or express mail.

In some cases, it can be helpful to use one of IQuest's special *InfoCenters*: special groups of databases and SmartSCANs that pertain to certain subjects. Examples of those InfoCenters are:

- IQuest Business Management InfoCenter (`GO IQBUSINESS`)
- IQuest Education InfoCenter (`GO IQEDUCATION`)
- IQuest Engineering InfoCenter (`GO IQENGINEER`)
- IQuest Medical InfoCenter (`GO IQMEDICINE`)
- IQuest Technology InfoCenter (`GO IQTECHNOLOGY`)

Informative files about IQuest

If you wish to know more about IQuest before you start using this service, `GO HELPFORUM` to visit the free CompuServe Help Forum (as always, communication surcharges still apply). The Reference Help library contains several files with lists of available databases, usage instructions and additional information.

9.3 Chatting and playing with the rest of the world

9.3.1 CB (GO CB)

If you like forum conferencing, the chances are that CB is just the thing for you. Imagine CB as a series of 36 conference rooms, each with its own audience. And what's more, there are three series each with 36 rooms, or *channels* as they are called in CB jargon: General, Adult 1 and Adult 2.

When you enter one of the CB bands, and after you have specified your *handle* (the name you will use while you are on CB), WinCIM displays the *Channel Selector*, shown in Figure 9.8. The Channel Selector contains the following fields and options:

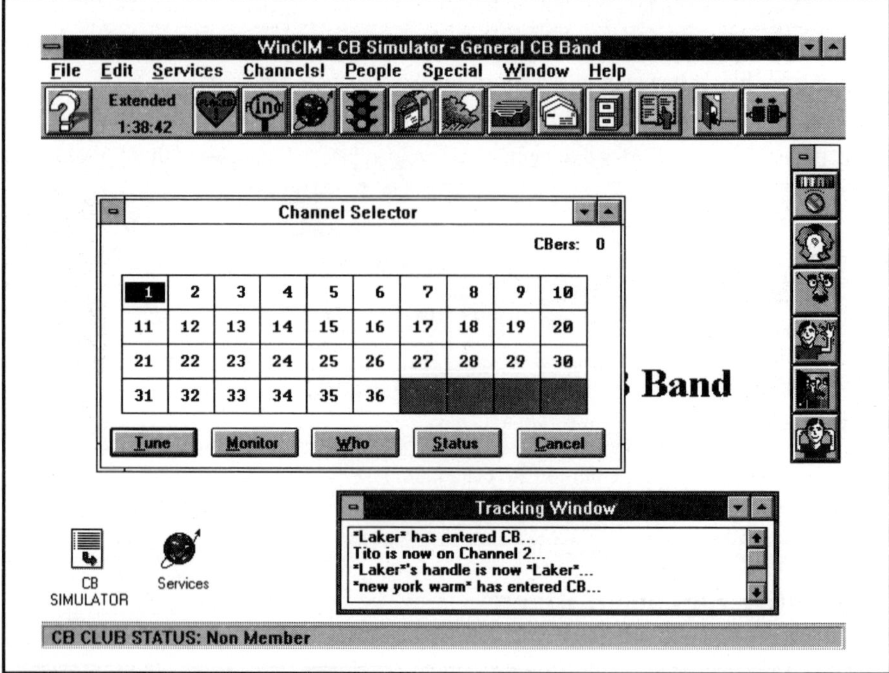

Figure 9.8 The CB Channel Selector

- *A list of available channels*: There are 36 channels per band. In the upper right corner of the Channel Selector window, the number of people currently on the selected channel is displayed.
- *Tune*: Press this button to 'tune in' to the selected channel. You cannot tune in to more than one channel. However, you can 'monitor' another channel (that is, listen to the conversation going on there, without actually participating).
- *Monitor*: Press this button to listen to the conversation on the selected channel. Unlike tuning in to a channel, you cannot participate in the conversation.
- *Who*: Press this button to see who else is on CB right now (see Figure 9.9). You can see either everyone on the current band or everyone on a particular channel. If you wish to talk to someone in particular, select that person and press the `Talk` button. If you wish to see a description of someone, select that person and press the `Profile` button. To enter your own profile, select the `CB Profiles` option on the `CB Simulator` menu.

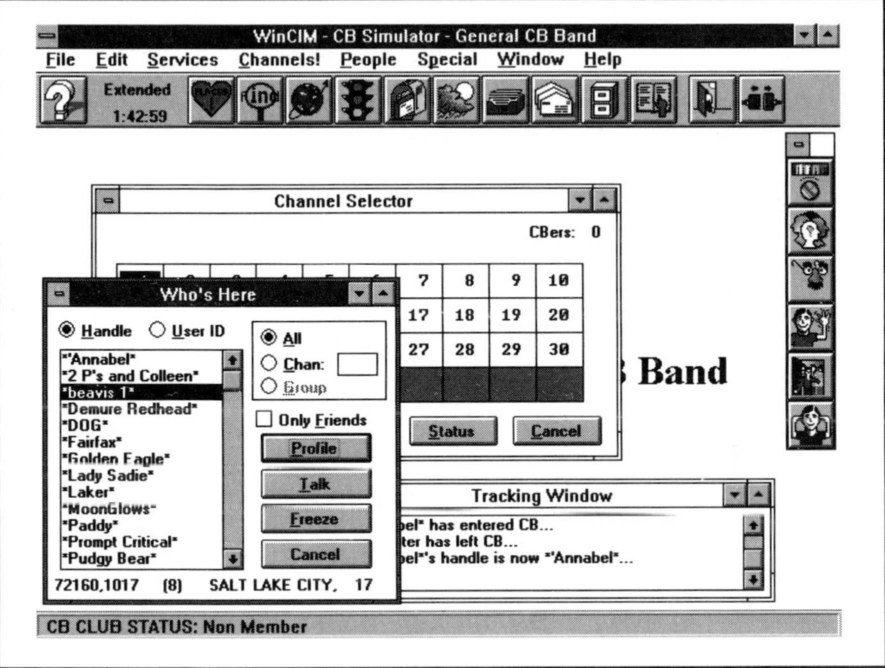

Figure 9.9 A list of other users on the current band

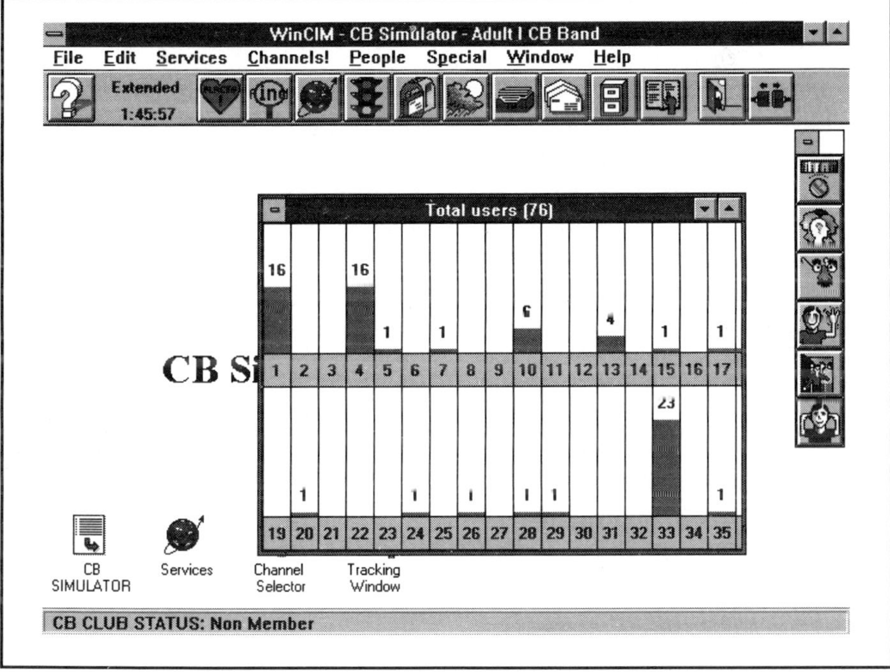

Figure 9.10 The occupancy of the various channels is displayed in this dialog

- *Status*: Pressing this button results in a graphical display of the various channels (see Figure 9.10). To tune in to a specific channel, double-click on it.

Once you have tuned in to a particular channel, everything you type can be read by everyone else who has either tuned in to or monitored that channel. Have fun!

CB is part of Extended Services. However, there are some special pricing plans available; paying a monthly fee gives you access to CB as well as the Entertainment Center at reduced prices. `GO RATES` for more information.

9.3.2 The Entertainment Center (GO ECN)

Have you ever played a game of backgammon with someone in Tokyo? Or would you like to beat your friend in New York at a nice game of chess? In that case, the Entertainment Center might be just the service that you are looking for. It allows CompuServe members from all over the world to meet and play games like chess, checkers, backgammon, and a science-fiction game called *StarSprint*.

To play the games available in the Entertainment Center, you have to download them. This can be done for a nominal fee (not more than a few dollars) *via* an option on the `Entertainment Center` Main Menu.

After you have downloaded one or more games and installed them (follow the directions in the README file that is included), you are ready to look for someone to play with. `GO ECN` and select the `Access the ENTERTAINMENT CENTER` option. You will now enter the lobby of the Entertainment Center.

The Entertainment Center is one of the CompuServe products that doesn't support HMI. Therefore, you will have to resort to Terminal Emulation mode, which means that you will have to type commands.

First, type `/help` and press the Enter key. You will see a list of available commands:

```
Note:  The user specification ('*') in the /SQUELCH and
/WHO commands may consist of a User Number, a User Id, or
a User Name.

Conferencing commands:
/EXIT         Leave the lobby (also /MENU)
/FIND x       Leave the lobby and find topic x
/GO x         Go to page x
/HELP         Request help
```

```
/NAME x       Change your name to x
/NOECHO       Turn off input echoing (cancelled with /ECHO)
/NOSEND       Suppress sends to you
/ROLL s n     Roll n s-sided dice (default is 2 6-sided)
/SEND # x     Send message x to user number #
/SQUELCH *    Squelch all lobby messages from user *
(disabled if no user specified)
/USERS        List all users in lobby or group.  /USERS ALL
lists all users.
/WHO *        Show user list information for user *

Group commands:
/BREAK        Exit a private group
/INVITE #     Invite user # to a private group
/JOIN #       Accept an invitation from user #
/NOINVITE     Suppress all group invitations to you

Game commands:
/GAMES        List all games in progress
/PLAY g       Join game g as an active player
/START x      Start a new game of title x
/TITLES       List all supported game titles
/VIEW g       Join game g as an inactive viewer
```

Normally, you will start with a **/USERS** command to see who else is currently in the Entertainment Center lobby. Note that you start a command with a **/** symbol: anything you type that doesn't start with a **/** symbol can be read by everyone else who is currently in the lobby. You can also send a message to a specific user; to do this, use the **/SEND** command.

To see a list of games that are currently being played, use the **/GAMES** command. To start a new game, use the **/START** command, followed by the name of the game you wish to play (Chess, Checkers, Backgammon or StarSprint). To view a game that is currently in progress, enter the **/VIEW** command, followed by the number of the game (as listed by the **/GAMES** command).

Don't let the seemingly complicated commands get in the way: manyCompuServe members find the Entertainment Center a fun place to be. If you are stuck, just type **HELP**; in most cases, another member will come to the rescue shortly. (That's how I got to play my first game not to mention the second!)

Because the game interfaces run under DOS and not under Windows, WinCIM users have to perform a few steps to be able to use them. After you have downloaded the games, proceed as follows:

1. From Windows, start the Control Panel application. Its icon can be found in the Main program group.
2. Click on the 386 Enhanced icon. This causes the 386 Enhanced dialog to appear.
3. In the Device Contention field, select, for each COM port on your computer, either the Never Warn or the Always Warn box.
4. In Program Manager, select the `New` option on the `File` menu to install a program item for each game that you wish to use.
5. When you arrive in the Entertainment Center, enter either `/START`, `/VIEW` or `/PLAY` and specify the appropriate game.
6. Next, minimize the WinCIM application (do **not** close it!). If, in step 3, you selected the `Always Warn` option, you will see a device contention warning. Ignore this warning and double-click on the icon corresponding to the game you wish to play.
7. You will now temporarily switch to DOS to play the game. When you have finished, you return to Windows. Finally, double-click on the minimized WinCIM icon to return to the lobby of the Entertainment Center.

The Entertainment Center is part of Extended Services. However, there are some special pricing plans available; paying a monthly fee gives you access to the Entertainment Center as well as CB at reduced prices. `GO RATES` for more information.

9.3.3 Games

Biorhythms (`GO BIORHYTHM`)

This is one of the oldest products on CompuServe. After you have specified your name and date of birth, CompuServe will calculate your biorhythms for the year and month(s) you have indicated. The result will be displayed as text and as a graphical image.

Biorhythms is part of Basic Services.

An adventure: BlackDragon (`GO BLACKDRAGON`)

BlackDragon is a so-called *role-playing game*. You will be placed in a labyrinth and find many treasures and hidden dangers on your journey. Because the game status information will be saved, you can return to the BlackDragon game later and continue where you left off.

BlackDragon is part of Basic Services.

The SHOWBIZQUIZ Games (GO SBQ-1)

If you think you know a lot about show business, try one of the quizzes that are part of the SHOWBIZQUIZ Games. There are quizzes about Frank Sinatra, Clint Eastwood, The Rolling Stones, Movies of Bette Davis, and Star Trek (my personal favourite), to name but a few. Apart from that, you can participate in several SHOWBIZQUIZ Trivias, or in a series of Beatles quizzes. There are lots of them, and new quizzes are added regularly.

The SHOWBIZQUIZ Games are part of Basic Services.

The Grolier Whiz Quiz (GO WHIZ)

As the name implies, this quiz is sponsored by Grolier's Electronic Publishing, Inc. It is based on the Academic Encyclopedia product, part of Basic Services. The quiz consists of 30 questions in a number of categories (which you can select) and can be played by four persons simultaneously.

The Grolier Whiz Quiz is part of Basic Services.

Air Traffic Controller (GO ATCONTROL)

If you can stand the stress of being an air traffic controller, or if you'd simply like to see what they have to deal with during a normal working day, Air Traffic Controller might be a game for you.

In Air Traffic Controller, you have your own sector of a large portion of airspace. It is your task to guide all traffic safely through your sector. If your sector contains an airport (and almost all sections do!), you need to guide planes from and to that airport as well. The Air Traffic Controller game can be played by several CompuServe members simultaneously; in that case, each member is assigned his or her own section of airspace. However, if there are no other members, the computer will generate a scenario for you.

You need no special game program to play Air Traffic Controller; CompuServe assumes that your terminal program supports ANSI (CIM and WinCIM are suitable as well). However, you'd better download the instructions and read them offline before you start playing. And if you use an MS-DOS computer, you might like to download the special ATSCOPE program, which acts as a communications graphics front end for Air Traffic Controller. To download this program, visit the MP Games Forum (GO MPGAMES). Look for the file ATSCPX.EXE.

Air Traffic Controller is part of Extended Services.

Island of Kesmai (GO KESMAI)

Island of Kesmai is one of the most popular and addictive games on CompuServe. When you play it, you enter a virtual, mysterious world, in which you will meet many characters. Some of them are created by the computer, but others are CompuServe members just like you.

Island of Kesmai is part of Extended Services.

9.4 Shopping on CompuServe

CompuServe provides plenty of opportunities to go shopping. The Electronic Mall is CompuServe's equivalent of a real, American shopping mall. And if you are looking for specific CompuServe software, merchandise or information, you can **GO ORDER**. Both services are free, except for communication surcharges.

9.4.1 The Electronic Mall (GO MALL)

The Electronic Mall is one of the most famous products on CompuServe. Just like a real shopping mall, a lot of famous American shops are represented. Because the Electronic Mall is a free service, lots of American users spend a lot of time there. Over here, in Europe, we still have to deal with communication surcharges and telephone bills, but nevertheless, it might be worthwhile paying a visit now and then. For starters, there are often free user credits to gain; sometimes stores give them even if you do nothing but order their free catalogue, to name an example. Besides, more and more shops deliver in Europe as well. You could therefore be in for some real bargains if you buy CDs and software, to name but a few articles, in the Electronic Mall!

Because the Electronic Mall supports HMI, WinCIM users will benefit from colourful graphics and easy-to-use menus and dialogs.

When you arrive at the mall, the opening menu appears on the screen (see Figure 9.11). You can either enter the Electronic Mall right away or stop at the Mall Information Booth to read instructions about ordering merchandise, getting in touch with merchants, and so on.

If you plan to use the Electronic Mall regularly, you might consider joining the Mall ELITE. Members of the Mall ELITE receive bonuses (free credits, for example), special discounts and the like.

After you have entered the Electronic Mall, you'll see the menu displayed in Figure 9.12.

Typically, you would select the option `Merchants Shipping Outside the US`, followed by `Shop By Department`. The rest is easy: just pick the shops that you are interested in, and look around for interesting merchandise.

HINTS & TIPS

Extra costs could apply!

Note that, in some cases, you will have to pay import duties and sometimes even additional taxes. When in doubt, contact the merchant for more information.

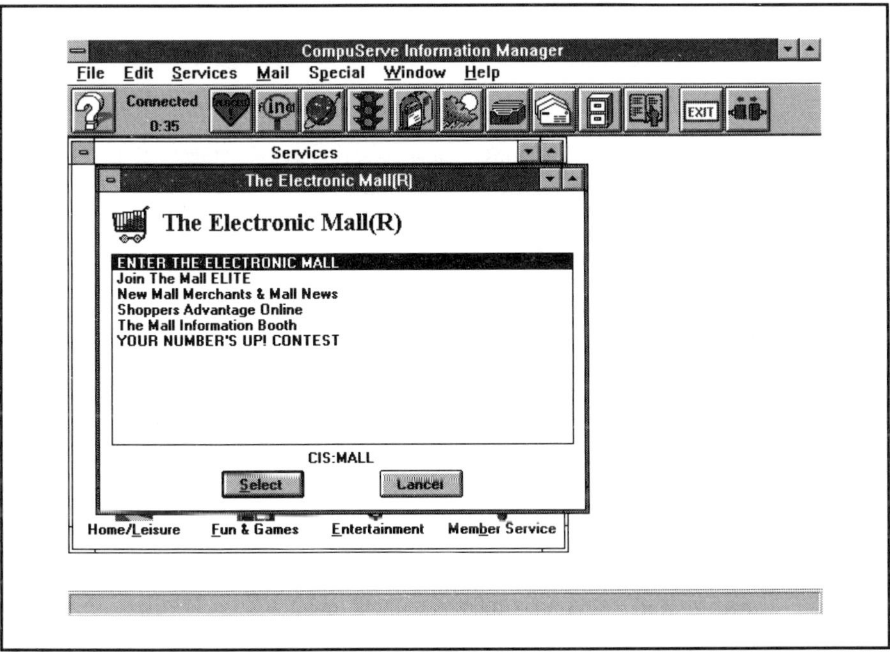

Figure 9.11 You have entered the Electronic Mall

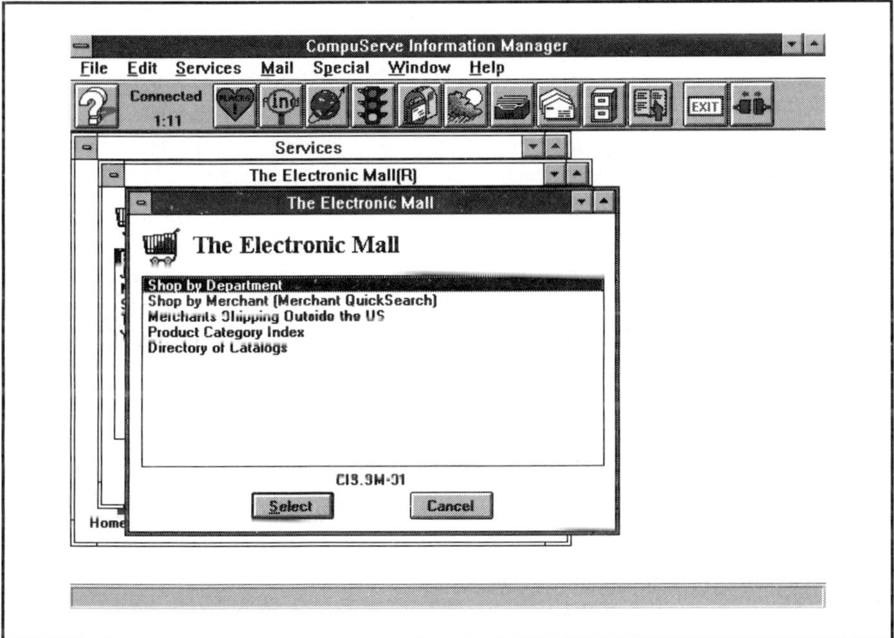

Figure 9.12 The Electronic Mall main menu

9.4.2 The CompuServe Store (GO ORDER)

CompuServe has its own electronic store. You can order anything from special merchandise (mouse pads, T shirts, and so on) to books, software and even gift certificates, if you wish to surprise another CompuServe member with some extra credits.

9.5 Travel services

If you are planning a journey, CompuServe can help you. Naturally, you can use forums (like the popular Travel Forum, for instance) to ask other members for information. But apart from that, it is even possible to make hotel reservations and order your airline tickets online. Two of the most famous services are Eaasy Sabre and WORLDSPAN Travelshopper.

9.5.1 Eaasy Sabre (GO SABRE/GO SABRECIM)

Sabre is one of the most comprehensive computer reservations systems in the world. You can book flights with more than 300 airlines, make room reservations for almost 20,000 hotels worldwide, and even rent your car. Apart from that, actual weather information is available, as well as scheduled flight information for all airlines. Once you have signed up for the Aadvantage Program, you can make reservations and start collecting frequent flyer miles. You can also fill out your personal profile; Eaasy Sabre will use that profile when searching for special offers, bargain prices, and so on.

There are two versions of Eaasy Sabre: one that uses Terminal Emulation (**GO SABRE**), and another that takes advantage of the WinCIM interface (**GO SABRECIM**).

9.5.2 WORLDSPAN Travelshopper (GO WORLDSPAN/ GO WORLDCIM)

The WORLDSPAN reservation system, owned by TWA, Northwest Airlines and Delta Airlines, is also available on CompuServe. You can look up flights and make reservations (either pay by credit card or *via* your local travel agency), and you can make reservations for hotel rooms and rental cars. In addition, WORLDSPAN Travelshopper offers information about the current weather at your destination, as well as the local time in other cities and currency conversion.

There are two versions of WORLDSPAN Travelshopper: one that uses Terminal Emulation (**GO WORLDSPAN**), and another that takes advantage of the WinCIM interface (**GO WORLDCIM**).

9.6 List of GO words

The following sections contain a summary of all public services on CompuServe.

9.6.1 Overview of CompuServe Forums

The following list contains an overview of all public forums on CompuServe. The plus sign (+) indicates that the forum is part of Extended Services.

ACI US Forum +	ACIUS
AI EXPERT Forum +	AIEXPERT
APPC Info Exchange Forum +	APPCFORUM
ASP/Shareware Forum +	ASPFORUM
AST Forum +	ASTFORUM
Accounting Vendor Forum +	ACCOUNTING
Adobe Forum +	ADOBE
African American Culture +	AFRO
Aldus Forum +	ALDUSFORUM
Aldus Software GmbH Forum +	ALDUSEU
Aldus Special Programs Forum +	ALDUSSP
All-Music Guide Forum +	AMGPOP
Amiga Arts Forum +	AMIGAARTS
Amiga Tech Forum +	AMIGATECH
Amiga User's Forum +	AMIGAUSER
Amiga Vendor Forum +	AMIGAVENDOR
Animation Vendor A Forum +	ANVENA
Apple II Prog. Forum +	APPROG
Apple II Users Forum +	APPUSER
Apple II Vendor Forum +	APIIVEN
Apple Support Forum +	APLSUP
Aquaria / Fish Forum +	FISHNET
Archive Photos Forum +	ARCHIVE
Artisoft Forum +	ARTISOFT
Artist Forum +	ARTIST
Ask3Com Forum +	ASKFORUM
Astronomy Forum +	ASTROFORUM
Atari GAMING Forum +	ATARIGAMING
Atari ST Arts Forum +	ATARIARTS
Atari ST Prod. Forum +	ATARIPRO

Atari Vendor Forum +	ATARIVEN
Attn. Deficit Disorder Forum +	ADD
Author of the Week Forum +	AOTW
Autodesk AutoCAD Forum +	ACAD
Autodesk Retail Products Forum +	ARETAIL
Autodesk Software Forum +	ASOFT
Automobile Forum +	CARS
Aviation Forum (AVSIG) +	AVSIG
BASIS International Forum +	BASIS
BORLAND +	BORLAND
Bacchus Wine Forum +	WINEFORUM
Banyan Forum +	BANFORUM
Benchmark & Standards Forum +	BENCHMARK
Blyth Forum +	BLYTH
Borland Application Forum +	BORAPP
Borland C++ for Win/OS2 Forum +	BCPPWIN
Borland C++/DOS Forum +	BCPPDOS
Borland DB Products Forum +	BORDB
Borland Dev. Tools Forum +	BDEVTOOLS
Borland GmbH Forum +	BORGMBH
Borland Paradox/Dos Forum +	PDOXDOS
Borland Paradox/Windows Forum +	PDOXWIN
Borland Pascal Forum +	BPASCAL
Borland dBASE Forum +	DBASEDOS
Broadcast Pro Forum +	BPFORUM
CA App. Development Forum +	CAIDEV
CA Business Partners Forum +	CAPARTNERS
CA Micro Germany Forum +	CAMICRO
CA Pro Solutions Forum +	CAIPRO
CA-Clipper Germany Forum +	CLIPGER
CA-Simply Forum +	CASIMPLY
CADD/CAM/CAE Vendor Forum +	CADDVEN
CASE DCI Forum +	CASEFORUM
CB Forum +	CBFORUM
CD-ROM Vendor Forum +	CDVEN
CDROM Forum +	CDROM
CIM Support Forum(FREE)	CIMSUPPORT
CP/M Users Group Forum +	CPMFORUM
CSNav-Win Support Forum(FREE)	WCSNAVSUP
CTOS/Pathway Forum +	CTOS
Cabletron System, Inc. +	CTRON
Cabletron Systems Forum +	CTRONFORUM
Cadence Forum +	CADENCE

California Forum +	CALFORUM
Cancer Forum +	CANCER
Canon Support +	CANON
Canopus Forum +	CANOPUS
Chess Forum +	CHESSFORUM
Cheyenne Software Forum +	CHEYENNE
ChipSoft Forum +	CHIPSOFT
Citrix Systems Forums +	CITRIX
Clarion Software Forum +	CLARION
Claris Macintosh Forum +	MACCLARIS
Claris Windows Forum +	WINCLARIS
Client Server Computing Forum +	MSNETWORKS
Clipper Forum +	CLIPPER
Collectibles Forum +	COLLECT
Color Computer Forum +	COCO
Comics Publishers Forum +	COMICPUB
Comics/Animation Forum +	COMIC
Commodore Applications Forum +	CBMAPP
Commodore Arts/Games Forum +	CBMART
Commodore Service Forum +	CBMSERVICE
Compaq Connection +	CPQFORUM
CompuAdd Forum +	COMPUADD
CompuServe Applications Forum(FREE)	CSAPPS
CompuServe Help Forum(FREE)	HELPFORUM
CompuServe Navigator, Mac(FREE)	MACNAV
CompuServe Pacific Forum +	PACFORUM
CompuServeCD Forum(FREE)	CCDSUP
Computer Art Forum +	COMART
Computer Associates Forums +	CAI
Computer Club Forum +	CLUB
Computer Consult. Forum +	CONSULT
Computer Language Forum +	CLMFORUM
Computer Shopper (UK) Forum +	UKSHOPPER
Computer Training Forum +	DPTRAIN
Consumer Elect. Forum +	CEFORUM
Consumer Forum +	CONFORUM
Cook's Online Forum +	COOKS
Corel Forum +	CORELAPPS
Court Reporters Forum +	CRFORUM
Crafts Forum +	CRAFTS
Creative Labs Forum +	BLASTER
Creative Solutions/Forth Forum +	FORTH
Crosstalk Forum +	XTALK

Cyber Forum +	CYBERFORUM
DATASTORM Forum +	DATASTORM
DBMS Magazine Forum +	DBMSFORUM
DEC PC Forum +	DECPC
DECPCI Forum +	DECPCI
DTP Vendors Forum +	DTPVENDOR
Da Vinci Forum +	DAVINCI
Data Access Corp. Forum +	DACCESS
Data Based Advisor Forum +	DBADVISOR
DataEase International Forum +	DATAEASE
Dell Forum +	DELL
Delrina Technology Forum +	DELRINA
Democratic Forum +	DEMOCRATS
Der Spiegel Forum +	SPIEGEL
Desktop Publishing Forum +	DTPFORUM
Detroit Free Press Forum +	DETROIT
Deutsches Computer Forum +	GERNET
Deutsches PC Direkt Forum +	PCDIREKT
Deutsches PCpro-Forum +	PCPRO
Deutsches Windows Mag Forum +	GERWIN
Deutschland Online Forum +	GERLINE
Developer Relations Forum +	MSDR
Diabetes Forum +	DIABETES
DiagSoft Forum +	DIAGSOFT
Digitalk Forum +	DIGITALK
Dinosaur Forum +	DINO
Disabilities Forum +	DISABILITIES
Dr. Dobb's Forum +	DDJFORUM
Dr. Neuhaus Forum +	NEUHAUS
Dvorak Development Forum +	DVORAK
ECTF Forum +	ECTF
ELSA GmbH Forum +	ELSA
Earth Forum +	EARTH
Education Forum +	EDFORUM
Educational Res. Forum +	EDRESEARCH
Eicon Technology Forum +	EICON
Electronic Frontier Foundation +	EFFSIG
Electronics Vendor Forum +	CEVENDOR
Encounters Forum +	ENCOUNTERS
Engineering Automation Forum +	LEAP
Entertainment Drive Forum +	EDRIVE
Epic MegaGames Forum +	EPIC
Epson Forum +	EPSON

European Forum +	EURFORUM
Family Handyman Forum +	HANDYMAN
Fed. Of Int'l Distributors +	FEDERATION
Financial Forums +	FINFORUM
Fine Arts Forum +	FINEARTS
Flight Simulation Forum +	FSFORUM
Florida Forum +	FLORIDA
Florida Today Forum +	FLATODAY
FocServices Forum +	FOCSERVICES
FocWizard Forum +	FOCWIZARD
Foreign Language Forum +	FLEFO
Fox Software Forum +	FOXFORUM
FundWatch by Money Mag.	FUNDWATCH
Game Forums and News +	GAMECON
Game Publishers A Forum +	GAMAPUB
Game Publishers B Forum +	GAMBPUB
Game Publishers C Forum +	GAMCPUB
Game Publishers D Forum +	GAMDPUB
Game Publishers Forums(FREE)	GAMPUB
Gamers Forum +	GAMERS
Gardening Forum +	GARDENING
Gateway 2000 Forum +	GATEWAY
Genealogy Forum +	ROOTS
General Computing Forum +	GENCOM
Glamour Graphics Forum +	GLAMOUR
Global Crises Forum +	CRISIS
Golden CommPass Support +	GCPSUPPORT
Graphics B Vendor Forum +	GRAPHBVEN
Graphics Corner Forum +	CORNER
Graphics Developers Forum +	GRAPHDEV
Graphics Forums +	GRAPHICS
Graphics Gallery Forum +	GALLERY
Graphics Plus Forum +	GRAPHPLUS
Graphics Support Forum +	GRAPHSUPPORT
Graphics Vendor Forum +	GRAPHVEN
Graphics Vendors C Forum +	GRVENC
Gupta Forum +	GUPTAFORUM
HP Handheld Forum +	HPHAND
HP OmniBook Forum +	HPOMNIBOOK
HP Peripherals Forum +	HPPER
HP Systems Forum +	HPSYS
HSX Adult Forum +	HSX200
HSX Open Forum +	HSX100

Hamnet Forum +	HAMNET
Hardware F	HARDWARE
Hayes Forum +	HAYFORUM
Health & Fitness Forum +	GOODHEALTH
Holistic Health Forum +	HOLISTIC
Home Forum +	TWHOME
IBM Applications Forum +	IBMAPP
IBM Bulletin Board Forum +	IBMBBS
IBM CAD/CAM Forum +	IBMENG
IBM COS Network Solution Forum +	IBMCOS
IBM Communications Forum +	IBMCOM
IBM DB2 Database Forum +	IBMDB2
IBM Data Products Forum +	IBMDATA
IBM Hardware Forum +	IBMHW
IBM ImagePlus Forum +	IBMIMAGE
IBM LMU2 Forum +	LMUFORUM
IBM Languages Forum +	IBMLANG
IBM Netview Family Forum +	NETVIEW
IBM New User's Forum +	IBMNEW
IBM OS/2 B Vendors Forum +	OS2BVEN
IBM OS/2 Developer 1 Forum +	OS2DF1
IBM OS/2 Developer 2 Forum +	OS2DF2
IBM OS/2 Support Forum +	OS2SUPPORT
IBM OS/2 Users Forum +	OS2USER
IBM OS/2 Vendor Forum +	OS2AVEN
IBM Object Technology Forum +	IBMOBJ
IBM PS/1 Support Forum +	IBMPS1
IBM PSP A Products Forum +	PSPAPROD
IBM PSP Deutschland Forum +	OS2UGER
IBM PowerPC Forum +	POWERPC
IBM Programming Forum +	IBMPRO
IBM Software Forum +	IBMDESK
IBM Software Solutions Forum +	SOFSOL
IBM Special Needs Forum +	IBMSPEC
IBM Storage Systems Forum +	IBMSTORAGE
IBM Systems/Util. Forum +	IBMSYS
IBM ThinkPad Forum +	THINKPAD
IBM Users N	IBMNET
IBM ValuePoint Forum +	VALUEPOINT
IBM Visual Product Forum +	IBMVISUAL
IRI Software Forum +	IRIFORUM
Ideas & Inventions Forum +	INNOVATION
Information Management Forum +	INFOMANAGE

Inn and Lodging Forum +	INNFORUM
Intel Access/iRUG Forum +	INTELACCESS
International Trade Forum +	TRADE
Internet Forum +	INETFORUM
Intersolv Forum +	INTERSOLV
Intuit Forum +	INTUIT
Investors Forum +	INVFORUM
Issues Forum +	ISSUESFORUM
JFK Assassination Forum +	JFKFORUM
Japan Forum +	JAPAN
Journalism Forum +	JFORUM
KnowledgeWare Forum +	KWARE
Kodak CD Forum +	KODAK
LDC Spreadsheets Forum +	LOTUSA
LDC Word Processing Forum +	LOTUSWP
LDC Words & Pixels Forum +	LOTUSB
LDOS/TRSDOS6 Users Forum +	LDOS
LOGO Forum +	LOGOFORUM
Lan Magazine Forum +	LANMAG
Lan Technology Forum +	LANTECH
Lan Vendor Forum +	LANVEN
Legal Forum +	LAWSIG
Lexmark Forum +	LEXMARK
Literary Forum +	LITFORUM
Living History Forum +	LIVING
Logitech Forum +	LOGITECH
Lotus Communications Forum +	LOTUSCOMM
Lotus GmbH Forum +	LOTGER
Lotus Press Release Forum +	LOTUSNEWS
MECA Software Forum +	MECA
MIDI A Vendor Forum +	MIDIAVEN
MIDI B Vendor Forum +	MIDIBVEN
MIDI C Vendor Forum +	MIDICVEN
MIDI D Vendor Forum +	MIDIDVEN
MIDI/Music Forum +	MIDIFORUM
MS 32bit Languages Forum +	MSLNG32
MS Applications Forum +	MSAPP
MS Benelux Forum +	MSBF
MS DOS Forum +	MSDOS
MS Foundation Classes Forum +	MSMFC
MS Fox Users Forum +	FOXUSER
MS France Forum +	MSFR
MS Italy Forum +	MSITALY

MS Mail and Workgroups Forum +	MSWGA
MS SQL Server Forum +	MSSQL
MS Spain Forum +	MSSP
MS Sweden Forum +	MSSWE
MS TechNet Forum +	TNFORUM
MS WINFUN Forum +	WINFUN
MS Win Multimedia Forum +	WINMM
MS WinNT SNA Forum +	MSSNA
MS Windows Extensions Forum +	WINEXT
MS Windows Forum +	MSWIN
MS Windows News Forum +	WINNEWS
MS Windows Objects Forum +	WINOBJECTS
MS Windows SDK Forum +	WINSDK
MS Windows Shareware Forum +	WINSHARE
Mac A Vendor Forum +	MACAVEN
Mac Applications Forum +	MACAP
Mac B Vendor Forum +	MACBVEN
Mac C Vendor Forum +	MACCVEN
Mac CIM Support Forum(FREE)	MCIMSUP
Mac Communications Forum +	MACCOMM
Mac Community/Club Forum +	MACCLUB
Mac D Vendor Forum +	MACDVEN
Mac Developers Forum +	MACDEV
Mac Entertainment Forum +	MACFUN
Mac Hypertext Forum +	MACHYPER
Mac New Users Help Forum +	MACNEW
MacNav Support Forum(FREE)	MNAVSUPPORT
MacUser Forum +	MACUSER
MacWEEK Forum +	MACWEEK
Macintosh Hardware Forum +	MACHW
Macintosh Multimedia Forum +	MACMULTI
Macintosh Systems Forum +	MACSYS
Macmillan Publishing Forum +	PHCP
Macromedia Forum +	MACROMEDIA
MagnaMedia Forum +	MAGNA
Masonry Forum +	MASONRY
McAfee Virus Forum +	NCSAVIRUS
Media Vision Forum +	MEDIAVISION
Medsig Forum +	MEDSIG
Mensa Forum +	MENSA
Micro Focus Forum +	MICROFOCUS
MicroStation Forum +	MSTATION
Micrografx Forum +	MICROGRAFX

Microrim Forum +	MICRORIM
Microsoft Access Forum +	MSACCESS
Microsoft BASIC Forum +	MSBASIC
Microsoft CE Systems Forum +	MSCESYSTEM
Microsoft Central Europe +	MSEURO
Microsoft Central Europe Forum +	MSCE
Microsoft Connection +	MICROSOFT
Microsoft DevCast Forum +	DEVCAST
Microsoft Excel Forum +	MSEXCEL
Microsoft France +	MSFRANCE
Microsoft Languages Forum +	MSLANG
Microsoft Spain +	MSSPAIN
Microsoft Sweden +	MSSWEDEN
Microsoft WIN32 Forum +	MSWIN32
Microsoft Word Forum +	MSWORD
Military Forum +	MILITARY
Missing Children Forum(FREE)	MISSING
Model Aviation Forum +	MODELNET
Modem Games Forum +	MODEMGAMES
Modem Vendor Forum +	MODEMVENDOR
Motor Sports Forum +	RACING
Multi-Player Games Forum +	MPGAMES
Multimedia B Vendor Forum +	MULTIBVEN
Multimedia Conference Forum +	MULTICON
Multimedia Forum +	MULTIMEDIA
Multimedia Vendor Forum +	MULTIVEN
Muscular Dystrophy MDA Forum +	MDAFORUM
Music Industry Forum +	INMUSIC
Music/Arts Forum +	MUSICARTS
NAIC Invest. Ed. Forum +	NAIC
NCR/ATT Forum +	NCRATT
NCSA InfoSecurity Forum +	NCSAFORUM
NeXT Forum +	NEXTFORUM
Netherlands Forum +	NLFORUM
New Age Forum +	NEWAGE
New York Newslink Forum +	NEWYORK
Newton Developers Forum +	NEWTDEV
Newton/PIE Forum +	NEWTON
Novell Client Forum +	NOVCLIENT
Novell Connectivity Forum +	NCONNECT
Novell DSG Forum +	DRFORUM
Novell Dev Support Forum +	NDEVSUPPORT
Novell Dev. Info. Forum +	NDEVINFO

Novell Hardware Forum +	NOVHW
Novell Information Forum +	NGENERAL
Novell Library Forum +	NOVLIB
Novell Net. Management Forum +	NOVMAN
Novell NetWare 2.X Forum +	NETW2X
Novell NetWare 3.X Forum +	NETW3X
Novell Netware 4X Forum +	NETW4X
Novell OS/2 Forum +	NOVOS2
Novell Press Forum +	NOVBOOKS
Novell Quattro Pro Forum +	QUATTROPRO
Novell Vendor A Forum +	NVENA
Novell Vendor B Forum +	NVENB
OS-9 Forum +	OS9
OZCIS Support Forum +	OZCIS
Office Automation Vendor Forum +	OAFORUM
Oracle Forum +	ORACLE
Other Ban Patchware Forum +	BANPATCH
Outdoor Forum +	OUTDOORFORUM
Outdoors Support Forum +	OUTSUP
PBS Applications Forum +	PBSAPPS
PBS Arcade Forum +	PBSARCADE
PC Computing Forum +	PCCOMP
PC Contact Forum +	PCCONTACT
PC Direct UK Forum +	PCDUK
PC Expert Forum francais +	PCEFORUM
PC Industrie Forum +	PCIND
PC MagNet +	PCMAGNET
PC MagNet Editorial Forum +	EDITORIAL
PC MagNet Programming Forum +	PROGRAMMING
PC MagNet Utilities/Tips Forum +	TIPS
PC Magazine UK Forum +	PCUKFORUM
PC Magazine UK Online +	PCUKONLINE
PC Magazine(Subscribe)(FREE)	PM
PC Plug and Play Forum +	PLUGPLAY
PC Plus / PC Answers +	PCPLUS
PC Vendor A Forum +	PCVENA
PC Vendor B Forum +	PCVENB
PC Vendor C Forum +	PCVENC
PC Vendor D Forum +	PCVEND
PC Vendor E Forum +	PCVENE
PC Vendor F Forum +	PCVENF
PC Vendor G Forum +	PCVENG
PC Vendor H Forum +	PCVENH

PC Vendor I Forum +	PCVENI
PC Vendor J Forum +	PCVENJ
PC Vendor K Forum +	PCVENK
PC Week Extra Forum +	PCWEEK
PC World Online +	PCWORLD
PC World Online Forum +	PWOFORUM
PDP-11 Forum +	PDP11
PEARL Forum +	PEARL
PR and Marketing Forum +	PRSIG
PSP BETA FORUM +	PSPBETA
Pacific Vendor Forum +	PACVEN
Packard Bell Forum +	PACKARDBELL
Palmtop B Forum +	PALMB
Palmtop Forum +	PALMTOP
Parsons Technology Forum +	PTFORUM
Pen Technology Forum +	PENFORUM
Pet Products/Reference Forum +	PETPRO
Pets/Animal Forum +	PETSFORUM
Photo Professionals Forum +	PROPHOTO
Photography Forum +	PHOTOFORUM
Play-By-Mail Games Forum +	PBMGAMES
Polaris Software Forum +	POLARIS
Political Debate Forum +	POLITICS
Portable Prog. Forum +	CODEPORT
Powersoft Forum +	POWERSOFT
Practical Periph. Forum +	PPIFORUM
Practice Forum(FREE)	PRACTICE
Prisma Deutschland Forum +	PRISMA
Quarterdeck Forum +	QUARTERDEC
Quick Picture Forum +	QPICS
Recording Industry Forum +	RECORD
Recreation Vehicle Forum +	RVFORUM
Religion Forum +	RELIGION
Republican Forum +	REPUBLICAN
Retirement Living Forum +	RETIREMENT
Reuter News Pictures Forum +	NEWSPI
Revelation Tech Forum +	REVELATION
Rocknet Forum +	ROCKNET
Role-Playing Games Forum +	RPGAMES
Rotarians Online Forum +	ROTARY
SYBEX Publishing Forum +	SYBEX
Safetynet Forum +	SAFETYNET
Sailing Forum +	SAILING

Santa Cruz Operation Forum +	SCOFORUM
Science Fiction Forum +	SCI-FI
Science/Math Ed. Forum +	SCIENCE
Scuba Forum +	DIVING
ShowBiz-Media Forum +	SHOWBIZ
Siemens Automatisierungs Forum +	AUTFORUM
Sight And Sound Forum +	SSFORUM
Smith Micro Forum +	SMITHMICRO
Software Pub. Assoc. Forum +	SPAFORUM
Software Publishing Forum +	SPCFORUM
Space Exploration Forum +	SPACEX
Space Flight Forum +	SPACEFLIGHT
Space/Astronomy Forum +	SPACE
Speakeasy Forum +	SPEAKEASY
Spinnaker Software Forum +	SPINNAKER
Sports Forum +	FANS
Sports Simulation Forum +	SPRTSIMS
Stac Electronics Forum +	STACKER
Standard Microsystems Forum +	SMC
Students' Forum +	STUFO
SunSoft Forum +	SUNSOFT
Sybase Forum +	SYBASE
Symantec AntiVirus Prod. Forum +	SYMVIRUS
Symantec Applications Forum +	SYMAPPS
Symantec CPS DOS Forum +	SYMCPDOS
Symantec CPS WinMac Forum +	SYMCPWIN
Symantec Dev. Tools Forum +	SYMDEVTOOL
Symantec FGS Forum +	SYMFGS
Symantec Forums +	SYMANTEC
Symantec Norton Util Forum +	SYMUTIL
Symantec Ntwrk Products Forum +	SYMNET
SynOptics Forum +	SYNOPTICS
TAPCIS Forum +	TAPCIS
TIMESLIPS Forum +	TIMESLIPS
Tandy Model 100 Forum +	TANDYLAPTOP
Tandy Professional Forum +	TANDYPRO
Telecommunications Forum +	TELECOM
Texas Instruments Forum +	TIFORUM
Texas Instruments News +	TINEWS
The Entrepreneur's Forum +	USEN
The Intel Forum +	INTELFORUM
Thomas-Conrad Forum +	TCCFORUM
Time Warner Crime Forum +	TWCRIME

Time Warner Trade Publishing +	TWEP
Time Warner-Dogs & Cats Forum +	TWPETS
Tips/Tricks From PC/Computing +	TNT
Toshiba Forum +	TOSHIBA
Toshiba GmbH Forum +	TOSHGER
TrainNet Forum +	TRAINNET
Travel Forum +	TRAVSIG
U. S. News Women's Forum +	WOMEN
U.S. News Forum +	USNFORUM
UK Communications Forum +	UKCOMMS
UK Computing Forum +	UKCOMP
UK Forum +	UKFORUM
UK Professionals Forum +	UKPROF
UKSHARE Forum +	UKSHARE
UNIX Forum +	UNIXFORUM
Ultimedia Hardware Plus Forum +	ULTIHW
Ultimedia Tools Series A Forum +	ULTIATOOLS
Ultimedia Tools Series B Forum +	ULTIBTOOLS
Ultimedia Tools Series C Forum +	ULTICTOOLS
Unix Vendor A Forum +	UNIXAVEN
UnixWare Forum +	UNIXWARE
UserLand Forum +	USERLAND
VAX Forum +	VAXFORUM
VNU BPA Forum +	VNUBPA
Ventura Software Forum +	VENTURA
Video Game Publishers Forum +	VIDPUB
Video Games Forum +	VIDGAM
Vines 4.x Patchware Forum +	VINES4
Vines 5.x Patchware Forum +	VINES5
Vobis AG Computer Forum +	VOBIS
WPCorp Files Forum +	WPFILES
WRQ/Reflection Forum +	WRQFORUM
WUGNET Forum +	WUGNET
White House Forum +	WHITEHOUSE
WinCIM Support Forum(FREE)	WCIMSUPPORT
WinNT Forum +	WINNT
Windows 3rd Party A Forum +	WINAPA
Windows 3rd Party App. D Forum +	WINAPD
Windows 3rd Party App. F Forum +	WINAPF
Windows 3rd Party App. G Forum +	WINAPG
Windows 3rd Party B Forum +	WINAPB
Windows 3rd Party C Forum +	WINAPC
Windows 3rd Party E Forum +	WINAPE

Windows Sources Forum +	WINSOURCES
Wolfram Research Forum +	WOLFRAM
WordPerfect Corporation +	WORDPERFECT
WordPerfect GmbH Forum +	WPGER
WordPerfect Users Forum +	WPUSER
WordStar Forum +	WORDSTAR
Working-From-Home Forum +	WORK
Worldwide Car Network +	WWCAR
ZD Benchmark Forum + +	ZDBENCH
Zenith Data Systems Forum +	ZENITH

9.6.2 Other CompuServe services

The following list contains a summary of available CompuServe services, with the exception of forums. To see a list of available public forums on CompuServe, refer to Section 9.6.1.

A plus sign (+) indicates that the product is part of Extended Services. A Dollar sign ($) indicates that the product is a surcharged service. Before using that product, consult its main menu for additional pricing information.

To obtain the latest copy of the complete list of all CompuServe services (remember that new services are added practically every day!), `GO INDEX`.

800 Listing +	XBQ-16
800 Flowers and Gift Shoppe(FREE)	FGS
AA Travel Services	UKTRAVEL
ABC Worldwide Hotel Guide +	ABC
ALPA +	ALPA
ANZ Company Library +	ANZCOLIB
AP France en Ligne	APFRANCE
AP Sports($)	SPORTS
Academic American Encycl.	ENCYCLOPEDIA
Access Numbers(FREE)	PHONES
Access Phone Numbers(FREE)	PHONE
Adventures In Food(FREE)	AIF
Adventures in Travel +	AIT
Aerosmith Coming Soon	AEROSMITH
African American Culture +	AFRO
Aids News Clips +	AIDSNEWS
Air France(FREE)	AF
Air Traffic Controller +	ATCONTROL
Airline Services Unlimited	ASU-1
Alaska Peddler(FREE)	ALASKA

Aldus Display +	ALDUS
All-Music Guide +	ALLMUSIC
Amazing Vacations	AMZ-1
American Heritage Dictionary	DICTIONARY
Americana Clothing(FREE)	AC
Amiga File Finder +	AMIGAFF
Apple Feedback(FREE)	APLFBK
Apple News Clips($)	APPLENEWS
Apple Tech Info Library +	APLTIL
Apple What's New Library +	APLNEW
Articulate Systems +	MACAVEN
Ask3Com +	THREECOM
Associated Press($)	ENS
Associated Press Online	NWS-47
Astrological Charting +	ASTROLOGY
Astronomy Download Area +	BLACKHOLE
Atari File Finder +	ATARIFF
Atari Users Network +	ATARINET
Audio Engineering Society +	AESNET
Austad's(FREE)	GOLF
Australian Associated Press	AAPONLINE
AutoQuot-R(FREE)	AQ
AutoVantage OnLine(FREE)	ATV
Automobile Info Center(FREE)	AI
Automotive Information +	AUTO
Aviation Menu +	AVIATION
Aviation Safety Institute +	ASI
BBC Music Magazine(FREE)	BBCM
BMG Compact Disc Club(FREE)	CD
BORLAND +	BORLAND
Basic Company Snapshot	BASCOMPANY
Basic Conversion Area	NEWBASIC
Basic Services	BASIC
Bassett Furniture(FREE)	BASSETT
Bed & Breakfast Database	INNS
Bertelsmann Lexikon	BERLEXIKON
Billing Information(FREE)	BILLING
Biorhythms	BIORHYTHM
Biz*File($)	BIZFILE
BlackDragon	BLACKDRAGON
Bonds Listing($)	BONDS
Book Of The Month Club(FREE)	BOMC
Book Review Digest($)	BOOKREVIEW

Books On Tape(FREE)	BOT-1
Books in Print($)	BOOKS
Borland Germany +	BORGER
Borland dBASE For Windows +	DBASEWIN
Brainscan +	BRAINSCAN
Breton Harbor Basket Co.(FREE)	BH
British Books in Print +	BBIP
British Legends +	LEGENDS
British Trade Marks($)	UKTRADEMARK
Broderbund Software(FREE)	BB
Brooks Brothers(FREE)	BR
Business Database Plus($)	BUSDB
Business Dateline($)	BUSDATE
Business Demographics($)	BUSDEM
Business Incorp. Guide(FREE)	INC
CB Club +	CBCLUB
CB Handle +	HANDLE
CB Profiles +	CBPROFILES
CB Simulator +	CB
CB Society +	CUPCAKE
CCML AIDS Articles($)	CCMLAIDS
CENDATA +	CENDATA
COMPUTRACE($)	TRACE
CS Lotus Notes Information Service	NOTES
Cabletron System, Inc. +	CTRON
Cadillac(FREE)	CADILLAC
Calculate Net Worth +	FINTOL
Canon Support +	CANON
CastleQuest	CQUEST
Change Your Password Program(FREE)	PASSWORD
CheckFree(FREE)	CF
Chef's Catalog(FREE)	CHEFS
Christian Children's Fund(FREE)	CCF
Cititronics(FREE)	CTR
Citizens Band Simulator +	CB
Claris Information Center +	CLARIS
Claris TechInfo Database +	CLATECH
Classic Adventure	CLADVENT
Classic Quotes +	TMC-45
Classifieds	CLASSIFIEDS
Coffee Anyone???(FREE)	COF
Colonel Audio Video	CVA
Colonel Video & Audio(FREE)	CVA

Columbia House Music Club(FREE)	FREECD
Comet/Jupiter Collision Files	COMET
Command Summary(FREE)	COMMAND
Commerce Business Daily($)	COMBUS
Commodities +	COMMODITIES
Commodity Pricing($)	CPRICE
Commodity Symbol Lookup +	CSYMBOL
Commodore Newsletter +	CBMNEWS
Commodore Users Network +	CBMNET
Commonly Asked Questions(FREE)	QUESTIONS
Company Analyzer($)	ANALYZER
Company Screening($EW)	COSCREEN
Compu-Cruise by Rosenbluth(FREE)	CRUISE
CompuBooks(FREE)	CBK
CompuServe Europe	EUROPE
CompuServe MS Mail Driver +	MAPI
CompuServe Magazine	OLI
CompuServe Mail	MAIL
CompuServe Mail Help(FREE)	MAILHELP
CompuServe Mail Hub +	MAILHUB
CompuServe Mail for PowerTalk	PTALK
CompuServe Navigator, Mac(FREE)	MACNAV
CompuServe Navigator, Windows(FREE)	CSNAV
CompuServe Operating Rules(FREE)	RULES
CompuServe Rates(FREE)	RATES
CompuServe Software(FREE)	CISSOFT
CompuServe Subject Index(FREE)	INDEX
CompuServe Tax Connection +	MMM-73
CompuServe Tour(FREE)	TOUR
CompuServe for GEOS Software	CS4GEOS
CompuServeCD(FREE)	CCD
Computer Buyers' Guide($)	COMPBG
Computer Database Plus($)	COMPDB
Computer Express(FREE)	CE
Computer Gaming World +	GAMEWORLD
Computer Library	COMPLIB
Computer Peripheral, Inc. +	VIVAMODEM
Computing Support	COMPUTERS
Concord Direct(FREE)	CATALOGS
Consumer Reports	CONSUMER
Consumer Reports Auto.	CRAUTO
Consumer Reports Drug Ref.	DRUGS
Contact Lens Supply(FREE)	CL

Contemporary Motion Images +	ENERGY
Continental Insurance Center(FREE)	CIC-12
Corporate Affiliations($)	AFFILIATIONS
Critic's Choice Video(FREE)	CCV-1
Crutchfield(FREE)	CFD
CupidGrams +	GRAMS
Current Day Quotes($)	QQUOTE
Current Market Snapshot +	SNAPSHOT
DEC Users Network +	DECUNET
DISCLOSURE II($E)	DISCLOSURE
DPA-Kurznachrichtendienst	DPANEWS
DTPONLINE +	DTPONLINE
Dalco Computer Electronics(FREE)	DA
Data Based Advisor(FREE)	DB
Data-Process. Newsletter($)	DPNEWS
Dataquest Online +	DATAQUEST
Department of State	STATE
Desktop Publishing Vendor B +	DTPBVEN
Desktop/Electronic Publ. +	DTP
Detroit Free Press Store	DFM-1
Deutsche Wahlen '94	WAHLEN
Dial-A-Mattress	BEDS
Digital Equipment Corp. +	DEC
Digital's PC Store	DD
Digitalk Database +	DBDIGITALK
Dissertation Abstracts($)	DISSERTATION
Dividends and Splits($)	DIVIDENDS
Download Pricing Data +	IQINT
Dreyfus Corporation(FREE)	DR
Dun's Canadian Mkt. Ident($)	DBCAN
Dun's Elect Business Dir($)	DYP
Dun's Market Identifiers($)	DMI
E*TRADE Securities +	ETRADE
E*TRADE Stock Market Game +	ETGAME
E-Span Online Job Listing	ESPAN
EAASY SABRE	SABRE
EAASY SABRE (CIM)	SABRECIM
EETnet +	EETNET
EMI Aviation Services($)	EMI
ERIC - Education Research($)	ERIC
Ei Compendex Plus($)	COMPENDEX
Electronic Books +	EBOOKS
Electronic Convention Ctr +	CONVENTION

Electronic Filing +	TAXRETURN
Electronic Frontier Foundation +	EFFSIG
Electronic Gamer(tm) +	EGAMER
Enhanced Adventure	ENADVENT
Entertainment Center +	ECENTER
Entrep. Small Business Square	ENTMAGAZINE
Entrepreneur Magazine(FREE)	ENT
European Company Library($)	EUROLIB
Examine Detailed Issue($)	EXAMINE
Executive News Service($)	ENS
Executive Service Option(FREE)	EXECUTIVE
Executive Stamper(FREE)	EX
Express America Mortgage(FREE)	EAM
FCC Access Charge Area(FREE)	FCC
FCCopy Utility Download +	FCCOPY
FTD Online(FREE)	FTD
Fantasy/Role-Playing Adv.	ADVENT
Fed. Of Int'l Distributors +	FEDERATION
Feedback to Customer Service(FREE)	FEEDBACK
Figi's, Inc.(FREE)	FIGIS
Finance +	MONEY
Financial Documentation +	FINHLP
Financial File Transfer +	FILTRN
Financial File/MQUOTE II +	MQUOTE
Financial Forecasts +	EARNINGS
Financial Interfaces +	INTERFACES
Financial Surcharge List	FINHELP
Florida Fruit Shippers(FREE)	FFS-1
Flower Stop(FREE)	FS
FontBank Online +	FONTBANK
Ford Motor Company(FREE)	FORD
FundWatch by Money Mag.	FUNDWATCH
Garrett Wade Woodworking(FREE)	GW
German Company Library($)	GERLIB
Gimmee Jimmy's Cookies(FREE)	GIM
Global Report($)	GLOREP
Gold Disk Astound Download +	ASTOUND
Golden CommPass Support +	GCPSUPPORT
Government Publications +	GPO
Graphics File Finder +	GRAPHFF
Green Mountain Coffee Roasters(FREE)	GMR
Guardian newspaper +	GUARDIAN
H&R Block(FREE)	HRB

HOMEFINDER BY AMS(FREE)	HF
HP Specials +	HPSPEC
Hammacher Schlemmer(FREE)	HS
Handicapped User's Data	HANDICAPPED
Hangman	HANGMAN
HarperCollins Online(FREE)	HARPER
Hayes +	HAYES
Health & Vitamin Express	HVE-1
Health Database Plus($)	HLTDB
Health/Fitness +	FITNESS
HealthNet	HNT
Hollywood Hotline	HOLLYWOOD
HoneyBaked Ham(FREE)	HAM
Hot Games Download Area +	HOTGAMES
Human Sexuality Databank +	HUMAN
Hybrid Technical Systems(FREE)	HYBRID
IBES Earnings Est Rpts($E)	IBES
IBM Clinton Health Plan +	IBMHEALTH
IBM File Finder +	IBMFF
IBM OS/2 Service Pak +	OS2SERV
IBM PC DOS 6.3 +	IBMPCU
IBM PCDOS 6.3 Upgrade +	IBMPCDOS
IBM PS2 +	IBMPS2
IBM Personal Software Products +	IBMPSP
IBM Users Network	IBMNET
IQuest($)	IQUEST
IRS Tax Forms/Documents +	TAXFORMS
Incue Online +	INCUE
Information USA +	INFOUSA
Int'l Dun's Mkt Identifier($)	DBINT
Intel Corporation +	INTEL
Intelligence Test +	TMC-101
InvesText($)	INVTEXT
Island of Kesmai +	ISLAND
Issue Pricing Interface($)	MQINT
JCPenney(FREE)	JCPENNEY
JDR Microdevices(FREE)	JDR
John Wiley Book Store(FREE)	WILEY
Justice Records	JR
KAOS AntiVirus +	ANTIVIRUS
Knowledge Index($)	KI
L'eggs Hanes Bali Playtex(FREE)	LEGGS
Land's End(FREE)	LA-1

Lanier Golf Database	GOLF
Legal Research Center($)	LEGALRC
Lens Express(FREE)	LENS
Library Of Science Book Club(FREE)	LOS
Lincoln/Mercury Showroom(FREE)	LINCOLN
Lotus 123 For Windows Upgrade	LOTUS123W
Lotus Technical Library +	LOTUSTECH
MECA TaxCut Download Area +	MECATAXCUT
MMS International +	MMS
MMS/Daily Comment($)	DC
MMS/Fedwatch Newsletter($)	FW
MQDATA($)	MQDATA
MS Client +	MSCLIENT
MS Software Library +	MSL
MTM Challenge Board +	MTMCHALLENGE
MacUser (Subscriptions)(FREE)	MC
MacWAREHOUSE(FREE)	MW
Macintosh File Finder +	MACFF
Magazine Database Plus($)	MAGDB
Magill's Survey of Cinema($W)	MAGILL
Marilyn Beck/Smith Hollywood	BECK
Market Highlights($)	MARKET
Market/Index Lookup(FREE)	INDICATORS
Market/Mgt Research Cent.($)	MKTGRC
Marquis Who's Who($)	BIOGRAPHY
Max Ule's Tickerscreen(FREE)	TKR
McGraw-Hill Book Company(FREE)	MH
Media Newsletters($)	MEDIANEWS
MegaWars I +	MEGA1
MegaWars III +	MEGA3
Member Assistance(FREE)	HELP
Member Directory(FREE)	DIRECTORY
Member Recommendation(FREE)	FRIEND
Members of Congress +	FCC-1
Membership Changes(FREE)	MEMBER
Mentor Technologies(FREE)	MENTOR
Message Handling Service Hub +	MHSADMIN
Metropolitan Museum of Art(FREE)	MMA
MicroWarehouse(FREE)	MCW
Microsoft Benelux +	MSBEN
Microsoft CE Systems +	MSEURO
Microsoft Central Europe +	MSEURO
Microsoft Connection +	MICROSOFT

Microsoft France +	MSFRANCE
Microsoft Italy +	MSITA
Microsoft Knowledge Base +	MSKB
Microsoft Plus Services +	PLUS
Microsoft Press(FREE)	MSP
Microsoft Sales & Information	MSIC
Microsoft Spain +	MSSPAIN
Microsoft Sweden +	MSSWEDEN
Microsoft TechNet Services +	TECHNET
Mirror Technologies +	MACCVEN
Mission Control Software(FREE)	MCS
Mobile Computing +	MOBILE
Modem/Modem Game Support +	MTMGAMES
Mortgage Calculator	MORTPAY
Movie Reviews +	MOVIES
Multi Issue Price History($)	QSHEET
Music Hall +	MUSIC
NCAA Collegiate Sports Network +	NCAA
NTIS - Gov't Sponsored($)	NTIS
NWS Aviation Weather	AWX
Narada Productions(FREE)	NARADA
Nat. Computer Security Assoc.	+ NCSA
National Public Radio	NPR
NavCIS Download Area +	WNAVCIS
Neighborhood Demographics($)	NEIGHBOR
New Car Showroom($)	NEWCAR
New Country Music(FREE)	COUNTRY
News Source USA($)	NEWSLIB
News-A-Tron($W)	NAT
NewsGrid +	NEWSGRID
NewsNet(FREE)	NN
Newspaper Archives($)	NEWSARCHIVE
Nicholas Direct, Inc.(FREE)	ND
Nifty-Serve +	NIF-5
Novell Files Database +	NOVFILES
Novell NetWire +	NOVELL
Novell Tech Bullet. Dbase +	NTB
Novell User Library +	NOVUSER
OTC NewsAlert($)	ENS
Official Airline Guide EE($)	OAG
Omaha Steaks Intl.(FREE)	OS
Online Surveys	SURVEY
Options Profile($W)	OPRICE

Options by IBM +	IBMOBI
Order From CompuServe(FREE)	ORDER
Outdoors News Clips($)	OUTNEWS
Overview of IBMNET +	OVERVIEW
PC Catalog(FREE)	PCA
PC Computing	PCCOMP
PC Computing (Subscribe)(FREE)	PCC
PC Computing(Subscribe)(FREE)	CMP
PC Expert En-ligne +	PCEXPERT
PC MagNet +	PCMAGNET
PC Magazine UK Online +	PCUKONLINE
PC Magazine(Subscribe)(FREE)	PM
PC Plus / PC Answers +	PCPLUS
PC Publications(FREE)	PCB
PC SERVER +	IBMSVR
PC World Online +	PCWORLD
PC/Contact Polls +	PCCPOLL
PRC Publishing(FREE)	PRC
PaperChase-MEDLINE($)	PAPERCHASE
Parlor and Trivia Games +	TTGAMES
Parsons Technology(FREE)	PA-1
Participate +	PARTI
Patent Research Center($)	PATENT
Paul Fredrick Shirts(FREE)	PFS
Peachpit Press(FREE)	PPP
Penny Wise Custom Print Shop(FREE)	PWP
Penny Wise Office Supply(FREE)	PW
Personal File Area +	FILES
Personal Menu +	MENU
Personality Profile +	TMC-90
Peterson's College Database	PETERSONS
Phone*File($)	PHONEFILE
Physicians Data Query($)	PDQ
Pontiac Showroom(FREE)	Pontiac
Portfolio Valuation($)	PORT
Premier Dining	DINE
Prentice Hall PTR(FREE)	PTR
Press Association Online	PAO
Price/Vol Graph($)	TREND
Pricing Statistics +	PRISTATS
Programming MS APPS +	PROGMSA
PsychINFO Abstracts($)	PSYCINFO
Quality Paperbacks(FREE)	QPB1

Quick Reference Word List(FREE)	QUICK
Quick Way Brokerage($)	QWK
RELO(FREE)	RELO
Rare Disease Database +	NORD
RateGram Fed Insured CDs +W	RATEGRAM
Rehabilitation Database	REHAB
Return Analysis($E)	RETURN
Reuters Financial Report($)	ENS
Review Your Charges(FREE)	CHARGES
Rock Video Monthly(FREE)	ROCKVID
Roger Ebert's Movie Reviews	EBERT
Rox +	ISDSUP
S&P Online($)	S&P
SAFEWARE Computer Insure(FREE)	SAF
SBCNet +	SBCNET
SHOPPERS ADVANTAGE Club(FREE)	SAC
SHOWBIZ Quiz	SBQ
SNIPER! +	SNIPER
SOFTEX +	SOFTEX
STAGEII +	STAGEII
SUPERSITE Demographics($E)	SUPERSITE
Science Tri*via* Quiz	SCITRI*VIA*
Sears(FREE)	SEARS
Seattle Film Works	SFW-1
Securities Screening($E)	SCREEN
Securities Symbols Lookup +	SYMBOLS
Shareware Depot(FREE)	SD
Shareware Registration +	SWREG
Shop-at-home	SHOPPING
Siemens Automation +	SIEAUT
Sierra Online(FREE)	SI
Single Issue Price Hist.($)	PRICES
Small Computer Book Club(FREE)	BK
SnapGraphics Download Area +	SNAPGRAPHICS
Soap Opera Summaries	SOAPS
Society of Broadcast Eng. +	SBENET
Softdisk Publishing(FREE)	SP
Software Publisher Online +	SPC
Specials/Contests Menu(FREE)	SPECIAL
Spring Gift Guide	SGG
Standard Indus. Class. +	SICCODE
State Capitol Quiz +	TMC-89
State-County Demographics($)	DEMOGRAPHICS

Stein Online +	STEIN
Sundown Vitamins(FREE)	SDV
Sunglasses/Shavers & More(FREE)	SN
Support Directory +	SUPPORT
Support On Site +	ONSITE
Syndicated Columns	COLUMNS
TICFIL +	TICFIL
TRADEMARKSCAN($)	TRADERC
TRW Bus. Credit Reports($)	TRWREPORT
TRW Credentials(FREE)	CRE
Tandy Newsletter +	TANDY
Texas Instruments News +	TINEWS
The 'GO GRAPHICS' Tutorial +	PIC
The Absolut Museum(FREE)	ABS
The Business Wire +	TBW
The Company Corporation(FREE)	CORP
The Electronic MALL(FREE)	MALL
The Electronic Mall Elite(FREE)	ELITE
The Escort Store(FREE)	ESCORT
The Focus Connection +	FOCUS
The Gift Sender(FREE)	GS
The Gutenburg Collection +	GUTENBURG
The Heath Company(FREE)	HEATH
The IAMS Company	IAMS
The Laser's Edge(FREE)	LE
The Mac Zone/PC Zone(FREE)	MZ
The Multiple Choice +	MULTIPLE
The Shadow Promotion +	SHADOW
The Tandy Users Network +	TANDYNET
The Whiz Quiz	WHIZ
The World of Lotus +	LOTUS
Thomas Register Online($)	THOMAS
Ticker/Symbol Lookup	LOOKUP
Time Warner Bookstore	TWEPB
Time Warner Trade Publishing +	TWEP
Tips/Tricks From PC/Computing	TNT
Travel Britain Online	TBONLINE
Travlers Advantage(FREE)	TRAVAD
Twentieth Century(FREE)	TC
U.S. News & World Report	USNEWS
U.S. News & World Report Store	USM
UK Company Library($)	UKLIB
UK Entertainment Reviews	UKREVIEWS

UK Historical Stock Pricing +	UKPRICE
UK News Clips	UKNEWS
UK Newspaper Library($)	UKPAPERS
UK Sports Clips	UKSPORTS
United Press Int'l($)	ENS
Univ of Phoenix(FREE)	UP
User Profile Program(FREE)	TERMINAL
VISA Advisors	VISA
Vestor Stock Recommendation +	VESTOR
Virginia Diner(FREE)	DINER
WORLDSPAN Travelshopper	PARS
WORLDSPAN Travelshopper (CIM)	WORLDCIM
Walter Knoll Florist(FREE)	WK
Wang Support Area +	WANG
War Games +	WARGAMES
Warner Bros. Song Preview +	WBPREVIEW
Washington Post($)	ENS
Weather Maps	MAPS
Weather Reports	WEATHER
West Coast Travel +	WESTCOAST
What's New	NEW
WinCIM Information	WINCIM
WinNav Information +	WINNAV
WordPerfect Corporation +	WORDPERFECT
Working Women Survey	WWSURVEY
Worldwide Car Network +	WWCAR
You Guessed It! +	YGI
ZZTop Contest +	ZZTOP
Zagat Restaurant Guide	ZAGAT

9.6.3 The ZiffNet Index

The following section contains the names and **GO** words of forums and services available on ZiffNet. To subscribe to ZiffNet, **GO ZIFFNET**.

ZiffNet Forums

Ziff Bendata Forum +	BENDATA
Ziff Cobb Applications Forum +	COBBAPP
Ziff Cobb Programming Forum +	COBBPR
Ziff Computer Shopper Forum +	COMPSHOPPER
Ziff Executives Online Forum +	EXEC
Ziff Software Center +	CENTER
ZiffNet +	ZIFFNET
ZiffNet FREE UTILS Forum +	FREEUTIL
ZiffNet Support Forum +	ZIFFHELP
ZiffNet/Mac +	ZMAC
ZiffNet/Mac Download Forum +	DOWNTECH

Other ZiffNet services

Ziff Editor's Choice +	EDCHOICE
Ziff Newsbytes +	NEWSBYTES
Ziff Online-Dienste +	ZIFFVO
Ziff Software Center +	CENTER
Ziff-Davis Press Booknet +	BOOKNET
ZiffNet +	ZIFFNET
ZiffNet Designer Templates +	FORMS
ZiffNet File Finder +	ZFILEFINDER
ZiffNet Membership & Benefits	ZIFFMEM
ZiffNet Polls(FREE)	ZPOLL
ZiffNet Reviews Index +	ZIFFINDEX
ZiffNet Surveys +	ZSURVEY
ZiffNet/Mac +	ZMAC
ZiffNet/Mac File Finder +	ZMC:FILEFINDER
ZiffNet/Mac Ordering +	ZMACEDITION
ZiffNet/Mac Seybold Newsletter	SEYBOLD
Ziffnet Surveys(FREE)	ZSURVEYS

10 CompuServe and the Internet

CompuServe and the Internet

During the past couple of years, the number of Internet users has grown dramatically. At the time this book was written, the estimated number of people with access to 'the Net' was about 20 million.

Until recently, there was a high virtual wall between CompuServe and the Internet. Although it was possible to send mail to and receive mail from people on the Net, there were no other links. For instance, the USENET Newsgroups, 'mailing groups' that can be compared, in a way, to forums on CompuServe, were not accessible *via* CompuServe. Other Internet facilities, like Gopher, FTP and Telnet, weren't available either.

Things are changing rapidly, however. While I was writing this book, CompuServe started to provide access to USENET Newsgroups. In the remainder of 1994 and the first half of 1995, additional Internet support will be added: Gopher, FTP and Telnet will all become available, as well as World Wide Web (WWW) access.

In this chapter, we'll focus on the first new Internet feature that was implemented, which will expand the horizons of CompuServe members: USENET access.

Get the latest information: `GO NLFORUM`

Visit the Netherlands Forum on CompuServe for up-to-date additions (in the English language) to the contents of this book. Browse through the `Engl. Lang. Files` library for available articles. Naturally, major expansions like Gopher, FTP and Telnet will be covered extensively.

10.1 What is USENET?

Let's start by getting rid of a common misunderstanding: USENET is not the same as the Internet. USENET is, in fact, nothing but a set of rules pertaining to *newsgroups*, which are, quite accidentally, distributed *via* the Internet. A newsgroup is a collection of messages, or *articles* in USENET jargon.

There are currently seven official newsgroup categories. Apart from that, there are a lot of non-official newsgroups in existence. Although these newsgroups are not officially part of USENET, they use the same structure as the official newsgroups. Not all of these newsgroups apply to a large audience; some of them are only available on one or more local Internet sites, while others are almost as widespread as the official USENET newsgroups.

The seven official newsgroup categories, which are normally available on any Internet site, are:

- *news*: this category covers subjects that are related to the newsgroups system. One of the most important newsgroups in this category is *news.newusers.questions*, in which questions are posted about usage of the newsgroups, *netiquette* (the way to 'behave' when you post messages to newsgroups), and so on.
- *sci*: this category contains newsgroups covering scientific topics.
- *comp*: in this category, newsgroups about a broad range of computing topics can be found.
- *rec*: the newsgroups in this category cover topics like hobbies and recreation.
- *soc*: the *social* newsgroups, in which people get together, discuss topics pertaining to a particular country or culture, and so on.
- *talk*: typical discussion newsgroups, about a broad range of issues.
- *misc*: if a newsgroup doesn't fit in any of the other six categories, it is placed here.

The seven official USENET categories contain lots and lots of newsgroups (several thousands). But that's not all: there is also a large range of non-official newsgroup categories. These categories came into existence because the founders didn't want to deal with the official, 'bureaucratic' USENET approach.

Some of the non-official categories are available at almost all Internet sites. A good example is *alt* (alternative). Subjects that you thought only existed in your wildest dreams are covered in their own alt newsgroup, besides more serious (and useful) newsgroups, of course. Believe me: the *alt* category contains some very, very weird newsgroups, dealing with subjects that would be edited out if I were to write them down...

As a CompuServe member, you will be tempted to approach newsgroups the same way you approach forums. However, don't expect the structure and elegance of CompuServe's forums to apply to newsgroups as well. A newsgroup is, in fact, nothing more than a series of mail messages, so-called *articles*, without any thread structure. In other words: every time you read newsgroup articles, you effectively read a bunch of mail messages. Articles posted in newsgroups contain subject and sender fields, but there is no recipient field! (Actually, there is: the newsgroup itself is the recipient.) If you wish to respond to the author of an article directly, you will have to send him or her your reply *via* mail. If you post your reaction in a newsgroup, it is effectively addressed to all its *subscribers*, and you have absolutely no guarantee that the addressee will read it.

The main differences between forums and newsgroups are listed in the following table.

FORUMS	NEWSGROUPS
Forums contain sections. In each section, messages about a particular subject or range of subjects are posted.	A newsgroup is, in fact, a section: it is part of a newsgroup category. If you look at it from a distance, a newsgroup category is, in fact, a kind of forum, with often several thousands of sections. In other words: there are seven 'forums', each with numerous 'sections'.
A section contains one or more threads: messages that are linked together. All messages in a thread share the same subject. If you reply to a message, you don't have to specify a subject: your reply becomes part of the thread.	A newsgroup contains separate articles: mail messages that were posted to the newsgroup. There is no way to reply to an article, other than *via* e-mail. To indicate that an article mailed by you to a newsgroup is a reaction to a previous article, you use the original article subject.
When you start a thread, you specify a subject or topic, as well as a recipient. You can also send a message to sysop or to all forum members.	There are no threads: you simply write articles and mail them to the newsgroup. There is no way to specify a recipient: the newsgroup is the recipient of your article.
You post a message in a forum. Every forum has room for a certain number of messages. Once that number is reached, the message that was posted first	You mail an article to a newsgroup. The number of articles that are visible when you look into a newsgroup depends on the capacity of your site. If you don't

FORUMS	NEWSGROUPS
will 'scroll off' the message board. If you have written a message to a particular forum member, it will be delivered to that member's mailbox if it scrolls off before he or she reads it on the forum.	visit a particular newsgroup for some time, and if the site only stores a limited number of articles for that newsgroup, you won't be able to retrieve all of the articles that were posted in the meantime. Because articles are mailed to the newsgroup and not to a particular person, there are no 'unread' articles.
Forums are managed by sysops.	A number of newsgroups are 'unmoderated': there is no 'sysop'. As you can imagine, this can lead to total anarchy, 'flaming' and other effects that are rare events on CompuServe forums. Be prepared for the worst!
Forums are, without exception, friendly places. New members are always welcome to post a message, and you will almost certainly get a nice reply.	If you are a 'newbie', watch out where you mail your articles to. Some newsgroup members can react very, say, 'aggressively' to new and inexperienced people. Don't expect your 'Hi, I'm here too!' messages to be responded to nicely; you are likely to receive a lot of 'flames' in your mailbox. The same applies if you post a message that is considered to be wrong, or in the wrong newsgroup. It can be a jungle, out there!
Forums have conference rooms.	Newsgroups are nothing more than series of mail messages. Internet members 'conference' *via* a feature called Internet Relay Chat, or IRC. This feature has nothing to do with the newsgroups.
Forums have libraries with files that you can download.	Some newsgroups contain binary articles, stored in a special ASCII format. These articles are 'UUENCODE-d': the sender has used a special program to convert the binary file into one or more chunks of regular ASCII articles. When you have retrieved those articles, you can use a decode program to convert the ASCII contents into a binary file.

10.2 Accessing USENET from CompuServe

As a CompuServe member, you have easy access to all USENET newsgroups, and to a number of non-official newsgroups. Can you guess the Go word? Right: `GO USENET`.

Although you can access USENET in Terminal Emulation, it is much easier when you use WinCIM. That way, you will be able to click your way through the messages, instead of reading them by typing in commands. In this chapter, WinCIM is used.

Typically, the process of accessing USENET newsgroups consists of two steps:

1. You select newsgroups that you are interested in. Next, you subscribe to those newsgroups. This is a one-time-only thing. When you have subscribed to a certain newsgroup, CompuServe will maintain internal information about the last message in that newsgroup that you have read.
2. You access the newsgroup and read all the messages that you are interested in.

10.2.1 Selecting and subscribing to newsgroups

Before you can subscribe, you need to find newsgroups that you are interested in. Proceed as follows:

1. `GO USENET`. After a few moments, the USENET Newsgroup entrance menu appears, as shown in Figure 10.1.

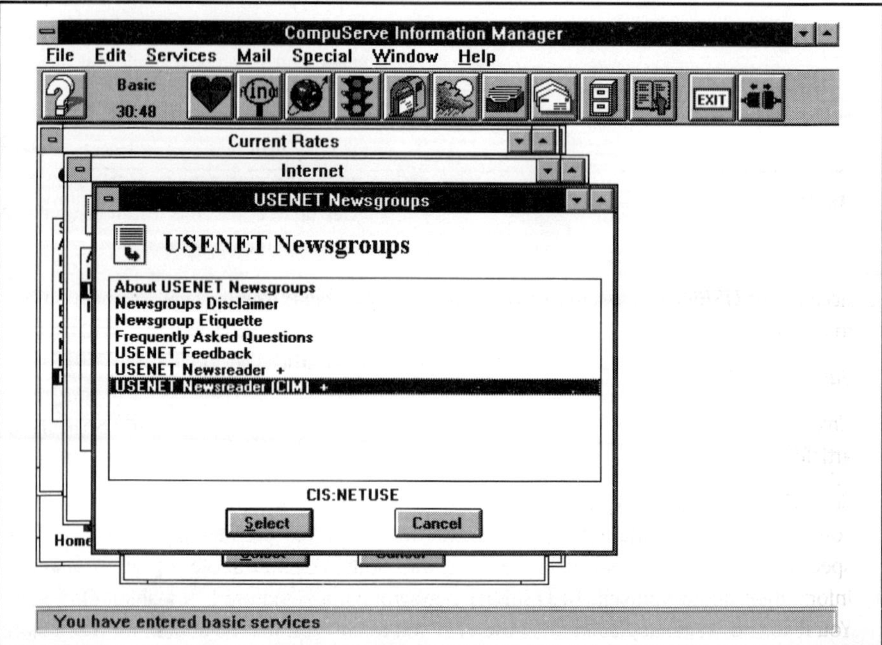

Figure 10.1 The USENET Newsgroups entrance menu

2. Select the `USENET Newsreader (CIM)` option. You might want to select options `Newsgroup Etiquette` and `Frequently Asked Questions`, first; these contain additional information about what lies ahead.
3. After a few moments, the `USENET Newsgroups` main menu is displayed, as shown in Figure 10.2. This menu contains the following options:

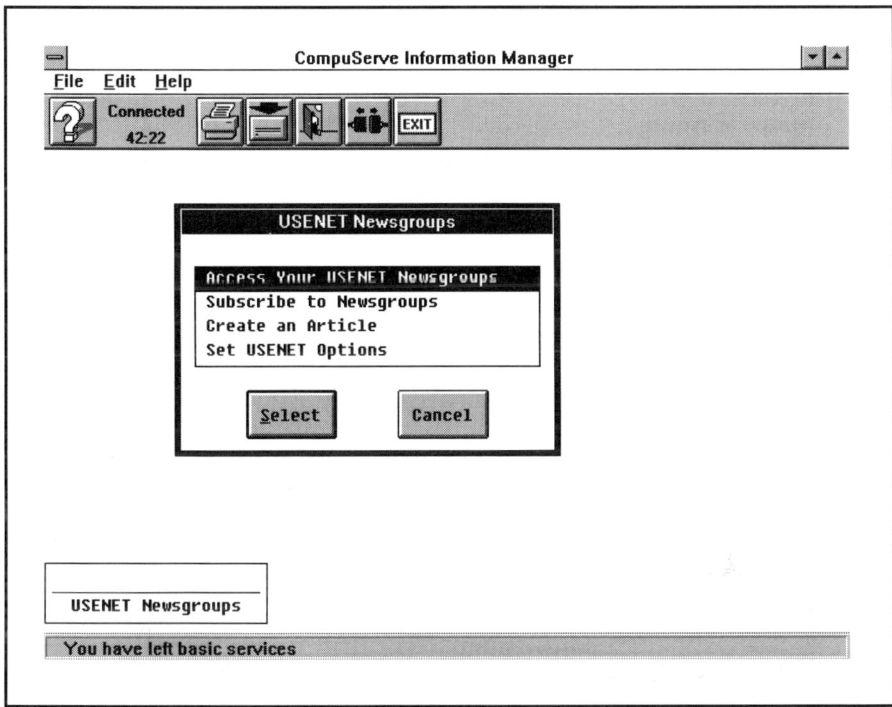

Figure 10.2 The USENET Newsgroups main menu

- *Access your USENET Newsgroups*. This option is available only when you have subscribed to at least one newsgroup.
- *Subscribe to Newsgroups*: This is the option we are about to select.
- *Create an Article*: This option, which will be discussed later, allows you to write newsgroup articles.
- *Set USENET Options*: Use this option to specify information about your name and company, and about the number of articles to be displayed per newsgroup. You can also specify your *signature*: one or more lines with some original quote, or with additional information about yourself. In USENET newsgroups, a signature is a fashion statement. You'll see no '`Regards, John`' over there! If you're curious: just be patient for a few more moments.

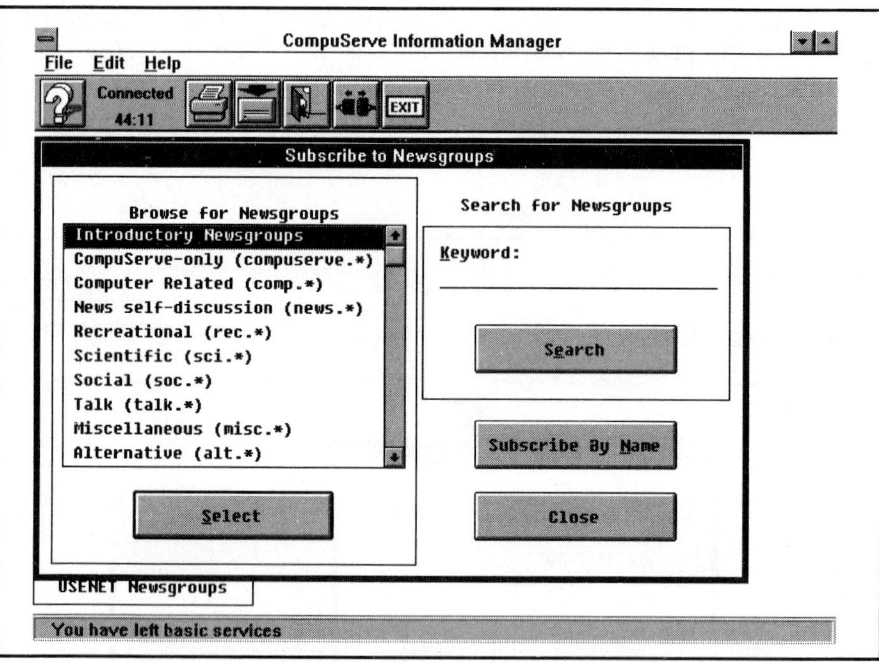

Figure 10.3 Select your newsgroups from this menu

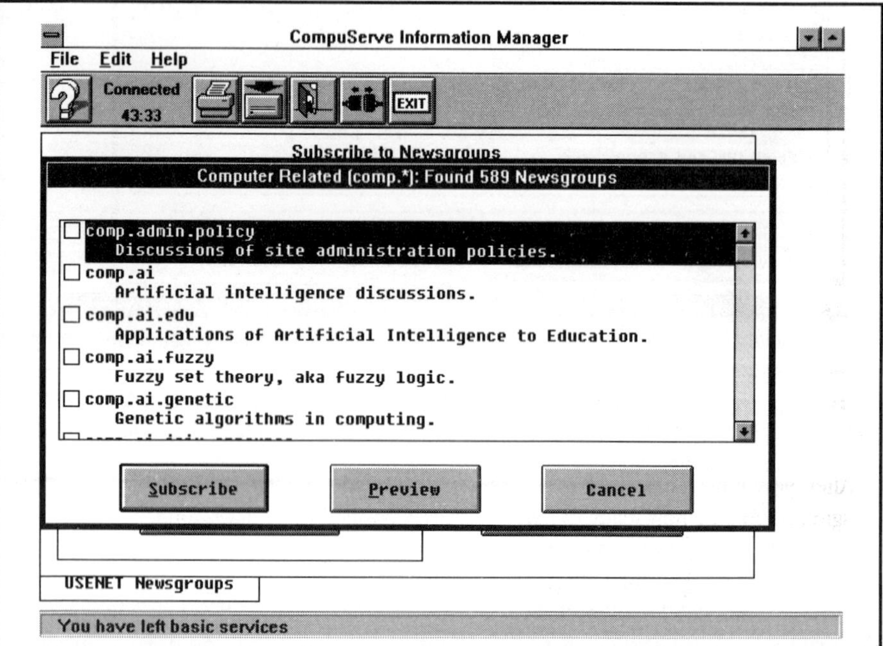

Figure 10.4 A selection of available newsgroups

Select the `Subscribe to Newsgroups` option. After a few moments, the 'Subscribe to Newsgroups' dialog appears, shown in Figure 10.3.

On the left-hand side of this dialog, you see a list of newsgroup categories. When you select a category and press the `Select` button, CompuServe will display a list of available newsgroups for that category. You can try this out for yourself: select a category, for instance `Computer Related`, and press the `Select` button. A possible result (remember: newsgroups are deleted and added all the time!) is displayed in Figure 10.4.

If you see a newsgroup that you like, check the box in front of it. If you wish to know more about the contents of a particular newsgroup, press the `Preview` button. WinCIM will display a list of current articles in that newsgroup, as shown in Figure 10.5. To subscribe to it, press the `Subscribe` button.

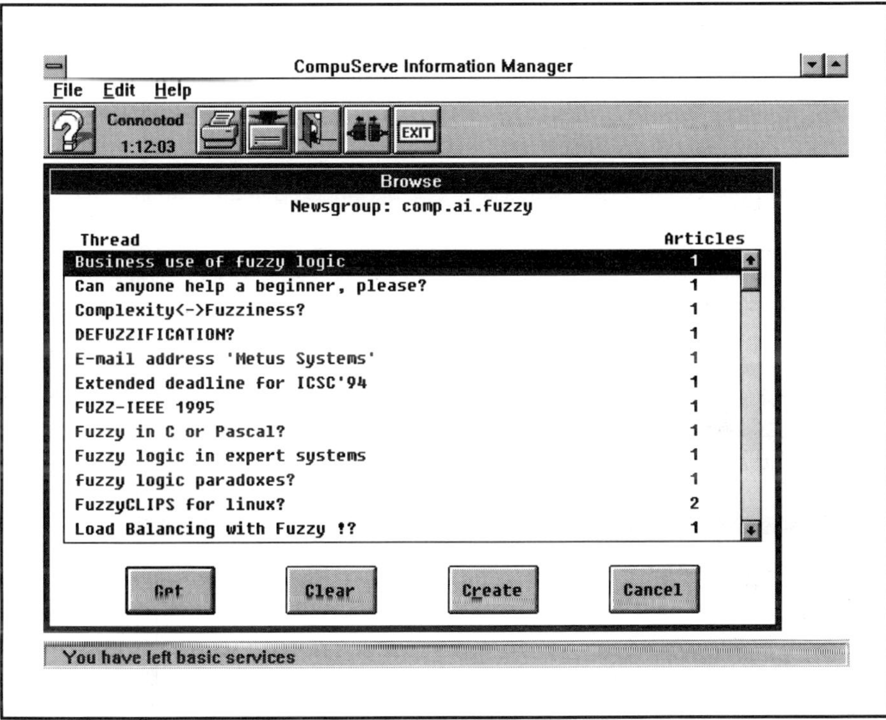

Figure 10.5 A typical list of articles in a newsgroup

After you have subscribed to a newsgroup, it will appear in your list of selected newsgroups. You are now ready to read the articles posted in that newsgroup.

10.2.2 Reading newsgroup articles

To read the articles that have been posted in newsgroups to which you have subscribed, select the option `Access Your USENET Newsgroups` from the USENET Newsgroups menu. You will see a list of newsgroups to which you have subscribed. To read the articles, select the appropriate newsgroup and press the `Browse` button. Next, a list of articles is displayed. Select the article you want to read and press the `Get` button. After a few moments, the 'Display Article Contents' dialog appears. Apart from the actual article, this dialog contains the following options:

- *Next*: Press this button to see the next article in the current 'thread'. (In USENET newsgroups, threads are simply groups of articles with the same subject. Unlike regular CompuServe forums, there are no links between thread messages.)
- >: Press this button to see the next 'thread' in the current newsgroup.
- <: Press this button to see the previous 'thread' in the current newsgroup.
- *Hold*: Press this button if you would like to see this article again the next time you access your USENET newsgroups.
- *Reply*: Press this button if you want to reply to the current article. You can send your reply *via* e-mail (in that case, only the sender of the original article sees your reply), or you can post it to the newsgroup. In the latter case, it is not ceratin that your reply will be seen by the sender of the original article. If he or she doesn't access that newsgroup for some time, your article will 'scroll'. Therefore, if you want to be sure that the sender reads your reaction, send it *via* e-mail as well.
  When you select the `Reply` button, you can *UPLOAD* a file that you have prepared offline. If necessary, CompuServe encodes binary and GIF files into a format that can be decoded with a UUDECODE utility.
- *Forward*: Press this button to forward this article *via* e-mail. You can either forward it to someone with an e-mail address or post it in another newsgroup.
- *More*: Pressing this button displays the next part of the article.

10.2.3 Tips

- There are many more newsgroups than are listed in the 'Subscribe to Newsgroup' dialog. Most of these newsgroups are also available, in spite of the fact that they are not listed. If you want to subscribe to such a newsgroup, press the `Subscribe By Name` button.
- If you want to see all newsgroups that discuss a particular subject, try the `Search` button in the 'Subscribe To Newsgroups' dialog. After you have entered a keyword, CompuServe will display a series of matching newsgroups.
- To cancel a subscription for a particular newsgroup, select the `Access Your USENET Newsgroups` option on the USENET Newsgroups main menu. Next, select the newsgroup that you don't want any more and press the `Remove` button.
- If you need a utility program to encode binary files, or to decode UUENCODEd files, use the IBM File Finder (`GO IBMFF`) to find the latest versions of those utilities. When asked for a keyword, enter `UUENCODE`.

Index

Notes

Notes

Notes

Notes

Notes

Notes

Notes

Notes

Notes

Notes

Notes

Notes

Notes

Notes

Notes

Books from

International Thomson Publishing

On The Internet

ACCESSING THE INTERNET
A Guide for the UK and Ireland

John W T Smith, UKOLN, The Office for Library and Information Networking, University of Bath

If you are looking to get connected – look here first!

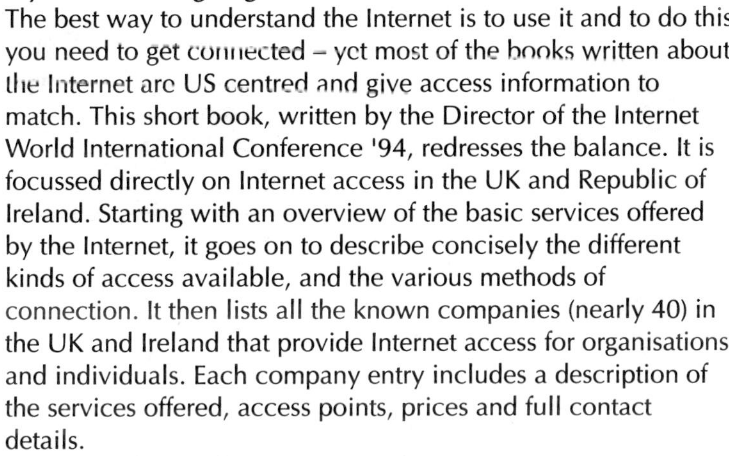

The best way to understand the Internet is to use it and to do this you need to get connected – yet most of the books written about the Internet are US centred and give access information to match. This short book, written by the Director of the Internet World International Conference '94, redresses the balance. It is focussed directly on Internet access in the UK and Republic of Ireland. Starting with an overview of the basic services offered by the Internet, it goes on to describe concisely the different kinds of access available, and the various methods of connection. It then lists all the known companies (nearly 40) in the UK and Ireland that provide Internet access for organisations and individuals. Each company entry includes a description of the services offered, access points, prices and full contact details.

December/224pp/1-850-32147-7/paper

SPINNING THE WEB
How to Provide Information on the Internet

Andrew Ford

An indispensable guide for all those who provide or intend to provide information on the World Wide Web, or want to make the most of their existing services, this book for the first time draws together all of the most up to date information and details of contemporary resources into one essential volume. Providing exclusive coverage of Web features, the book includes an overview of Web facilities, how to create hypertext documents, security issues, how to set up a server and the selection and evaluation of software. A variety of examples from current Web sources are included.

December 1994/250pp/1-850-32141-8/paper

PIECING TOGETHER MOSAIC
Navigating the Internet and the World Wide Web
Steve Bowbrick, 3W Magazine

Mosaic is the most widely used browser for the Internet's World Wide Web and runs on UNIX, Macintosh and Microsoft Windows. Providing a multimedia interface to the Internet, Mosaic helps the user navigate the Internet and the World Wide Web, and explore the information superhighway. This title provides a user-friendly introduction to Mosaic. Fully illustrated throughout, this invaluable guide explains what Mosaic is and how it works, including: a quick start session for those people who already have a browser set up; details of how to obtain Mosaic from the Internet and configure it for your platform; Web navigation and search strategies; how to use Internet tools and services via Mosaic; an appendix listing useful World Wide Web sites; a glossary of terms; beyond Mosaic – how to set up a Web server and write HTML documents.
Spring 1995/300pp/1-850-32142-6/paper

Where to purchase these books?
Please contact your local bookshop, in case of difficulties, contact us at one of the addresses below –

ORDERS
International Thomson Publishing Services Ltd
Cheriton House, North Way, Andover, Hants SP10 5BE, UK
Telephone: 01264 332424/Giro Account No: 2096919/
Fax: 01264 364418

SALES AND MARKETING ENQUIRIES
International Thomson Publishing
Berkshire House, 168/173 High Holborn, London WCIV 7AA, UK
Tel: 0171-497 1422 Fax: 0171-497 1426
e–mail: Information@ITPUK.CO.UK

MAILING LIST
To receive further information on our Networks books, please send the following information to the London address –
Full name and address (including Postcode)
Telephone, Fax Numbers and e–mail address

Free $15 CompuServe Credit!

CompuServe is pleased to offer new and existing members a usage credit woth $15*.
Non-members wishing to take advantage of this offer should follow the instructions on the enclosed disk.
Existing CompuServe members can take advantage of this offer by simply completing the coupon below, clipping and sending the coupon to:

'CompuServe for Europe' Offer
CompuServe
No. 1 Redcliffe Street
PO Box 676
Bristol
BS99 1YN
UK

DosCIM or MacCIM is available free of charge to both existing and new members who are unable to use WinCIM (Windows). Please contact the address above, or call the following number, quoting 'CompuServe for Europe': 0800 289458 (Freephone within UK) or (+44) (0)117 976 0680 from outside the UK.

Conditions: One coupon redemption per ID number. Coupon is not transferable. Send this original only, photocopies will not be accepted.
All queries relating to this offer should be directed to CompuServe at the above address.

** CompuServe is an international service and is priced in $US. Billing is in local currency at the prevailing rate.*

CompuServe
for Europe

Bonus Coupon Offer: $15 usage Credit for existing user

Name ____________________

User ID Number ____________________

Address ____________________

Postcode ____________________

Signature ____________________